SVERRE FEHN THE PATTERN OF THOUGHTS

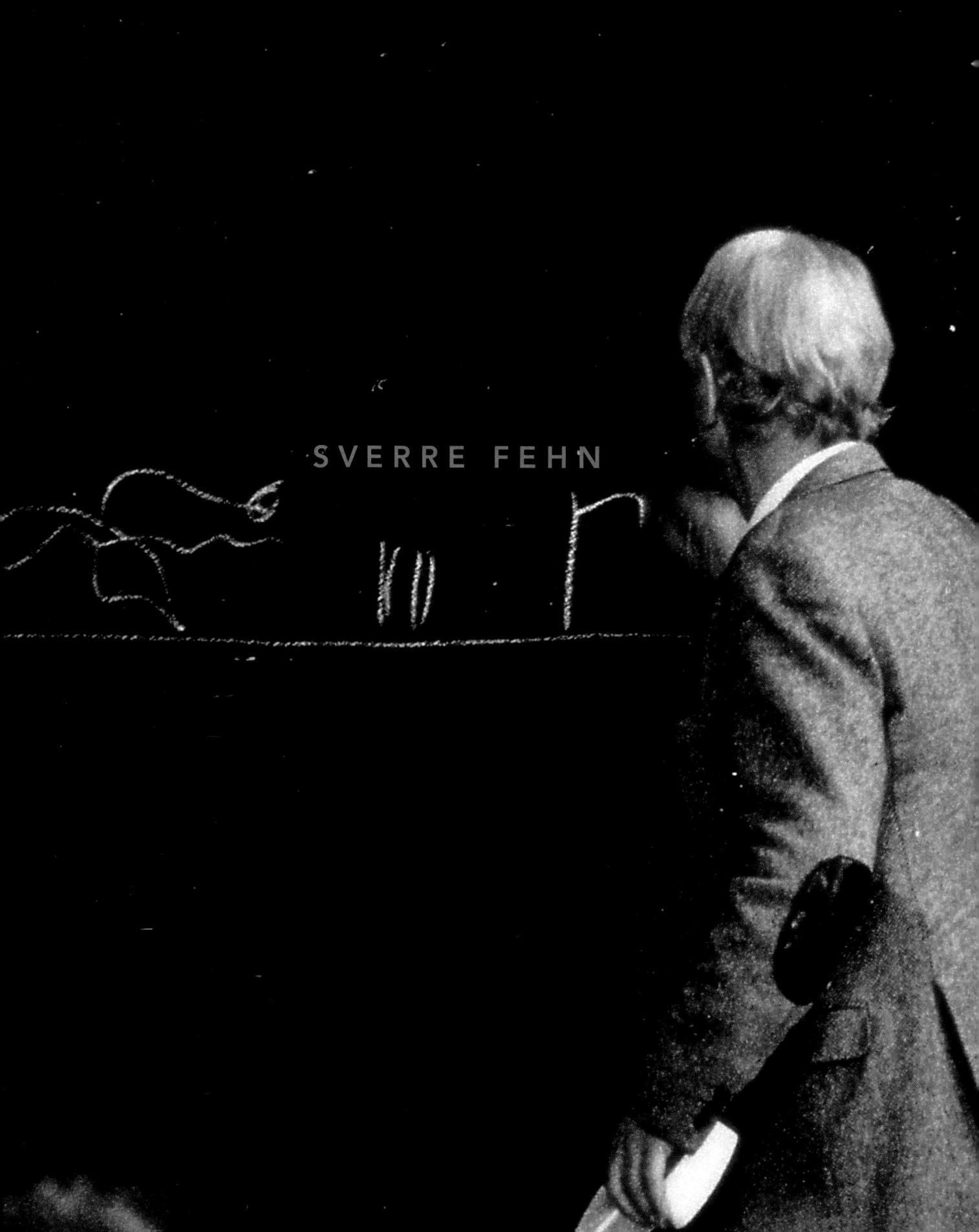

SVERRE FEHN
THE PATTERN OF THOUGHTS

PER OLAF FJELD

THE MONACELLI PRESS

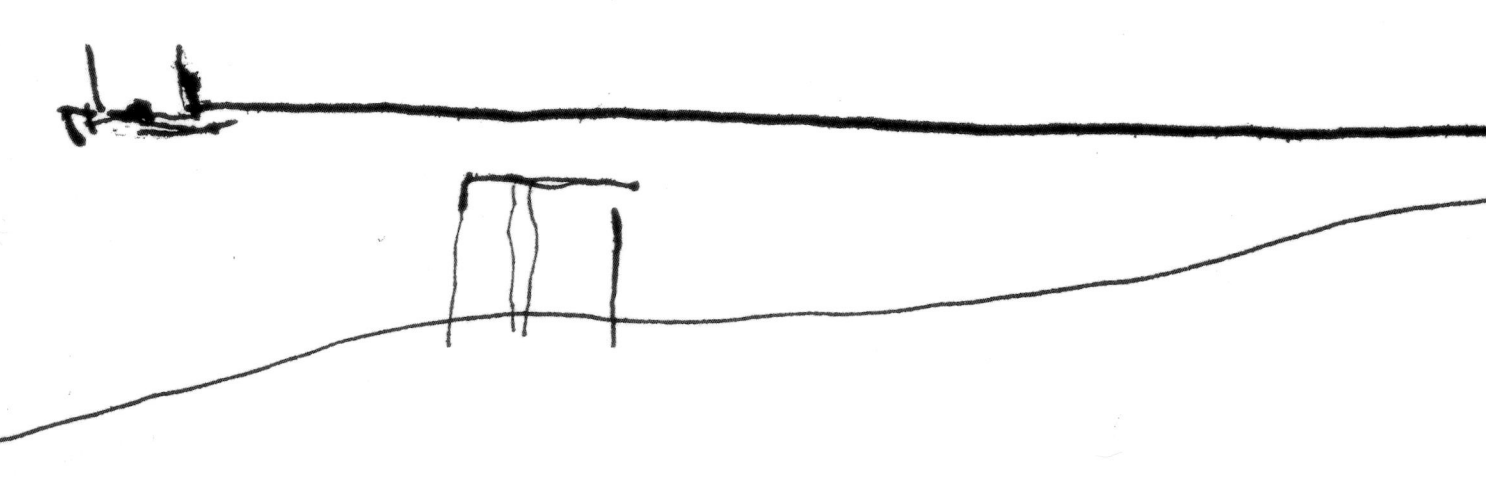

Copyright © 2009 by The Monacelli Press, a division of Random House, Inc.

All rights reserved. Published in the United States by The Monacelli Press, a division of Random House, Inc., New York

The Monacelli Press is a trademark of Random House, Inc.

Library of Congress Cataloging-in-Publication Data
Fjeld, Per Olaf.
Sverre Fehn : the pattern of thoughts / Per Olaf Fjeld. — 1st ed.
p.　cm.
ISBN 978-1-58093-217-2
1. Fehn, Sverre, 1924– —Criticism and interpretation. I. Fehn, Sverre, 1924– . II. Title.
NA1273.F45F54　2009
520.92—dc22　　　　　　　　　　　2009003720

Printed in China

www.monacellipress.com

10 9 8 7 6 5 4 3 2 1
First edition

Designed by **Think Studio, NYC**

CONTENTS | Preface and Acknowledgments 6 | Midsummer Frames 9 | The Beginning of No Return 29 | Early Fame 45 | Beyond the Image of Home 67 | The Return of the Horizon 107 | Public Conversations 137 | A Twenty-Year Pit Stop 171 | Connecting Heaven and Earth 189 | The Mask and the Cut 207 | Paraphrasing Nature 233 | Before Closing the Gate 259 | Notes 288 | Chronology of Works 292 | Collaborators and Consultants 301 | Selected Bibliography 302 | Photography Credits 303

PREFACE AND ACKNOWLEDGMENTS

A thin rectangular brass nameplate hung on his door: Sverre Fehn—Architect. That was all. I knocked, he opened the door, and I started my first job as an architect. Thirty-five years later, Fehn has finally placed this thin strip of brass into his drawer. During those thirty-five years, I listened to his stories, worked with him, and visited his buildings. In this book, it is my aim to bring to life his voice as an architect, educator, and storyteller with the capacity to transform a personal narrative and its essence into physical space.

In my first book, *Sverre Fehn: The Thought of Construction*, published in 1983, Fehn was at a midpoint in his career. He had little work in that period and was able to set aside time for a publication. The background material for that book consisted of several notebooks recording conversations and interviews that took place from 1978 to 1980. Not everything in those notebooks was used or relevant at the time, since the purpose of that volume was to introduce Fehn's work to a broader international audience.

Beginning with my early association with Fehn's office and continuing as I taught with him at the Oslo School of Architecture until he retired in 1994, I took notes on all his lectures I attended and, whenever possible, our conversations. On and off we talked about putting together a second book, but neither one of us had the time or focus such a project required. Yet one day as I looked through some of my old notebooks, it became clear that without an effort to transcribe, organize, and make the connections between my notations and Fehn's work, this information would be lost. When I finally set to work, I discovered I had boxes of notebooks not only on Fehn's lectures but also on his friends and colleagues, which gave further depth and immediacy to the material. But the most rewarding discovery has been to find that my notes correspond to and compliment his sketches, which have always been an essential tool in his creative process.

This book encompasses most of Fehn's built work and projects. I have tried to hold these works to a series of themes in order to convey an aura of Fehn's approach. My wife, Emily, catalogued and organized Fehn's drawings and translated most of the notes. She has in every way been part of this book, and without her this project would not have been possible.

Fehn received numerous awards and prizes, including the Gold Medal from the French Academy of Architecture in 1993 and the Pritzker Architecture Prize in 1997, and there have been a number of publications on his work. The significance of his insight and freshness of his approach in architectural thinking is rare: with this attitude and with his built work, Fehn now seems to attract more interest than ever. His cultural and spatial reflections form a language quite foreign to today's architectural debate; yet indirectly his thoughts are open and seem to anticipate changes and attitudes on issues that will face the profession in the future. I am also aware that the documentary has historic value and will thus attract another type of reader, one who will place Fehn as one of the last great Scandinavian modernists. He shares a heritage with Gunnar Asplund, Sigurd Lewerentz, Jørn Utzon, Mogens Lassen, and others with strong individual approaches and deep respect for social engagement as architecture. The career of Sverre Fehn has followed the pattern of many other prominent European architects of his age: it has been filled with struggle, which is magnified by the fact that he comes from a small nation. There have never been more than five collaborators in the office at one time, but as a teacher, he has influenced an entire generation of Norwegian architects. His total production is not large, but there is a consistency in its quality that is impressive.

Not long ago, an architect who worked in Fehn's office for a considerable period of time commented on the relatively small number of collaborators. He pointed out that we share something even if we do not know one another well, that there is a bond. This also applies to the assistants who worked with Fehn at the Oslo School of Architecture. They are part of this story as well, and I would like to thank all of them.

Sverre Fehn has had neither the energy nor the health to follow and comment on the development of this book as he did so intently twenty-five years ago with *The Thought of Construction*, but we have discussed content and memories whenever possible over the past year. If I have been unsure about a sketch, its meaning, or an event, he has been there to correct me. He generously gave me full access to his archive. From the material in my notebooks, I have selected pieces that connect to specific sketches, ideas, and built work. Few if any of the lectures were taped; in the transcriptions of lectures and conversations, there are places where material is missing, and I have deliberately not tried to fill in those blanks. It is my hope that this new book will bring further insight and depth to his work.

On the morning of Sverre Fehn's eighty-fourth birthday, many from his office, both past and present, stopped by his home for a visit. Our present was a large heavy book on Le Corbusier that had just come out, which we set up on the bedside table. The small room was packed, and for a moment it was as if the entire office through time was there. Fehn began to leaf through the book; it was not really the content that struck him but the size. Almost at once he began to form stories: "The next book on Corbu will be so large, you will have to bring it sideways through the door."

On my way home a collage of memories from our relationship surfaced. My walk slowed, and I stopped outside the old apartment where he drew two of his most important early works. His brass nameplate flashed through my mind, Sverre Fehn–Architect. His work and creative thinking have been and will continue to be an inspiration for many.

Sverre, this book is a small thank you note from Emily and me.

PER OLAF FJELD

CHAPTER 1

MIDSUMMER FRAMES | Very few Scandinavian architects educated just after World War II have been able to capture the Nordic tradition and transform it into a vibrant modern architectural language in the manner of the Norwegian architect Sverre Fehn. His work has an intuitive confidence in how to use the Nordic landscape and its particular light conditions within the built culture, and yet throughout his career each period has reflected a refined sensitivity to international changes and attitudes in architecture. It can be compared to a poetic work conceived on an isolated mountain by a writer with an uncanny, intuitive sense of what is going on in the towns below. The result is a fresh identity for each project and, behind that, a conceptual framework that is equally surprising and demanding.

Fishing village in Lofoten, Norway.

PAGE 8 Watercolor painted at Hvasser.

For many years, situating Fehn's talent and impact within modern Scandinavian architecture was not clear. He was born in a remote and, at the time, poor country, but this isolation was also an advantage in that he met the world outside with energy and curiosity and without expectations. Today, he has gained a place alongside other important figures in architecture and has influenced a new generation of Scandinavian architects through his years as a teacher. Yet this recognition has been slow to take hold at home in Norway. Sverre Fehn's work has the same meticulous workmanship, clarity of construction, and use of material found in the best of prewar Scandinavian architecture and design. It is a heritage he has always respected but at the same time has reworked and added new layers. Fehn's creative process is rather complex. He edges around a given topic or project, nearing it by way of a myriad of poetic stories, phrases, and sketches, and through this process strips the constructive thought down to its most basic state. Conceptually, he places material in two distinct categories: material as mass, most often represented by concrete, and material that through its intrinsic nature carries a precise or clear set of dimensions, most often represented by wood. Parallel to this deliberation on material, Fehn considers a range of inventive stories and images. At the point he is able to bring a particular story into his material concept, a creative resistance force belonging to structure evolves. A conscious use of sequential movement is also part of this plot. And similar to the best in Scandinavian architecture, the architect deems catching light and bringing it into an interior spatial presence more important than focusing on the view out.

Fehn often refers to the past, but never as history. For centuries, Nordic architecture had a strong, clear, and specific architectural context based on three important factors, which were understood and accepted by the population of the region: climatic conditions, potential of place, and a common definition of social consciousness. The perception of these factors may have differed slightly from nation to nation, but their similarities were far greater than those Scandinavia shared with the rest of Europe. Equally important, much of the Scandinavian population shared a language base and history. Whether documented through prehistoric rock carvings or the remains of Viking ships, the sea has been an important vehicle for communication, but it appears to have been a fairly one-sided exchange. Many sailed south to trade, but few Europeans traveled north, and the connecting element or go-between was the sailors and what they brought home. The isolation of the North translated the world beyond the horizon into dreams and fairy tales. The farther north one traveled, the more natural barriers formed through the harsh climate, and this influenced society. For prolonged periods each year many people had minimal contact outside their immediate family or village. Until the late nineteenth century, a large portion of the population in the North lived in rural farming societies. In the long and cold winter, life was spent indoors; in the short summer, life was a rush of activity outside. The darkness of the winter and the midnight sun of the summer set the patterns for activity and social interaction. Because of the isolation imposed by climate and geography, family units were as self-sufficient as possible, not just in terms of supplying food for themselves but also in terms of craftsmanship.

Understanding the landscape and interpreting that reading with regard to the climate were essential. Finding the best possible site for a house in relation to nature's forces could have life-or-death consequences. The sea, strong winds, areas with heavy snowfall, avalanches, spring floods, and fertile land were all considered carefully in the choice of an advantageous site, and this accumulated information was passed down from generation to generation. The house as protection was dependent on maximizing the potential of the place. There is an almost religious respect for nature's power that sets Scandinavia and Finland slightly apart from central Europe. The farther north one goes, whether in Finland, Sweden, or Norway, the stronger a sense one finds of nature's immensity and power. This is not an altruistic relationship, since anything in the landscape that represents a real or imagined threat to survival is addressed on some level. In relation to cultural expressions from poetry to architecture, many writers have remarked on Europe's inclination to view rather than to step out into nature, but on this point Scandinavia differs. In the North, one's position in relation to nature has always been clear. Here, prior to the benefits of modern technology, the abstraction of nature was a pause before jumping back into an extremely physical comprehension of survival. In the North, architecture was always responding to or acting on or in nature. The exceptions were the result of ideas slowly making their way up from central Europe, and only the wealthy could indulge in a "view." As a result of these common factors, modern Nordic architecture has been able to build on a base strong enough to translate and use other spatial conditions and ambiguities, yet still retain its intimate interior space and ascetic use of material and light in relation to climate.

With improvements in transportation, communication, and energy sources and a population moving toward urban centers in the beginning of the twentieth century, Norway along with the other Nordic nations developed

Sketches, 1947, of the Woodland Cemetery, Stockholm: Holy Cross Chapel, waiting room for the Chapel of Hope, courtyard (Gunnar Asplund).

a new layer of place identity. The recent urban dweller retained a clear regional differentiation and sense of past through a heightened appreciation of the simple or ordinary. Traditional folktales, music, and architecture experienced an intense revival on a grass-roots level. The first serious archaeological investigations and preservation programs in relation to early wood structures, burial mounds, and ruins intensified this sense of Norwegian identity. Although European theories, styles, and politics influenced Norway, architecture was able to pragmatically straddle the two worlds of Europe and Scandinavia. This period was clearly influenced by the European Arts and Crafts movement, but it was not necessarily motivated or propelled by the same foundations. The move into urban areas and the subsequent industrialization took place in record time, often in only one generation. The memory and skills built up over centuries from a rural past were still intact in the city or town, and so were the rural traditions and beliefs; what was gradually lost through a lack of personal experience was an identity connected to a physical landscape.

After World War I, economic growth and international influences were noticeable even in the smaller towns, but Norway was the last of the Nordic countries to benefit, and it was also the poorest. There was an expedient approach to new technology: on one level, Norwegians remained connected to a basic and shared understanding of everyday life; at the same time, they quickly incorporated any and all technologies that eased harsh daily realities. By the end of the 1920s, influence from the architectural discussions taking place in France, Germany, and the Netherlands was apparent in all of the Scandinavian capitals. The World Exhibition in Stockholm in 1930 brought together many latent creative forces in Nordic architecture. Ironically, Le Corbusier was asked to head the exhibition, but he did not accept the offer, and the Swedish architect Gunnar Asplund was appointed to the job. In retrospect, this move helped Scandinavia form its own definition of Functionalism, a "new modern" identity that looked to the future through everyday physical and social concerns. The exhibition featured everything from simple household goods and handcrafted objects to experimental buildings to specific schemes for improving living conditions on a large scale. Many groups of society were caught up in this uplifting momentum, not least the political parties. There was a sense of working together toward a state of well-being for all, and the exhibition garnered an immediate response. From the viewpoint of the average visitor, the buildings and exhibition objects may have had new and different forms and spatial aesthetics, but there was nothing foreign in the values and the direct applications that prompted them.

The core motivation behind Functionalism was in many ways a mirror of the motivation behind Nordic society surviving in its harsh climate: there was little room for excess. Nordic architecture reinterpreted the intellectual discussion coming from central Europe. What evolved was a potentially interesting spatial ambiguity in relation to nature, since the concept of the view and the viewer entered the brief late by way of central Europe. The initiative generated an expression of optimism anchored in the hope that nature's force could be controlled and exploited architecturally. Equally, architecture took a far stronger social stance and was expected to support and develop the existing social content. Bruno Zevi has commented that Nordic Functionalism was based not on dreams or programs but on a social consciousness related to a social content.

The optimism of the World Exhibition in Stockholm reflected the sentiments of a broad

Scandinavian population, not just architects and craftsmen. The logic behind Functionalism was interpreted as a method to apply technology and new materials to immediate problems. Visitors to the exhibition, most removed only a generation or two from an isolated, traditional agrarian life, understood the practical implications this new architecture would have on daily life. This situation allowed for a broad and elastic interpretation of the explorations coming out of central Europe as well as an opportunity to disregard arguments, theories, and visual perceptions that did not contribute to the particular conditions in Scandinavia. Each of the Nordic countries adapted and used what suited its specific circumstance, and the architects of the time felt confident enough to modify expressions and attitudes as needed. It is interesting to note that Asplund's Villa Snellman was built after his success with the World Exhibition in Stockholm: his position as a proponent of the modern movement was secure. Sigurd Lewerentz, Asplund's collaborator, competitor, and friend, also went through a number of changes and adaptations in his work.

Woodland Cemetery, Stockholm: Forest Chapel (Sigurd Lewerentz), stair to Memory Grove (Gunnar Asplund).

OVERLEAF Lofoten, Norway.

In Norway, the implementation of Functionalism and other cultural influences coming out of Europe was strongly influenced by its history. Freed from Danish and Swedish political dominance only decades earlier, there was an intense need for a national identity, and at the same time, large parts of the Norwegian population were still quite isolated, with few of the new technologies available in urban areas. The National Romanticism movement in architecture, evident before World War I, continued to develop after the war, but simultaneously Functionalist ideas were quickly adopted in the larger cities; both on some level reflected the country's political and social aims. By the late 1930s, Norway supported a number of interesting Functionalist works as well as an individual form of National Romantic architecture, and to some degree there was a polarization. But what is also interesting is the mutual, pragmatic borrowing of expressions and solutions. During the first half of the twentieth century, there were a number of very good architects practicing in Norway. Knut Knutsen was regarded as a strong proponent of the National Romantic movement at this time, but he was not beyond adapting or revising ideas received from Europe. Another architect working at the time and deeply inspired by the new European tendencies he observed during his many travels abroad was Arne Korsmo. Knutsen and the younger Korsmo, who represented seemingly opposing positions, collaborated on a project for the International Exposition in Paris in 1937. The distance and isolation from European centers of architectural discourse allowed Norwegian architects to develop personal interpretations without the hindrances of loyalty to or consistency with a movement. Knutsen interpreted the situation in his own way: "Architecture shall be human by being unimportant . . . It shall age with beauty and be inexpensive in both upkeep and construction."

Immediately after World War II, Norway set up a crash course in architecture at the National Arts and Crafts School in Oslo. Due to years of German occupation during the war, which also closed educational institutions, there was a great demand for both housing and architects. The colloquial name for this program was the Crisis Course, and it was set in motion before the war was officially over. Many of the architects active before the war directly or indirectly influenced the content of this program. Knutsen and Korsmo in particular had a strong impact on the students, Knutsen with his profound belief in traditional Scandinavian architecture and its capacity to meet future requirements and Korsmo with his close ties to many important figures in architecture of the time. Fehn remembers the first lecture he attended by Korsmo opening with: "I am not able to teach within the differences of beautiful and ugly, neither can I discriminate the Renaissance over the Gothic. But when I go over a bridge and see two houses, one on each side as if the landscape opens and closes before us, I think the following: on one side I want to look out, and on the other I ask for protection. This is the essence of my architecture: to open or take away from the landscape."

But it was not just the teachers, undeniably a strong group of noted architects, that set the course content. An unusual number of the first students entering this course were also very talented, among them Sverre Fehn. This class additionally included the internationally recognized architectural historian Christian Norberg-Schulz, architect Wenche Selmer, Fehn's good friend Odd Østbye, and Fehn's early partner Geir Grung, along with many others who would later form the backbone of architectural firms in Norway. Even today, it is remarkable to consider how many important Norwegian architects were in this same class

at the Arts and Crafts School. Many of these students would return to teach at the school. As a member of the next generation, and having been educated abroad, I often found it difficult to understand the inner workings of this group. They had disagreements and at times could polarize the school with their differences, yet they were strangely cohesive as a result of their memories of the Crisis Course and the associated activities and trips—in particular, a bicycle trip through Europe one summer.

I asked Fehn about Knut Knutsen as a teacher, and he gave this short description:

The key to the formal expression lies in reading the ground's formation and the area's vegetation. In this context, Knut Knutsen became a teacher and with this quiet attitude he created his work.

The first impression I had of Knut Knutsen was in the wide corridors of the art school with its deep white windowsills full of light. Here we put up our student work, and his footsteps were decisive. If he stopped and had a few comments, everything he said was important, more important than all the world's juries or grades, and I think he stays that way in our minds. If we have finished a drawing we are always

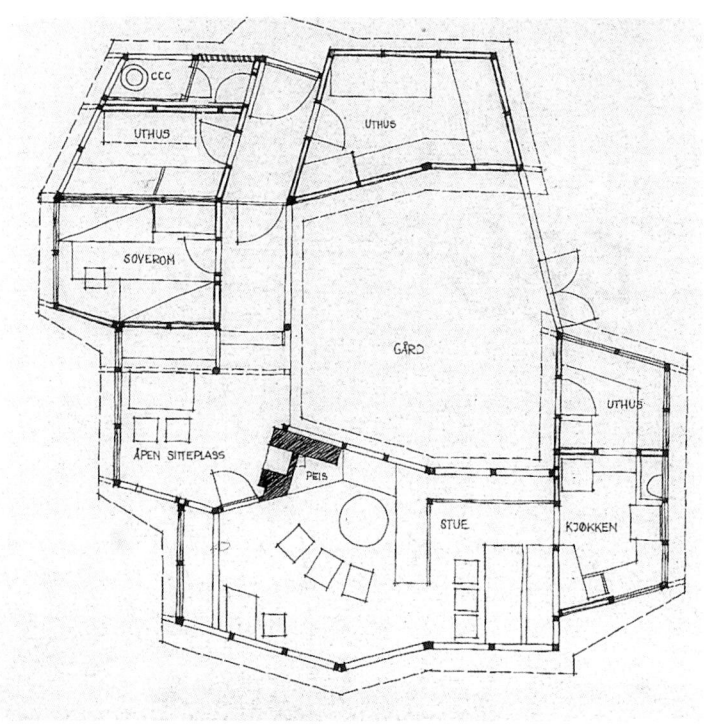

Thorkelsen Cottage, Portør, Norway (Knut Knutsen): View, plan.

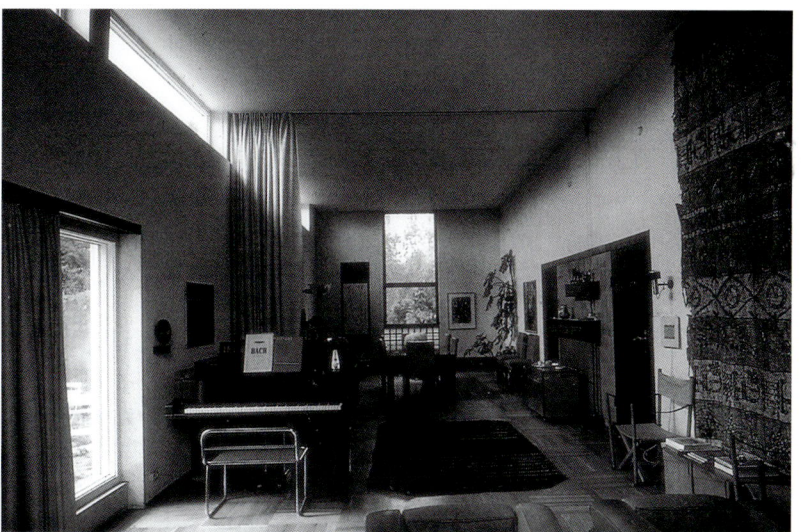

Villa Damman, Oslo (Arne Korsmo): View and interior from the period the Fehns lived there.

MIDSUMMER FRAMES 19

Oslo School of Architecture soccer team: Fehn is in the upper row, second from right, and Odd Østbye is in the lower row, center.

Crisis Course students on a bicycle trip through Europe: Odd Østbye, Fehn, and Geir Grung.

OPPOSITE Sketch of the great bicycle trip.

asking ourselves, What would Knutsen say about this? He, who taught us that a little space can have a big window.

A few years later, in an article, Fehn commented on Korsmo as a teacher: When the construction was completed on Arne Korsmo's Villa Damman, where I now live, I was eight years old, and on my father's bedside table lay *A Day in October* by Sigurd Hoel. Fourteen years later he was my teacher in design. The year was 1946.

"I don't know a thing about form. If it's beautiful, it's beautiful, and if it's ugly, it's ugly" was his first remark. And he continued: "You can erect a wall so that man can see what is beautiful and hide what is hideous," and then he left.

We were tossed back and forth through art history with reckless subjectivity. Without dates, without a plan. The way to Africa was via Leo Frobenius. The journey from Egypt to neoclassicism was never undertaken. Thirty years after Arne Korsmo's great lecture on Sumerian sculpture, I find myself standing in front of a display case in the Altes Museum in East Berlin. All of these Persian statues are suddenly mine.

We were both at the opening of Le Corbusier's apartment building in Nantes in 1955. On the train back to Paris he spoke only of Charles Eames and his own glass house in Oslo. In the flat French landscape that passed our train window, it was as if Le Corbusier had never existed. I didn't see him much after that. He received a professorship in Trondheim—and in the end, his professional foundation was only to be found in the breast pocket of his tweed jacket where he kept his letters.

My last meeting with him was on an airplane between Oslo and Stockholm. He had lost his glasses, so we spent our time looking for some new ones in Stockholm. A few weeks later I received word that he had died in Peru.

P.S. After having written down these few sentences, I have a feeling of having struggled with a translation from an unknown language.

After graduating from the Crisis Course at the Arts and Crafts School, Fehn remained in Oslo. He married in 1952, and as soon as it was feasible he and his wife, Ingrid, bought a summer cottage on the island of Hvasser, not far from Tønsberg, a coastal town south of Oslo where Fehn spent most of his childhood. During his youth, Tønsberg was still heavily involved in fishing and shipping. But his father's family owned an old farm in the mountainous area to the west of the town, and since Fehn was an only child it was expected that he would eventually take over the farm. These two places and his first years in the mining town of Kongsberg established a divergent sense of place for the young boy. Fehn attended an agriculture college after graduating from high school. Stories and impressions from this period often came up in lectures at school, and in many ways this period had some indirect influence on his architectural development and how he differentiates between the cultivated landscape and nature.

I had to keep a workbook on horses. We were on our knees weeding all summer and this eighty-year-old farmer, huge man, sat on his little tractor and kept an eye on us. The animals . . . well, wild animals run around, and the domestic, the pragmatic, the scientific, the industrial animals, they stand still. There is something incomprehensible when looking straight into the eyes of an animal. The cows know when spring is approaching. The animal is in itself rational in the knowledge that it will die.

The small white house at Hvasser would become an important retreat for the Fehn family, a crystallization of the Nordic lifestyle. Simplified to bare necessities—a table, chairs, shelves, telltale signs of its inhabitants' professions—and a few sparse personal objects, the space was compact and direct. There was a pump outside, a central fireplace, and a minimal area for cooking. Fehn made a few things himself with pine straight from the local lumberyard, in particular the lamps, variations of which would later appear in a number of his house commissions; and most of the other furnishings and fixtures were put together by local carpenters. Outside, the traditional sailor's house was discreet, sober, and tucked into the landscape. It is possible that the initial move to buy a summer house was inspired by Jørn Utzon and other Scandinavian architects' vacation homes, and of course he was familiar with Le Corbusier's retreat overlooking the sea; but the house at Hvasser soon developed its own distinct routines and influences on Fehn's life. Many old friends and students have memories of seeing Sverre Fehn early in the morning, with his bathing suit, towel, and sketchbook clipped to the back of his bicycle, riding along the gravel road leading to the beach, the rocks, and the cold water. In many ways this picture captures how Fehn perceives and lives in nature. He exists in the physical world without buffers, testing nature's force.

For years, the cottage's neighbors were local residents of the island, and the summer invasion of tourists was kept at a distance. Hvasser was not in a direct sense a haven for experimentation; rather, it was so uncluttered that it did not require Fehn to do more than to just be in the house or its surroundings. Here, for short periods of time, he could block out the pressures of the office. The island's physical distance peeled away all but the most important issues or problems, and what was left was a focus on the elementary needs of the day. In this environment Fehn was able to ruminate.

Ingrid worked hard at keeping this small window of time private in the summer. Office work remained in Oslo, and the architect made it clear that these few weeks were to relax. Hvasser in all its simplicity was a mechanism for Fehn to confront and reflect on his work. The rock formations meeting the sea, the stretches of grass and sand, and the thick band of blue sea were there day in and day out, with nothing to add or subtract, and it is here that one senses some of the most basic themes that recur in Fehn's work. This is not a location that set in motion his imagination; there were other places that served that purpose. (His stories from in and around Venice are a good example of this form of inspiration.) Rather, the simplicity of the immediate and sparse landscape around the cottage at Hvasser allowed for another type of focus, and Fehn's thoughts entered an abstraction of this landscape.

Two of the most important themes in Fehn's work trace their origins in part to his observations of the landscape at Hvasser, particularly his abstraction of the horizon. He built an intellectual connection between heaven and earth, and in this exploration he found another important theme: the built structure's meeting with the earth. These two themes, the establishment of a new horizon and the meeting of a structure with the earth, almost independent of a project's brief, set a challenge or signaled a method of attack. And it is an attack, just like the sea meeting the rocky shoreline at Hvasser is an attack. For the thought of construction to achieve physical space, there had to be confrontation with the landscape. Even in Fehn's very first works, including commissions that had no given site, he invented a site in order to find a method of attack. Villa Norrköping, 1963–64 (see page 73), in Sweden, is perhaps the clearest example of this tactic. When he returned from painting watercolors at the beach, Fehn would almost always comment if a sailboat with red-brown sails had crossed the horizon. That was a lucky day for painting the horizon.

Each summer had its novel. It could be something Fehn found abroad, a gift, or simply a volume picked up on his way home from school. I was never really quite sure if he liked or read all of them, but in each he would find a sentence or phrase that would follow him throughout the summer. It would come up over and over again, slightly changing with time, but he would continue to explore his selected passage passionately and with great humor, and it would eventually evolve into architectural content. If the book was not popular current reading material, he had far more latitude to explore and interpret his chosen phrase—no one could take exception, and the focus could remain on the phrase and not the novel. With popular novels, this approach was often confusing, since few of his colleagues understood it was a method of approach, an attack, on an architectural thought, and not a comment about the book.

Fehn always saw the landscape as a "room" that nature created, but this sensitivity does not imply any control over nature's growth. He has always had an uncanny sense of how far nature can run wild and still retain the sense of a room. At Hvasser, he was preoccupied with a hedge that separated the house from the gravel road, keeping it carefully trimmed all summer. The cottage was enclosed by nature, secure in its little world; the only visible human control was this hedge, which contrasted sharply with the overgrown bamboo thicket on one side of the house and the pear and apple trees entangled in vines on the other. Running parallel to the hedge, barely two meters from the back of the cottage, was a long, high granite ridge that formed a pronounced narrow space. In one sense, this narrow space reappears in many of Fehn's later projects. Fehn's understanding of when to step into nature's process and take control and when to let go was never more evident than in the "room" around the house at Hvasser. It was secluded, complete, and it asked nothing of him. He was simply there with Ingrid and nature.

Unfortunately, the financial situation in the office became so difficult in the late 1980s that the couple sold the cottage, keeping only the red barn directly across the road. The move was one of just a few meters, and the summer rituals remained much the same, but the memory was split in two. I cannot recall that Fehn was truly attached to any single object or space. His search was always beyond attachment, rooted instead in an acute understanding of a spatial setting and its objects, but this little cottage had touched another sensitivity. Life in the red barn was in many ways even more primitive. In the cottage, the view outside was not an issue, since the house was enclosed and formed its own world; but the barn's small entrance platform as well as a large window in the main room, which looked out over the neighboring farm and a distant view of the sea, spurred another agenda. It was as if the view took over, and the farmer's field with all its activity was the only topic. Fehn has often questioned the twentieth-century need or obsession with the view, and with the move into the barn it did not take long before he went to work on the scenery. Within a short time bamboo protected the little platform and window. The large central room had a fireplace, and soon everything fanned out from this point: the focus was interior. There really was nothing left other than to sit in front of the fire or at the dining table. The meals that came out of an extremely small and rustic cooking area were delicious, and the conversations around the table were for a guest as lively as ever. I have often felt that Fehn's period in the red barn pushed his concept of the basic physical aspects of dwelling to an extreme. There was no comfort, no view, no technology: if something was "useful" enough, it would find its place. Just as the granite formation and hedge across the road had established a framework around the horizon and the meeting with the earth, life in the red barn, while a much simpler journey, was strong enough to set both nature and individual thoughts in motion.

Hvasser was also where Fehn prepared his notes for the coming school year. Written notes were followed up with sketches that represented the core of his investigation. This was the material he would present at the first

Hvasser: The rock formation meeting the sea.

The two retreats at Hvasser: The white house and the red barn.

The white house, Hvasser: This recent photo shows the granite ridge, but an addition has replaced the bamboo thicket at the end of the narrow passageway.

OPPOSITE Sketch, "At sea."

Sketch, "Midnight sun and winter darkness."

meeting with his teaching team, and it was also the method he used to approach competition projects in his office. The conceptual direction of a competition project would often be established during the weeks at Hvasser, but it was a deliberation that stayed private until Fehn sensed a certain maturity in the idea, one that could withstand a conversation with others. There was no lack of books and magazines on architecture at the school or in his office, and Fehn was always interested in what was being built or discussed abroad. But the weeks at Hvasser helped him strip a project or semester plan down to its bare core, and in a sense he gained control over outside input.

To put so much emphasis on an architect's summer house cannot fail to bring to mind architects' vacation homes all over Europe. For a Scandinavian, however, this touches on a deep cultural tradition. For centuries, the shift between summer and winter carried with it a change in dwelling in an attempt to make the most out of the few warm months of the year. This transfer did not encompass just humans but also farm animals and pastureland. A great number of influential Scandinavian architects in the early and mid-twentieth century had a summer (or in some cases, year-round) retreat in which to grapple with and test architectural ideas and, equally important, to live as close as possible to the social framework and culture so clearly expressed in their architecture. Probably the most internationally famous of these Nordic summer retreats is Alvar Aalto's summer home on the island of Muuratsalo. Perhaps even more telling in the sense of a Nordic mind-set was Ingmar Bergman's home and film atelier on Fårö Island, a very simple cluster of buildings integrated into the local community. In Fehn's case, the summer house was for many years a vital instrument in relation to his creative process. The mental baggage from Oslo was carefully chosen; and all that was left was the sea, the horizon, and the rocky landscape. He entered this landscape physically—he did not treat it as a "view"—and he took what he experienced into his work.

Fehn's red barn was sold in 2007. I had a conversation once with Peter Smithson in Siena during a session of the International Laboratory of Architecture and Urban Design, and he talked about his summer house, how much it meant to him, and how difficult it was when it was sold. Strangely, Fehn once mentioned to me a visit to Smithson's home. Fehn (of all people) commented on its sparseness and on how he and Smithson sat on wooden crates in the garden. This was a generation of architects who had a passionate relationship to architecture. It went beyond work; built space was still rooted in a deep understanding of existence and responsibility.

MIDSUMMER FRAMES 27

CHAPTER 2

THE BEGINNING OF NO RETURN | Arne Korsmo set in motion activities and choices that were pivotal not just for Fehn but for many of his classmates. He opened doors abroad, pressed a number of young Norwegian architects to participate in the Congrès International d'Architecture Moderne (CIAM), and later was instrumental in founding Progressive Architects' Group, Oslo, Norway (PAGON), which included Fehn and other notable Crisis Course students. Just after the war, he arranged to meet Jørn Utzon in the Japanese Tea House in the garden of the Museum of Ethnography in Stockholm. This meeting and Korsmo's thoughts on Japanese architecture were described in an important article in the Norwegian architectural journal *Byggekunst* called "Japan and Western Architecture" and were later expanded on in a 1961 article in *Kamera* magazine. It was not long after this meeting in Stockholm that Utzon arrived in Oslo from Denmark and, together with Korsmo, designed several competition projects. Utzon was also active in PAGON. When Christian Norberg-Schulz neared retirement, he gave a series of lectures at the Oslo School of Architecture. From a lecture in 1995, I took down the following quote: "In 1949, Jørn Utzon and Arne Korsmo took a trip together to the United States. They saw everything: Mies, Wright, Eero Saarinen, and Neutra. Utzon visited the Robie House [Wright] and the IIT campus of Mies and was very excited about their work, but Utzon was critical of Neutra's and Saarinen's work."

Almost immediately after graduation Fehn started a small practice with his Crisis Course classmate Geir Grung, an architect he would collaborate with for about seven years. They worked in the City Planning Office by day and designed competition projects by night. In 1949, they won a competition for a museum to house the Sandvig Collection, consisting of Norwegian artifacts, in Lillehammer. Considered rather radical and modern at the time, the building drew a surprisingly positive response from the public. The structure, based on a modular order, was designed in relation to the topography of the site and may be seen as a continuation of the landscape. Even today, despite the many alterations and the fact that the project's intentions were never fully realized,

In 1952, Fehn and Grung began work on Økern Home for the Elderly. **We drew this after a program for a hotel,** Fehn later noted. This sophisticated one-story building is organized around two open interior courts, and the design focuses on the well-being of each individual. Each resident had his or her own room and bath with a view to the exterior, a luxury unknown at that time in Norway; criticism quickly followed because the home embraced a level of comfort and social care that many felt was unnecessary.

Grung and Fehn also teamed up with Jørn Utzon to design a housing project for the outskirts of Oslo, presented as a Norwegian submission to CIAM in 1953. Fehn commented once that they designed

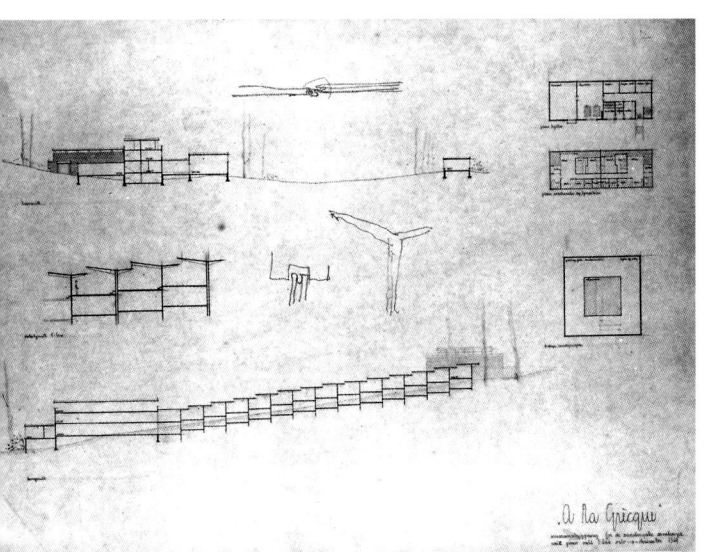
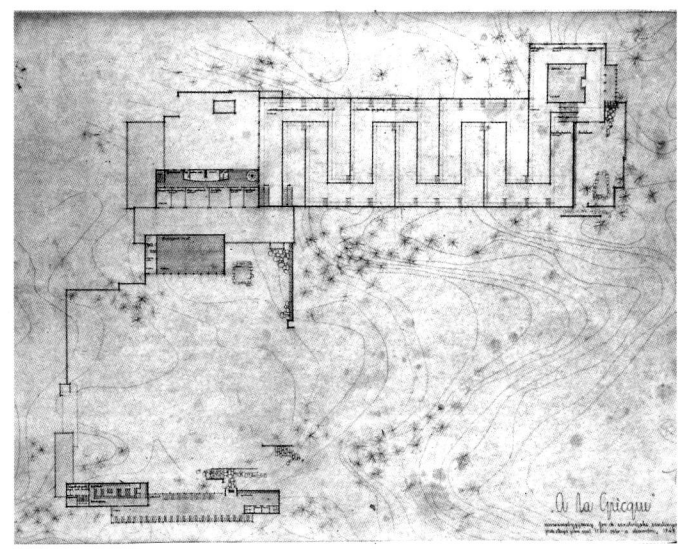

Sandvig Collection, Lillehammer, Norway (with Geir Grung): Section, plan.

PAGE 28 Crematorium, Larvik, Norway (with Geir Grung): Clay model.

the building's relationship to the site is still an essential component. The workshops and the adjacent exhibition areas, never built, were in some ways the most interesting part of the project, with a winding path that follows the slope of the land down to the main museum area. Natural light enters both from openings in the wall and from above as a result of the repetitive cross section.

the competition project in Copenhagen. Utzon's wife and children left for their summer house ("it was healthier"), and the three architects set to work in what Fehn remembers as an apartment that was painted a dark blue color throughout. Grung and Utzon concentrated on the models and Fehn on the drawings, and to save time an eraser was used to stamp the houses on the site plan.

Utzon followed in Korsmo's wake, and he brought with him all of America and firsthand stories about Mies and Wright. Utzon's way of living, his house, his children, his wife, and himself seemed at a distance so informal, but Utzon's being belonged to a sense of wholeness. Utzon was global. He lived on the earth and had a book from each continent, and at the same time he searched for inspiration in everything.

In my friendship with Utzon I met a constructor. He thought in constructions. I think more in stories, in content. Utzon goes directly into construction, immediately. His father was a marine architect. Utzon has never been afraid of foreign forms in architecture. He had seen his father's boat drawings. Through Utzon I came very close to Europeans. Up here, one is over-enthusiastic. He could just sit down on the beach and make his sand castles, and in these he placed wedges. In this way, he built his works.

The partnership of Fehn and Grung was a mix of two strong and talented young architects. Once construction was underway for Økern and the first set of final plans for the museum at Lillehammer was completed, it became apparent that working as a team could not last. They were both uncompromising in their ideas of what and how the buildings should develop, and meticulous in following up details with great care and precision; there was no middle ground. The various trips that they took during this period did not help the affiliation, not least because long-distance communication was difficult. Just the same, this partnership left its mark on

Økern Home for the Elderly, Økern, Oslo (with Geir Grung): Model.

Økern Home for the Elderly: Views of interior court.

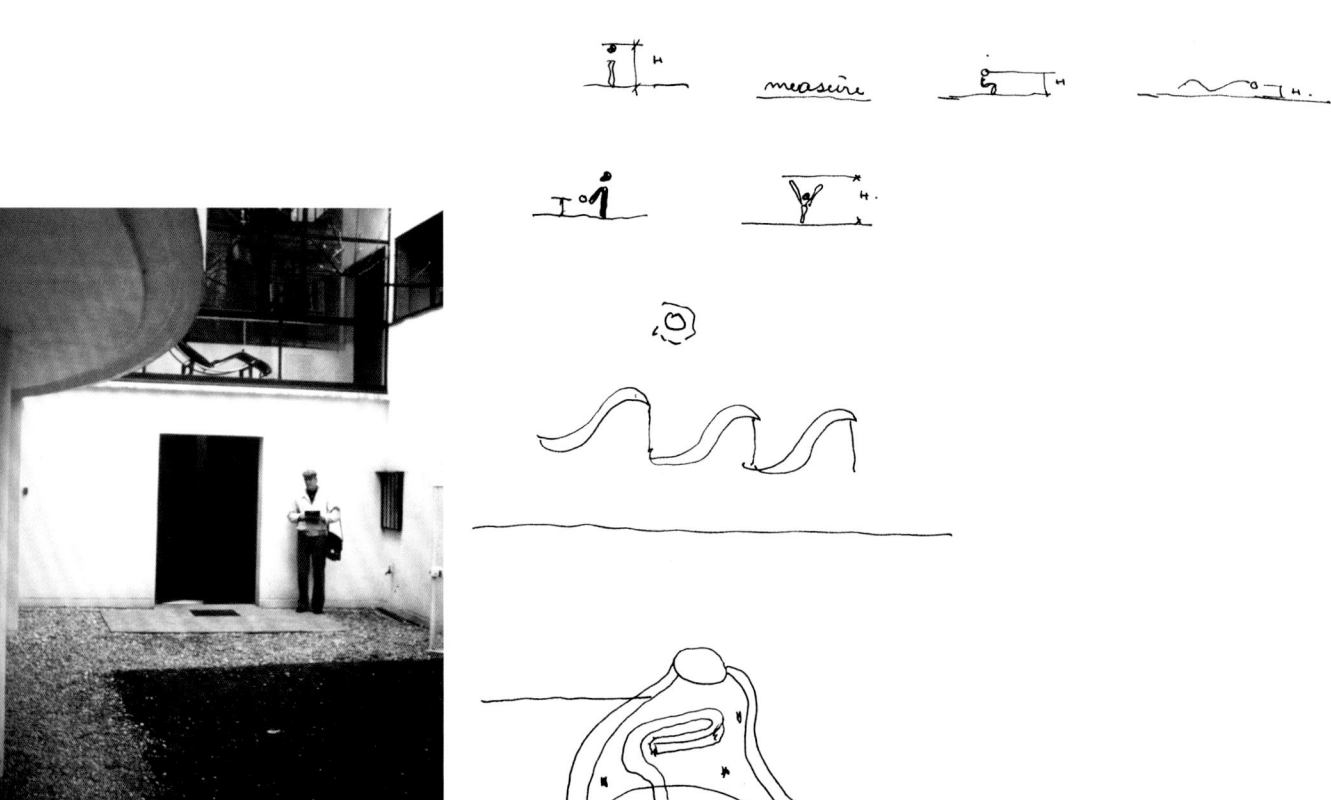

Sverre Fehn sketching at Le Corbusier's Villa La Roche.

Sketch, "Jørn Utzon. Moving in the room."

both architects. A competition project Fehn designed with Geir Grung for a crematorium in Larvik, 1950, reveals a conceptual spatial direction that would be evident in much of Fehn's later work. On a beautiful site facing the sea, one long concrete wall with a single opening parallels the shoreline. In Fehn's personal vocabulary, there is a relationship between the trivial and the tragic. The opening facing the sea offers a dimension without scale, the sea and the horizon. Here, ashes are scattered within nature's "room." The other side of the wall faces the town. Through the single opening one returns to the "room" of the living, to human thoughts and constructions. In *The Thought of Construction* I wrote, "The breeze from an opening is the pause from which to enter, the last reminder of a bodily dimension." Fehn would return again and again to this theme of the dividing wall and the way in which it sets in motion a profound spatial interaction. The partnership ended with the two built commissions, but the architects remained good friends.

It was also at this point that Fehn's wife was offered a job in Paris as a pianist. Korsmo was instrumental in helping Fehn secure a place in Jean Prouvé's Paris studio. At first glance, Prouvé's office may seem to have been a strange choice for Fehn, but the French architect's work on prefabricated houses had interested him for some time, and with Le Corbusier's *Vers une architecture* in mind, he became fascinated with the house as an absolute construction, a machine for living. Prouvé integrated the necessary technical systems into the basic form of the house and through industrial production gained the precision of a machine. Fehn took this experience, distilled it, and adapted the thought process to his own work.

During the year in Paris, Arne Korsmo often asked Fehn to help him with various arrangements and translations. **My French was soon much better than his, so I was asked to make hotel reservations, all sorts of things. But Korsmo spoke very good English.** Korsmo was generous in promoting his old student and sharing

Crematorium, Larvik:
Model views.

THE BEGINNING OF NO RETURN

Sketches of the sea and the horizon.

OPPOSITE Sketch, "The house in the desert with a clay pot. This must be simplicity."

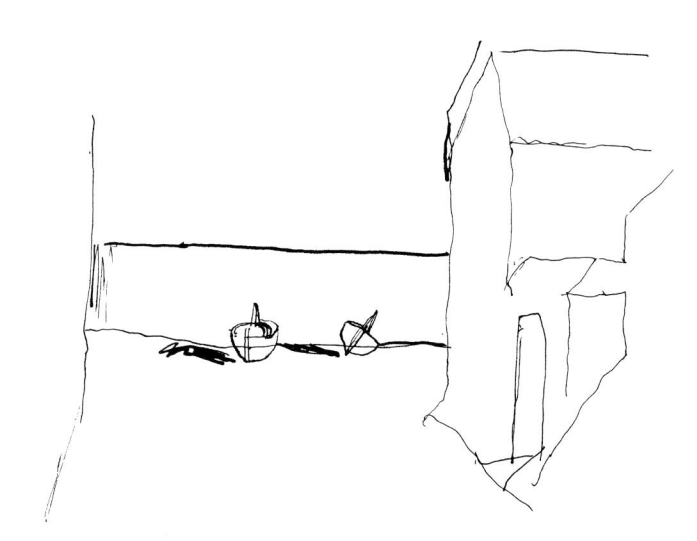

Konstruksjonen   A

Corbusier g Egypt
Marseilles.

Boken faller ned
og hun måles opp
akkurat. Modular

Corbusier g reieffet.
Symbolet ordrer eller dimensjonen

den egyptiske fra
uendeligheten til øyet

Ordene tall er 0 ⟶ høyere matematikk
den arabiske matematikk

Intetheten   og altet.
0 beskriver intetheten.   og uendeligheten.

his contacts. Fehn attended CIAM meetings and a number of important lectures and events, and the year in Paris allowed him time and access to better understand Le Corbusier's work and milieu. Equally significant, he met a number of architects of his own generation who would in time become important in architecture and architectural theory. **When I was living in Paris I met Prouvé, van Eyck, Corbusier, Baccama, and the Smithsons. One was floating in this group, and we sought out the same places, but this was before the pavilions in Brussels and Venice.**

Fehn's return to Norway from Paris marks a point at which the first signs of creative isolation begin to take form. There were fewer openings for conversations on architecture in which the situation carried a creative resistance, and in turn inspiration. Fehn often commented that keeping up with his international friends was not just an economic problem: many were soon connected with a university and could use that affiliation to attend meetings and publish work; in addition, they were living in large active metropolitan areas relatively close to one another.

Once he returned home, Fehn faced a relatively insular profession in Oslo and a closed university system; I believe this state of affairs weighed heavily on Korsmo's career as well, and he would soon leave Oslo and take a professorship in Trondheim. Fehn would not receive a tenured position at the Oslo School of Architecture until 1971. Later, when I was active in Siena at ILAUD with Giancarlo de Carlo, many old friends complained over Fehn's tendency to isolate himself in Oslo. His contact with Utzon was also difficult to keep up after the break-up of his partnership with Geir Grung, and it was seldom that they met or spoke with one another. For Fehn, this was a loss. He never ceased to have interest in or admiration for Utzon's work. Years later, Fehn would occasionally complain of lack of stimuli, but it was also clear that this isolation gave him plenty of room for personal interpretation, with little interference or correction. Still a young architect, it was his ability to draw that saved him on many occasions. No one could resist his sketches and drawings, along with the personal stories; his architectural vocabulary, however, was not always appreciated or understood. In this early period, Fehn also designed several competition projects with classmates from the Crisis Course, in particular his friend Odd Østbye.

In 1951, Fehn won a grant to study vernacular architecture in Morocco. Some of his close friends were also traveling at this time, but their focus was more directed toward the East. Fehn's study trip opened a window to another spatial understanding, and over time, this journey influenced many areas of his thought process in relation to architecture. On his return, he published a four-page article on Moroccan architecture—the longest and most comprehensive of all his writings. A small notation in his sketchbook, which is dated November 2, 1951, comments on Marrakech: **I don't really know what I should write. This is hell's city. There is so much noise and we humans are the cause. The only place where there is any calm is the tower of the mosque by the large square. And then the mountains with their snowy tops—it is unending and quite a sight. One can walk along the street in the shadows of orange trees and look up at the snow-covered mountains. It is this the city has to offer, and oh yes, the snake charmer. Well honestly, it has all sorts of jugglers/buffoons. And buffoons, that is what we in our world call intellectuals. So free me and protect me. I am beginning to see the whole of our culture through the marketplace in Marrakech, and it is not an orange tree! Had I taken it seriously enough, I would have gone home and become a farmer.**

For Fehn, the next ten years would set a direction from which there was no return. In 1987, with his class of students from the Oslo School of Architecture, he would visit the same villages and landscape that had inspired him in 1951. Fehn was totally absorbed with the prospect of this return visit, so much so

Sketches, "Construction: Corbusier and Egypt, Marseilles," "The book falls down and he makes the exact measure. *Modulor*," "Corbusier and the relief. The symbol over all dimensions," "The Egyptian identity, from endlessness to the eye," "The number belonging to the desert is 0, the Arabic mathematics," "Endlessness and 0 give the scale."

The desert.

Fehn's Citroën 2CV stuck in a snowstorm in the Atlas Mountains, Morocco.

OPPOSITE Sketch, Morocco, 1951.

THE BEGINNING OF NO RETURN 41

that he was almost oblivious to both teachers and students during the trip. In September of that year he gave a lecture on Morocco to his class:

It is in the desert, in the border area between Morocco and the Sahara, that one reaches the interminable, a place without dimension. Here mass as material, between oneself and heaven, is nothing more than one's shadow, light, and sand. It is a situation that creates an unending mass, but where does it stop? Is it the only dimension of our time?

The desert encourages you to think about nakedness. But you are not; instead it is the spirit that begins to dress you. The turban is fifteen meters long. Construction begins in the mosque; inside, the spatial story begins at once. The mosque denies shadow and sends the sun out again unto itself. In this landscape the well is the most precise point. The well and the damp build downward into the sand. It is only the shadow that gives the wall a story.

There is a zone between the plain's earthen walls and the mountains. Wood construction slips through in this belt, and the trees are down to nearly the size of a human, and you can walk on top of the wall. It is a conscious reduction of the constructive dimension.

Nothing is protected; both children and adults can fall off a wall. That there is no railing has something to do with nature.

After this last trip to the desert, Fehn would often refer to his experiences in Morocco. The idea of strong architectural precision wrapped in a cloud of endlessness and timelessness would always continue to inspire his imagination.

I went to Morocco not to discover new things but to recollect what has been forgotten. And when you enter the valley at sunset and hear a man call from the highest rooftop, you will still think: I don't know anything about this. The only answer to this architectural simplicity and clarity is that it exists in a culture that for us seems timeless. Architecture's work is perfect, because it is working in a timeless space. Its signature is anonymous, because it is nature itself.

Sketch, 1951, "Today I experienced these rooms above the trees. I saw how the women folded out their carpets, sat down, and drank their tea."

OPPOSITE Sketch, 1987, "I was thinking of Josephine Baker. For a period I drew her constantly."

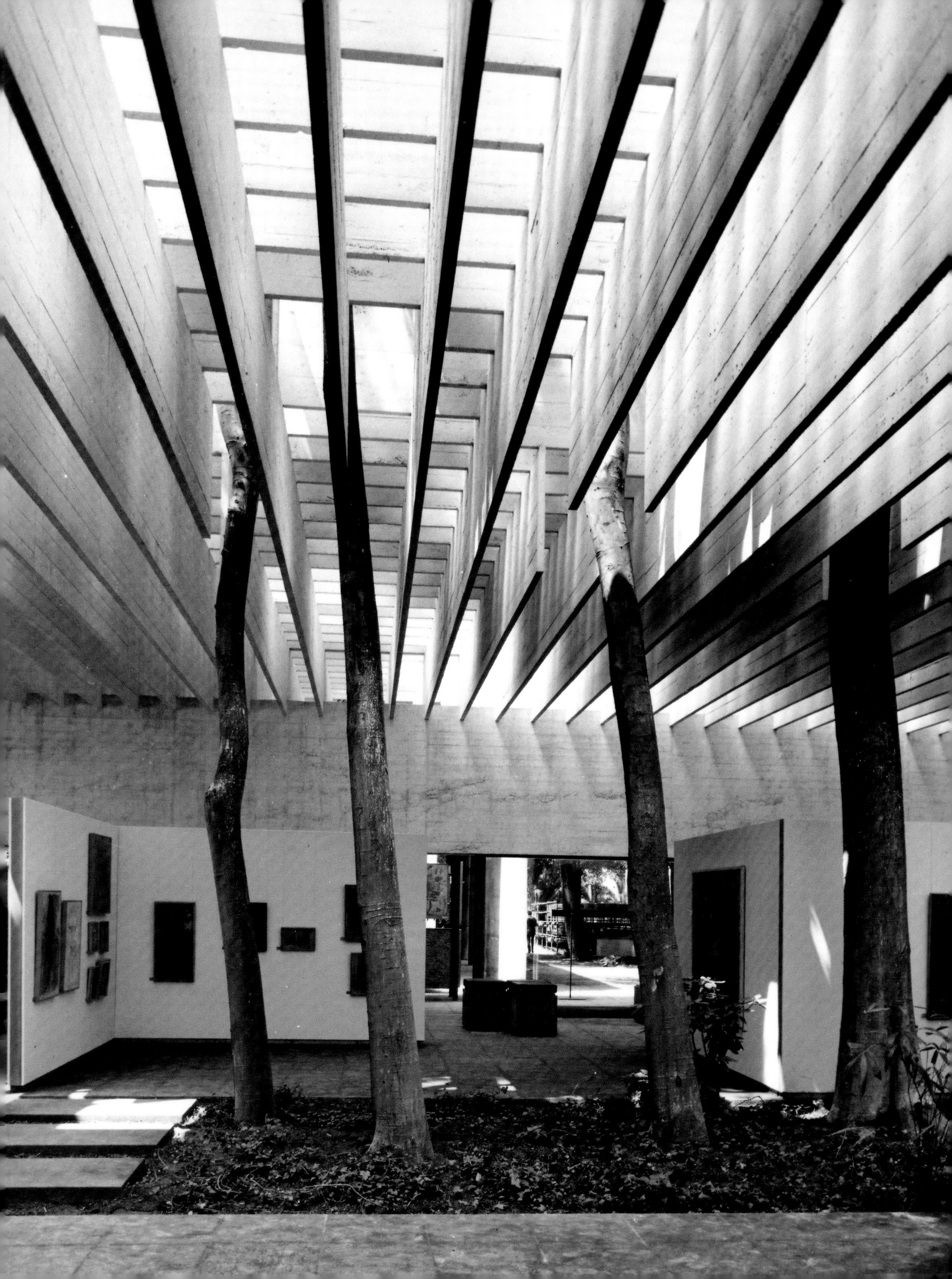

CHAPTER 3

EARLY FAME | Fehn's determination and commitment to architecture must have been at a high point during the period he submitted designs for two major competitions, the Norwegian Pavilion for the World Exposition in Brussels, 1956–58, and the Nordic Pavilion for the Venice Biennale, 1958–62. He drew both pavilions alone, at home in a small apartment where Ingrid was also working on her music. Meetings with various authorities and committees in relation to these two projects took place in the apartment's windowless entrance hall, which was painted black for the occasion. Ingrid often commented on hiding clothes and shoes before meetings and spending hours in the public room at the nearby National Broadcasting Center waiting for the apartment to empty. It was a tough but exciting time, not only for the Fehns but for the whole country. Despite the optimism of rebuilding Norway after World War II, the nation's economy in this pre–North Sea oil period was constricted.

The competition jury for the Norwegian Pavilion for Brussels was headed by a noted architect and teacher from the Crisis Course, Knut Knutsen, and fortunately for Fehn, the leader of the building and exhibition committee was strong and committed to the project. From the start, the working drawings for the pavilion indicated that it would be a rather complicated and experimental project dependent upon fine craftsmanship and material precision. The pavilion had a simple layout. Tucked into the terrain and enclosed on three sides, it worked as a filter for light and air. Plexiglas columns and a translucent roof gave great variation to the intensity of light and shadow, and this quality was instrumental for the display of objects.

Fehn stayed in a hotel in Brussels for the entire period of construction, visiting the site every day. He has often laughingly commented, **I stayed in a good hotel that served breakfast in the room, and my fee went to paying the hotel bill.** Possible complications—and there were many, to be sure—were caught early. In a sense, the pavilion was conceived as a package to be shipped in a container to Brussels. The interest was not focused so much on the logistics and integration of design elements, as it is today, but rather on a precise understanding of physical material and how a minimal use of physical material could achieve a particular spatial identity. The process was equally a conceptual investigation. The fact that the structure would arrive in a container was simply a logical conclusion.

Norwegian Pavilion for the World Exposition in Brussels: Views of construction site.

OPPOSITE Fehn's office in Tiedemans, Oslo.

PAGE 44 Nordic Pavilion for the Venice Biennale.

Each material's characteristics worked toward a specific light and spatial presence. Like the other pavilions at the fair, this one was to showcase the nation's production, culture, and technology, but many of Fehn's ideas required expertise far more advanced than what was found in Norway at that time. Just forty-eight bolts held the main construction, thirty-seven meters square, together. The laminated-wood beams atop the concrete walls were of Norwegian timber, but the lamination process took place in Belgium. For secondary supports, he experimented not only with Plexiglas but with transparent concrete. In the end, the columns were made and tested in Germany, and the idea of transparent concrete was dropped for lack of time. The semi-transparent roof material was Co-Coon, an epoxy sprayed over nylon threads. **It became very apparent after the first rain shower that Co-Coon was not waterproof. The roof leaked, and we had to punch a hole in it to run the excess water off faster.**

The pavilion was influenced by the work of Mies and Wright, but Fehn's time with Prouvé was also evident in the assemblage of different structural components. What interested him most in terms of space was the relationship between material and light. The pavilion had three distinct zones of light: the open sky, the translucent roof, and the opaque roof. Each of the zones was connected with sets of large sliding doors running between the massive laminated beams, which together with the changing quality of light generated a variety of spatial sequences both inside and outside the pavilion. Fehn often commented that good space has a particular sound: **The project had silence; it worked with sound as a vital part of the space. It was sectioned off from the main road and this helped with the noise. The Japanese sat right down and seemed to stroke the silence. The Co-Coon worked as an acoustical** ceiling. The object's essence was placed in a glass world filled with silence. In this sense, there was something mystical with the space.

I joined the film club in Brussels. The experience of the Brussels pavilion enticed me to hold out with architecture. The pavilion was withdrawn from the competition for the best pavilion by the Norwegian government. The reason the pavilion was withdrawn, according to Fehn, was the project's experimental attitude and the resulting technical complications.

The contents of the pavilion reveal Fehn's tenacity in retaining a sense of immediacy and authenticity in all his work. He insisted that the exhibition objects be originals, not copies, and among these objects were an Edvard Munch painting and an important prehistoric rock

EARLY FAME 47

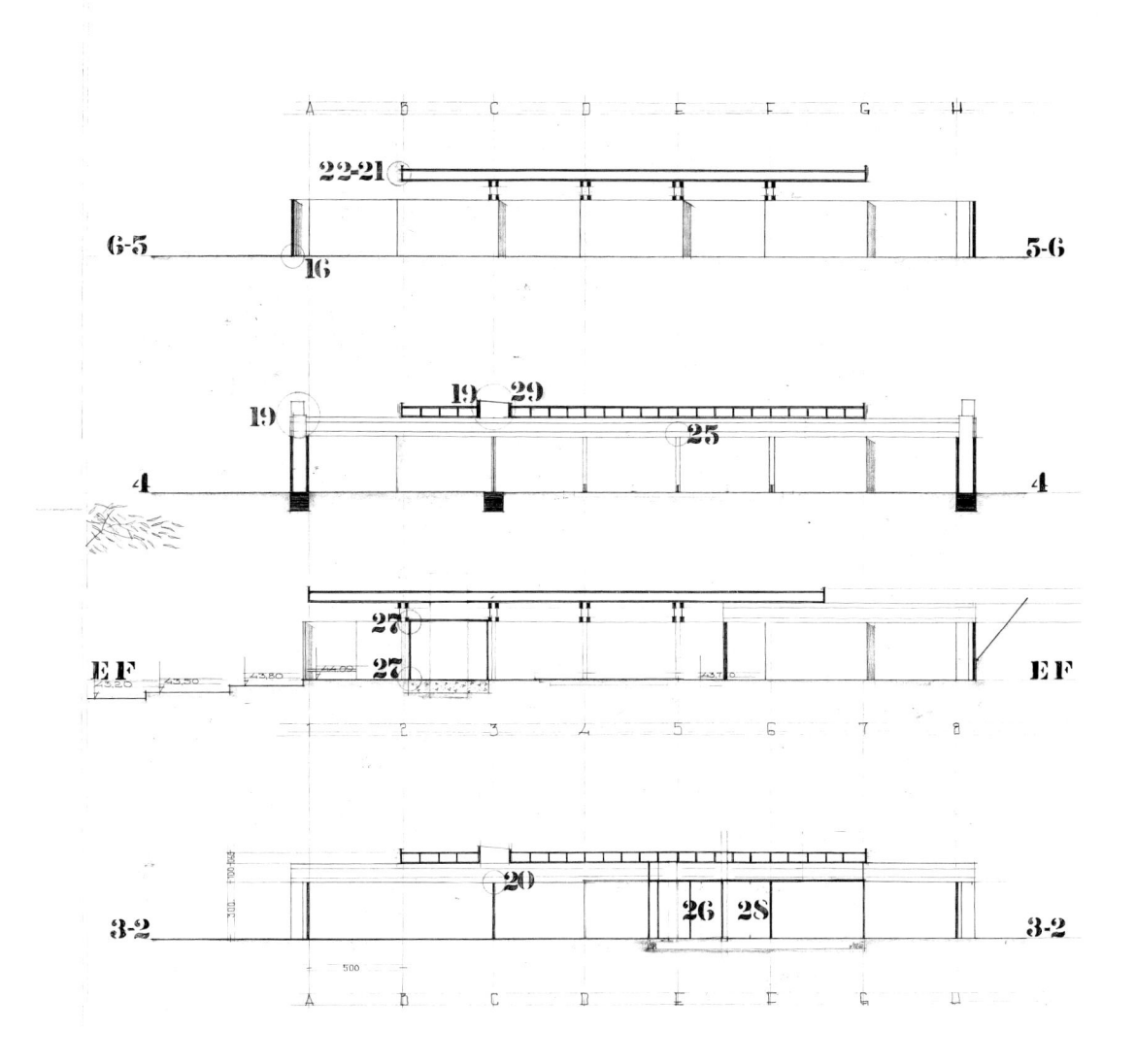

Norwegian Pavilion, Brussels: Sections, entrance facade.

carving. The painting and rock were placed without fanfare or overt protection within the open, semitransparent pavilion; visitors experienced them in a new light and a new vulnerability. Glass objects were placed on glass shelves; the shadows cast on the floor and walls themselves became objects in the display. Fehn later commented, **I visited various museums in Norway collecting items I wished to exhibit. I drove around in my [Citroën] 2CV to pick up the objects, and in the end I had to put in a new motor.**

The Brussels display signifies the beginning of Fehn's long-term interest in the exhibited object.

During the construction and opening of the fair, Fehn met a number of prominent figures in architecture and was exposed to attention quite different from what he received in Oslo. The Japanese and French architectural press showed particular interest, for the pavilion was architecturally advanced, especially for a small country with rather limited resources. Later he told me that work on the site was truly a struggle. He was young, he did not have an easy time with the contractor, and he envied the lightweight structures he had come to know in Prouvé's studio. Once he ended one of his lectures with: **Corbu denied Newton's fall, and I was just left there with a large wooden beam.**

The pavilion is no longer standing. At the close of the exhibition, it was offered to the Norwegian government, but the offer was

EARLY FAME 49

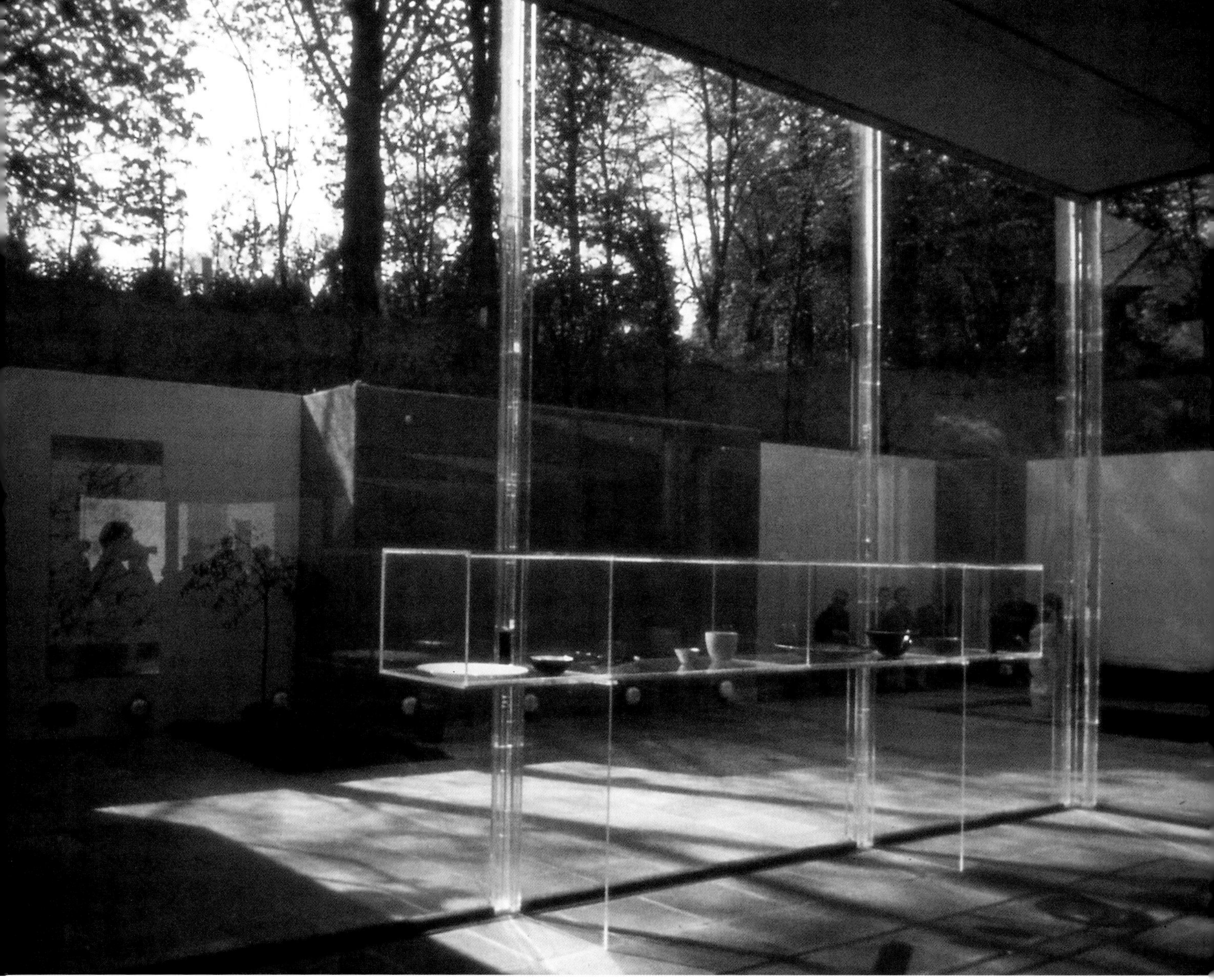

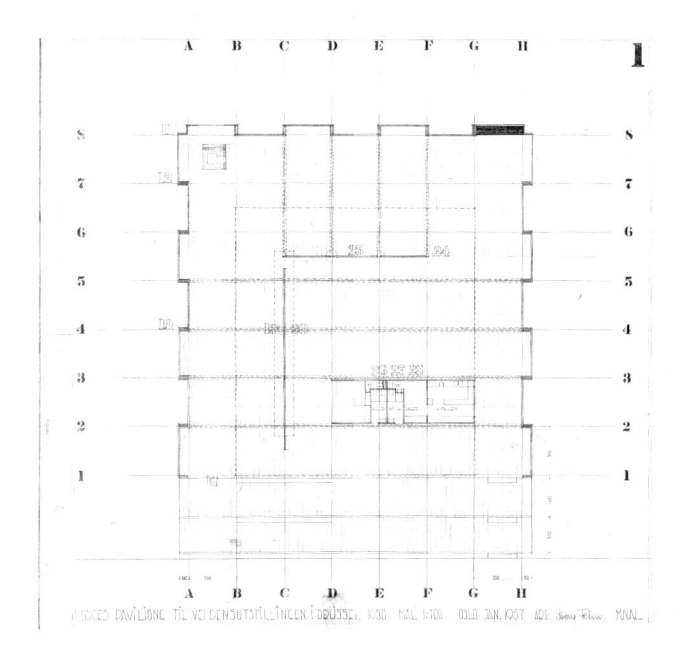

Norwegian Pavilion, Brussels: Views of display, plan.

EARLY FAME 51

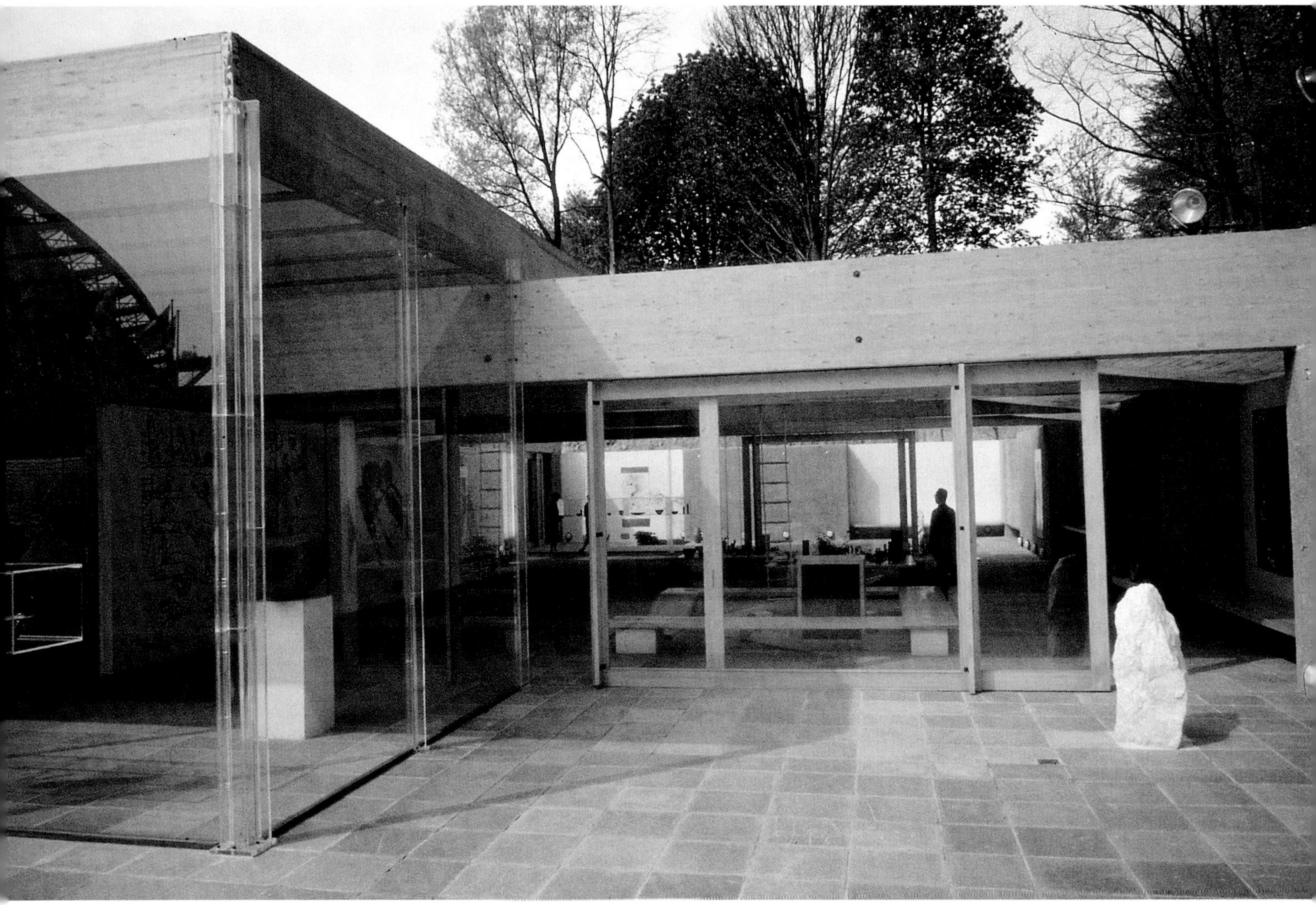

Views of Norwegian
Pavilion, Brussels.

rejected, and the pavilion was moved outside of Brussels and used as a day-care center for a few years.

A small camera store, 1960, in Oslo indicates further study of the concept of display that first came up in the Brussels pavilion; it also demonstrates Fehn's great care in detailing. This work no longer exists, but it is important in that it reveals an acute functional precision of an interior, which is later apparent in all of his houses. It also illustrates a spatial/visual story that evolves around the use of glass as the main material; reflection and transparency, shadow and light, are all part of the story line as one looks both into and out of the storefront. Fehn said, **The goal is to rediscover a dimension that never existed in the premise's original form.**

The second major competition in this early period of his career was the Nordic Pavilion for the Venice Biennale. Having completed his project in Brussels with all of its problems but also with a taste of recognition and early fame, it must have been exciting to turn the focus to Italy, and in particular to Venice, which would play an important role in Fehn's comprehension of urban life. Containing all the ingredients needed to set in motion his storytelling imagination, the city has never ceased to inspire him. His ability to simplify architectural complexity meant that his prolonged stay in the city during the construction of the Nordic Pavilion was a lucky and beneficial circumstance. Days of walking to the site and observing the city formed a special place in his architectural memory, and ever since he has been preoccupied with this unique city's boats, relationship to the sea, handling of goods, and integrity of circulation. Before a class trip to Venice, Fehn lectured on the city: **Venice is a city that has stolen its expression. It offers a form of coexistence out from its strange position between Asia and Europe. It grows earth, water, and luxury.**

Venice is the thief's city, the salesman's city. Every possible commodity passes through this city that is a meeting of the earth, the sea, and the landscape. **The city's birth is that the earth splits up, a fantastic instrument for urban function, and the canals are the urban streets.**

Venice discovered light and color. The carpets reached St. Mark's Square in a special way as ornaments born in the desert, in infinity, and they are laid down on the floor of St. Mark's Square. It is a powerful story. And the bridge . . . in it lies the desire for the stormy sea. When I look at Carpaccio's paintings I can imagine myself through the entirety of Venetian life. He is always on the lookout for dimensions that belong to the human body. Venice has dimensions that follow you, and it always welcomes you. The painter Turner also loved this city, and treated it as a concept.

It belongs to an unsocial revolution; it gave birth to interest rates and the villa. The beginnings of our suburban towns are in reality Palladio's villas; the center of a world image is torn to pieces and everything is measurable . . . Venice has a dimension that follows you, and it is always willing to accept you into its space.

The Nordic Pavilion for the Biennale continues to be one of Sverre Fehn's major works, and an important midcentury work for Scandinavia as a whole. The simple, open, but classic plan free from interior structure was carefully placed not just in the site but over the site: pieces of the roof were cut away for nature's objects. Fehn often commented that in Venice every tree is precious, and the lot assigned to the Nordic Pavilion had a number of them. One particular tree, part of an old avenue, stood on the edge of his appointed site. The authorities had planned to remove the beautiful old tree, but Fehn refused and instead embraced it in the main structure. The floor in dark Norwegian slate was a choice made in order to abstract the floor as site. The intention was that the dark slate would neither delineate interior and exterior nor float as a platform above the ground. Whatever was blown or carried into the space was drawn into the situation. There was no spatial hierarchy between nature, people, and the displayed

Camera store, Oslo:
Display, interior.

EARLY FAME 55

Sketch, 1993, "The column takes away the sky. The treetop removes heaven."

OPPOSITE Nordic Pavilion, Venice: Tree embraced by the structure.

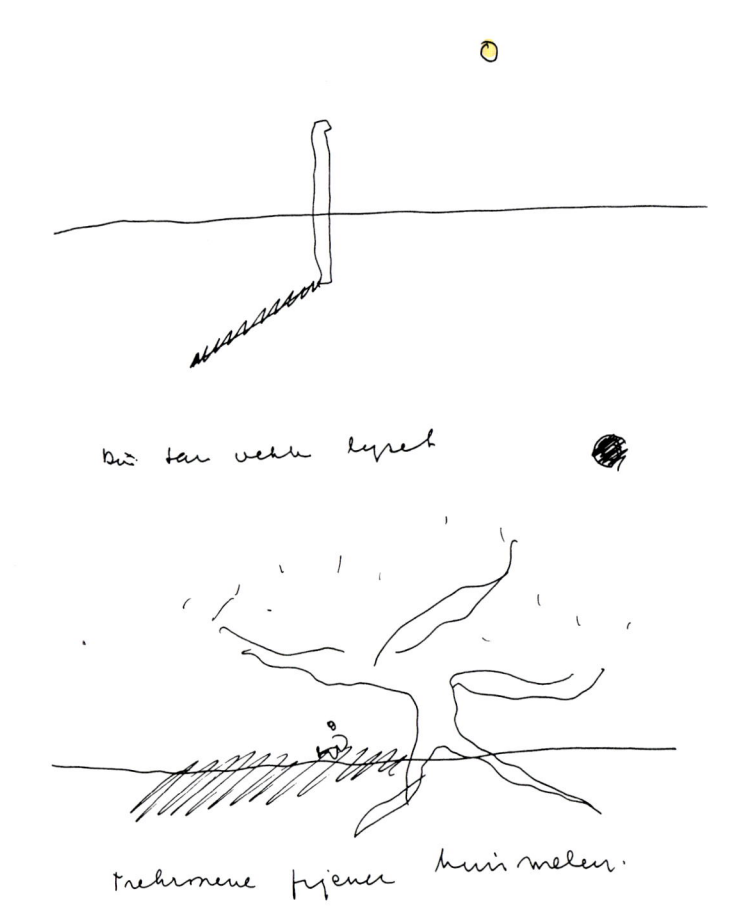

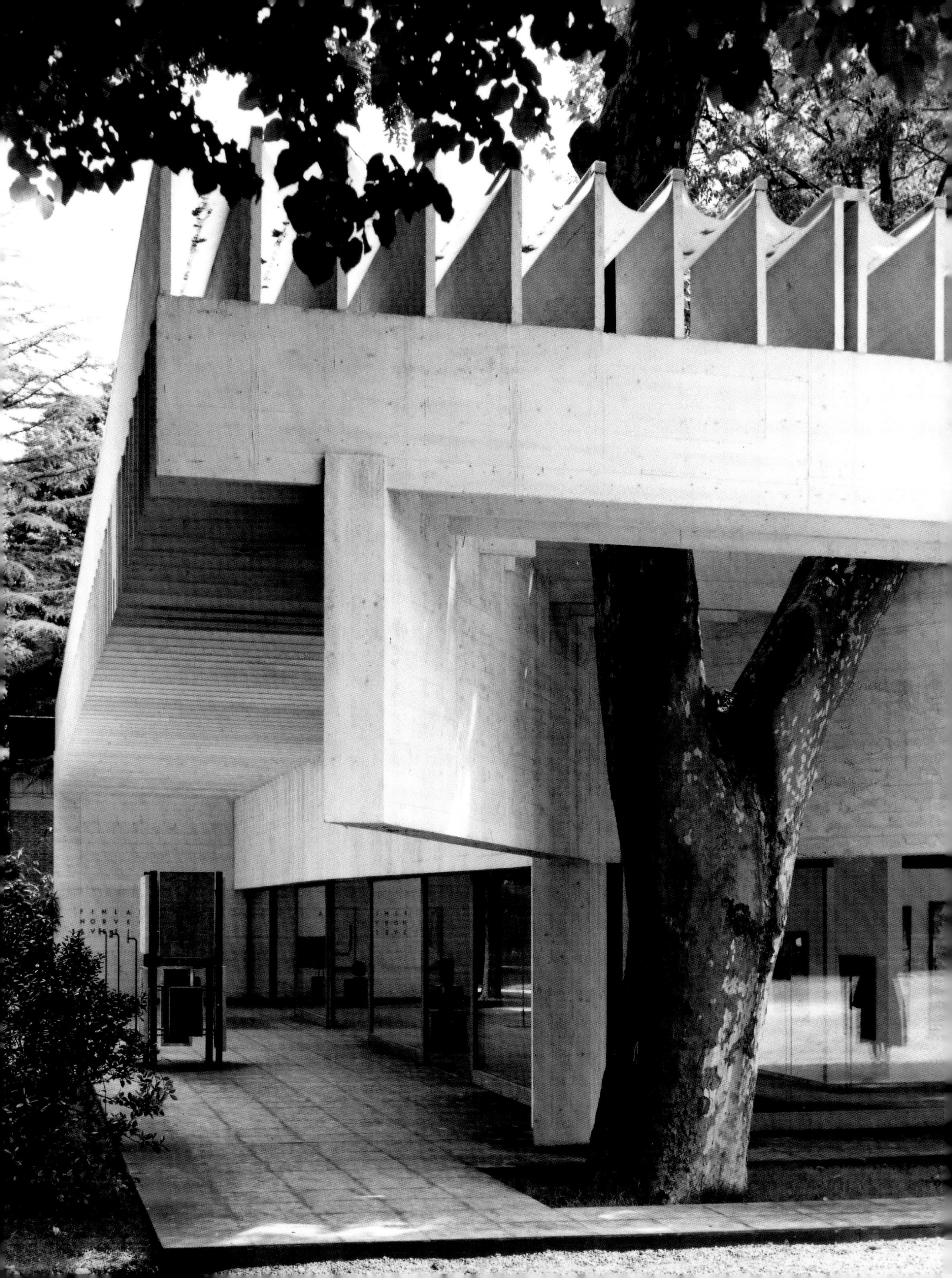

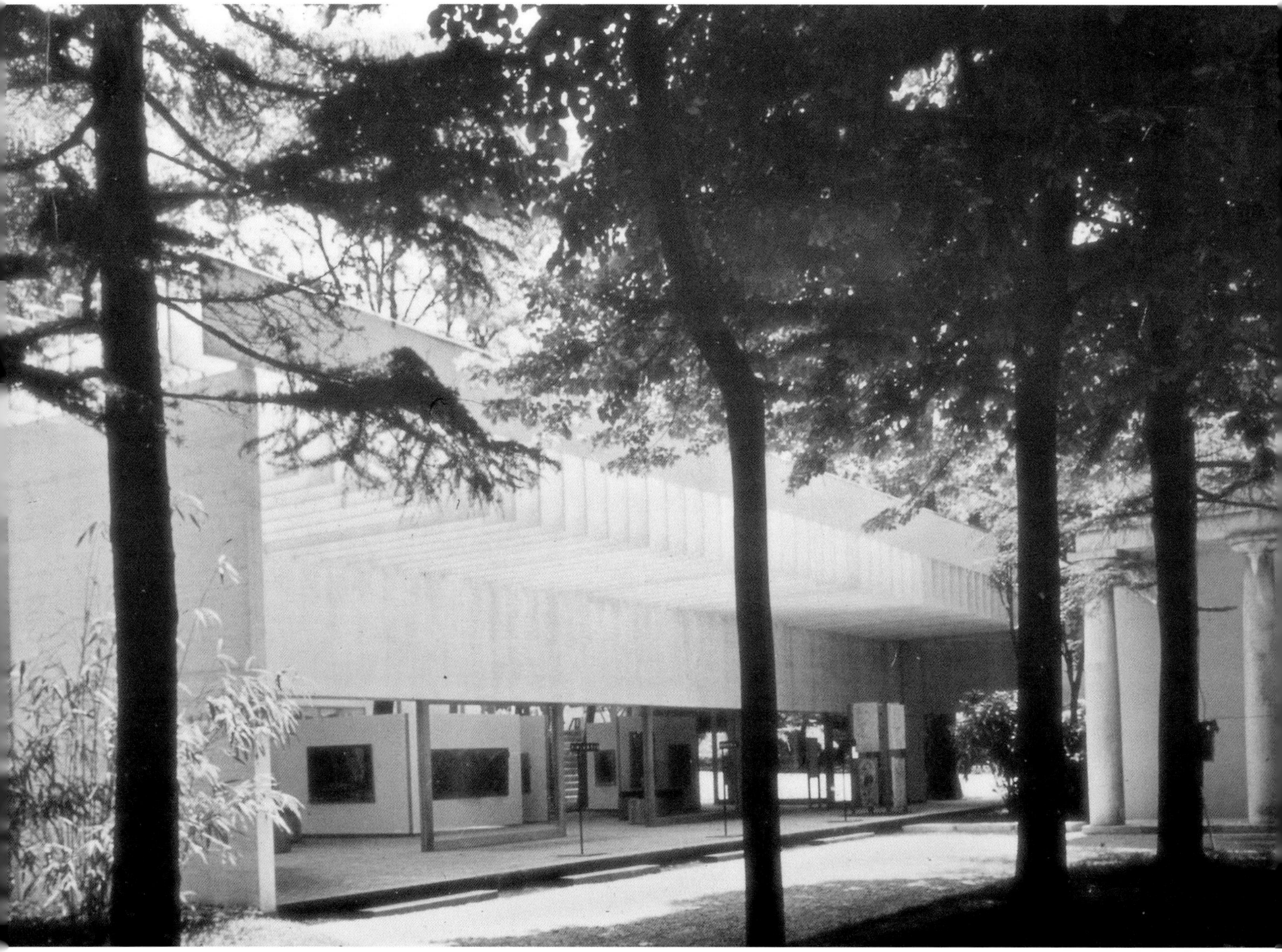

object. Unfortunately, a marble floor replaced the slate floor in the early 1980s, deflating some of its spatial energy.

The roof construction was integral to the realization of the pavilion's architectural intentions. Thin concrete beams form a two-layer grid that catches and diffuses natural light into a soft presence, a mass without shadows. The trees on the site grow through the grid, toward the sky. Atop the beams is a transparent fiberglass roof. Inside the pavilion, visitors are caught up in a Nordic light and spatial silence that sharply contrast with the bright light and surroundings of late-summer Venice. The completion of this pavilion established Fehn's international reputation as a young, up-and-coming architect; yet as time passed and other works gained recognition, such as the museum at Hamar, the pavilion was at times mistakenly credited to other architects.

Fehn drew two sets of furniture for the pavilion. The first included a leather and chrome chair, a small table, and a stool. The chrome chair prototype was later used in the Villa Norrköping during the Villa Parade housing exhibition in Sweden, 1964. Because the first set was so expensive, another chair, table, and stool were submitted; the design was modified to use Norwegian pine. None of these items was ever commercially produced, but Fehn made several prototypes. Two of the chrome chairs were for years a familiar part of his household.

Fehn has often commented on how difficult it was to complete these two pavilions to a level of uncompromising quality: **Some days before the opening of the pavilion I stood together with the lawyer for the Biennale Gardens at the bottom of the pyramidal stair that follows the landscape. He complained that the stair was too steep and asked if I would consider changing it. During the conversation the Biennale's president also joined us and politely inquired which language I preferred for the opening, and I answered, "Italian, Mr. President." And afterward, the president almost hopped up the steep pyramid steps. The lawyer turned and said,**

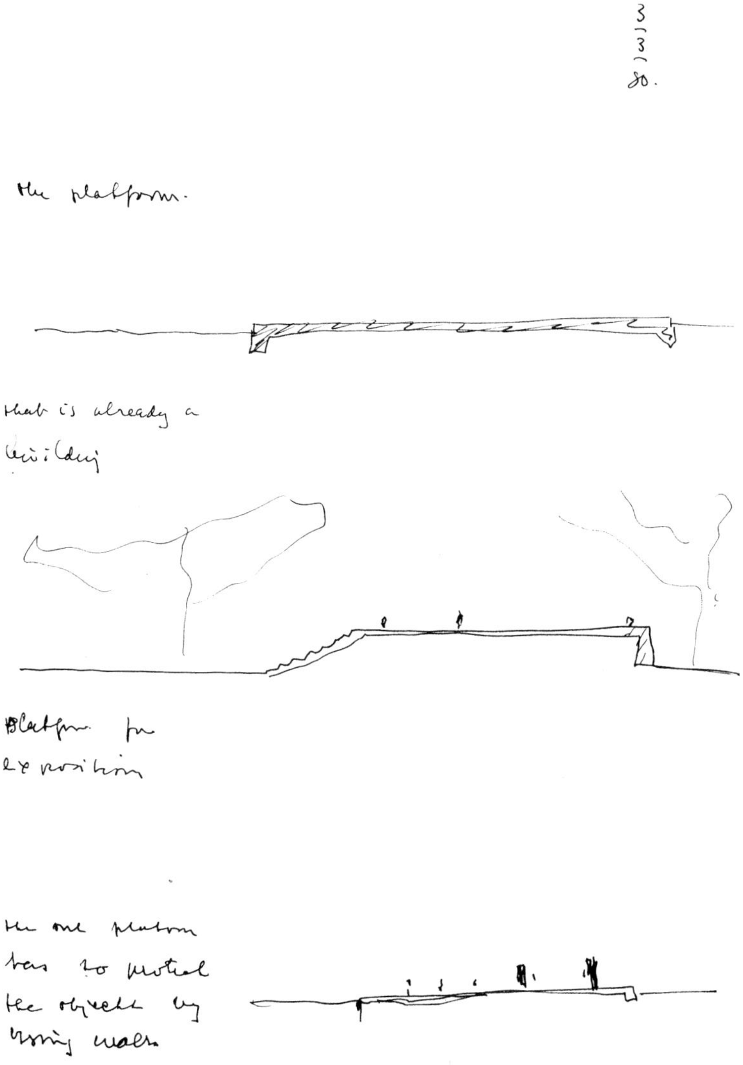

Sketch, March 3, 1980, "The platform. That is already a building. Platform for exposition. The one platform has to protect the objects by moving walls."

OPPOSITE Nordic Pavilion, Venice: Facade with large sliding doors.

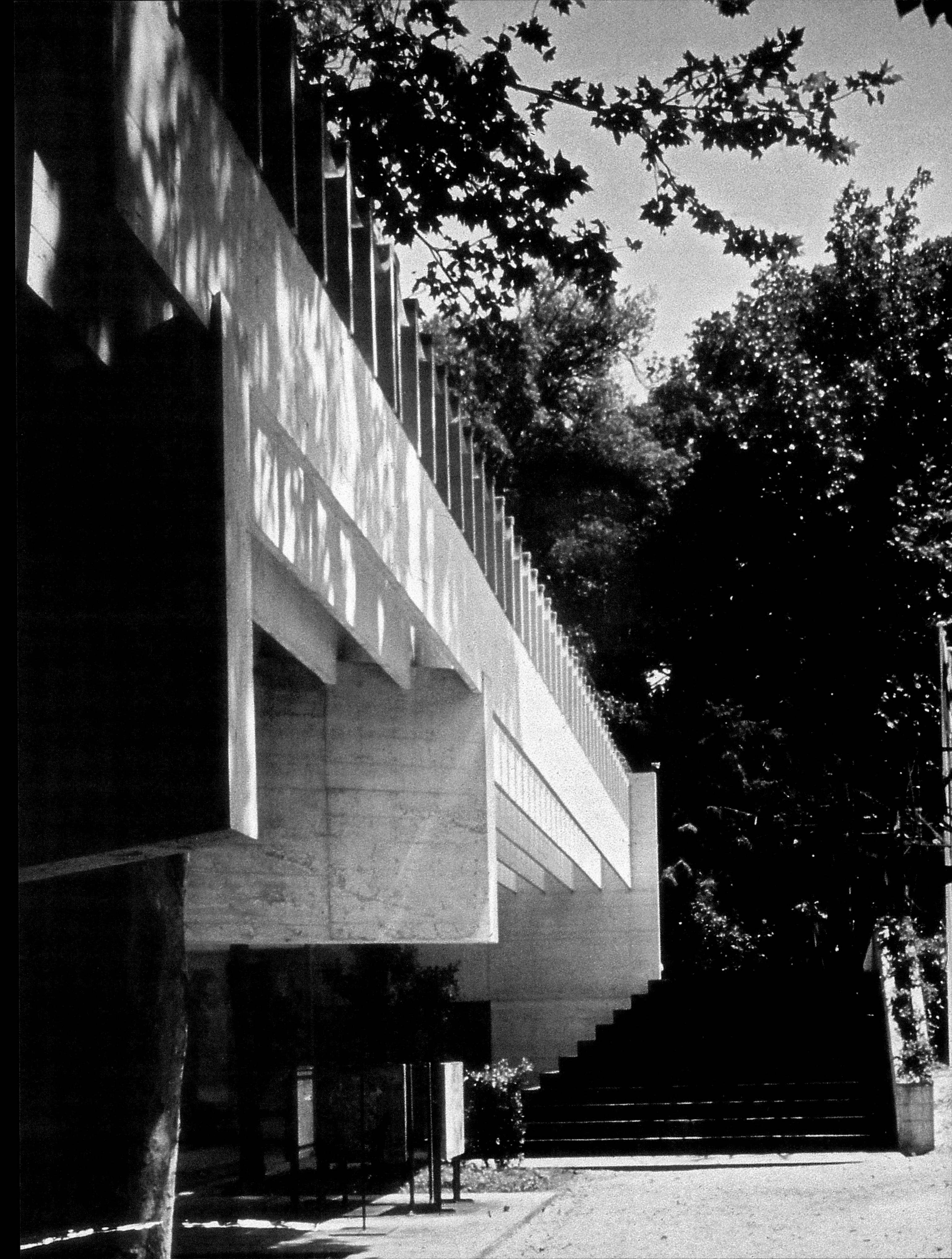

Nordic Pavilion, Venice: Continuation of an old allée, section, elevation.

OVERLEAF Nordic Pavilion, Venice.

"Well, if the president can manage them, so can I."

At this point in his career, Fehn had little experience in handling such a prestigious international commission. There were things that went wrong, but he had the capacity to keep his focus, stay with the project, and not give in to compromise. He has often spoken of the optimism that pervaded in this period, and the sincere belief in architecture's capacity to fulfill whatever role it was given. I have since heard many of his friends of the same generation make similar observations. In a sense, Fehn has been fearless in his ability to follow his own direction guided by his own intuition. The architectural backdrop of modern pre–World War II Scandinavia was quite strong, which gave a sense of authority and confidence, as did his teachers Knutsen and Korsmo. To this inheritance Fehn appended a deep concern over a structure's meeting with the earth. The visitor was always part of the conceptual discussion, and the pavilions were affixed to the earth in the same physical world as the visitor.

The Brussels and Venice pavilions gave Fehn early fame, contacts abroad, and a certain degree of confidence in his future, but they had little impact on the amount of work coming into his office in Oslo. **After the Venice pavilion was completed I kept up my contacts with Finland and Helsinki. They saved me internationally. The Venice pavilion received a lukewarm response at home. Christian [Norberg-Schulz] said he could have thought of building something like it. Blomstedt and Pietilä became very**

EARLY FAME 61

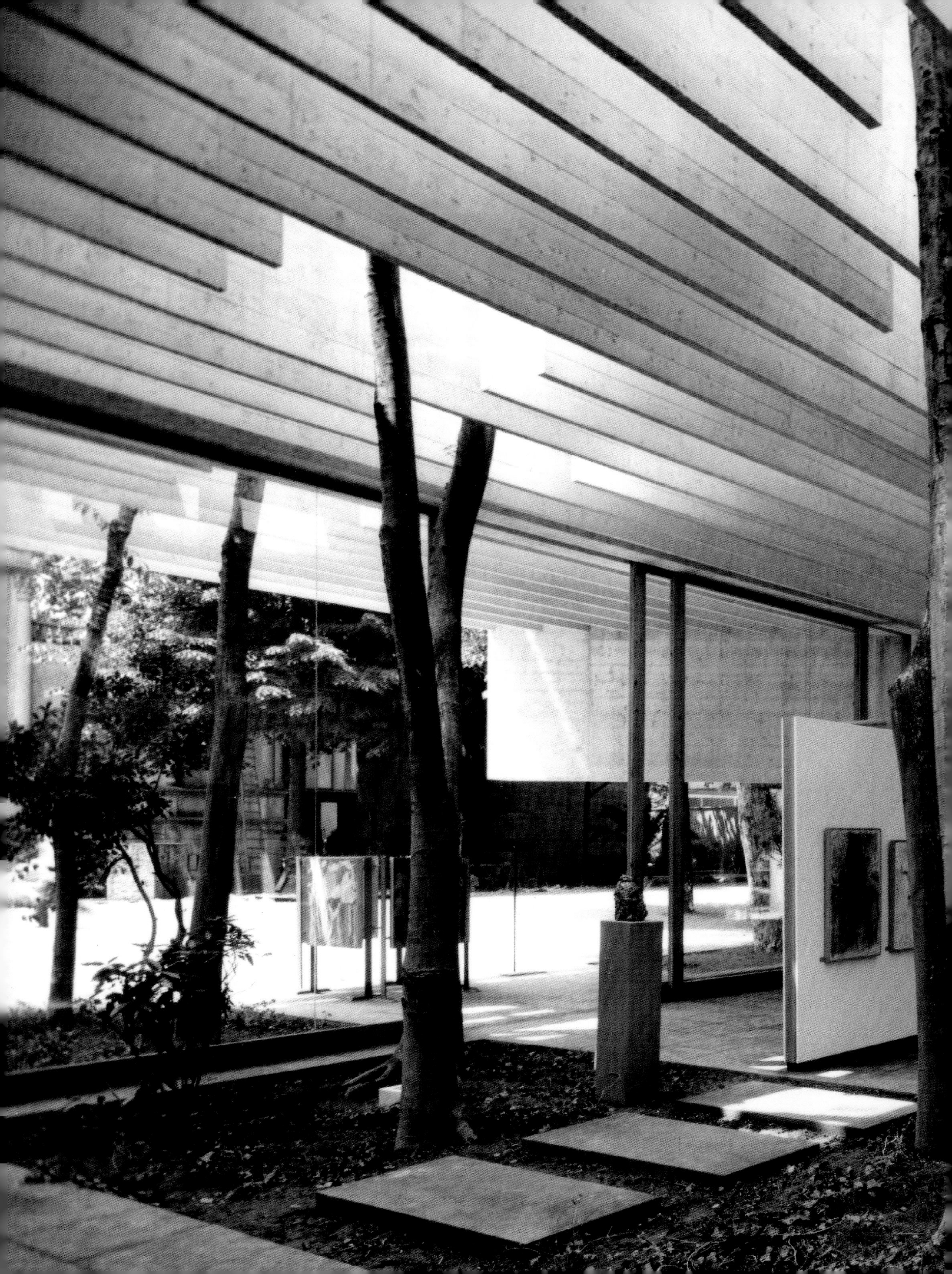

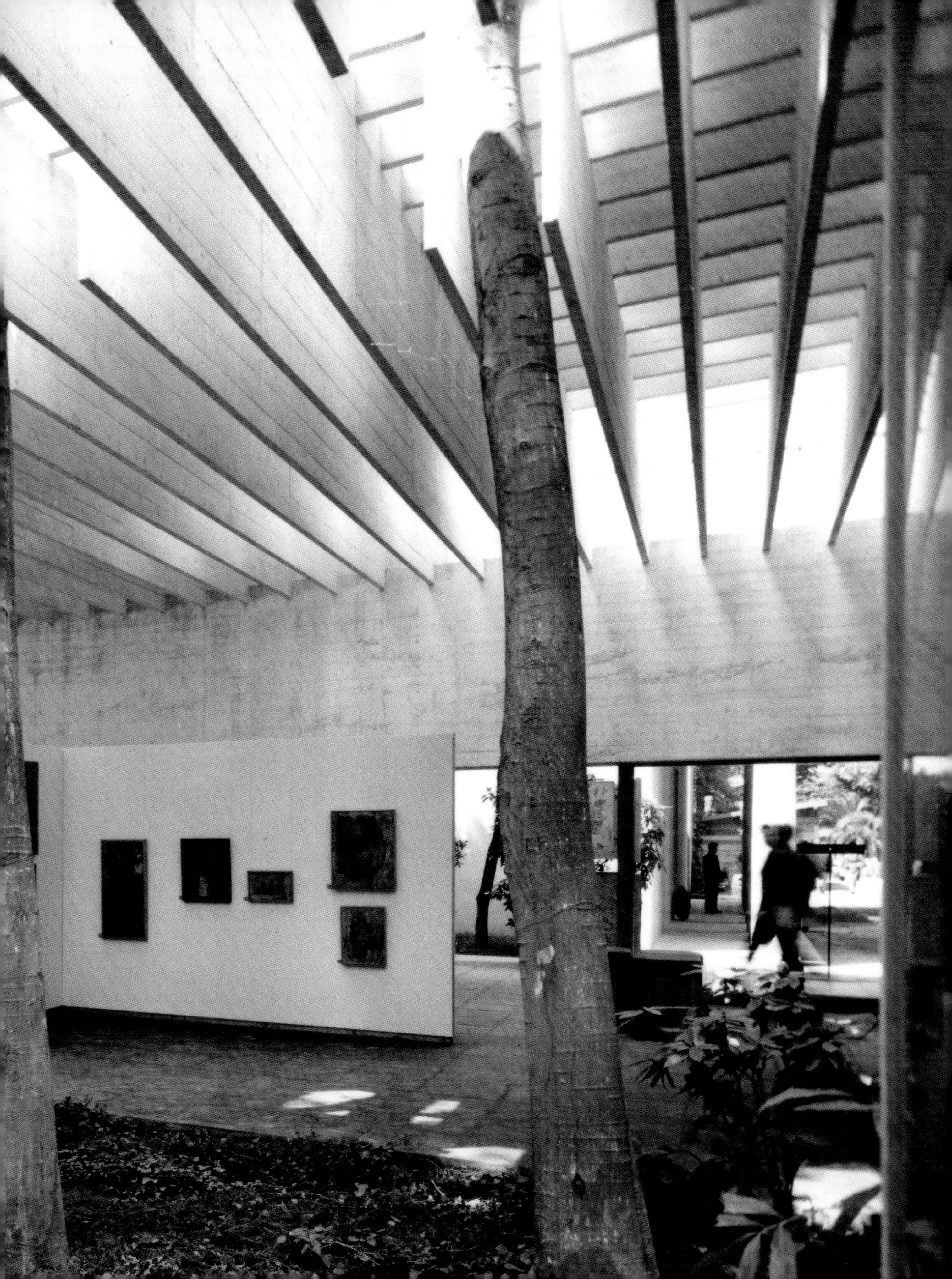

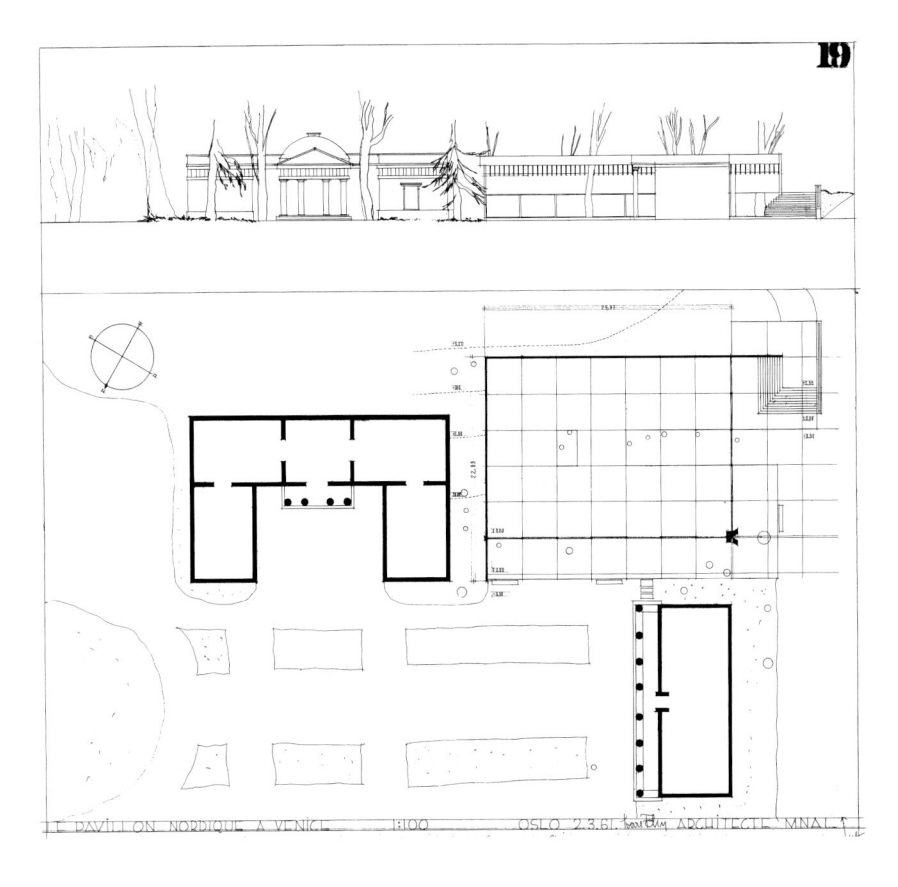

Nordic Pavilion, Venice: Plan of Nordic Pavilion (upper right) with American and Danish Pavilions, pyramidal stair.

important for me; the Finnish have always supported me and have been incredibly loyal. CIAM crossed me off the list, and it wasn't so easy to follow up. For a while I didn't have money for anything, and for this reason it was impossible to build up a network. I had the Schreiner House and some teaching on the side, but I couldn't afford to enjoy or accept applause. At the start of the Villa Norrköping project, I had to sleep in the car [the 2CV] in order to see the site.

In years to come, when the situation in the office was again quite grave, this period and memories of these two pavilions kept alive for Fehn a sense of purpose and drive. The observations he made during his stay in Venice would continue to influence and color his lectures and conceptual thinking around new projects. Here he also met another passionate architect: **I remember my short meeting with Carlo Scarpa in Venice. I had an appointment, but he arrived very late. I talked about Oslo, but for Scarpa** it was somewhere beyond the Alps, and he remarked, "For me, there is no culture north of the Alps."

In a later lecture Fehn said: [**Scarpa**] **is in material. He thinks material. He manages to pull together a project in such a way that it tells you it has always been there.**

At the core of Fehn's architectural nature is a spatial attitude that is quite different from that of Scarpa. His work carries a clear posture belonging to structure, structure as a screen differentiating inside from outside, light from shadow. For Fehn it is the structure that calls and directs the story: **How much should structure direct the architectonic story? How much should it decide? Shall I put forth only portions of my room picture? How much of this room shall I hide and how much shall I deliver for those out there? The entire architectonic story is played out in an orchestra of structure, and daylight is the material that strengthens the plot.**

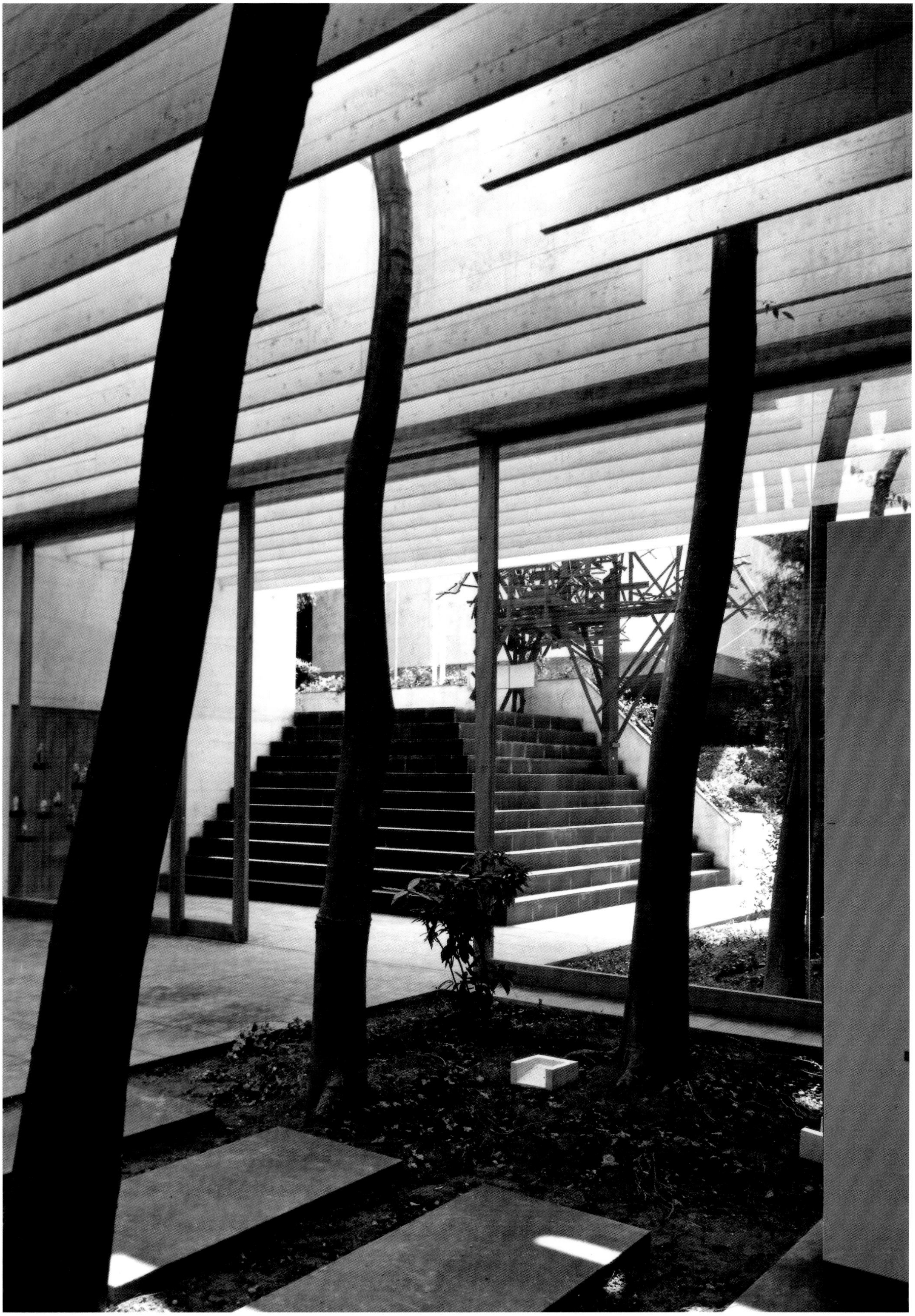

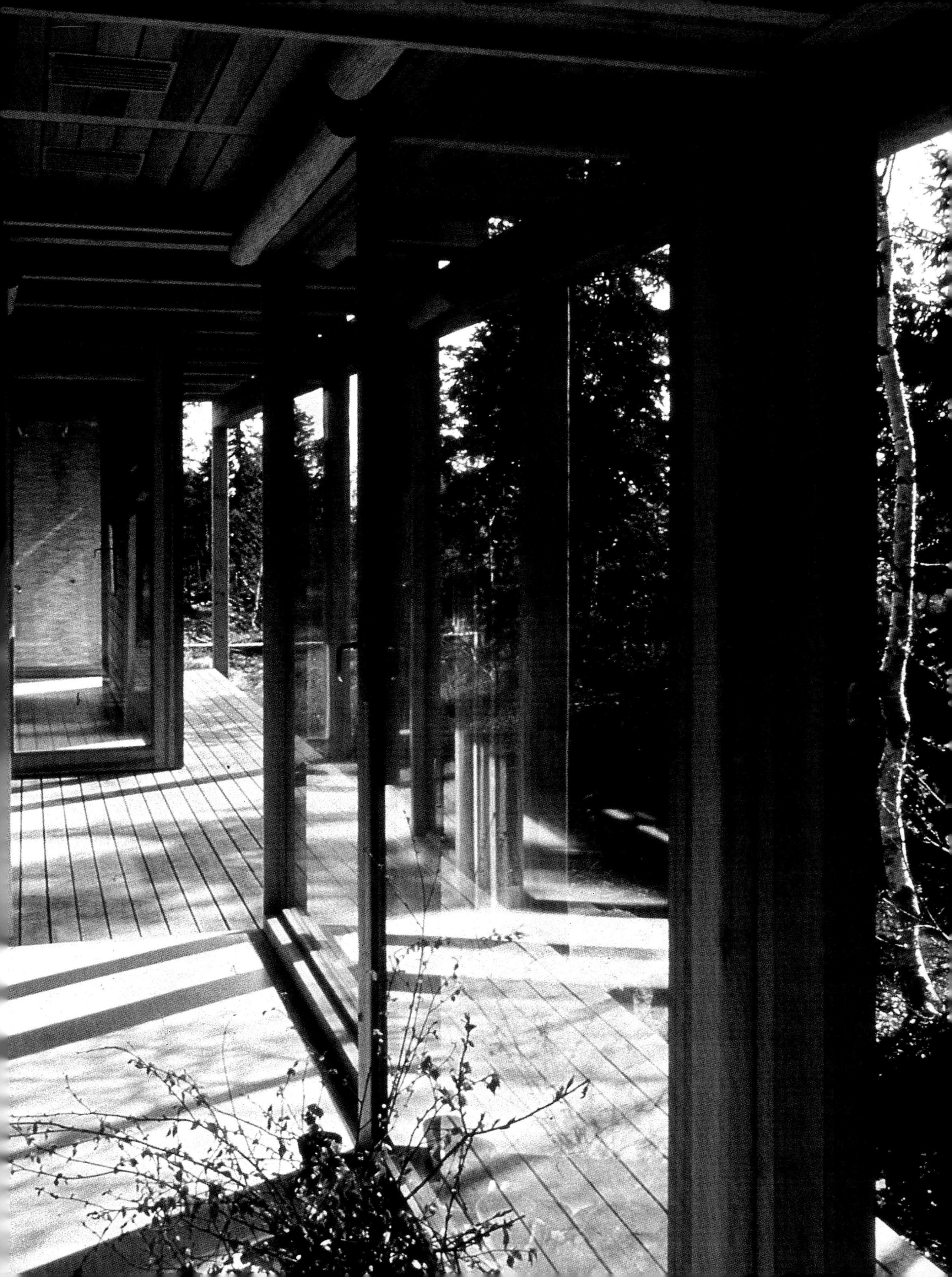

CHAPTER 4

BEYOND THE IMAGE OF HOME | A precision related to proportion and scale is evident in all of Fehn's work, but it is most clearly felt in his private houses. These homes always developed through a long process of interpretation in which the client's desires, needs, and inner nature found a reciprocal scale and the physical result gained an unmeasurable dimension.

Architecture must travel from a spiritual dimension over to the concrete world. It should manifest itself in a variety of dimensions, and all thoughts are in relation to one size. It is always a discussion on how one shall relate to human size—the inner personal space and the violent space, the world—and how one tumbles into this reality as a human being. How fast shall you let this person reach the door? The stairs and the length of a footstep decide everything, even the way a priest goes up to his pulpit. It is these precisely measured stories you give to the craftsman: how you want the inhabitant to react to a communication. Material is involved in giving a dimension. It becomes a character in this story. It has inherent rules and limits.

What type of sensitivity should architecture radiate? Shall a column be so slender that I can circle it with my hand or does it need a circumference of two people to go around it? Architecture's choices feel intuitive when you enter a room. The constructive history lies in judgments, a story between yourself and material. What do you want to say, what are you looking for in your proportioning? I draw a space for seven people, high. One is working with one scale in relation to another scale. One does not control the architectural space before one attacks the human scale. This is a dimension you must submit to, and out from this confrontation, you build up an extraordinary world because you have something to work against. How should a door be? If you follow the standard you won't know where you are. Do you wish to be polite? Well, offer a small door. Generous? I draw a large open door. Thus the inhabitant receives a dimension in relation to his own scale. Look at palaces: a little door in the large door so they can be comfortable in their everyday life. Corbu never lost his careful attention to what he observed. He intentionally destroyed the servile standard meter. We need different "user" scales. African towns can appear dimensionless, but if you enter the inhabitant's thinking mechanism, you will find they have a very precise scale.

The single-family house has always played an important role in Fehn's office, especially as a testing ground for ideas. Fehn could be as absorbed in these modest jobs as he was in much larger commissions, and at times it was just these small projects that kept the office going. His houses span the breadth of his career and reflect all the changes of attitude and interest that came and went over the years. Some houses continued to be an inspiration long after completion. It was often the large, complex programs in combination with the limited square meters available that intrigued him the most. At the same time, he felt that understanding the relationship of house to home was an essential architectural theme that challenged him anew with each project. He used to say to his students: **If you know how to draw or sketch the essence of a given program for a villa, you can more or less draw anything.** The sober and controlled use of space and material that typified Scandinavian living was very evident in the first houses, and Fehn retained this sensibility despite changing attitudes in relation to comfort and consumption brought about by increased prosperity and easy communication. In fact, he responded not by retracting earlier positions but by adding another layer. The houses built in the mid- to late 1980s have the same exacting physicality, but they anticipate the impact of modern visualization. In his later work, his inventive stories and sketches, which once functioned as a method to reach a core understanding of a project's spatial identity, came to act as visual signposts. His final house, completed in 1997, carries all these elements yet also reiterates a characteristic present in each one of Fehn's houses, a clear geometrical plan.

He started from scratch with every commission, but two essential elements, fire and water, always directed the early conceptual development. Fire and water formed the permanent units, the fixed core of the house. These spaces, connected to the earth and

Johnsrud House, Bærum, Norway: Early plan sketches.

PAGE 66 Schreiner House, Oslo.

BEYOND THE IMAGE OF HOME 69

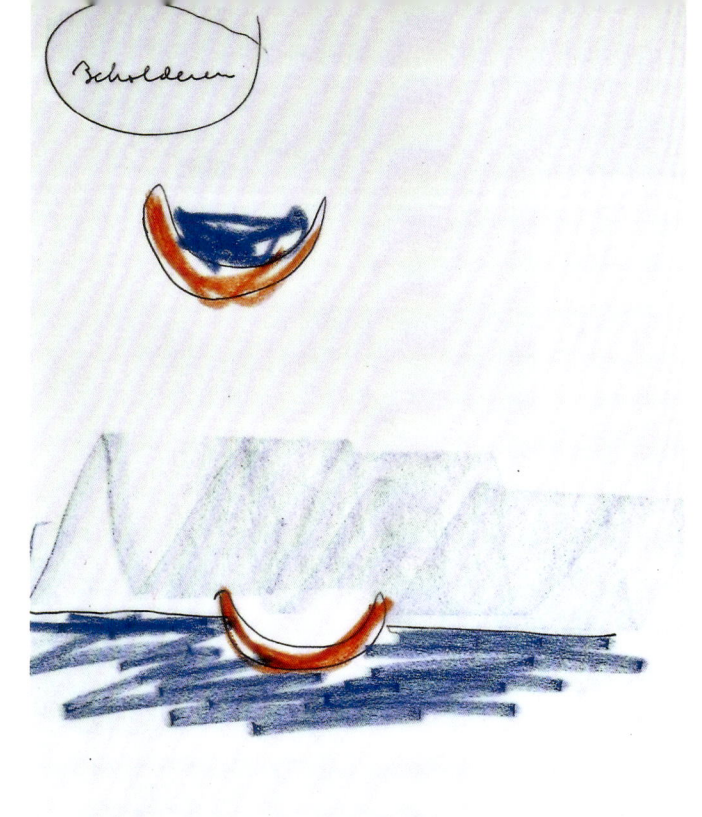

Sketch of bowl as a container to gather water.

OPPOSITE Sketch, "The pot for boiling water."

filled with essential materials for living, were conceptually more complex and, from an emotional and human point of view, were not at all what Louis Kahn rationally considered "servant spaces."

Once water is regarded as a central source of survival, once fire is regarded as a central source of protection and nighttime light, the house gains an exceedingly physical orientation. Other spatial decisions fan out from these two central themes, and there is little material waste due to visual concerns. While this is perhaps a symbolic attitude, Fehn achieves very tight and precise space. He has often commented on the effect of the slow loss of the understanding of a fire/water/earth relationship within a house: the changing conceptual awareness of places of rest and nourishment is moving the house away from a basic understanding of home to that of a temporary rest stop. In contemporary residential design, the volume of the house increases with each decade, and fire and water are placed everywhere. The kitchen is far more an image of cooking, and the fire a computerized flame. Fehn does not attempt to go back in time—he does not envision his clients sitting around an open fire or bringing water from a well—but he endeavors to retain an awareness of what one is consuming and how. Fehn argues that in the day-to-day rituals embedded in these two elements lies an aspect of time, in particular an aspect of "waiting," and that this time aspect is a resistance force: it sets limits. Today the house is equipped to perform everything at all times with little or no effort. Basic no longer exists. **Tragedy arrived when one had to live with instant light everywhere. Tied to the fireplace was a ritual belonging to a time aspect. Now you can no longer hide in the darkness. When light conquers the night, the wall is born, shame's wall, the interior. When a house contains night's light, it erases age. It was generous with the old.**

Fehn's houses are all modest in size even when the brief indicates a large home. They do not effuse wealth, but they are spatially rich and elicit an architectural performance. The client must inhabit or activate the interior space. Each perceived activity results in a spatial decision that reaches toward the fundamental core of that activity. Whether it is a kitchen or a place to relax, the space is not passive in its limitations. In an interview, Fehn said, **The bathroom is an extension of your clothes. It is a big costume that includes waste.** The projects are drawn in minute detail, but this is not the same as unlimited space or invention, because everything in the program is questioned in relation to size and the pressure it puts on the total interior space.

In one sense, Fehn's houses are like small fortresses protecting their inhabitants but also closing and opening up to nature as appropriate. In their precise articulation the homes respond on many levels to seasonal change. Opening a sliding door does more than create an opening: one in fact takes away a wall, as in the Schreiner House, or opens up a corner, as in Villa Norrköping. What is in the winter an exterior space becomes in the summer part of the interior. Each house has a precise and particular relationship to the immediately adjacent exterior space. This interstitial area

gepfens/hitler
wor Wannes
bee paint kohl

ag.

og

Simme nugi   null

is as carefully considered as the interior space, activating the total area to a maximum. This reflects the economic utilization of seasonal change found in early Nordic homes: technology is not a cover-up for poor use of space and material. In an interview from 1978, Fehn gives some insight into how he uses the spatial condition of night and his perception of its light:

The night gains an incredible value in that it erases space. The fire invents light and heat, and through this light the darkness gains new importance: it creates the story, it entertains. The fire invents a room where there is light. The fire is a producer of space, and in the shadow mystery is born.

Villa Norrköping, 1963–64, generated public and professional interest from the start, and it would continue to attract attention over the years. Equally it has been a source of inspiration for many of Fehn's stories that would accompany articles on his work. The house along with five others was part of a housing exhibition in Norrköping, Sweden, interpreting the Scandinavian home of the future. In plan, the house is a Greek cross. The central core contains all functions centered around water, including kitchen and bathrooms. Around the core, the arms of the cross sponsor different activities; through the use of sliding walls, they transform from one room to nine rooms. At each of the four intersections of the cross, large glass doors and windows offer natural light and unhindered access to the exterior. The houses were put up for sale at the close of the exhibition; one year later, a Swedish weekly magazine interviewed the owners of Fehn's design, presenting it along with one other house from the exhibition. The article, titled "Please, Come Without a Moving Van," provides a portrait of the Sylvan family and also gives a good idea of what Scandinavians desired and expected from a modern house in the early 1960s: "The radical plan and use of new building materials was foreign to this area, and many expressed their skepticism with a warning of 'ugh,' but museum director Bo and his wife Anna Sylvan knew from the very first second this was home. Six-year-old Märten and Tova, two and a half, could not

Sketch, "Today everything is driven by the same type of energy."

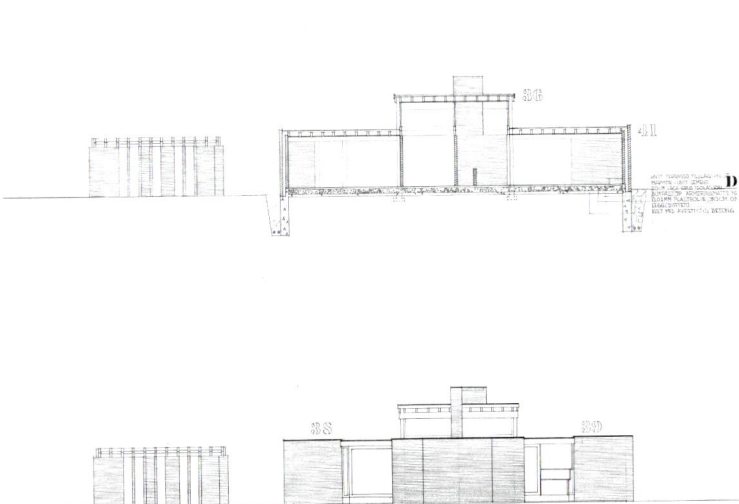

Villa Norrköping, Norrköping, Sweden: Sections and elevations, model of roof structure, exterior view.

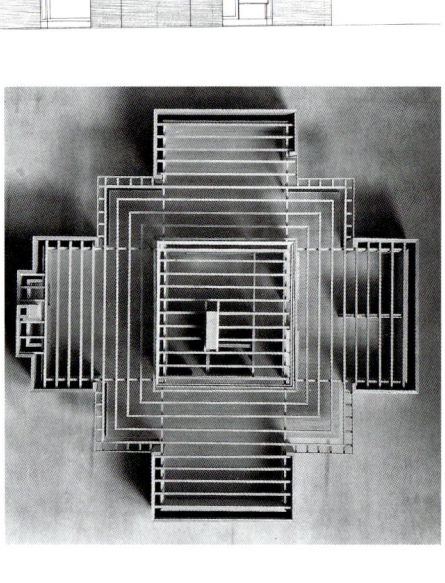

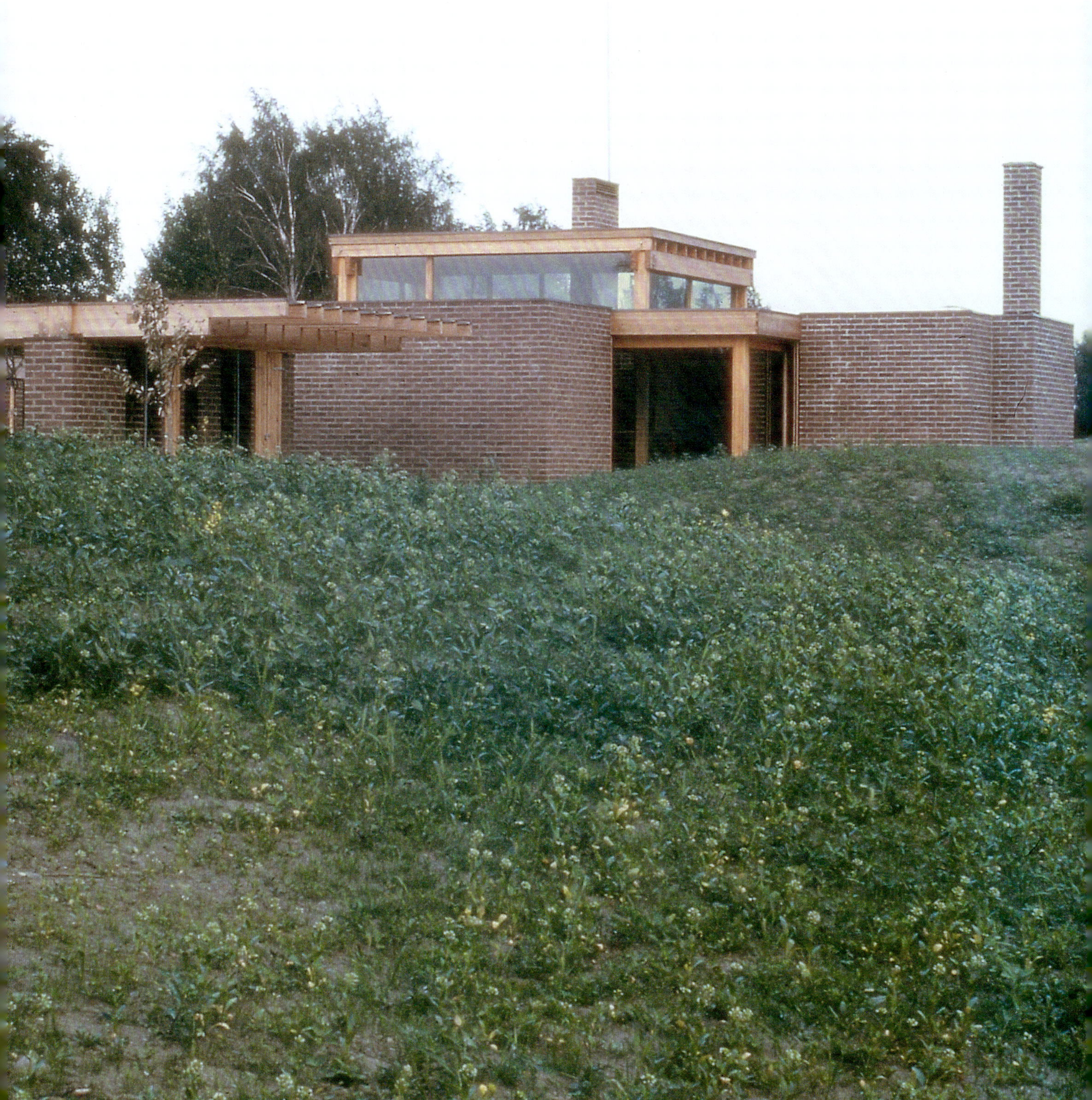

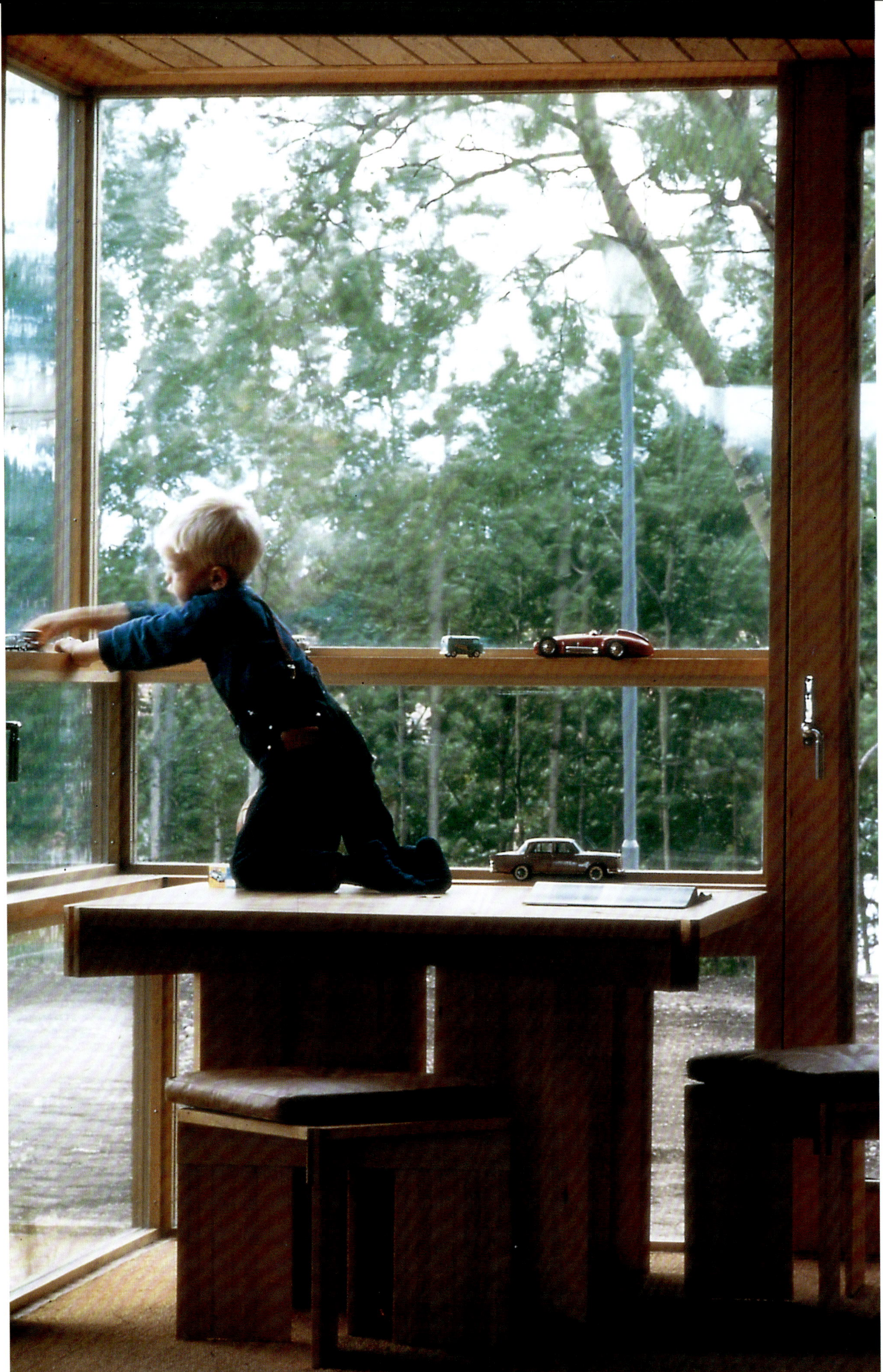

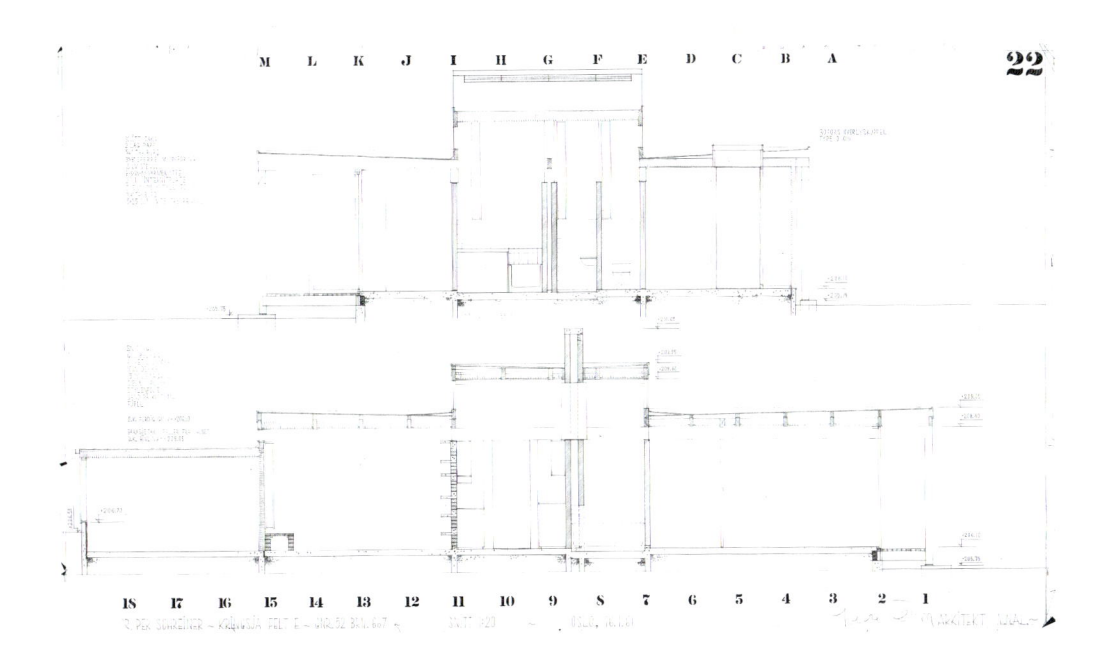

Villa Norrköping: Glass corner, sections, views of interior.

78 THE PATTERN OF THOUGHTS

Villa Norrköping:
Open corner, kitchen
in central core.

Villa Norrköping: Plan showing sliding walls.

OPPOSITE Sketch, 1984–85, with Villa Rotonda.

express their feelings about the house, but it was noticeable that it suited them very well, too. You must not move in here with sentimentality or nonchalant thinking but rather with a minimum of possessions, otherwise the whole concept of the house is lost. This is what the Sylvans did—parted with their old furniture without complaining and with this discovered that this unusual house worked well and all practical chores were much easier. The house demanded a more informal and simpler lifestyle."

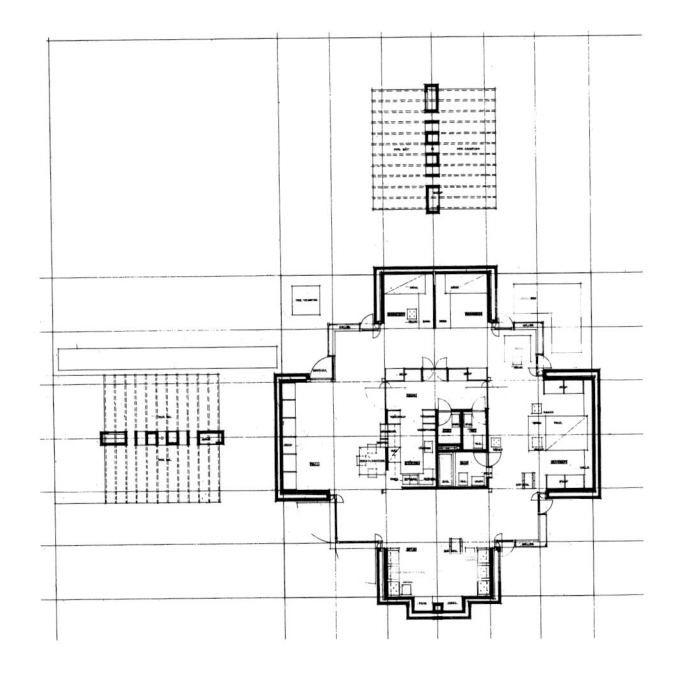

Fehn described the house in a lecture at the Oslo School of Architecture: **The house is constantly giving darkness a scale. It has a precise division of mass in relation to wood and brick. It is the glass corners that direct the light, and from here one can withdraw into a situation that is almost dark if desirable. One enters a cavelike situation. Pietilä dreamed about making caves in wood.**

In Villa Norrköping, the focus and polarity of fire and water is very clear; along with its geometry and a site that was assigned only after the design was completed, this factor resulted in a house that would generate a number of Palladio stories over the years. Fehn had many variations on these "conversations"; the following is one of his earliest:

Corbusier: How are things going with your Villa Rotonda?

Palladio: I think the same family still owns it. I think they still live there.

Corbusier: Ah, my Villa Savoie is already a historic monument.

Palladio: You are challenging infinity.

Corbusier: I thought I was challenging nature.

Palladio: Yes, of course.

A long pause.

Palladio: What do you think about eternity?

Corbusier: Boring.

Palladio: Yes, we both belong to the earth.

Corbusier: The wind has carried us both to the same acknowledgement.

Palladio: You have challenged infinity.

Corbusier: I thought I challenged nature.

Palladio: Yes, exactly.

A year later Fehn gave a lecture in Urbino for the International Laboratory of Architecture and Urban Design, and he presented a new conversation. This time it was between himself and Palladio; Villa Norrköping is clearly the subject. **The interior is a stage play with light. The sliding doors that give you darkness change the plan from nine to one room. In this house I met Palladio. He was tired.**

Palladio: You put all the service rooms like the bath, the toilets, and kitchen in the house's center . . . I made a big room there, and you know the dome with the overlights was without glass in those days. I drew the room as an ovation to nature. It could be filled with rain, heat, and cold.

Sverre Fehn: And the four directions?

Palladio: Ah yes, you know (and he began to grow much smaller) at that time we lost the horizon.

He stopped for a moment.

You opened up the corners . . . you are about to lose the earth.

BEYOND THE IMAGE OF HOME

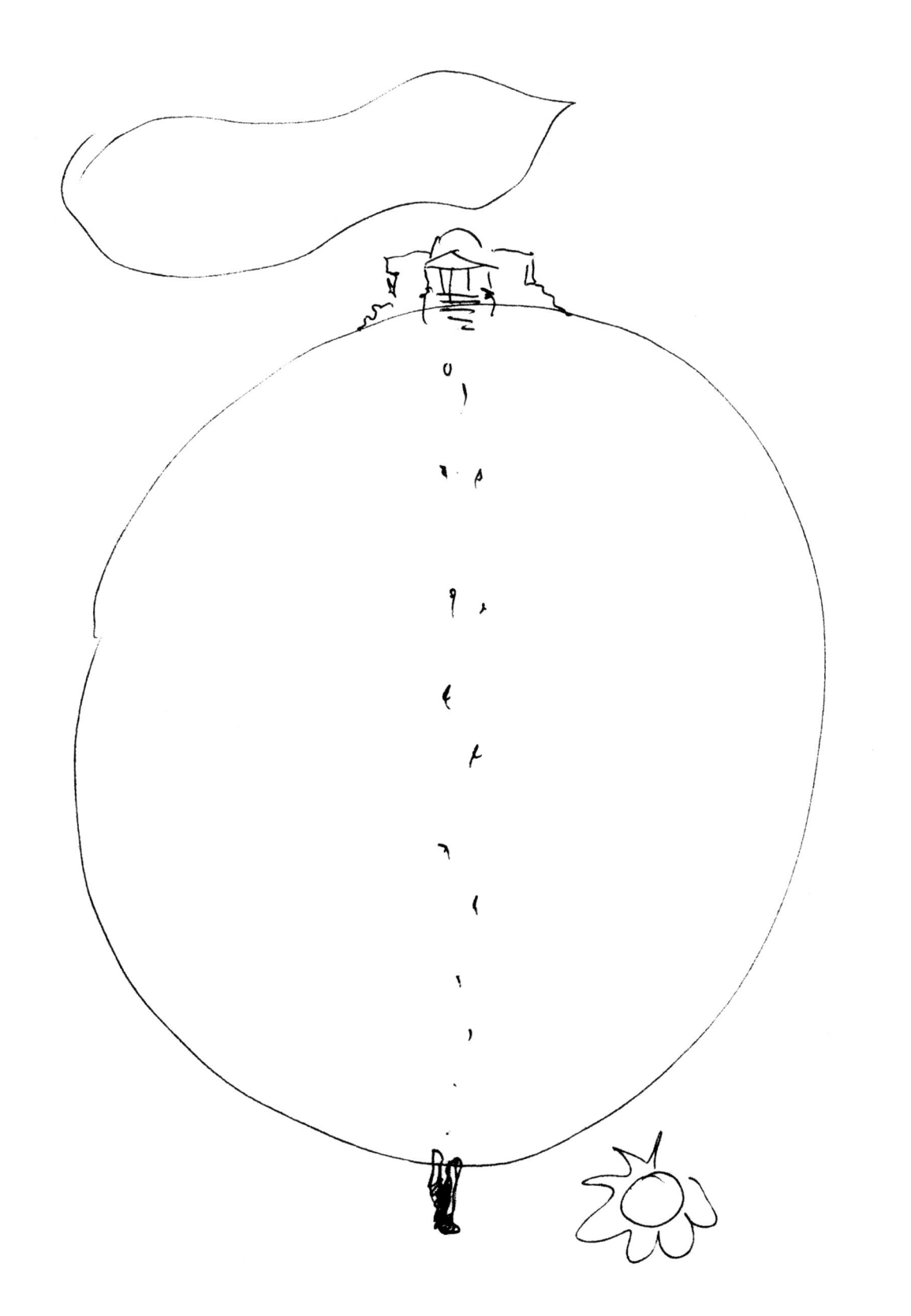

82 THE PATTERN OF THOUGHTS

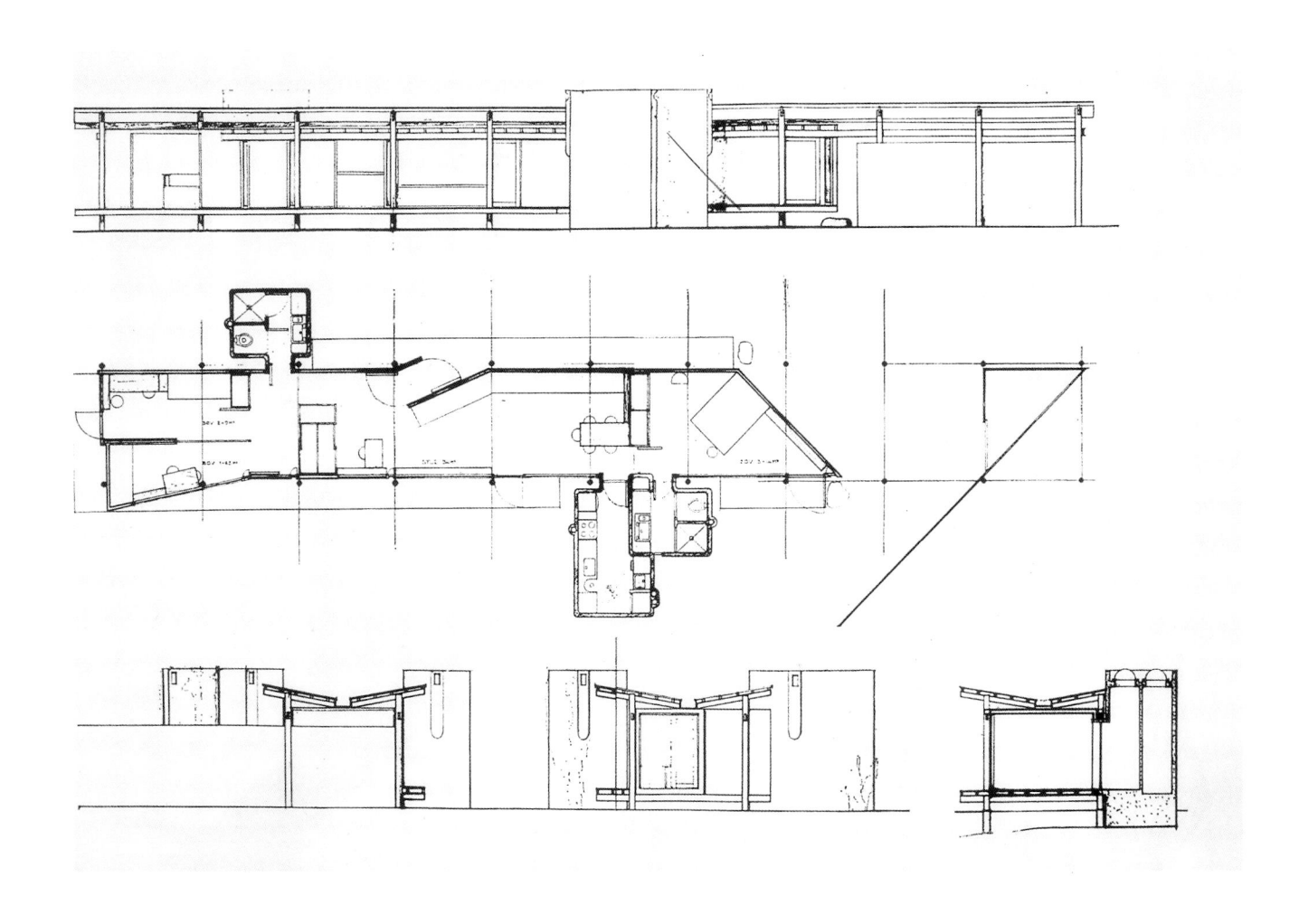

Schreiner House, Oslo: Exterior floor, roof detail.

OPPOSITE Eternit Prototype House: Plan, sections.

Sverre Fehn: Tell me more.
Palladio's voice was fainter.
Palladio: All constructive thoughts are related to death.
And then he was gone.

When entering one of Fehn's houses one is almost always taken by surprise. The interest or need to orient oneself in relation to objects or details as objects is absent, and instead one is given spatial content, compact and energized. It is an intensely personal space, yet it carries no article or direct signal of the private domain; rather it embraces one's body and one cannot escape. The scale is always at the minimum; thus the interior space never takes over. None of the houses carries a room plan in the traditional sense, but the plan is always individualized, with clear forethought to possible adaptation. Sleeping and living areas expand and contract or extend out into the exterior; everything adapts and moves around the stable central core of fire and water. The Johnsrud House, 1968–70, is the most extreme. In what is almost an inversion of Villa Norrköping, service areas are located along the periphery of the house, and the main living space is at the center. Originally all the interior walls were bookshelves on wheels, but this entailed so much discipline that eventually the walls around the sleeping areas were made permanent. The Schreiner House, 1959–63, which Fehn often referred to as his homage to Japan, is compact but at the same time open. The street facade is, for the most part, a closed wall; the opposite facade with its sliding glass doors insists on a direct relationship to the exterior and to the adjacent forest. In this home, the kitchen and the fireplace again play a central role. While the Schreiner and Johnsrud Houses and Villa Norrköping all represent an interpretation of the unit, the project that explores this concept most profoundly, but with a more mechanical approach, is the Eternit Prototype House, 1963–64. The bath and kitchen are prefabricated entities plugged into the rectangular structure of the house as two focal points. A clear inspiration from Fehn's time in Prouvé's office is evident, yet this scheme also carries Fehn's own tight simplicity of plan.

84 THE PATTERN OF THOUGHTS

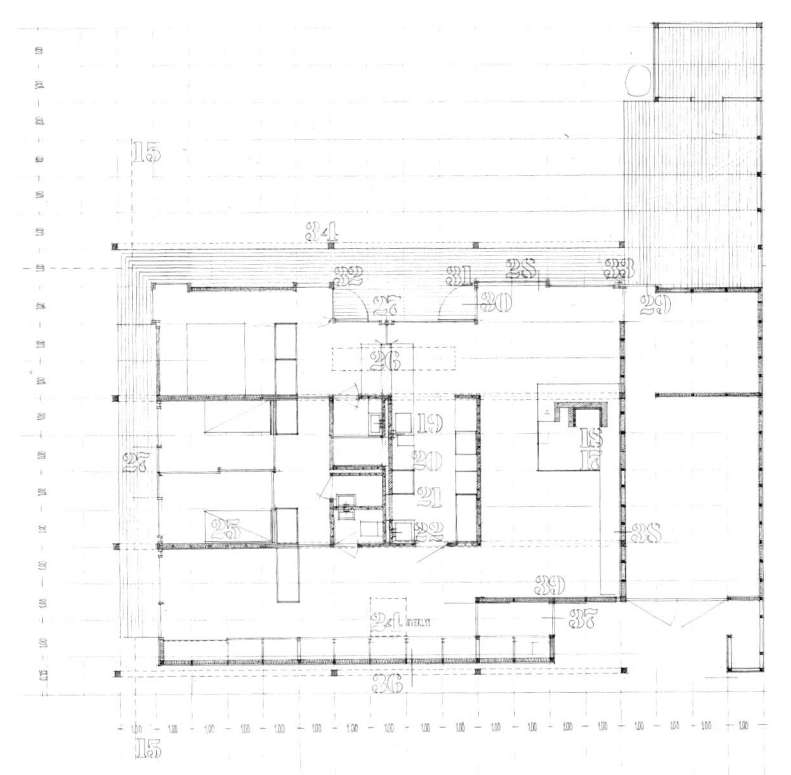

Schreiner House: Plan, interior view, day and night views.

BEYOND THE IMAGE OF HOME 85

X

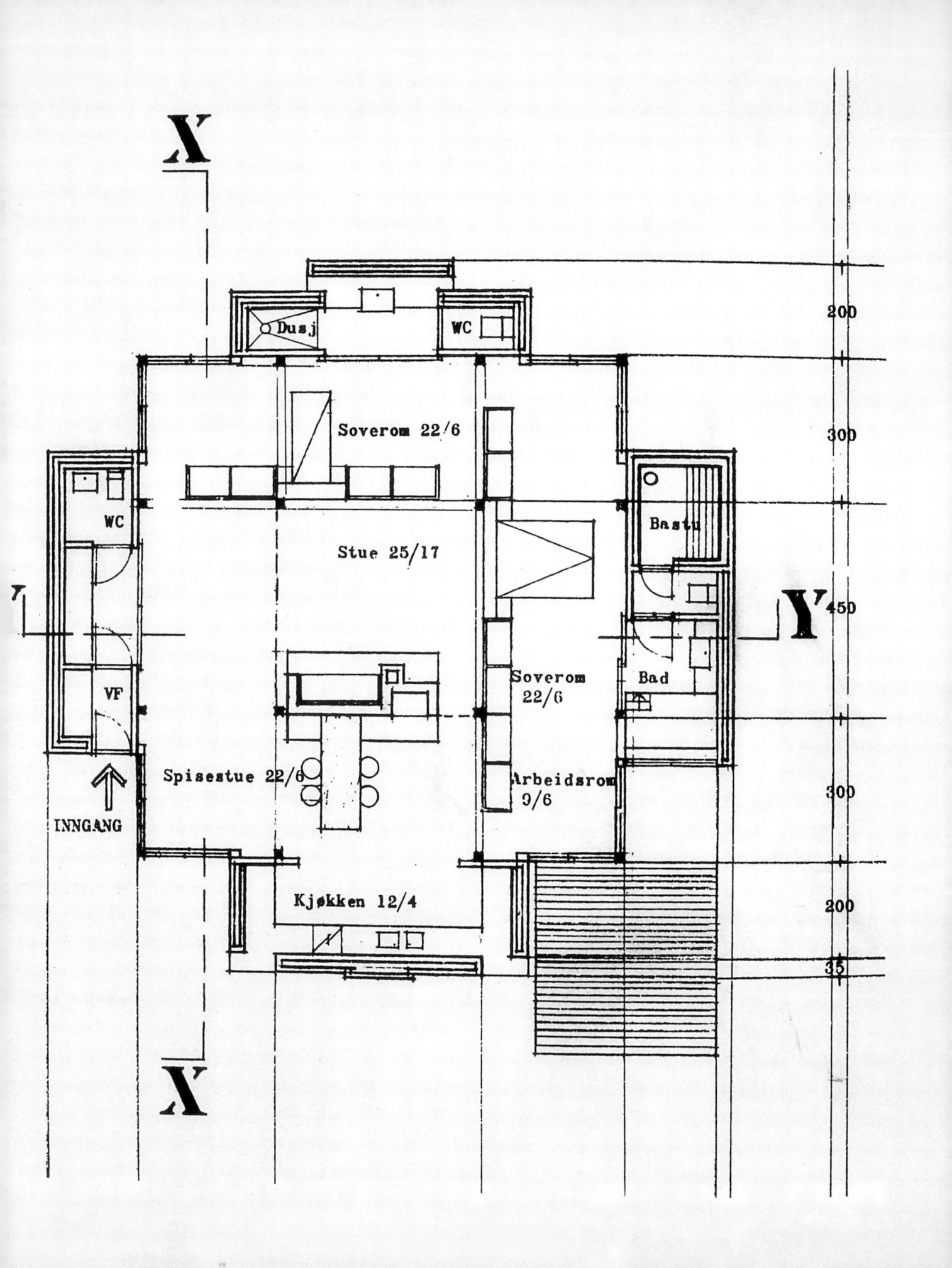

Dusj WC

Soverom 22/6

WC

Bastu

Stue 25/17

Y' 450

Soverom 22/6

Bad

VF

Spisestue 22/6

Arbeidsrom 9/6

INNGANG

Kjøkken 12/4

200

300

300

200

35

X

Johnsrud House: Plan, exterior view, interior view.

BEYOND THE IMAGE OF HOME 87

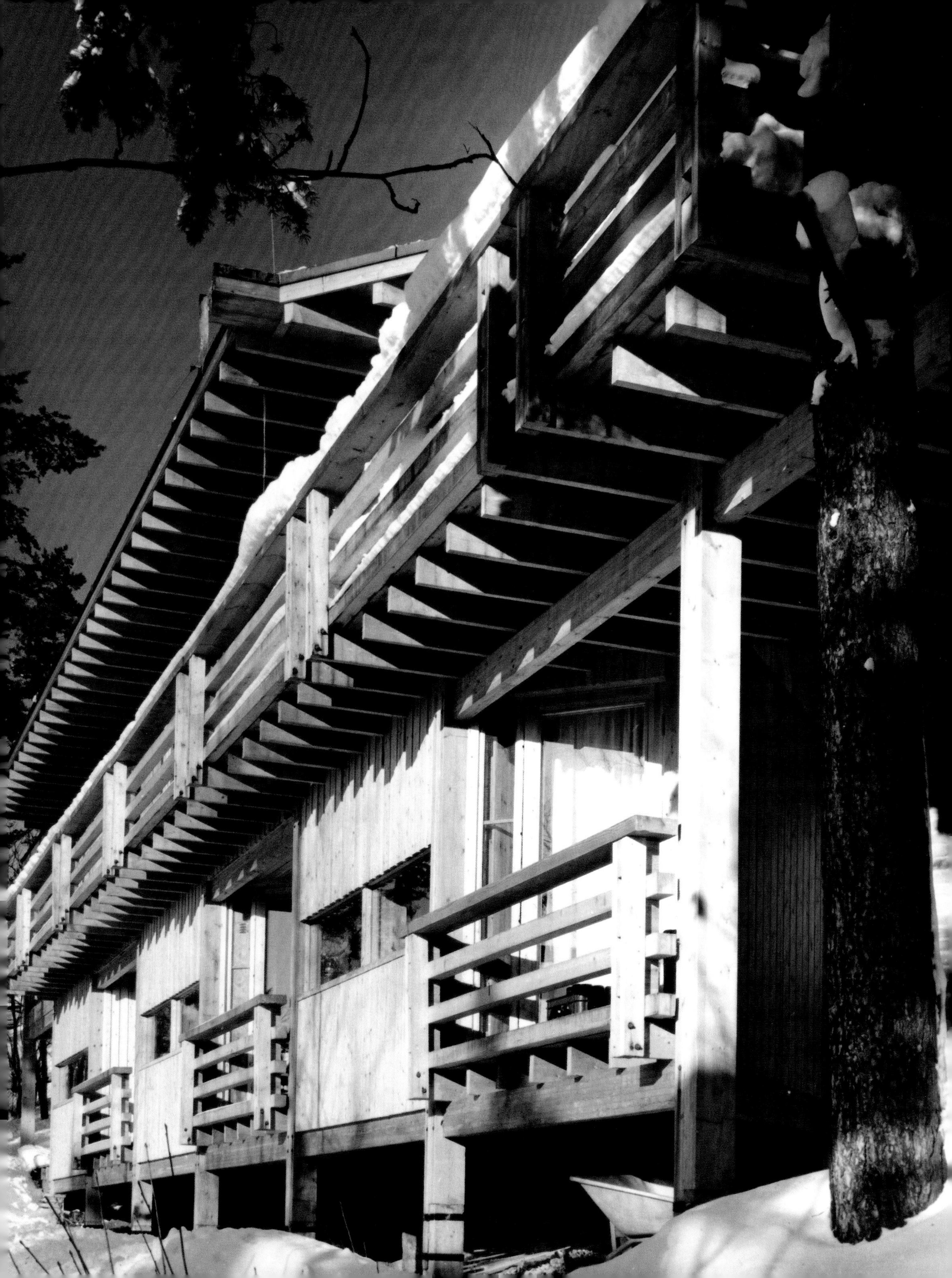

The zigzag house built for Arne Bødtker, 1961–65, deserves more attention than it has received over the years. From the exterior, it is deceptive: at first glance it appears quite ordinary, but its interior spatial diversity and complexity are so strong and active that it requires strength of mind from the inhabitant. In plan, the building is a parallelogram; in the middle are three V-shaped masonry walls that set in motion an inner and outer spatial sequence over two floors. The back of the house hugs a steep hillside, and the passage between building and slope is dim and private, almost cavelike; the front of the house looks into the treetops and to a view over Oslo and its fjord. **The Arne Bødtker House is like a thin line drawn between heaven and earth. The sea hawk uses it as a perch and feels safe.** This house explores some core issues that would not become evident until Fehn's later work: the cave, the horizon, and the modern sense of view.

A few years later, Fehn designed a house for Arne Bødtker's brother, Carl, on a site nearby. A strict geometrical approach lends the residence a sense of formality both inside and out. The main body of the house is a cube with a central core—stairwell and light shaft—set on the diagonal. The top or entrance floor is a large public family area that fans out to the corners; movement revolves around the diagonal core that leads down to the more private rooms. The private and public areas are separate, but the stairwell offers spatial communication; though one is able to retreat from activities in the public area, one is not isolated. Clinging to the steep site, the house is a fortress with high brick walls, but it is a fortress that protects family life with spatial openness and functional order. Later Fehn would muse, **A house is not nature: it is culture. Humans live in an unnatural nature. The swallow's nest is precise, but the same every time. Architecture demands new challenges. To come back twenty years later, I experience the house almost as a type of skin. In one sense, I said farewell to timber heritage with this house.**

Almost twenty years later, a second house was attached to the original building; Carl Bødtker and his wife, Erna, moved into the smaller house, and one of the sons and his family moved into the original house. As a dual house, some of the original clarity is diminished; nevertheless, the two dwellings work together, although each has its own temporal aspect.

Almost all of Fehn's houses were built in a time when the Nordic climate was still a practical issue of great importance. All of the houses have an excellent quality of craftsmanship, which itself affects the spatial experience: material and structure communicate through tactility. Light or the lack of light is also an important factor in understanding each house's individual identity.

For a number of years after the excitement around the pavilions in Brussels and Venice had died down, it was Fehn's houses that were widely published and gave the office international exposure. These houses have been an inspiration for the succeeding generation of Norwegian architects, and most of the owners were generous in allowing Fehn's students to visit. The houses of the 1960s and 1970s are timeless, seemingly lacking in trendiness, and have served as important references for many architects. They are impossible to copy in that they are derived from an understanding of a specific physical situation and not a visual cognition.

Arne Bødtker House, Oslo.

Arne Bødtker House: Model, interior views, plans of ground floor and main floor.

90 THE PATTERN OF THOUGHTS

BEYOND THE IMAGE OF HOME 91

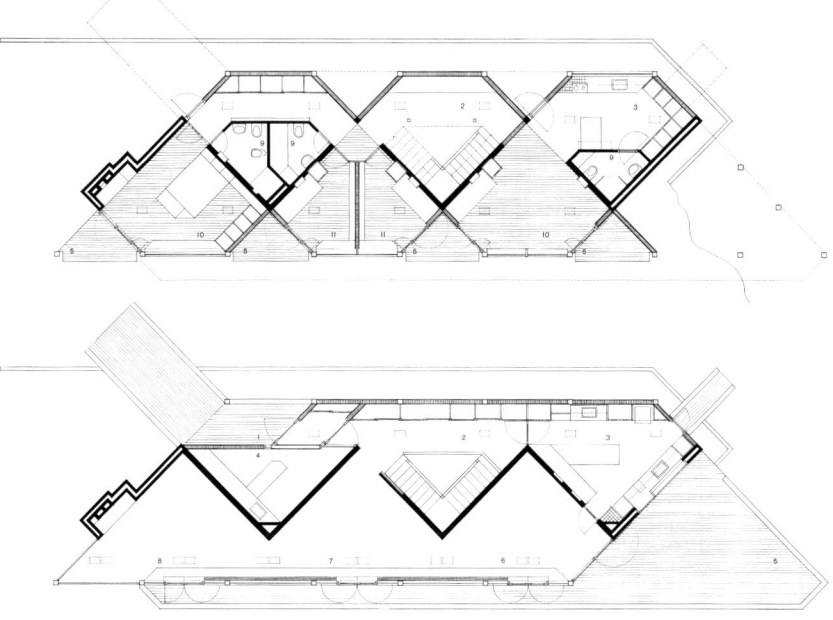

Carl Bødtker House, Oslo: Exterior views, entrance pergola, diagonal core.

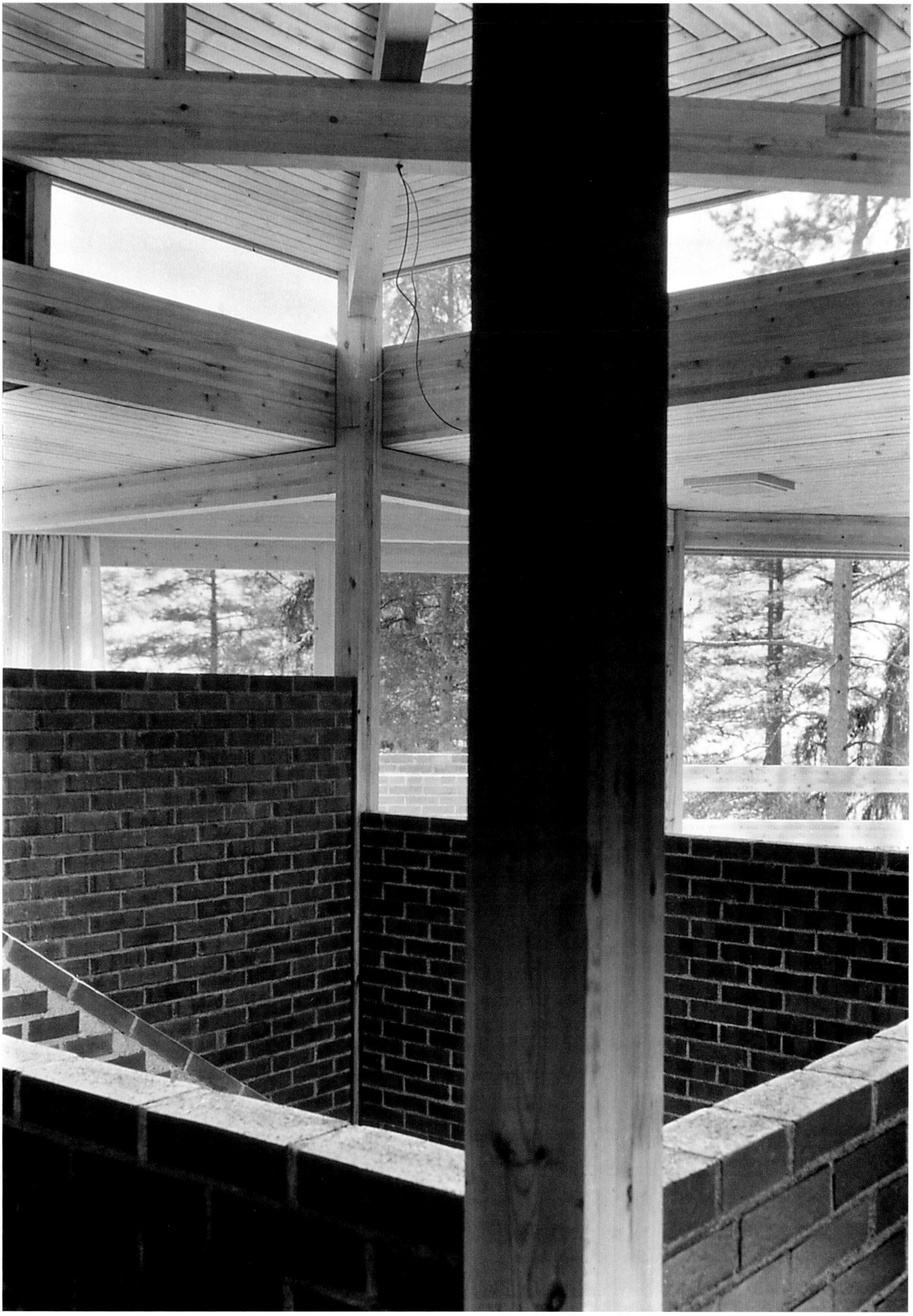

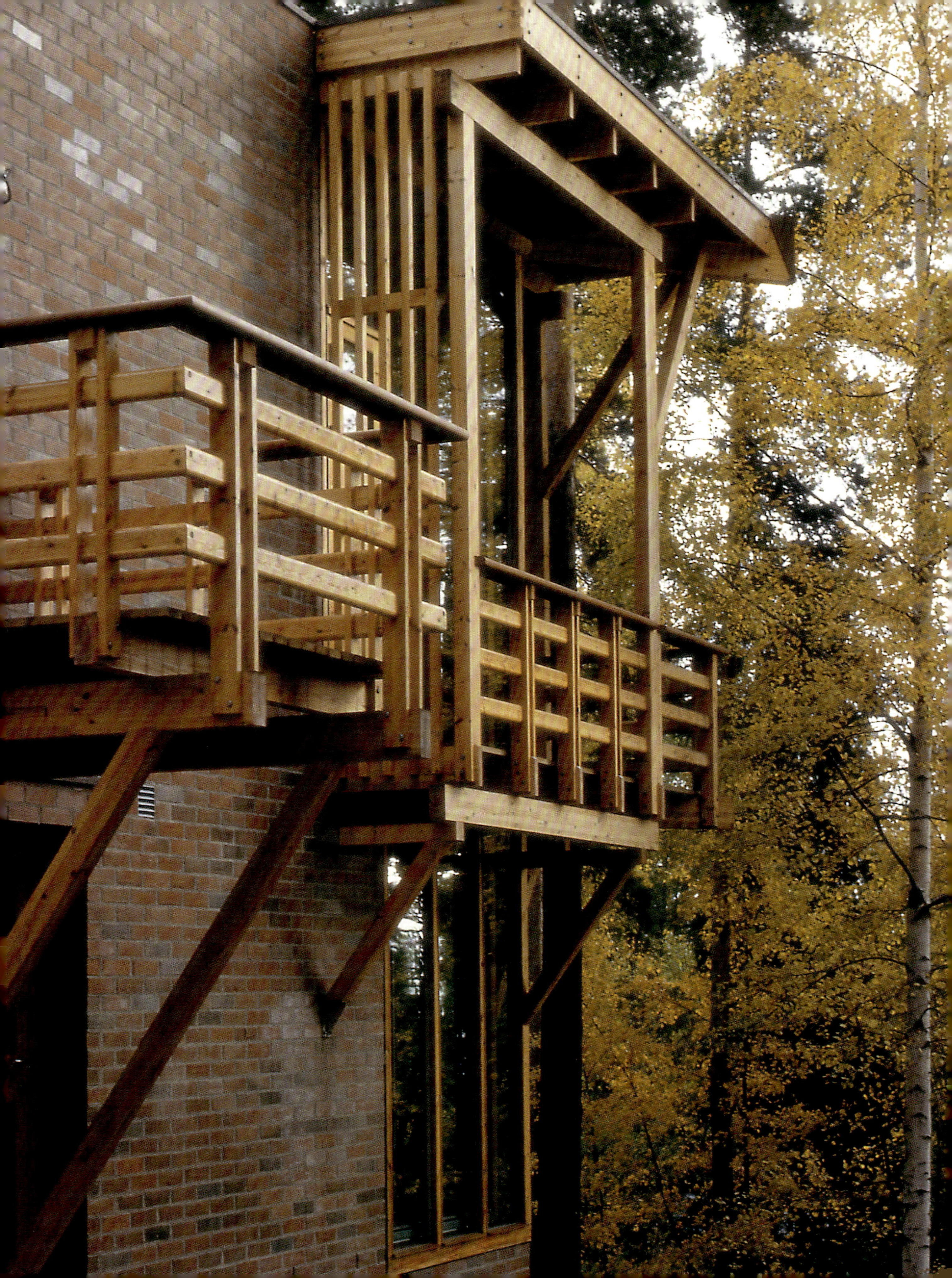

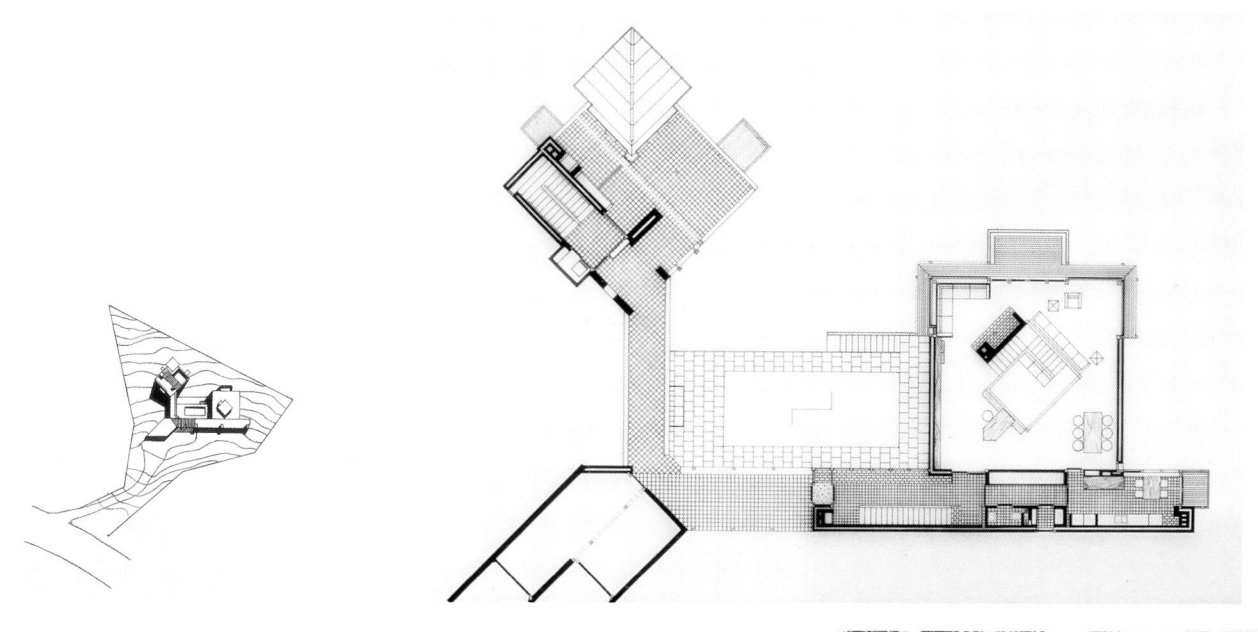

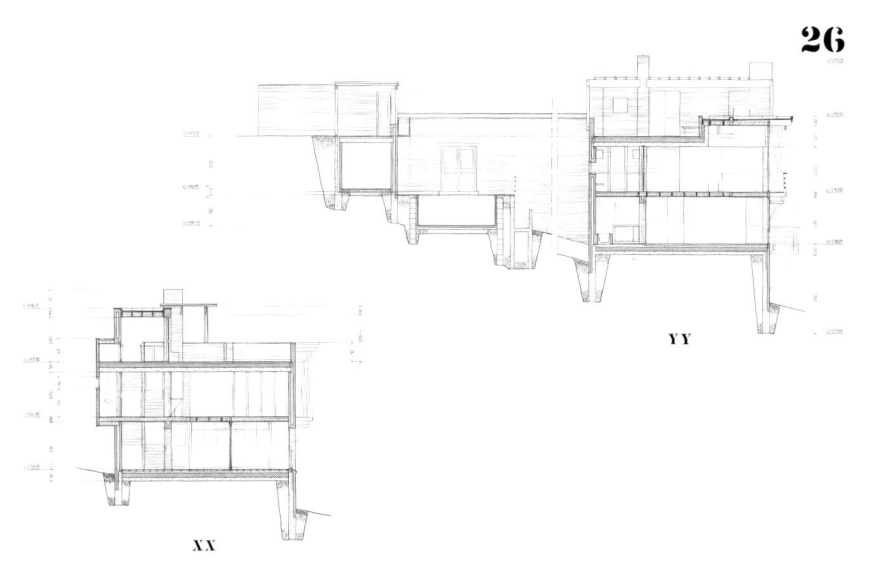

26

XX

YY

Carl Bødtker House:
Balcony on second
house, site plan, plan
with second house,
sections of first house,
exterior view of
second house.

BEYOND THE IMAGE OF HOME 95

OPPOSITE
Mauritzberg Prototype House, Mauritzberg, Sweden.

In the mid-1980s, Fehn embarked on a new period of house commissions. The Brick House and the Busk House (see pages 209, 212) reveal a definitive change in approach and clarify how Fehn added a new layer to his work process. He also had two commissions to build what were called "ecological houses," one in Sweden as a prototype for the Mauritzberg Vacation and Conference Center and the other in Kolding, Denmark. Fehn was acutely aware of, and often joked about, the limitations of a singular ecological improvement if the basics of the overall project functioned within a framework that was without ecological merit. In light of the extreme simplicity of his summer house at Hvasser, it is easy to see why these two houses, promoted as modest, ecologically sustainable dwellings, presented him with some complicated issues.

The prototype house at Mauritzberg, 1991–92, was built with a light wood skeleton supporting walls of pressed-clay blocks consisting of 10 percent clay and 90 percent straw. These walls were topped with a simple laminated triangular beam that supported the roof construction, which was of plywood arches treated on the exterior with a tar mixture. The house was built in eight weeks with the help of architecture students from Sweden, Norway, Finland, and Latvia. The Nordic Ecological House in Kolding, 1994–96, which was built by Scandinavian students, was more or less a version of the same project, though compacted and simplified as much as possible in relation to the program. The prototypes were attractive houses, but Fehn was never able to investigate fully the capacity and capabilities of sustainability in relation to architecture. I have always felt that this is an area in which Fehn had a great deal more to give, especially given his precision of scale and his ability to minimize.

The many house projects the architect designed for his friend Knut Wiggen in the period 1968–72 give an indication of just how compact Fehn could make private living space. During these years, he developed a number of houses. One was circular, with bath and kitchen in the center; another was rectangular. In the latter, the elements of fire and water are not isolated but nonetheless create rooms in themselves, dividing the volume into zones of activity. The open plan provided spaces for an intense and receptive social interaction among its inhabitants. **The house welcomes you without a costume; it has no mask. You are left standing there with your inner thoughts and your body. Here one just lives with others, and the core [bath and kitchen] is not dissolved/hidden.**

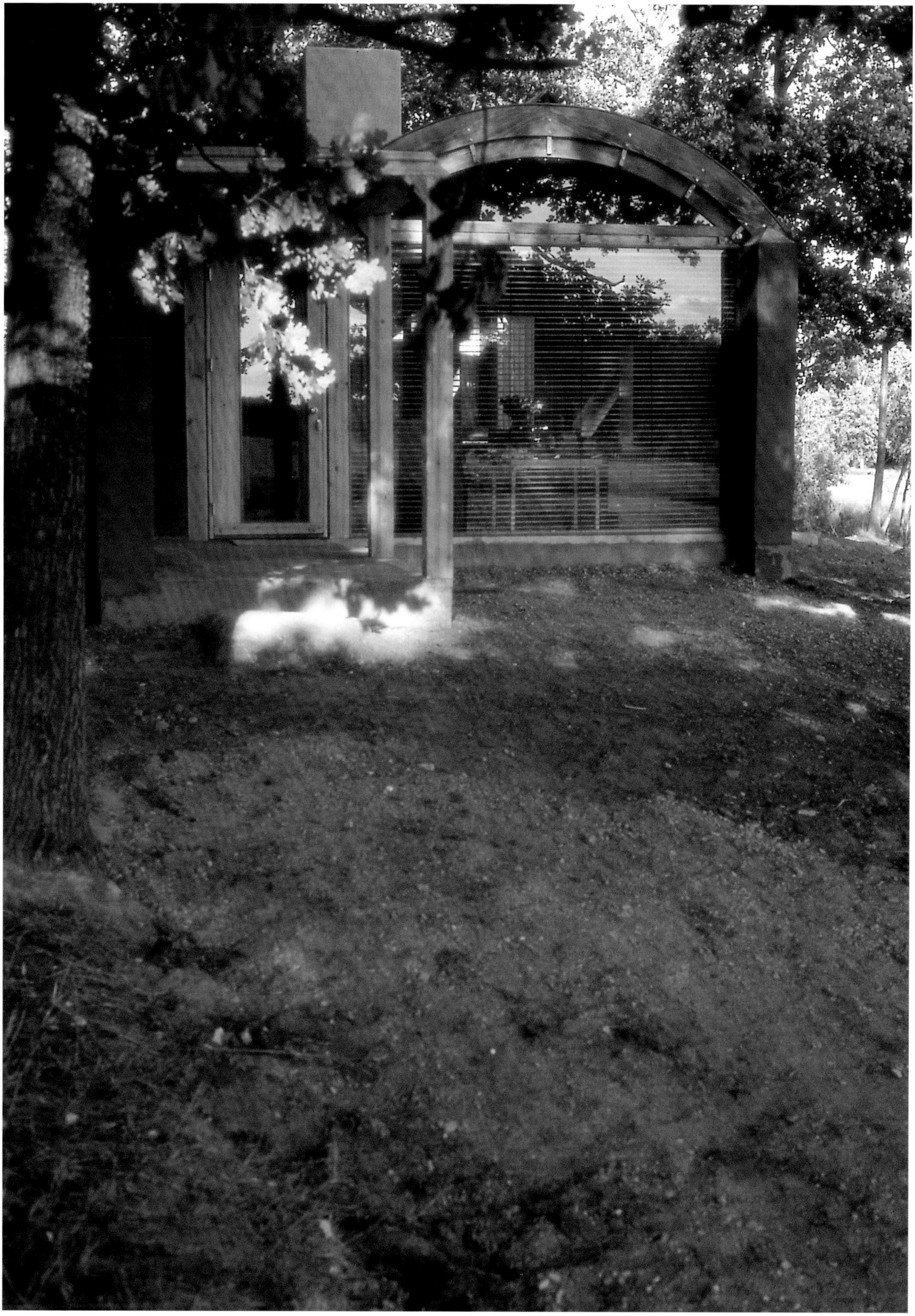

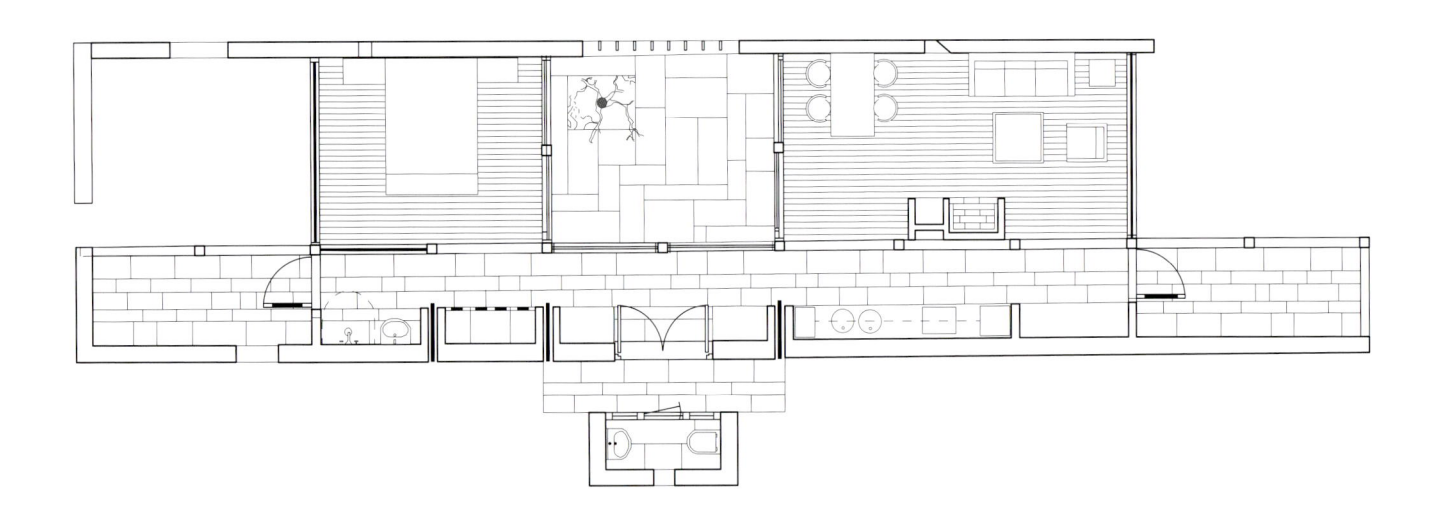

Mauritzberg Prototype House: Plan, interior view.

Each of Fehn's house projects is in some way a translation of social and lifestyle concerns into an architectural interpretation of the client. Even when there was no client, Fehn would invent one. The process of envisioning a client was always a challenge, and the end product was never neutral. Though the client might come with a shopping list of needs and preferences, Fehn's interest lay in what was behind the requests: a deeper, more direct reflection of personal space. He always said that it took courage for clients to face the spatial picture of themselves, and those who hesitated seldom considered him as their architect. Regardless, quite a few clients have remained in contact throughout the years, and some became close friends. The last house-studio Fehn built was designed for a painter. Ingolf Holme commissioned several houses over the years, and finally in 1995–97, he was able to realize one of these projects. The main body of the house sits diagonally on the site, taking advantage of a rock formation to the rear of the dwelling. The rather forced geometric plan suggests a static formality in its spatial sequence. Though the house is open, it does not give the same sense of adaptability as the earlier houses. The Holme House, like a spatial painting with its own logic, offers an argument, a resistance force for the painter. After he had lived there for a while Holme commented, "I have to confess, the house has influenced my paintings in a very positive way."

Fehn drew every house down to the smallest detail, and work would not begin before the drawings—typically about fifty to seventy per project—were complete. If the site was in the Oslo area, there could be up to three meetings a day during construction. Fehn would arrive early in the morning, an assistant would visit during the day, and usually, Fehn would pass by again on his way home from school. The drawings were meticulously followed; there were no compromises in relation to materials or finishes; and no shortcuts were taken. To some extent his relationship to the building site is reminiscent of that of the Swedish architect Sigurd Lewerentz, who followed his projects with a similar intensity. But to my knowledge, Lewerentz developed a rapport with each individual workman on the site, which in turn influenced the final result. Fehn relied more on his finished drawings, and if anything needed adjustment, the drawings were the basis for discussion. He did not work quite so directly on the site, but communication with the construction manager and perhaps specific craftsmen followed the same pattern. **When you build with brick, you are always building orderly; it runs in courses. It is a ruin that goes back into itself, and it is finished with every layer of brick. It is as if you go back to the past. When you build in brick you experience the past.**

In all of Fehn's houses, material identity supports and even influences the conceptual idea. It was very seldom

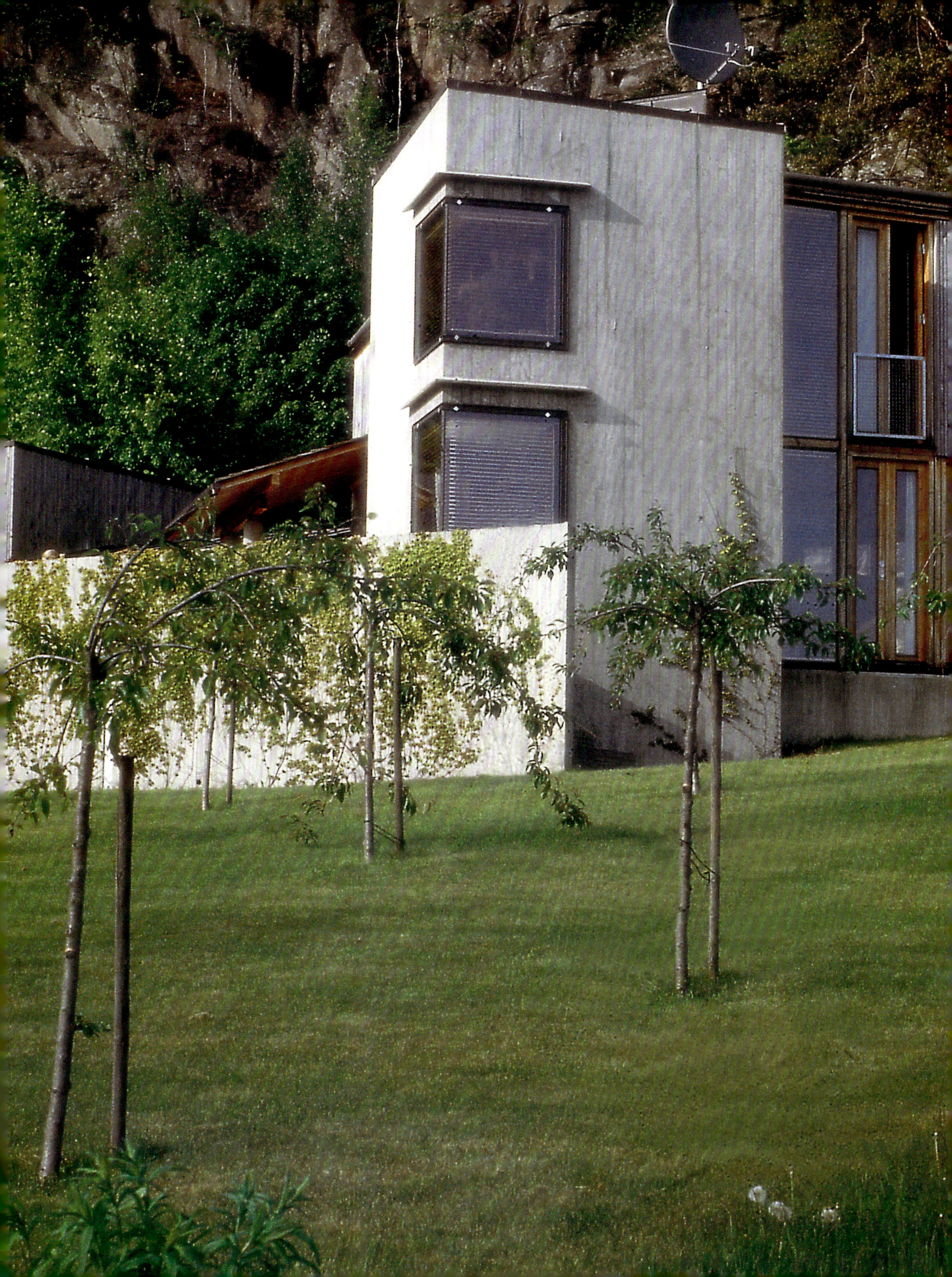

Holme House,
Holmsbu, Norway:
Exterior view, door to
back garden.

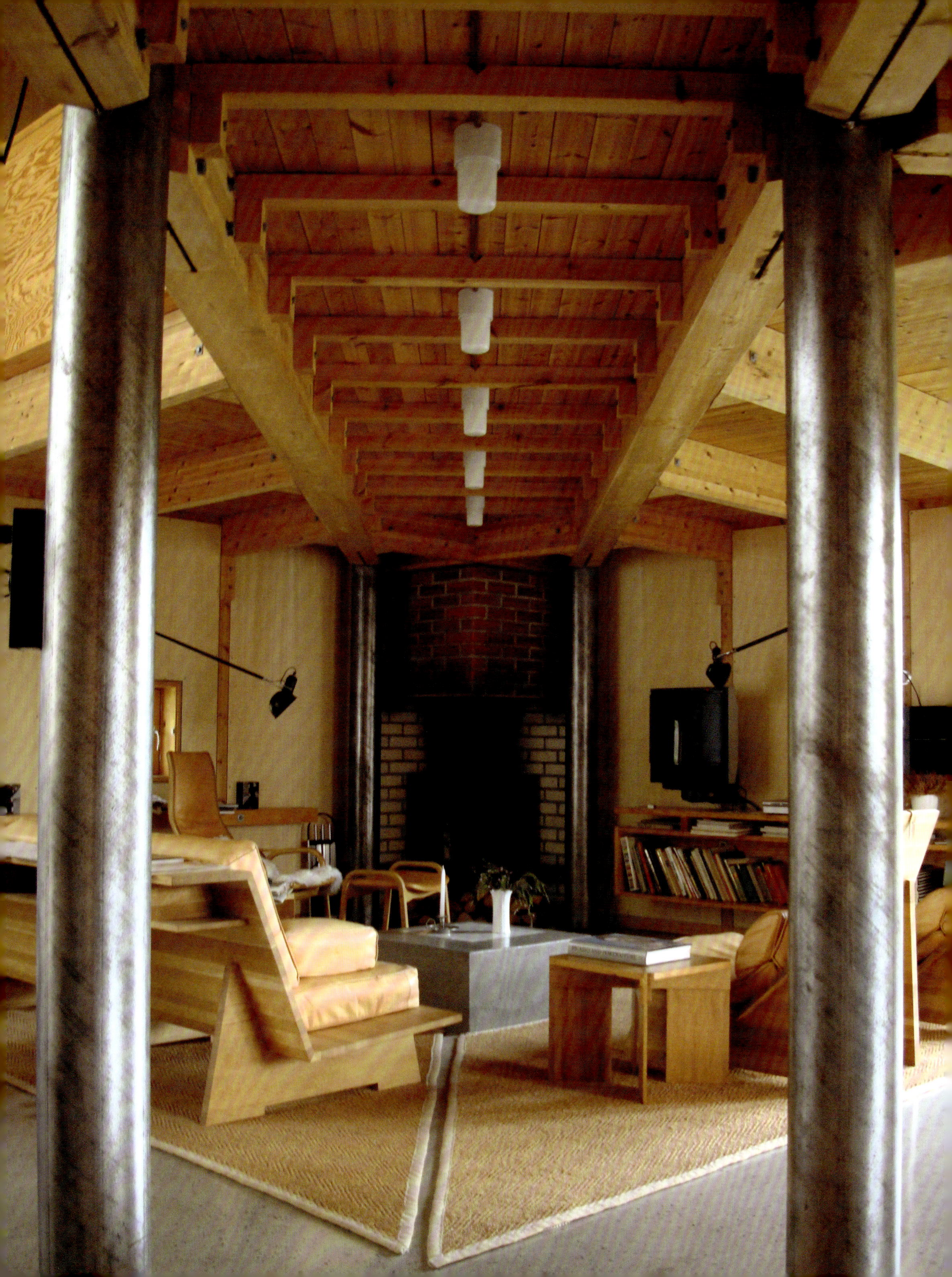

Holme House: Views
along diagonal axis.

Church of St. Peter, Klippan, Sweden (Sigurd Lewerentz): Detail of brick wall.

OPPOSITE Sketch, 1993, "A child's meeting with its first column."

that the inherent dimension of a material (tiles, bricks, lumber) was altered or forced into an overall idea; rather, the material and the idea developed together as they gradually reached a structural integrity. This architectural discipline is not only a respect for material but a reaction to waste. If the project called for a different dimension, a cut, or an added element, Fehn would have anticipated the situation in advance. His pre-computer-era plans are beautiful and careful drawings in which the office took great pride.

Fehn's houses extend beyond the image of house. They are physically active, homes in the fullest sense. Family activities take place in a space that is very precise; and yet there is room for interpretation. The spaces developed in relation to the client's inner spatial identity gain in intensity. All of the houses demand something of the inhabitants: the days and weeks after moving in were often difficult; possessions and habits (not just objects) needed to be reconsidered. Clients did not cast off their old lives but rather readjusted. Once past this point, many of the original owners developed strong ties to their homes and kept them as they were originally conceived as long as possible, often fearing the changes that would come with new owners.

The child holds himself up with the help of its mother's leg, the first column in its life. The child conquers and conquers, walls, doors, the toilet, everything. It grows into the room and becomes the little individual that forms the world.

søjler.

det frie [Rom]   søjlen

Barnets møte
med den
største første søjle

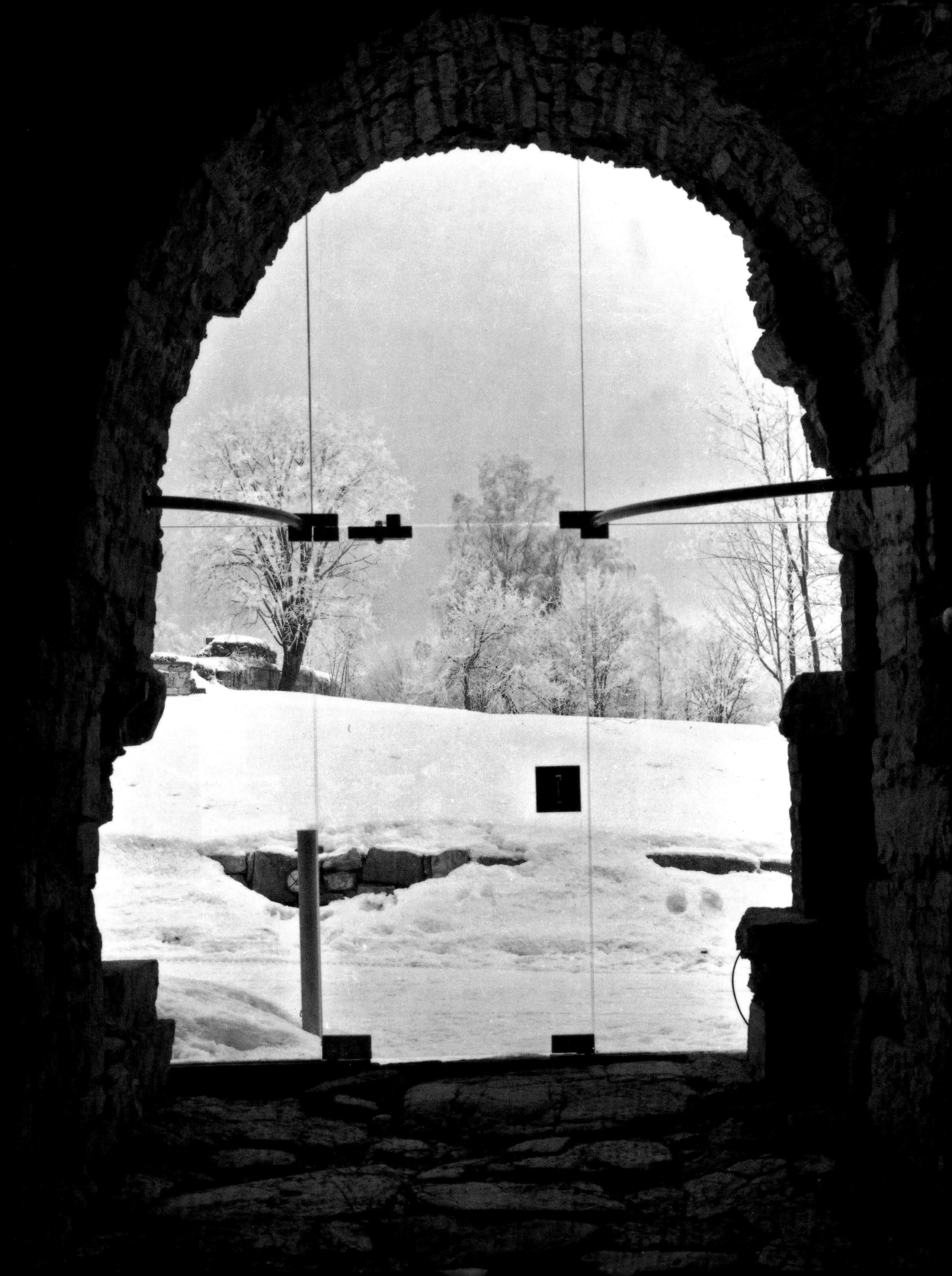

CHAPTER 5

THE RETURN OF THE HORIZON | Every artist has an internal vocabulary, words forced into being by the desire to express. I believe the articulation of subliminal thought is one of the most authentic forces within the creative process. The internal vocabulary follows the artist like a shadow; it is an instrument or tool of the creative process. How the artist formulates his or her expressions is singular, since they are a reflection of the individual's personality; but common to all is the manipulation of intuition. These subjective translations of thoughts are part of the internal vocabulary, and it is this vocabulary that the artist leaves behind in his or her creation.

Fehn's sketchbooks, which span his entire career, are filled with drawings and notations on the earth, the sky, and the horizon line. The architect is absorbed by heaven and earth in relation to various aspects of time, with ways in which one might move from one horizon to another. In order to carry a concept of heaven and earth into the core of a project, Fehn developed a personal interpretation of the two issues. He explored some of these relationships in an interview conducted with him in 1985.

THE SECOND HORIZON

How shall we respond to man and his objects affixed to the surface of the earth? Everything we build must be adjusted in relation to the ground, thus the horizon becomes an important aspect of architecture. My interest has always been where to put man in relation to the horizon in a built environment. What qualities shall he draw out of the open landscape?

The simplest form of architecture is to cultivate the surface of the earth, to make a platform. Then the horizon becomes the only direction one has, and the moment a dialogue between the earth and the horizon is established, one can start to consider it as a room. Once the room exists and an object is placed inside, all decisions yield to the horizon. At least it was so a long time ago. When the earth was perceived as round, the horizon disappeared as a mystery. The earth's surface was finite, an assessable number. I believe this to be the greatest architectural statement affecting the idea of room. With Palladio, the concept of the horizon changed. In the Villa Rotonda, he almost lost the horizon as an unlimited force. The house gives no orientation; it is a labyrinth within itself.

The moment you lose the horizon, your desire is always to reinstate it. It is trapped somewhere between the cave and the tower, and at the same time, the earth reveals its limitations. The architect becomes the surgeon who cuts open the earth and is unafraid to tear the sail that has moved the horizon and defended the unlimited. He can establish places under the ground, and these become the new way to travel into the past, as the horizon faces a new journey. The room of darkness confronts the precise decision of light. In lack of courage, we give life to restoration. The cultural artifacts that are uncovered are now placed on the surface of the earth, but where is each object's personal shadow? The problem is, where shall each object meet its new light?

I think my projects penetrate this struggle. The projects of Spiraltoppen Restaurant and Hotel and Voksenkollen Medical Conference Center dealt with simple horizons in an open landscape. The Nordic Pavilion in Venice established a plateau, a floor, as an instrument for an architectural horizon. In the museum at Hamar, the physical horizon disappeared. Here the objects are displayed above and below the horizon; you might say the horizon is everywhere. In my project for the Mining Museum at Røros, I made a bridge to span the gap between heaven and earth. The Tullinløkka Square project gave a clear statement of an architectural journey above the horizon, but the idea culminated in the Wasa Ship Museum, where the entire museum was an underground journey.

When I flew to Vienna a couple of weeks ago, something happened. Having flown through the clouds and just coming out on the other side, I looked out of the window. Intuition called for God and his angels to be there, but they were not...what I discovered was the second horizon.

MARKS IN THE LANDSCAPE

The Scandinavian landscape has determined much of my production. The land is the architect of my buildings; the way in which the building is set in the landscape gives the project its precision. The script with its definite number is given by society, but it is the land that gives the answer. Luckily the terrain is fearless of any script. The architect finds architecture with the help of nature.

At one time, man's fear placed the landscape in a far more exalted position, as fear forced a search for safety by way of the contours of the terrain. Today,

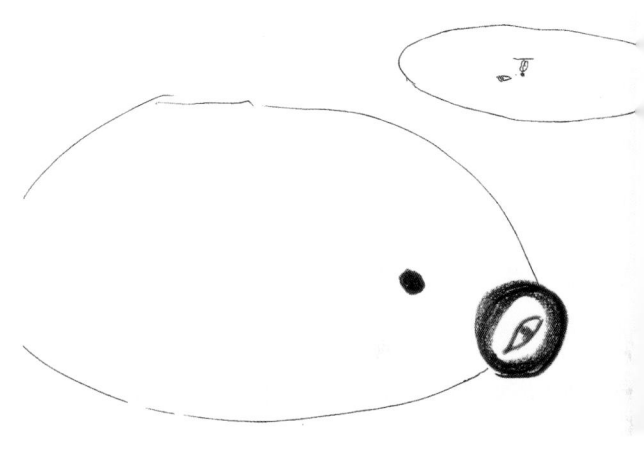

Sketch, 1992, "The object and the human."

Sketch of the bullet eye.

PAGE 106 Hedmark County Museum, Hamar, Norway: View to exterior.

fear is not a problem, as it is everywhere, in the city and in the country. Rather, it is an integral part of our consciousness. The fortress or city wall set into the landscape no longer bears the same importance. The bullet can see you everywhere, thus how the architect reads the landscape has also changed. It is useless to rely on topography alone, since the landscape has ceased to afford the same safety. We now learn to read the land primarily in relation to aesthetic and historic terms. It appears as though the only discussions that establish a new set of marks in the landscape are based on aesthetic determinations. Human survival has shifted its focus ever so slightly, equating itself not so much with work but rather with recreation. The poetic side of man's comprehension of nature—the sun, the moon, the sea, and the mountains—still stimulates strong forces, since we call upon these to fertilize new places of well-being. In this sense, historical marks seem to have a revival. New York, on the other hand, has it all figured out. If everyone agrees to put the landscape on a grid and the sky is free, there is no fear in relation to size. The city is alive within these decisions as it reaches for a size beyond numbers.

DEATH

The largest constructions have always been connected to the enigma of eternity. The constructions around death are the most irrational of all. Once man required a space where the journey into the unknown could take place, the shadow had a place within the irrational thought. The moment life after death ceases to exist as a dream, death is an absolute; its construction simply is a configuration of numbers. As the world becomes more and more rational the shadow forfeits its place, since there is nothing there for it to inhabit. Is there a construction for this complete emptiness of dreams, once death is finite? How are we able to materialize this into a space? How can we construct a space for the shadow after death when it no longer has its place? This is my concern.

When "I am dead" becomes an endpoint, an absolute, there is no desire to give it an expression leaning toward an irrational thought. In a sense, we are about to lose a very important construction, the construction around the irrational. As such, the whole essence of architecture is about to change.

THE RETURN OF THE HORIZON

We have attacked the ground. We have cut into the surface of the earth and forged rooms with no shadow. In my project for the Wasa Ship Museum, the boat and a scenario of the death of men and their objects continue their journey under the horizon.

The moment the construction meets the earth, it substantiates its dimension. The construction is the force that occupies nature and provides room for an architectural journey. One of the most elegant constructions is the swing. The little man sits on his plank with his feet almost touching the ground, and with every move the swing cheats the earth of its meeting. "No, it is not here I shall meet you." The constructive force travels through the plank into the tree and finally takes root in the ground. With new interpretations of the horizon, our perception has changed. The horizon ceases to evoke the same mystery, and one cannot take for granted that the constructive forces belong solely to the ground. Today the mystery belongs to the weightless work in space. We are working with a new set of spatial considerations, and we are about to change our vocabulary.

Fehn has continued to find new aspects or angles of interpretation of the horizon throughout the various phases of his work. I think it is almost a love-hate situation. He has never been able to escape his conceptual construction around eternity or the immeasurable, and how he connects this to a life-death relationship. The horizon serves as an image of this eternity, and yet the same image without limits has the ability to move. It moves in relation to one's position on earth. The opposite circumstance is the artifact buried in a fixed position below the earth's surface. Bringing the object up into the light gives it a new life with an ever-moving horizon. Fehn's focus is on finding the object's position: **The moment it is again offered its horizon, it also finds its shadow.**

Very early on, his approach was quite straightforward, but by the time the Hedmark County Museum in Hamar was underway, the horizon and built abstract horizons had become tools to understand spatial concepts. Summer after summer spent painting sailboats breaking the blue horizon at Hvasser replicated in many ways his labors on the elusive horizon in the Hamar project.

The Hedmark Museum required a conceptual approach that both hit at the core of the project and included the temporal aspects of moving from one horizon to another. **Where between heaven and earth do I place people?** was a fundamental question Fehn asked throughout this project. With each new or historic layer there was an associated abstraction of horizon. Interior and exterior ramps form a sequence of spaces that allow much of the ground to remain untouched or available for archaeological research. Over and over again the comprehension of horizon adjusts, and the only fixed point is the earth. It is the abstract point somewhere between earth and heaven that captures Fehn's imagination. This point is unreachable, immeasurable, and yet it inspires numerous spatial constructions.

On several occasions Fehn has referred to a Viking wagon removed from a burial mound; it is now in an Oslo museum. The wagon has large, clumsy wheels, but the trunk, or cradle, is intricately carved. Fehn imagines an infant in this "cradle" and, further, the cradle as a construction lifted above the earth to give the child his own horizon. Similarly, Fehn would present a stave church as a structure that raised itself off the ground, and almost in the same sentence he would characterize log dwellings as "lazy structures." Or he would bring up, in his lectures, Viking ships, not just for their beauty and precise structure in relation to material but because they had the capacity to move the horizon. **The secret of the boat was to fight the horizon. The mast moved the horizon while those on land gazed at its line and the horizon until they became one. The concrete and the abstract melted together as these inseparable elements united. With this moment of union, the horizon was ruined. Nature with its enormous scale was no longer the uncharted, since the unknown had been usurped by man.**

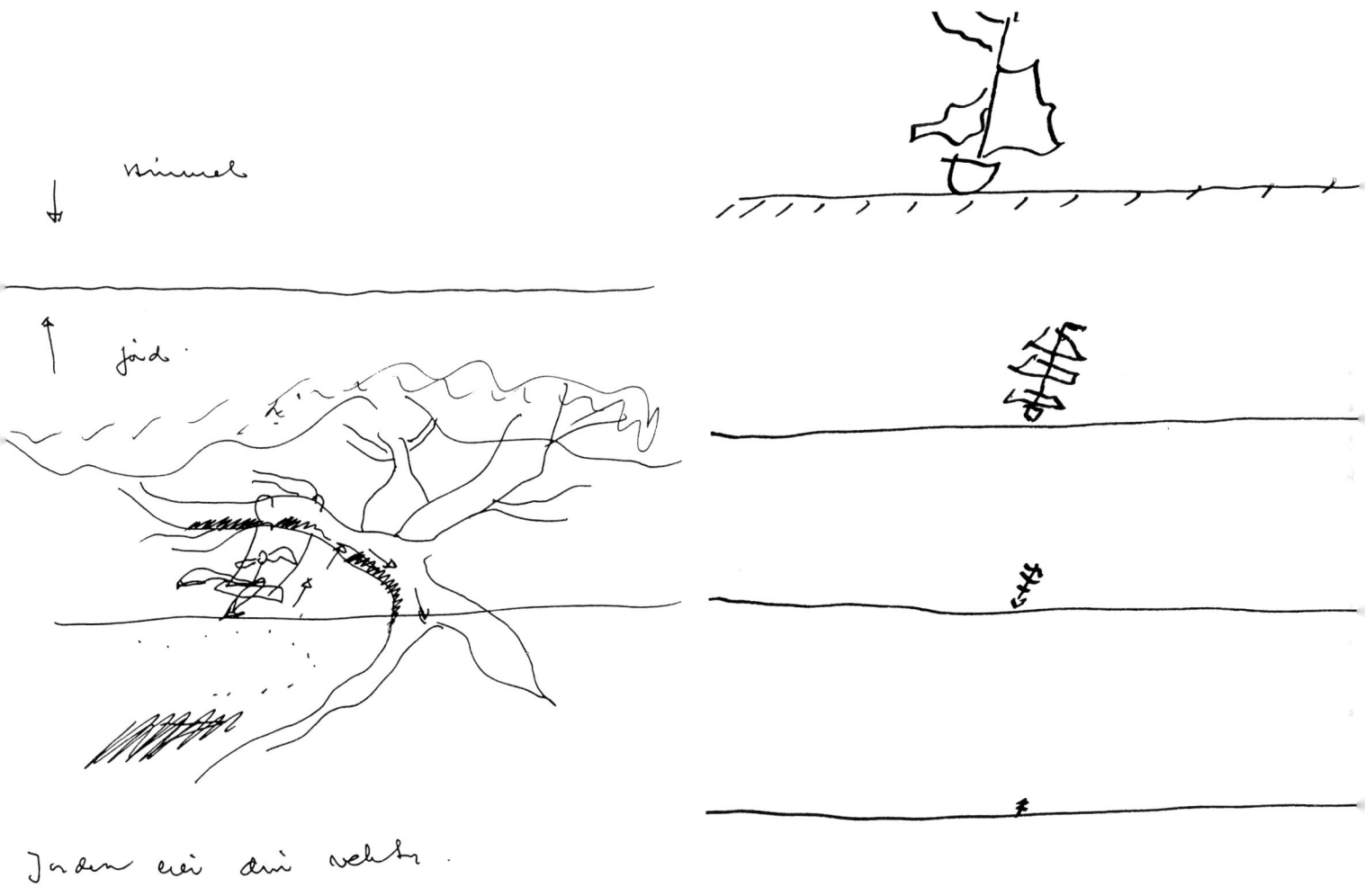

Sketch, 1984,
"The earth becomes your weight."

Sketch, 1992, of the ship moving the horizon.

THE RETURN OF THE HORIZON

Hedmark County Museum: Interior ramp in west wing, interior view of north wing.

OPPOSITE Sketch, "And even the tree got the same poetry."

In 1967, a late-twelfth-century bishop's manor at Hamar, which had been used as a barn for more than a century, was in such bad shape that the town decided it would have to be demolished if it did not receive immediate repairs. A former student of Fehn's proposed a radical plan to save the ruin, asking the architect to transform the barn into a museum for the county of Hedmark. It was to be a "cold" museum, to cut heating costs, and archeological work would need to continue there after the project was complete. Fehn arrived on the scene with his usual engineer, Arne Neegård; together they devised a plan to stabilize the walls. It was at this point that a long and meticulous process of transformation began.

The interior of the former barn is now a constructed landscape. New ramps and plateaus together with the ruins form a varied spatial sequence. The old structures remain untouched with the clear intention of allowing all paths and marks in the "landscape" to continue their now slowed decay. Yet it is still open for new discoveries. According to Fehn,

The Norwegian Forestry Museum [unbuilt project from this period] is a forerunner to the museum in Hamar. This building has to do with a map and the river. It has to do with going down to the river, stopping, and going back up again.

The similarity between the Forestry Museum and Hamar is most apparent in the plan. The former has a ramp and two parallel platforms separated by an exhibition space. The display area is defined by a double row of columns that runs the length of the museum and extends down into the river. The two rows of columns are also the main structural support for the roof. The Hedmark Museum and the Nordic Pavilion in Venice also have some similarities of approach. The pavilion's structure and material carefully worked around the original fixtures of the garden, the trees and ground. In Hamar, each new structure respects the building's origins and previous transformations. The thick exterior stone walls continue as the main structural element;

and even the tree got the same poetry.

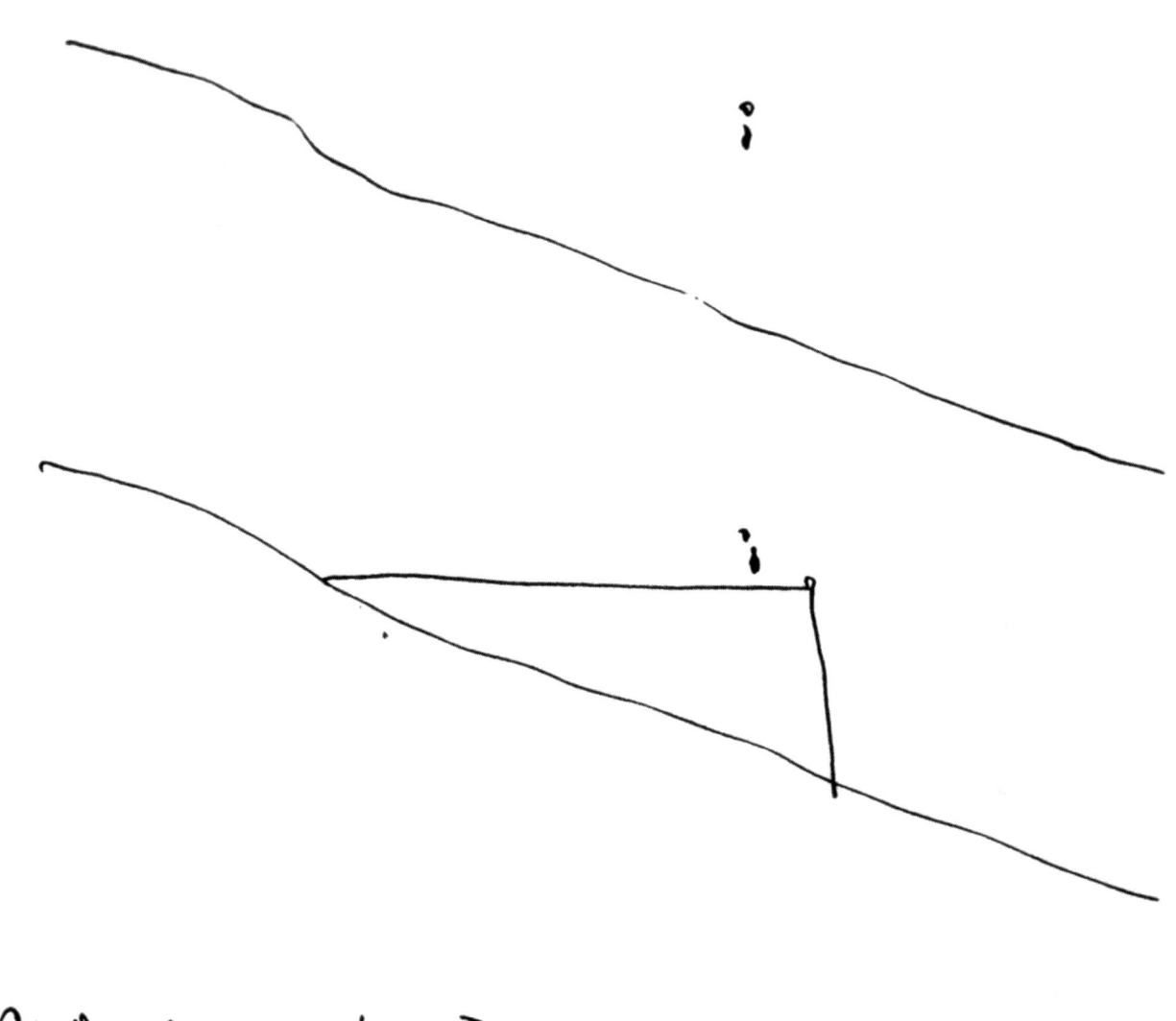

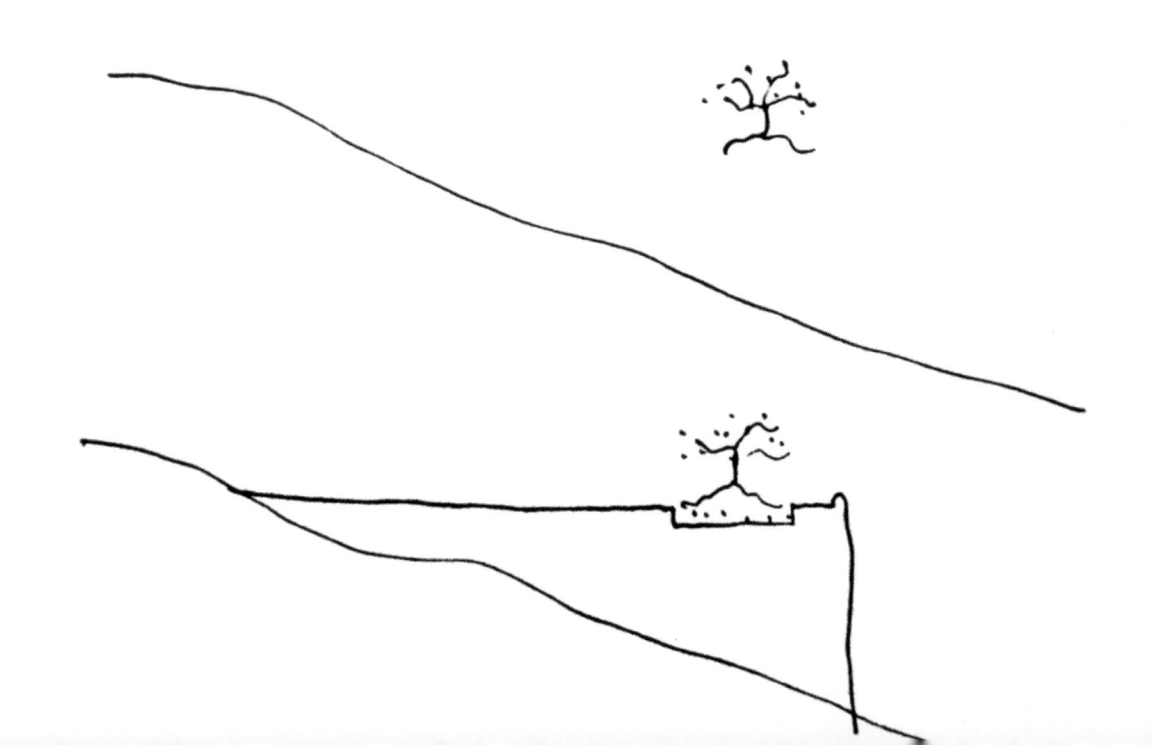

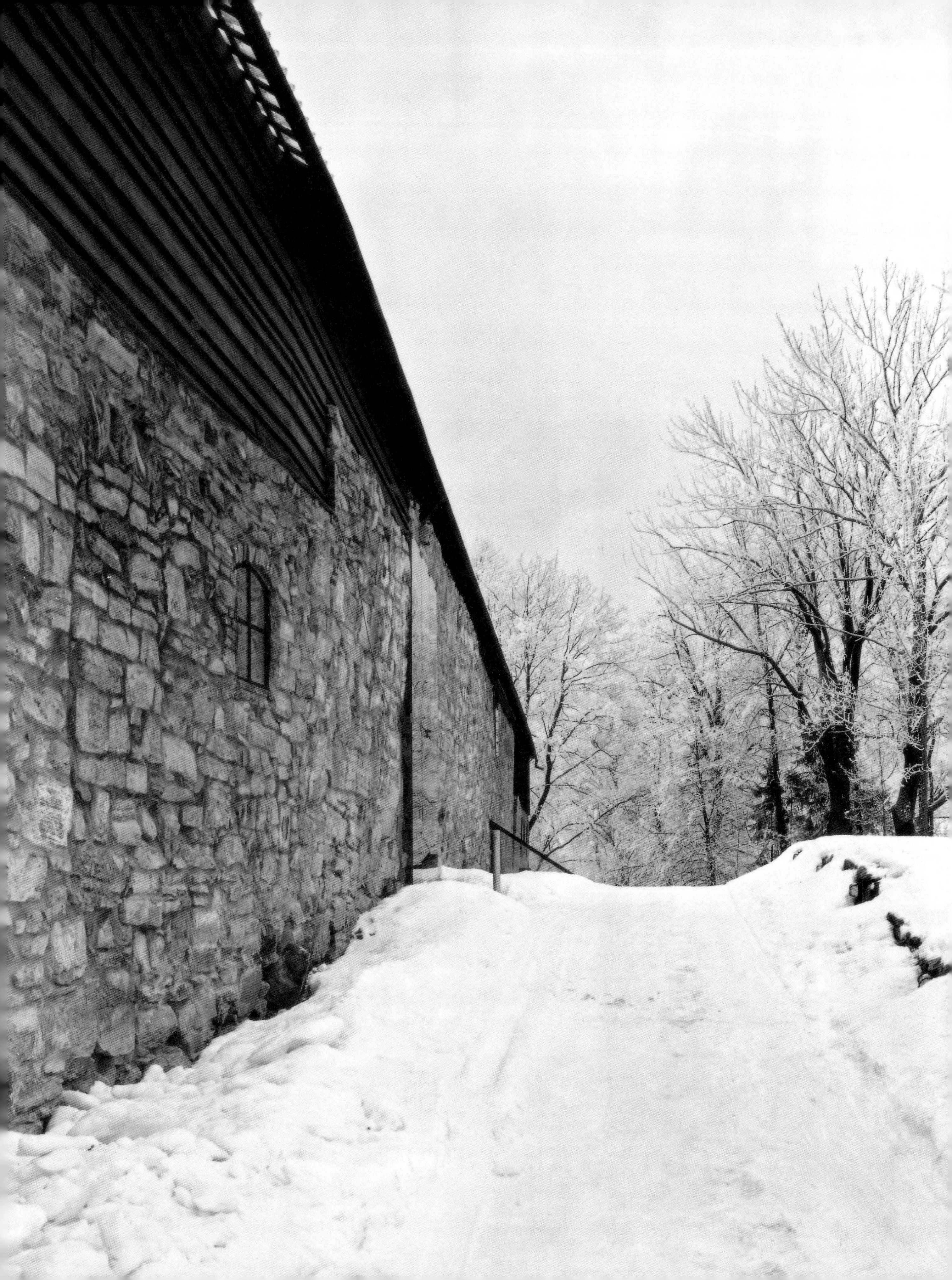

Hedmark County Museum: Path leading to entrance, views before restoration.

THE RETURN OF THE HORIZON 115

Hedmark County Museum: The opening in the ruin, concrete ramp and adjacent wooden structure, exterior detail.

the openings remain untouched, with sheets of glass simply attached to the exterior. The interior and exterior ramps meticulously steer clear of original openings and archaeological finds. Fehn brings into being through a physical structure a mental construction of heaven and earth. The bridges and ramps stage new horizons, and thus he is always able to place the visitor somewhere between heaven and earth.

My story is, where do I put the horizon? As an architect one works over and under the horizon. When an airplane takes me up to the other horizon there is no one there.

There has been no attempt to repair or to restore a specific period in the barn's history. It gives no signal of time in suspension; the building and objects openly continue a process of disintegration, but the temporal aspect is slowed. Rather than working with history as information, Fehn approaches history as memory. The excavation and small ruins in the exterior courtyard, while protected, are still in nature, in time. The same situation occurs in the interior. Material contrast highlights the inner nature or story of an object, and the glass layer over the openings in the barn's exterior wall slows the distance between past and present, but neither object nor barn is frozen.

My interest is not to continue destroying what is already destroyed. The barn was rotten, a sad creature, this enormous barn that still had something of the bishop's manor in its spirit. I looked upon it as an old horse, a place with an animal-like character. When things die, new ideas are born. The tree's leaves fall, rot, and disappear. For me, this building's history, all the marks on the ground that should

117

Hedmark County Museum: Auditorium, spiral stair, plan, sections and elevations.

118   THE PATTERN OF THOUGHTS

THE RETURN OF THE HORIZON 119

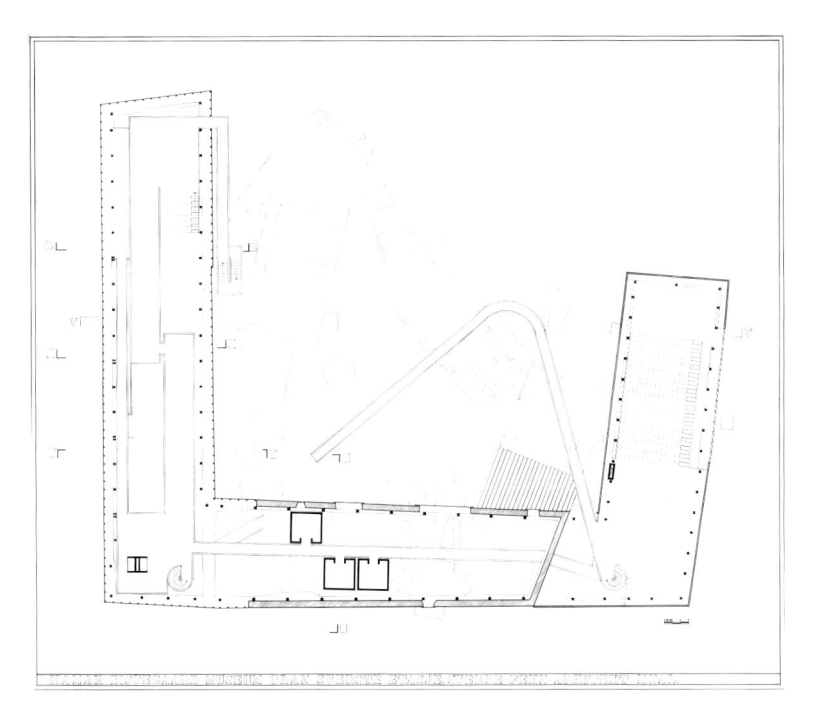

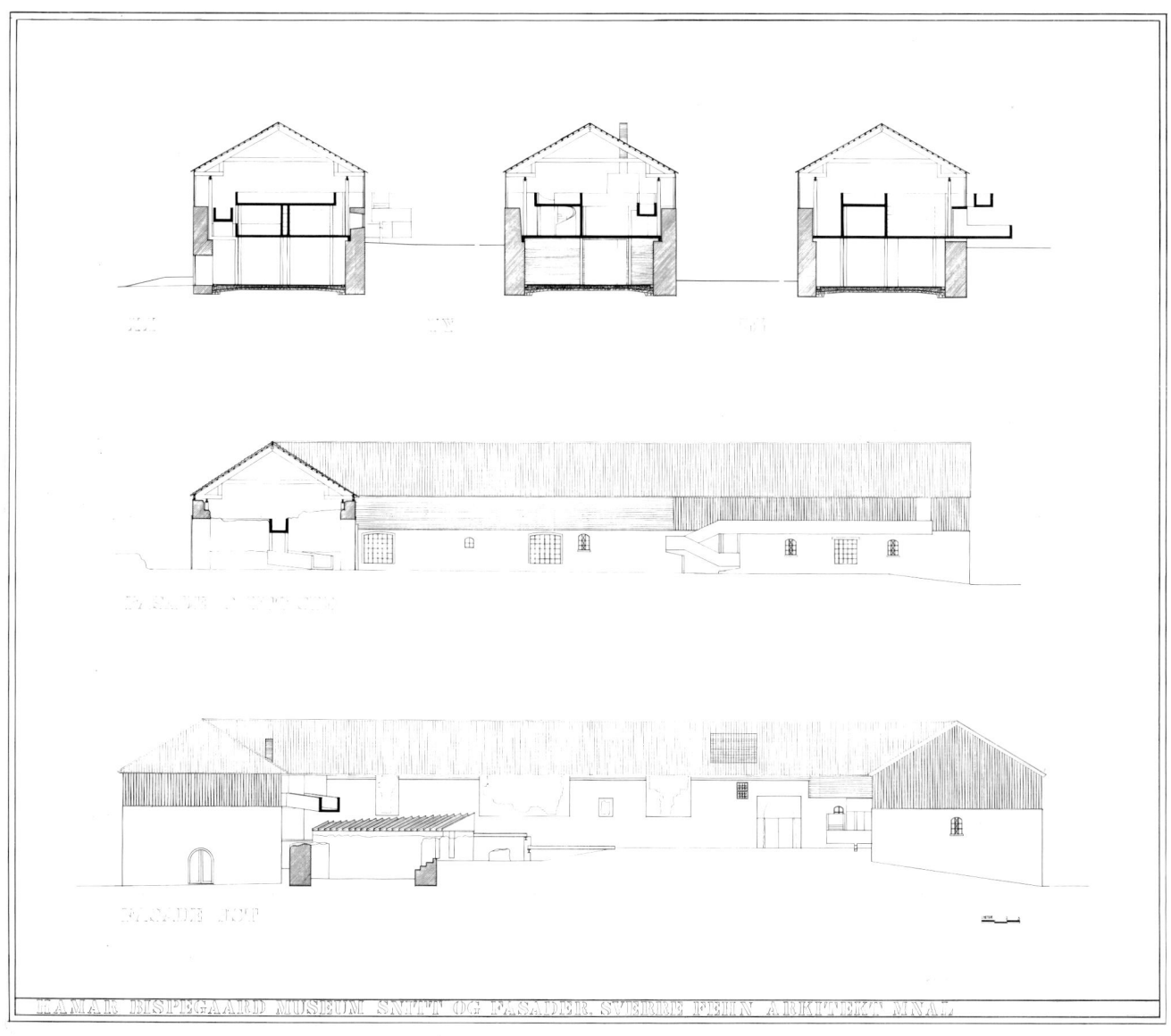

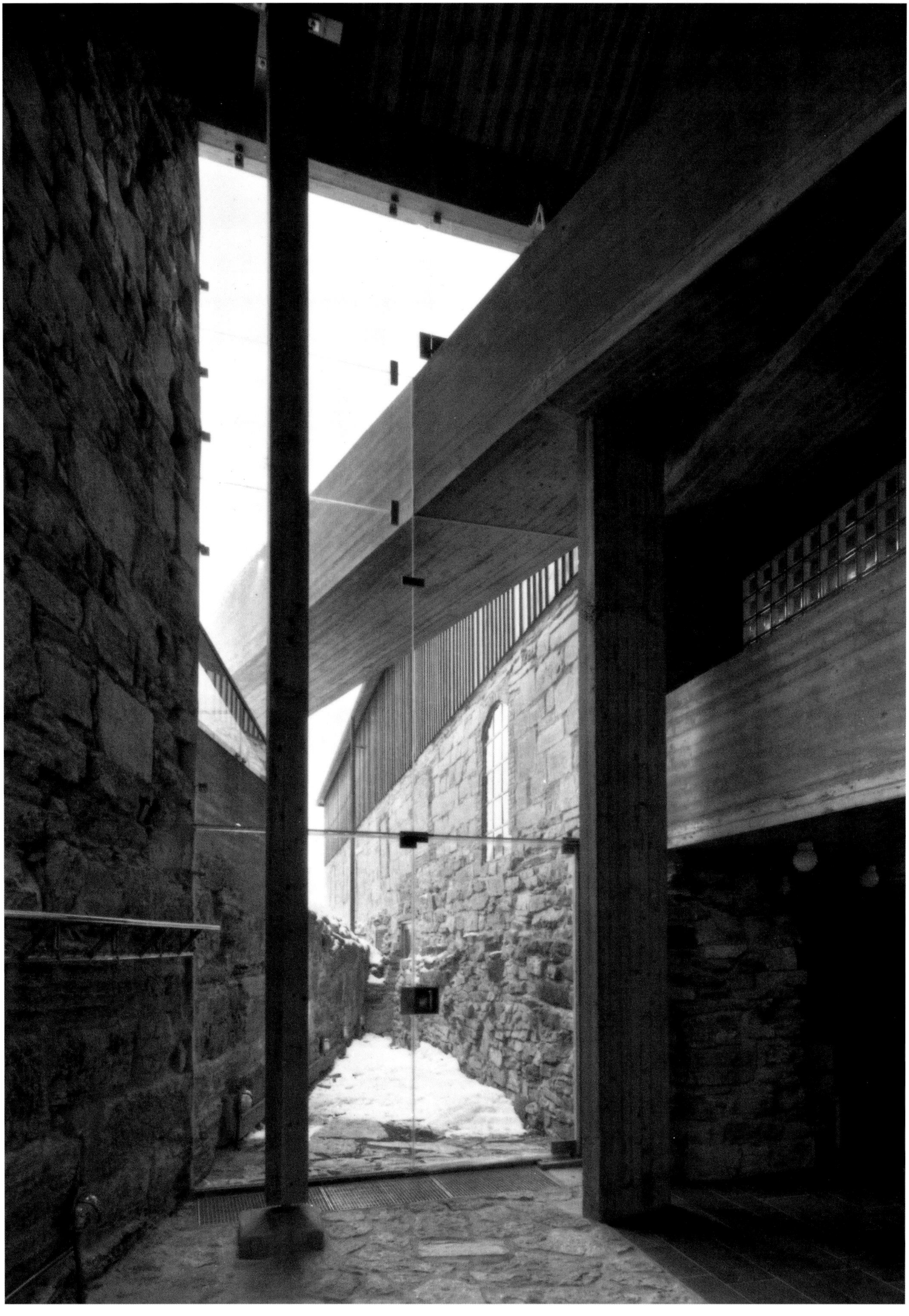

Hedmark County Museum: Exterior/interior ramp, exterior ramp leading up to auditorium.

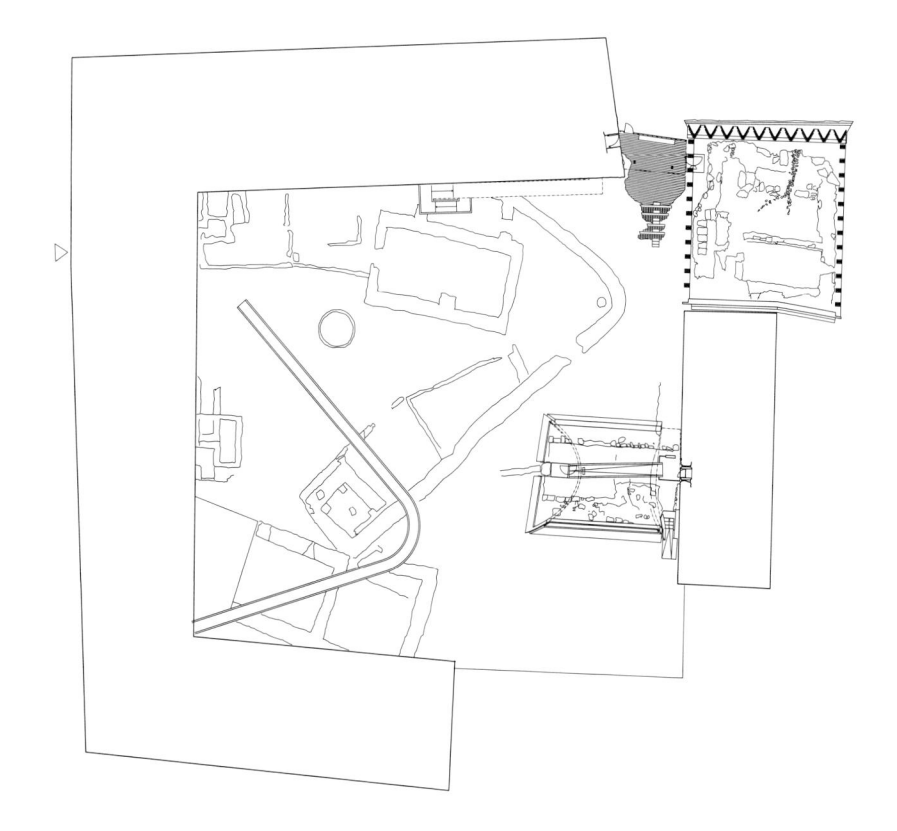

Hedmark County Museum: Plan showing addition, exterior view of addition.

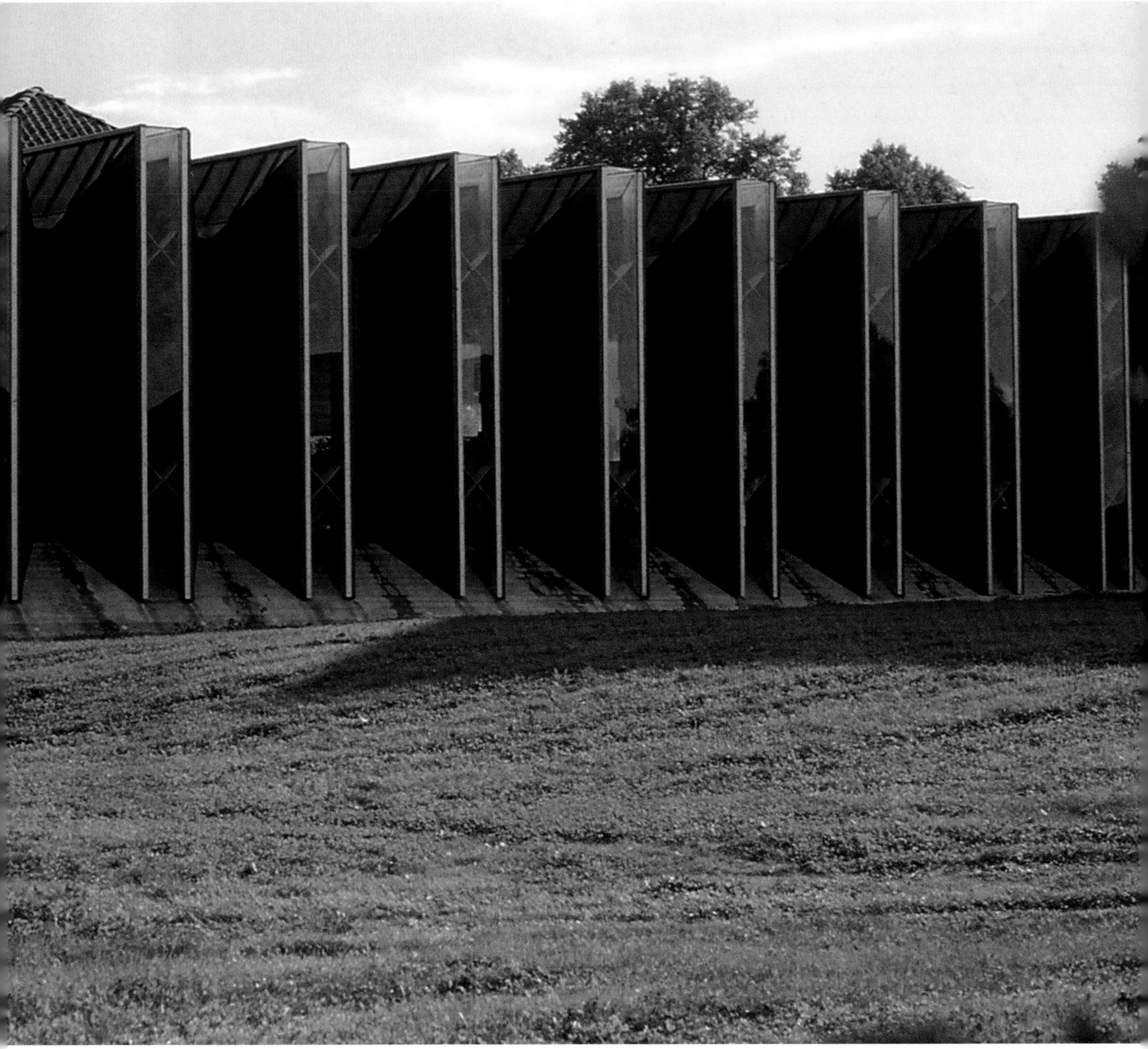

Hedmark County Museum: Roof structure of addition, detail.

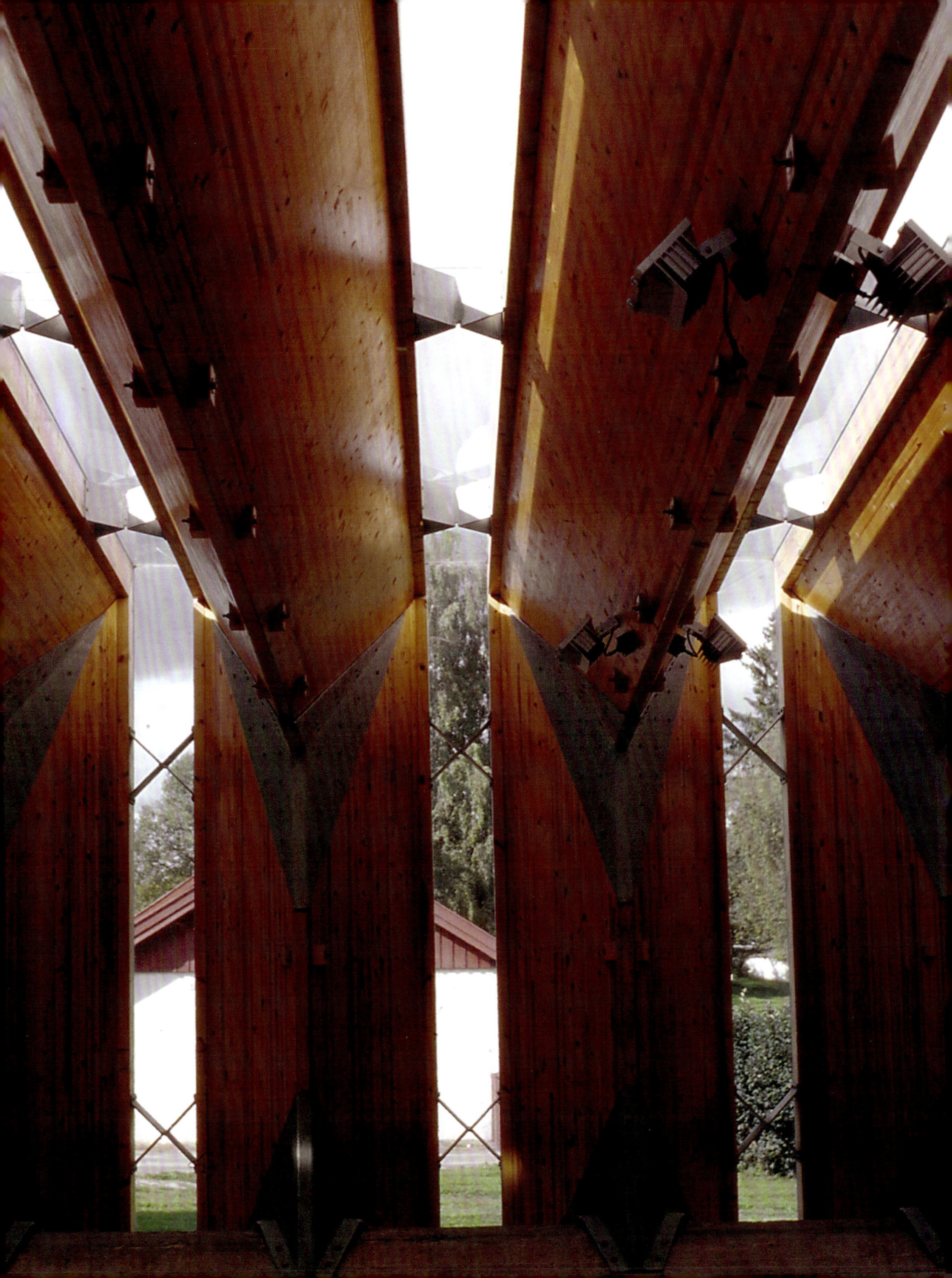

The deconcueit blue objcohn.

not be touched, were what should be emphasized, and it was this thought that gave birth to the ramps and the bridge. In the ground lay the remains of the Middle Ages, and the children [living nearby during the construction period] were like small ghosts: they crawled in from everywhere.

Beside the museum is a twelfth-century cathedral ruin; its preservation provides an interesting contrast to Fehn's approach. This project was not instigated until several years after Fehn's museum was complete. Originally the remains of the cathedral were out in the open, exposed to the seasons and decaying in and with nature, and there was a certain tension between the barn and the ruin. The cathedral was transforming more quickly than the barn, but the physical decay was parallel nonetheless. A protective glass structure, built over the cathedral ruin by Lund + Slaatto Architects in 1998, approached the brief from a different point of view. Once the cathedral ruin and its history as an image are regarded as equivalent, technology as protection serves as a savior. For centuries the townspeople of Hamar faced the remains of the sidewall of the church nave head-on. By reinstating the orientation of the cathedral as an illustration of history, the physical ruin becomes a backdrop for its protector, the glass structure. The structure over the cathedral has claimed the horizon, and its placement in the landscape is an interpretation. This juxtaposition is a curious contrast of two approaches to the past.

Once the first stage of the museum building was complete, Fehn turned his attention to the installation. He began to develop a relationship to each of the intended objects. In the Norwegian Pavilion in Brussels, he gained an intimacy with the objects through material, but he found new stimulus in the museum at Hamar. To revitalize a forgotten artifact or lift a mundane object into the light has always intrigued and fascinated Fehn. He insisted on gathering whatever background material there was for each object, whether it was excavated from the site or crafted in the surrounding district, not merely to relay information but to strengthen memory. The simplest everyday item or the most fragile, priceless church relic: each needed its horizon.

He began as usual by inventing stories around the objects. From these stories he recognized a potential within each object and a rationale for its placement. His office at this point was down to a minimum; remarkably, Fehn and one assistant took care of most of the work. Every object was carefully studied and sketched; a considerable number were fashioned in lead for the large working model of the exhibition area. **The time an artwork can feel that it is great is when it no longer has any form of reference. When the object moves itself into a museum, its dialogue with the past, with the space where it was made or belonged, disappears. The person who created the work is also gone. But time is fixed into the picture, and the object is left with its aesthetic and its energy. It must survive on its own magic. If the magic is not strong enough, it will disappear. Some objects demand a continuation of history, and once the artist disappears, so the picture's process into the future changes. Its beauty and inner strength will confront time as well as the object's legitimacy. The bullet in relation to an exhibition has always been an interesting object for me. What kind of space does a bullet demand? For me, it does not belong to movement, but to rest. It is in the space of rest that the bullet's movement can be described. To give an object its space, you must be alone with it. It must speak to you, and you must initiate this lonely dialogue on your own. If you are going to manage to communicate through the way an object is displayed, you must understand its magic and power. You need to become the bullet in order to tell about its importance and to form the space around it. No one can imagine himself or herself as a battle-ax without mentally cutting the head off a man. My space around the bullet carefully puts it to bed, the sleeping bullet. It keeps its magic within itself, and together with the space around it there is potency.**

It is the object that is constant, but the visitor experiences the exhibited object differently. It is

Sketch, 1992, "The discovery of the object."

the way in which the object communicates with the space that makes the individual communication possible. The exhibitor injects a new personality into the object, but it is the visitor who decides if it is understood. Thus it is not a final static placement. Time passes, and the object may demand a new place from someone who can convey new thoughts into it. The object will signal that a new placement is necessary. At that very moment the senses take a different hold on the object, and it will gain its new placement. Its placement and corresponding journey identify how it can be the embodiment of an object's essence. Its wandering in time is on one level totally irrelevant, because the object is strong enough on its own to signal "come, live inside of me." A pearl is not a pearl until it is loved; if an object blushes with modesty because it has been given a unique placement, it will begin to talk.

The object's movement in relation to time is a strange phenomenon. If you take time out of it, our experience of the object begins to move. The various objects and their orientation to one another begin to react and communicate. The bullet has reciprocal dialogue with the shield and the ax. The space is not filled with solitude once the visitors leave; the objects continue through their eloquence to speak to one another. They survive and continue on within their own solitude.

Fehn is a poet in his conversation with the object. When the dialogue between the architect and the object evolves into an expression, the object and the way it is exhibited will demand a dialogue with the viewer. In this situation, the viewer takes an active role in the room around the object. For instance, Fehn placed in a rather small concrete room (3.66 by 3.66 meters) an overpainted Madonna from a local village and part of a crucifix where the Christ figure reaches to the heavens. Just outside the door is the head of a devil. The position of the crucifix is a confrontation between the individual and his god. The shadow is death's own shadow. Here, alone with light, the suffering becomes the visitor's own. In this same room is a cannonball, an object that controls life, but it is death that is the high point. A bullet, lying completely imprisoned in a box, underlines movement. Architecture is a spatial participant in this defined event, allowing a story to unfold as one enters the space. A scythe casts its shadow across a rough concrete wall. A plow reveals its strength through a cut in a steel plate. The relationship between the object and the choice of material explodes through events in a readily understandable expression. Jewelry is placed on leather to evoke the texture and warmth of human skin. A painting is hung on its easel. A drinking glass is placed on a glass shelf near a window to expose its material identity. These poetic images are in their comprehension of the object very concrete and reveal Fehn's uncanny ability to inhabit each object.

To exhibit an object, I have to become the object . . . The invisible museum belongs to the earth's crust. In its dark depths the objects talk. Once the surface is broken, the objects are lifted out into loneliness's light. The reason is history. The old stone walls of the Middle Ages draw ornaments in the sand. And the visitor casts shadows into the past from the bridge's concrete structure. All the answers are given from the individual's position between heaven and earth . . . The largest museum is the earth itself. In its surface lost objects are preserved. The sea and the sand are the great conservationists and they make the voyage into eternity so slow that we find the key to culture's birth through the patterns left behind.

It is interesting to note how Fehn on the one hand focused on the minute details of each exhibition object and on the other retained a clear comprehension of the overall task. In a conversation I had with him in 1979, he reflected on his work at Hamar, and in many ways these few lines sum up his personal approach or attitude in relation to this

Hedmark County Museum: Objects on display.

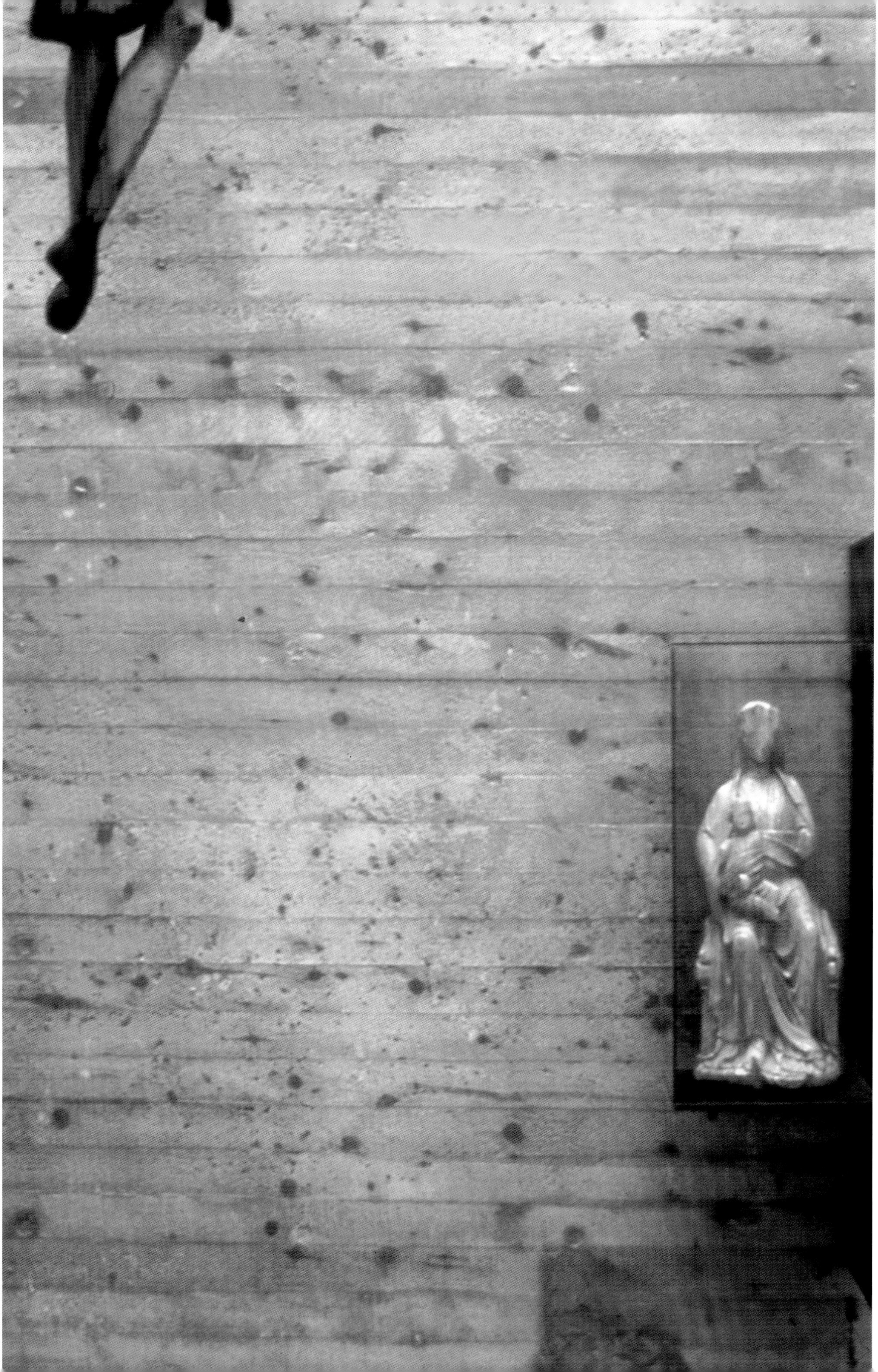

Hedmark County Museum: Objects on display.

OPPOSITE Mining Museum, Røros, Norway: Site plan.

130 THE PATTERN OF THOUGHTS

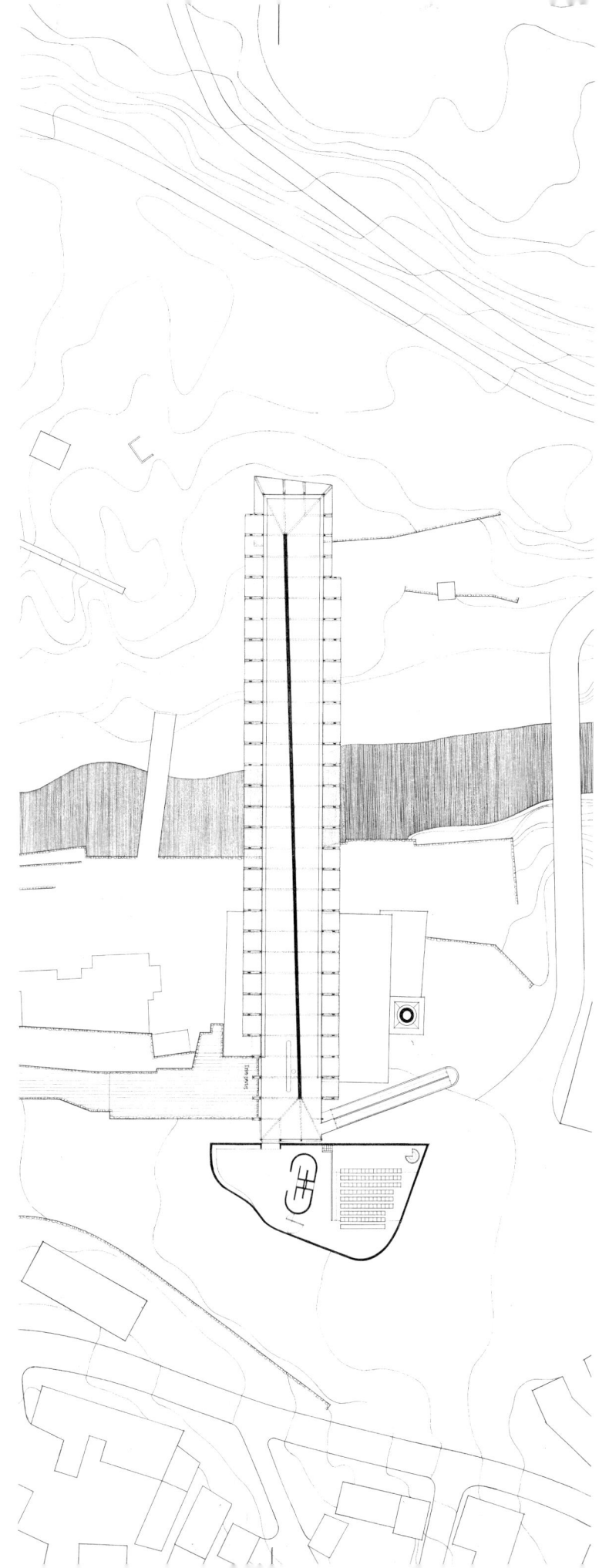

important work: **Someone without an urban sensibility in his or her subconscious could not have solved Hamar. One must understand the building as an urban reality. The exhibition became culture born again, new.**

Some years after the completion of the first stage of work at Hamar, Fehn drew a project for the Røros Mining Museum, 1979–80. It reveals a strong relationship between light and structure that in turn indicates the possibility of a unique space. There is nothing to add or take away; the architecture is complete. It lies within the spirit of Louis Kahn's work in that there is neither a secondary structure nor a need for additional walls. The single line of the building has an architectural complexity that finds its expression in a precise, tapering structural repetition, and its urban image is set as a spatial bridge that forms the museum. As a span, it connects two distinct site features: the open plains of the highlands and the silver-mining town of Røros. It straddles the open landscape but reflects the urban activity of the town. As a structure, the bridge lends comprehension to the whole: it directs how and where objects are placed, since it is inside the diagonal wall that one finds the displayed objects. The intensity of daylight varies in the long interior as a consequence of the diagonal wall. Light from the roof mixes with light reflecting up from the slag of the silver mine. The singular structure allows for an integrated spatial expression where light gives identity.

The building mimes the diagonal lines of a perspective drawing of the street plan. The eternal themes of a voyage, a boat and a bridge, the first impulses in relation to a straight line, were spatially treated in

132 THE PATTERN OF THOUGHTS

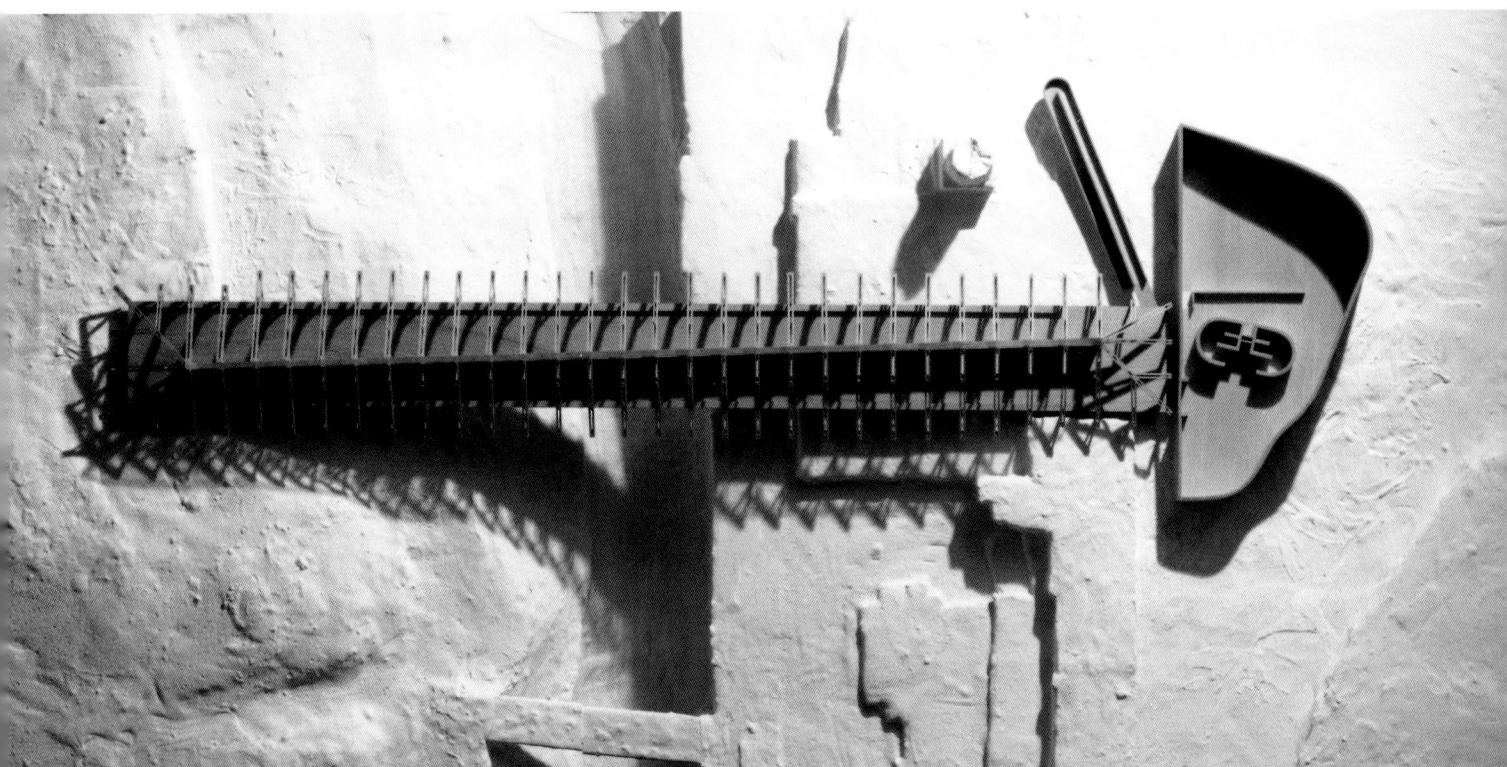

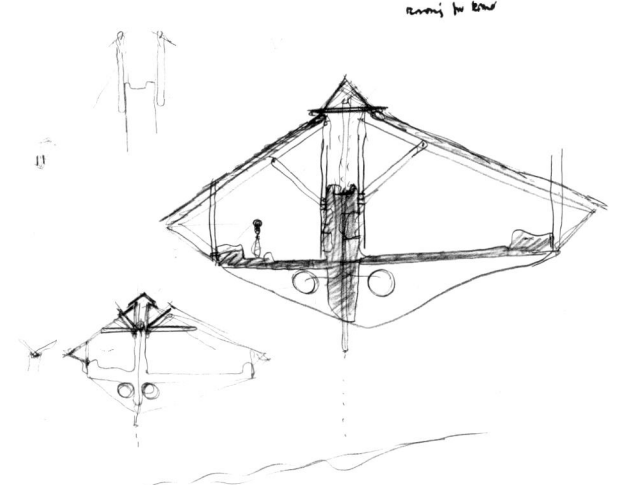

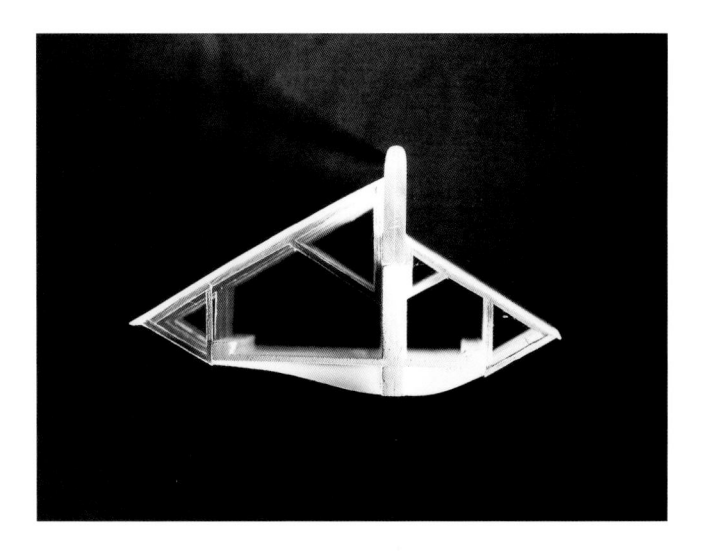

Mining Museum:
Model views, sketch, section model, elevations and sections.

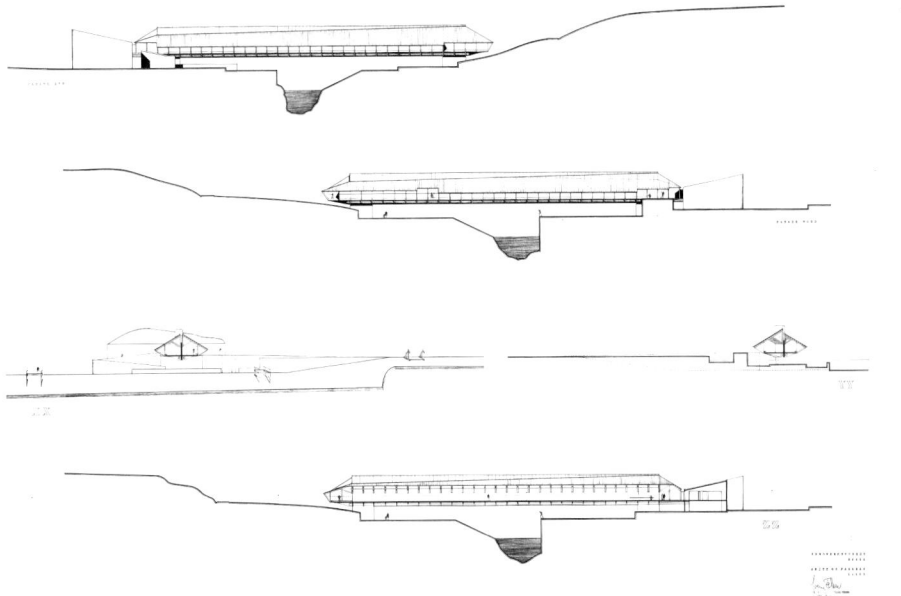

THE RETURN OF THE HORIZON

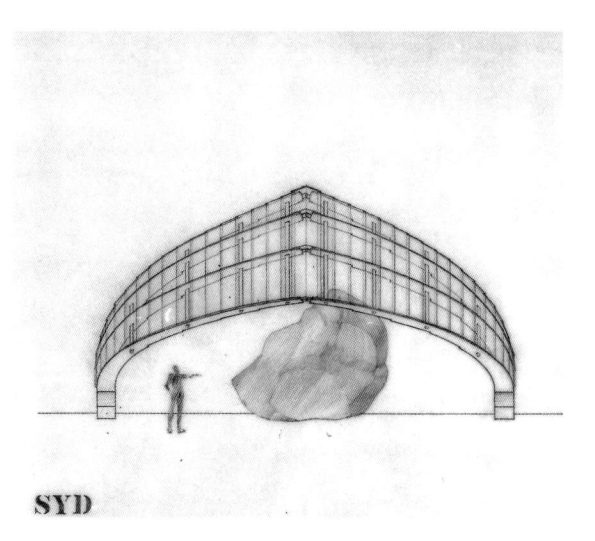

Protective covering for a prehistoric rock drawing, Svartskog, Norway: Elevation, rock carving.

OPPOSITE Sketch, 1982, "The dream of being between heaven and earth."

this project. In animal and human movement, there is no straight line, but once you lift the building up from the ground the straight line appears in the same way that a wheel creates a straight line, a straight path. The building's structure contains the boat's construction. Looking out, one sees the waterfall and the slag piles. The waterfall rushes freely under you. In one sense, my architectural discussions converge in this project.

A project from 1978 for a small protective structure over a rock carving is an interesting supplement to Fehn's conceptual dialogue around the idea of the museum. The relationship between heaven, structure, and ground is at its maximum because the displayed object is the earth itself. **Rock carvings have no horizon; they are in space. From this, the earth itself, the sun, the moon, and the heavens are carved into the surface. Large and small symbols affix themselves to a universal picture. The drawings rely on nothing more than the earth's surface. What then should a rock-carving museum be about, the keys to heaven or to the landscape? Or should it transfer an understanding of ourselves?**

The competition project for the Trondheim Library, 1977, again confronts an archaeological site: a city block in the old section of town. In this proposal, Fehn drew a new floor under the existing ground level where the ruins once touched the earth. The roof works as a skylight, creating a relationship between the cut in the town landscape and its new natural light. The roof structure varies in relation to the sequential positioning of the ruins below the level of the street outside. One meets silence together with the library books. Here, the room of the past is not given a new architectonic motif: the tilted glass roof is just a lid that offers protection.

The buildings and projects from this era, especially those that engage with a site belonging to the past, dwell upon position, that is, position in relation to an ever-changing horizon. But it is a horizon attached to the earth, an earth that is far more than a surface skin. The earth is a deep structure, a historic mass that contains traces of all living things. When Fehn cuts into this mass in order to form a room, he connects the room of earth and heaven through light: light pulls the past into the present. The physical connection between heaven and earth through bridges and ramps is not so much a celebration of the sky as it is of the earth and its contents.

Træet og fuglen

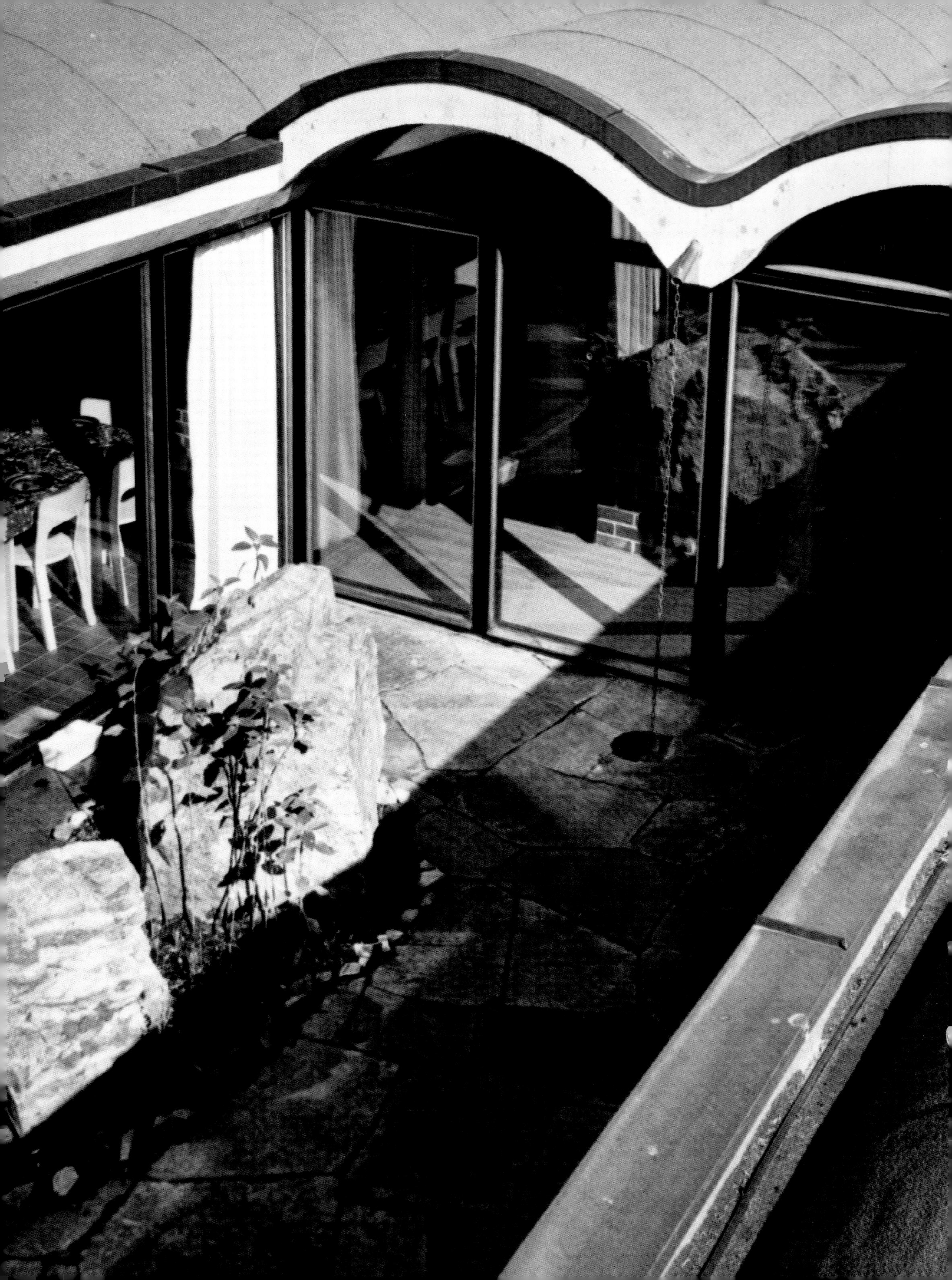

CHAPTER 6

PUBLIC CONVERSATIONS | Sverre Fehn has never been very active in public debates or discussions, and he seldom expresses publicly opinions about current issues or politics in architecture. Perhaps the only place a stated position might surface is in the classroom. Newspaper articles, conferences, and radio and television shows were infrequent, and a more general public interest in his work has occurred only at the end of his active years. Fehn has clear opinions about the work of others, but he keeps them within the private sphere and, for the most part, to himself. Yet he is curious about new architecture projects and the professional gossip around them. He has great respect for the effort that goes into any built work; he considers this effort in many ways independent of the architectural quality of the structure. All other aspects of building—architectural history, theory, or public opinion—are for him information and inspiration related to the act of building. He centers his thoughts and energy on his own architectural work, and it is here one finds standpoints in relation to public and social issues. The goal has always been the same: to build. It is within the language of architecture and its limitations, its physical result, that he offers a public or social dialogue. Fehn speaks through his buildings.

Palladio's Villa Rotonda and Le Corbusier's Villa Savoie often come up in Fehn's lectures, not so much as individual works but together, since it is in their comparison that Fehn finds what inspires him. These lectures give great insight into his views on larger public projects. This is particularly true with regard to the relationship he sees between architecture and nature: many have gradually come to view nature as a picture, as scenery belonging to aesthetics, rather than working with nature's forces and capacities in order to strengthen architectural content. The built is no longer able to draw a line between the urban and the natural landscape, since the urban tissue eats away at the landscape and imprisons it as a view.

The minute interest was legal, and one could earn money from money, it gave freedom to enter the world in another way. Money became more money, and some no longer needed to work. This changed our relationship to the house. What was one supposed to do? One had to concentrate on aesthetics, beauty, the view, and the aesthetic consideration of where it is beautiful to live. This enabled one to move away from the site's characteristics embedded in the specific relationship between nature and production, but there had to be enough of a nature concept that the breeze from the river or sea could brush through a silk shirt.

For Palladio, the city house is a simple drawing, but when he places it out in the landscape, he draws the house like a little village. Palladio, the farmer from the Po Valley, takes his drawings with him from Venice, and yes, almost screws his spatial object to the earth, and the columns almost stand in line to enter. He builds a new room in an existing landscape room. Earlier the farmer worked within nature's cycle, and the forest and landscape were seen as unending. What was finite belonged to heaven; it was the earth that was unlimited. The map of the earth came late, but the map of the heavens was early.

In the Villa Rotonda, Palladio forms the earth into a labyrinth. In the Villa Rotonda, I have gone around the earth and come back to the same point where I started. Three hundred years later, Corbusier builds the Villa Savoie, and he says to himself, "I am not going to touch the ground; for me, it is unimportant. It is not enough for me anymore. I will conquer the sky." The earthly maps are over. Livingstone and the others have done everything.

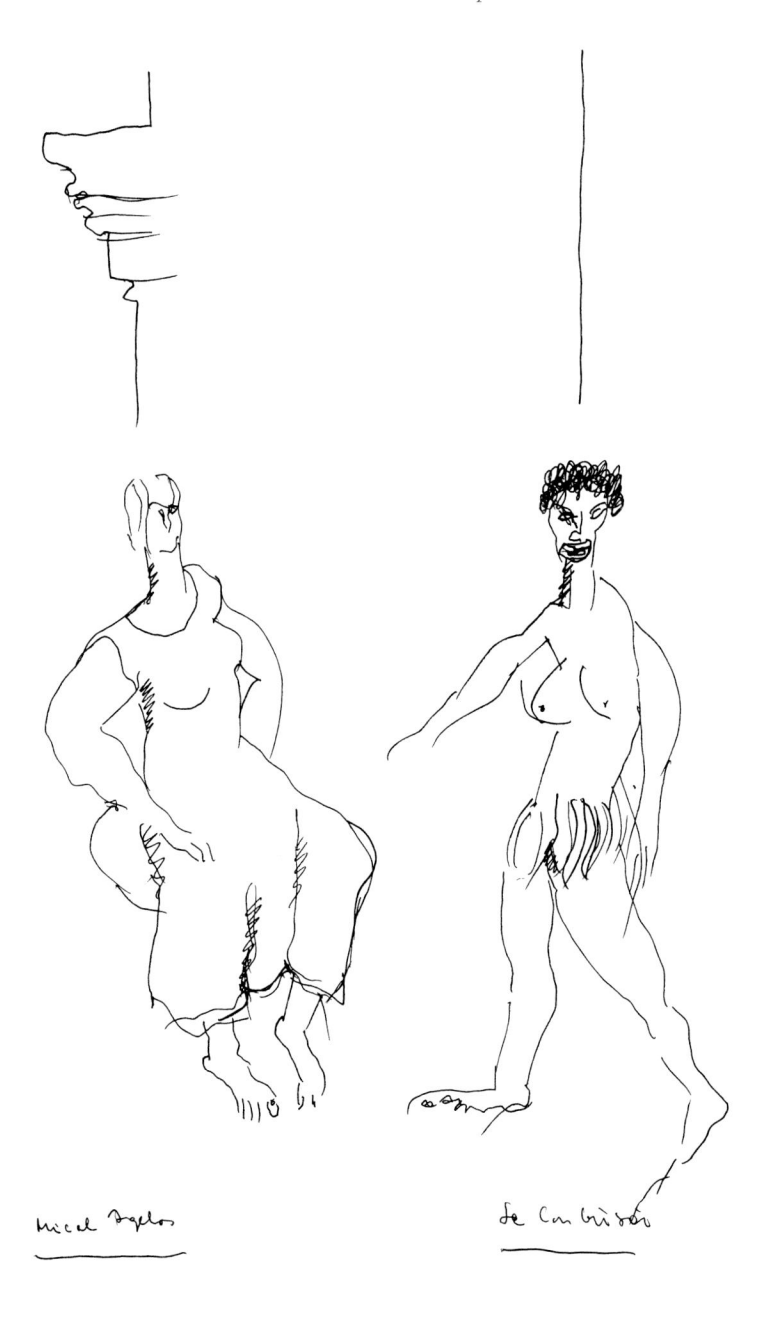

Sketch, "Michelangelo. Le Corbusier."

PAGE 136 Skådalen School and Accreditation Center for Children with Hearing Impairment, Oslo: Interior court in dormitory.

OVERLEAF Sketch, 1996, of Villa Rotonda and Villa Savoie with conversation between Palladio and Le Corbusier.

In the Villa Savoie, with the sun and sunbathing on the roof, the sky was no longer a mystery for Corbusier; it was rather an aesthetic consideration. He gave people a house that no longer had a mystery, no attic and no cellar. It was too much for many; Corbu built a philosophy. He unveiled the mysterious. The moment he conquered the sky we lost the mystery, and at the same time, we approached the earth in a new way.

It is possible to see some parallels between Fehn's projects and commissions from the late 1960s to about 1980 and what was being built by and discussed within certain groups in Europe, in particular some members of Team 10, who were old acquaintances from the architect's stay in Paris. Fehn was keenly aware of the writings and built work produced by Team 10 members, their conflict with Le Corbusier, and their reasons for dropping out of the Congrès International d'Architecture Moderne. He was torn between a master and a group with an ideological dream. He has often commented that he seldom participated in international meetings at this time due to expense, but I think the reason lies closer to the fact that the time, effort, and personal cost to bridge the distance were too great. Instead, the ideas coming from Europe were mulled over, reexamined, and run through a Nordic sensibility; only then would they reappear in his larger public projects. Fehn had a unique way of filtering information. The smallest incidents or details could at the right moment translate into a phrase that gave him architectural insight. In 1985, I jotted down Fehn's beautiful and personal comment on Aldo van Eyck's Hubertus House. He knew the building well, and he condensed what was for him its essence into four words: **He knits his light.**

The changes in attitude that the Nordic form of socialism brought to Norway after the war filtered down into the built environment unevenly. In Norway and especially in Sweden, the development of architectural space was not followed by an internal understanding of physical space and its properties as a shared experience; rather, political statements set an agenda, and the space that followed was more a reflection of this expressed agenda. Fehn's architecture had a level of abstraction that was demanding and not always understood. He did not transform the political agenda into an architectural image, nor did he treat the functional requirements of a building as items on a specific list. Both personal and general preconceptions in relation to public space needed to be reexamined. Politicians were aware of the problem and thus were eager to take part in the discussions around developing programs for new buildings and urban planning schemes, but the resulting innovative work was not always what they envisioned. For Fehn, a good response meant innovation, and it was almost as if his work needed to be tried and accepted abroad before it found approval in Norway. Many architects at that time faced a similar challenge. Nevertheless, the local opposition Fehn experienced in relation to his public buildings did not alter his energy or creative focus.

Similarly, Louis Kahn, in his relationship both to his own work and to that of others, was occupied with this quandary. What is it that released in the general public a form of acceptance? Kahn referred to it as "the acceptance will, or the will to accept," meaning that in the end it is the people or inhabitants who must have a readiness to accept the work. The moment the work leaves the subjective, coddled realm of the architect it attains an objective quality that is offered without the protection of a user's manual. There is a spatial boldness in Fehn's buildings, but also a certain type of innocence. They are neither directly political nor based on a predictable

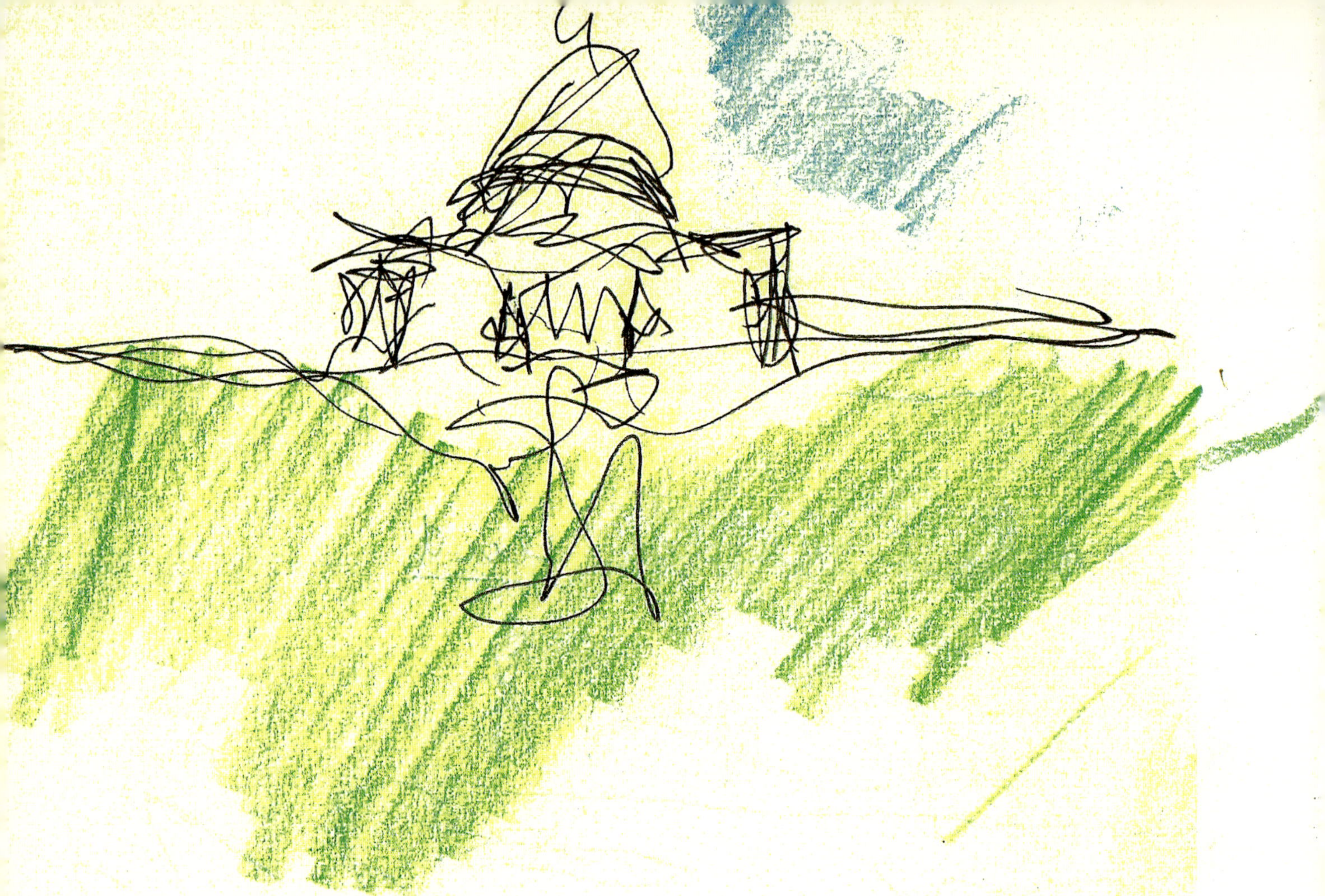

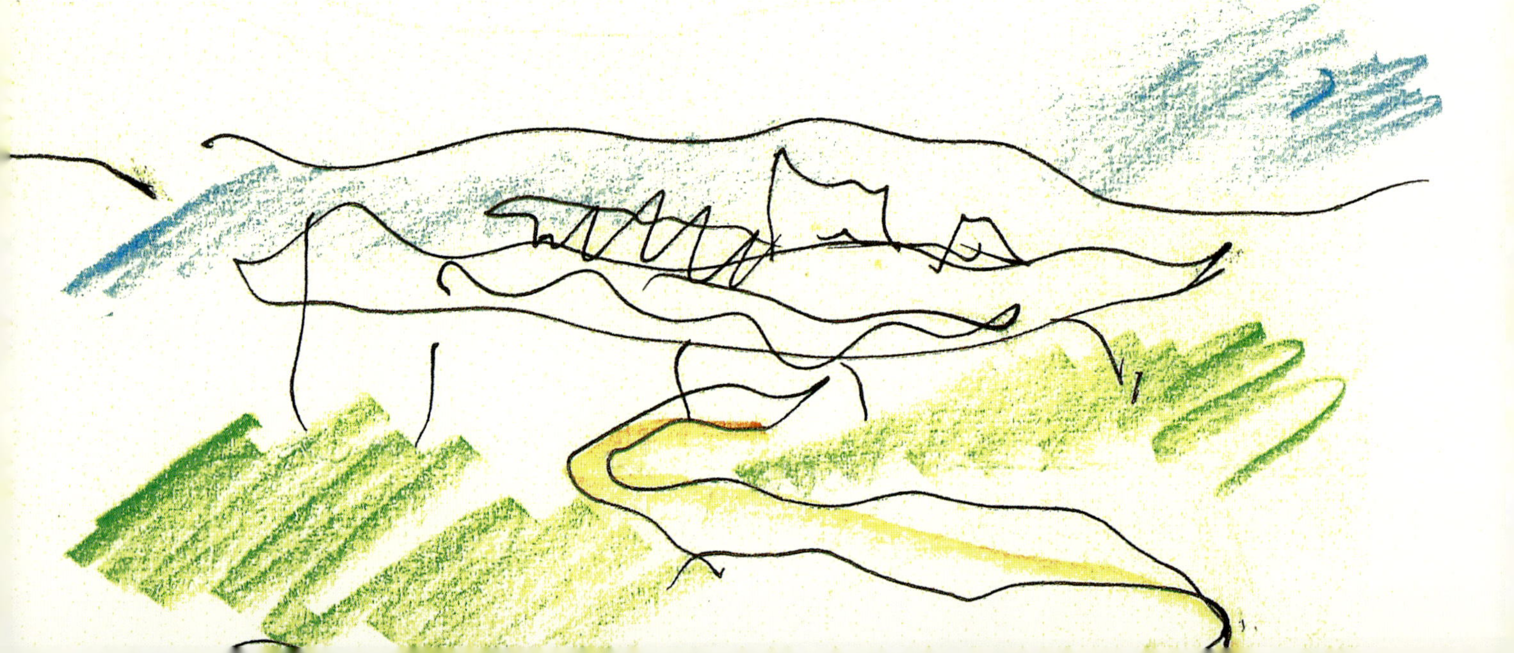

a.C. ... columbia.

P. O.K. I think I think
    see some families still
    use it.

J.C. Hardly don. nobody lives
     there. (it has become
     a monument historic)

P. We have changed
    nothing too (1 ...
    ...

J.C. I thought I changes.
     the nature.

J. Precisely

method of success. Each work stands alone as an individual reading of a singular situation.

Fehn's project for a church at Honningsvåg, 1965–67, in the far north of Norway, was the first-prize winner in a design competition. This particular project has always meant a great deal to Fehn. **When constructing a church in Honningsvåg, a town whose existence is based on the boat, thoughts of the tree are not far away. It is in the nave, the ship of the church in Norwegian terminology, that one meets, as a town citizen, the story of heaven and hell. When the "teaching" becomes difficult and the mind becomes filled with fear for the total demands of religion, it is good to raise one's eyes to the ceiling. If one finds again the curved construction with some of the closeness of the hull, or if one leans against the column that has the secure dimension of the mast, the church becomes filled with symbols that are one's everyday references. For the mast is the construction that has been given the means of catching the wind, and has given the world to men.**

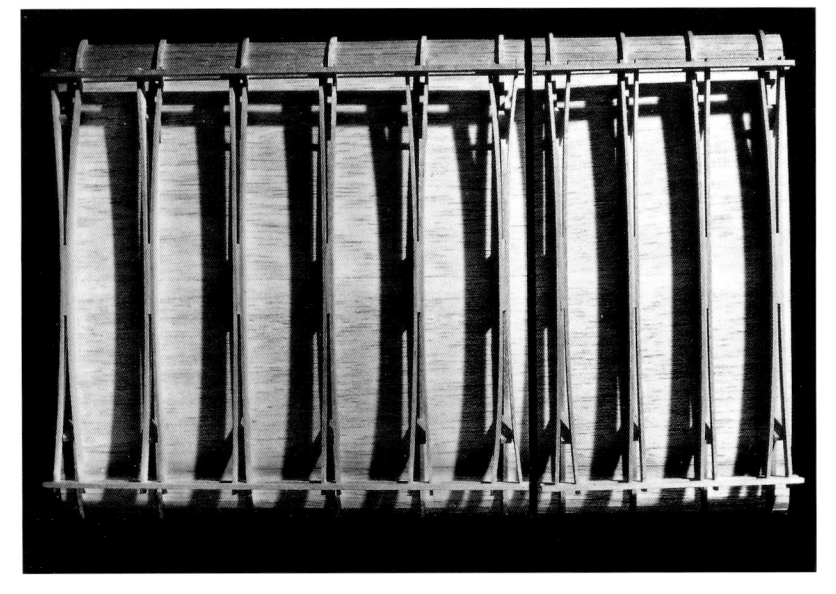

Fehn also referred to this church project as a turning point in relation to his structural composition: **I was so tired of the large mass construction involved with the Brussels pavilion. I wanted to experience the simple column and the intricate beam. The church's constructive components and their various dimensions in building up a spatial layer were my protest against the rather heavy construction diagram in the Brussels pavilion. In the church I wanted to release the structure and find a particular scale for each of the different elements.**

The competition asked for a multipurpose central church room, and Fehn's entry answered the program directly. All scheduled activities would take place in a central space with adjacent service rooms; though this room could be divided in two by large sliding doors, everything from a bazaar to a funeral would share the same space. In order to combine the sacred and the everyday, Fehn balanced the openness of the multipurpose room with a careful choice of structure and material. The exterior concrete walls formed a shell that offered protection from the harsh polar climate, and the interior wooden construction bespoke an image familiar to the congregation. In the architect's remarks on the church at Honningsvåg, it is always the boatbuilder and his precision related to material that come into focus: **The boatbuilder is familiar with nature's technology. The tree and its curves contain the boat's dimensions. Today even the tree has become a mass, like the earth, and we demand of it all dimensions. The Viking ship's construction, a proportioning of parts put together into a precise assemblage that is based on an understanding of the sea's movement, has**

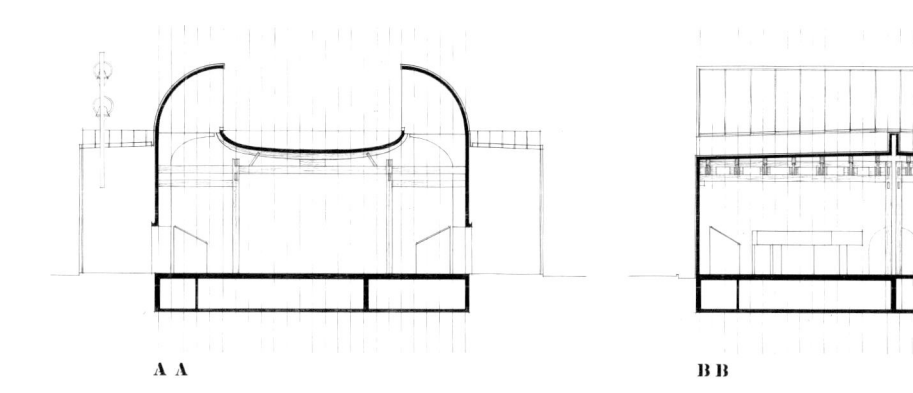

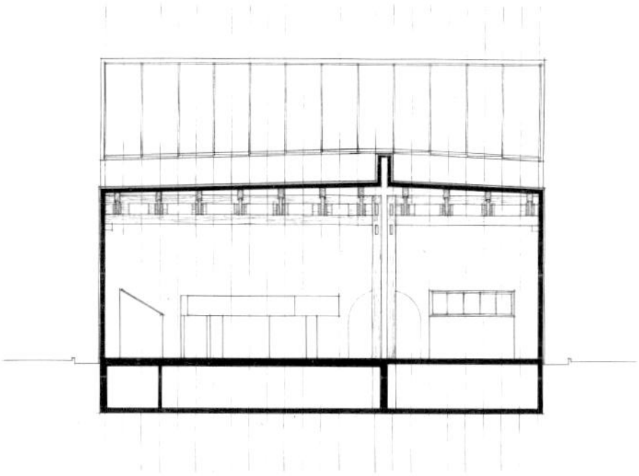

A A B B

Church, Honningsvåg: Model of roof structure, interior model, sections, detail of roof structure.

inspired the roof construction in this church. The fisherman feels comfortable and is familiar with the construction covering his room. The central church room becomes a large open space, a marketplace for many activities, some that can only take place in the church, and this is important for an area where half of the year is experienced as one long night. This was the idea, but the committee could not agree: "We can't have death in our midst; the corpse must go down in the cellar!"

 Shortly after I started to work in Sverre Fehn's office, he drove me out to the Bøler Community Center and Library, 1962–72. I had recently returned from Louis Kahn's master class at the University of Pennsylvania, and that day the connection between Fehn and Kahn became clear. It was not a question of visual likeness but of simplicity and essential energy.

 This small community center on the outskirts of Oslo comprises a multipurpose space and an administration and library building. A planned swimming and recreation hall was never built, and this was particularly unfortunate because it was these two functions that would have attracted a broader audience to the center. In addition, the plaza that would have been formed by the three buildings was never developed.

 Ramps clearly indicate an easy way in and out of the building complex. The open multipurpose space could accommodate a number of activities. The second floor opened up to this central room, inviting communication and participation on many levels. One was always part of the large social room, but one could also opt for distance and intensity; Fehn achieved through his spatial decisions a built-in discrete pressure on the visitor to interact at some level with the main room.

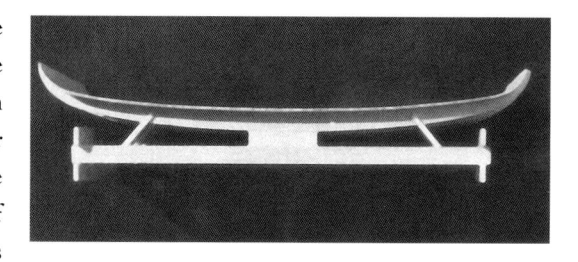

 This work is greatly underestimated in relation to Fehn's production as a whole. Unfortunately, the building never had a chance. The center entered the public arena to the surprise of the inhabitants of the small suburban area. Local politicians and leaders of the center were also caught unawares. The initial concept behind the project was misunderstood almost from the start. The spatial openness and possibility for the inhabitant to engage, transform, and take over the space in a more personal way reflect the changes in public architecture in Europe at that time. In fact, the building expressed a cognizance of social change that would be apparent to politicians and social workers only many years later. Over the years, changes required in relation to new building codes were enacted in a way that did not attempt to preserve the original spatial intentions, and in order to satisfy the more conventional understanding of space in public buildings of the time, the center gradually disappeared as architecture. Some years later, politicians and planners came to prefer this type of spatial integration in designs for schools and youth centers.

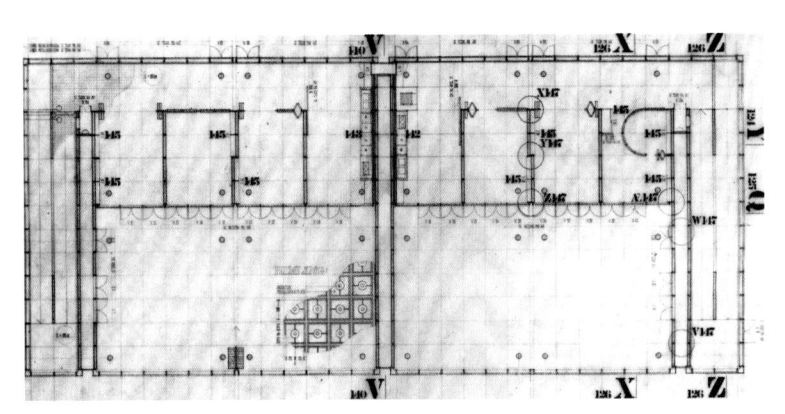

In the Bøler Community Center, Fehn once again attempted to use Co-Coon, this time in a form called Dekaphan, which he had first employed in his pavilion in Brussels. Fire regulations made this a complicated process, but it was finally decided that the semitransparent material could clothe the box. At night, the facades lit up like a lantern with a soft yellow glow, and during the day, a diffused light filtered through the walls. It took only a few years before the Co-Coon was replaced with glass, emphasizing a questionable view and giving a sharp light. At this point, the building was lost. Sadly, even today there are some who congratulate themselves on the fact that all traces of Fehn were erased. If the complex had been completed as planned, it would have given the area a distinct identity. But after twelve years of proposals and revisions, after the site for the recreation hall was cleared and the plans approved, a single telephone call from the authorities ended the project.

The Skådalen School and Accreditation Center for Children with Hearing Impairment, 1971–79—which was underway at the same time that Fehn's office was working on the Bøler project—did not fare much better. Again it was a commission in which Fehn used architecture to express a social point of view. He struggled to understand the world of a child with a serious hearing impairment, and possibly poor eyesight as well. What type of space should address this situation? Fehn wrote about his approach to the Skådalen School in the article "Four Stories."

THE CHILD AND THE OLD MAN

When I was a young architect of twenty-six, I designed a home for elderly people. Twenty years later I was asked by the government to build a school for deaf children. Confronting the elderly as a child, you concentrate on the physical differences in their bodies: the joints are weak, the bones are fragile, and the heart beats slowly. Stairs are like mountains. After observing these simple facts, it was natural to construct a one-story building. Meeting the child

Bøler Community Center and Library, Oslo: Plan of community center, site model, detail of exterior, interior view of community center, interior view of library.

OVERLEAF Bøler Community Center: Interior ramp.

PUBLIC CONVERSATIONS 145

BRANNSLANGE

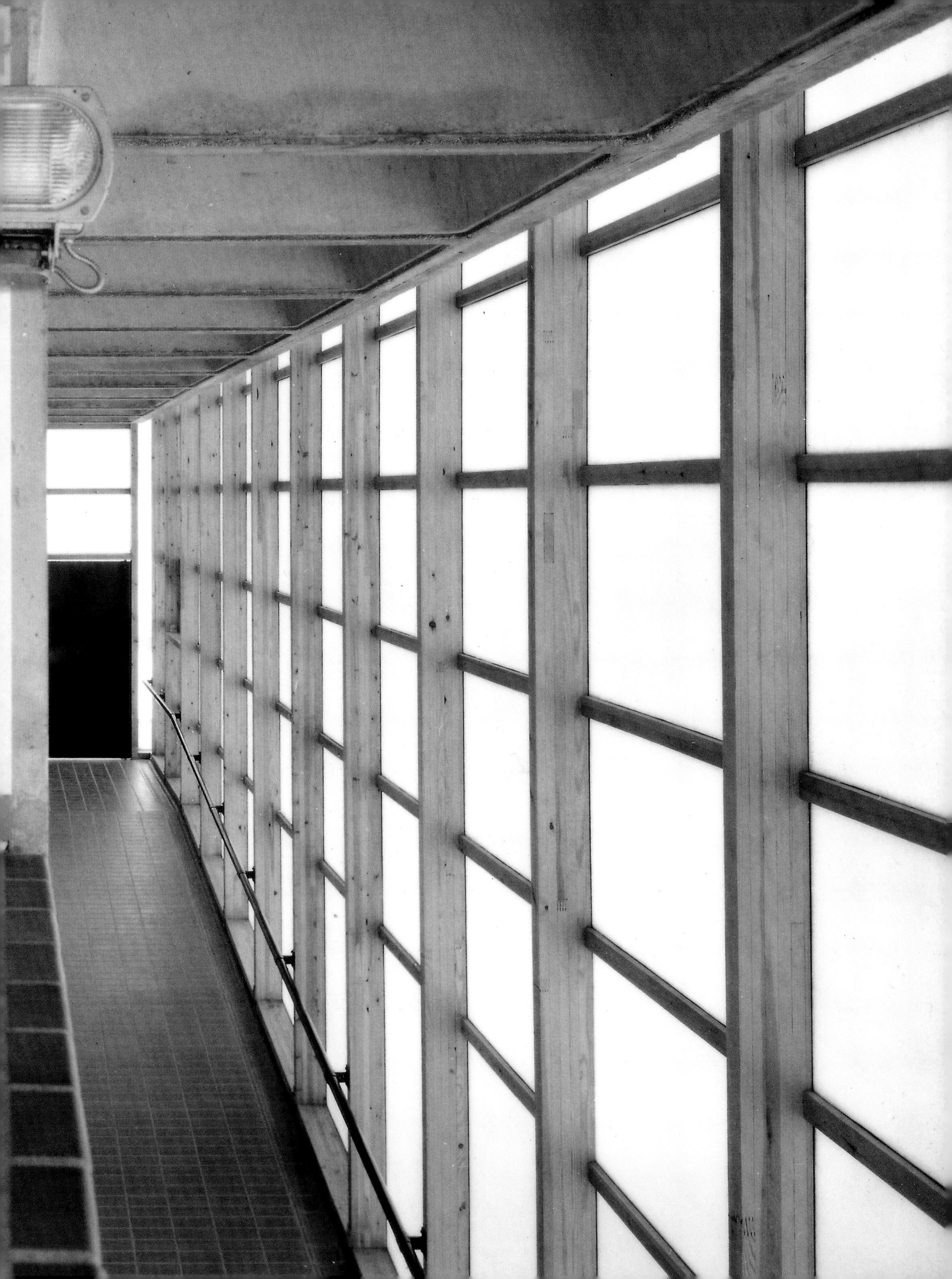

Skådalen School: Site model, exterior view of dormitory.

as an old man you realize that nature must be conquered by the child. So your buildings must be set into the landscape as gently as when the little child makes his first step into the woodlands.

The wall is the partner that returns the ball to the child and gives shadow to the elderly. Both sense the nearness of the elements of architecture. Distance lives only in the memories of the old and the fairy tales of the young. When a child mixes sand and water with his hands, making a cake of mud to transform his face into a mask, it is the child's homage to the earth. If you hide the concrete column, you rob the child's possibility of having a conversation with architecture.

"It has been snowing outside," the mother says from her window, but the child sees nothing in an architecture where you must reach the age of twenty-one before the construction fits your body, and you end at eighty-two with just one key in your pocket, the key to your drawer, your last "room."

The school at Skådalen is a community consisting of several new structures—six dormitories, kitchen-dining room, classrooms, administration, and workshop and observatory space—and a new gymnasium with a swimming pool in a restored building. The buildings are molded to the contours of the wooded suburban site. Fehn was particularly interested in the physical dimension of space as a response to the size of a child, and in the possibility that a spatial awareness could be reached and strengthened through tactility. The intrinsic surface of materials—brick, concrete, and wood—gave texture to the form of each space. In this respect, daylight also became a material. The light and the view—through openings calibrated to a child's size—worked with the interior space to intensify the children's understanding of both their place within the building and the room's relationship to the exterior. The furniture, designed to be moved around and arranged for the needs of the day, avoids a static classroom effect. Smaller semicircular rooms off the larger classrooms—areas for small groups of students or a private conversation—made reference to a fundamental image of children gathered around the teacher as a storyteller. It was not just the interior that was meant to provide orientation and sense of place; the surrounding landscape too was intended to remain an untouched forest setting that would give the school and dormitory complex layered contact with the neighboring area. Simple paths connected the buildings, road, and nearby trolley stop. The haphazard paths, homemade ski slopes, and tree forts were securely contained within the grounds yet also beheld a sense of adventure in the carefully preserved wooded area. On a number of occasions during this period, Fehn would refer with great respect to the Suresnes Open-Air School in Paris, 1935, by Baudoin & Lods and to the Municipal Orphanage in Amsterdam, 1960, by Aldo van Eyck.

Skådalen was the first open-classroom school for hearing-impaired children in Scandinavia. The architecture staged a new relationship between the teachers and the children, and the staff was faced with not just a demanding building complex but with new pedagogical methods as well. In December 1975, just before the first phase of the school complex was finished, one of Norway's largest newspapers ran a front-page article with the title "Concrete Hell," and from this point a cloud hung over the project. Much of the final stage toward completion suffered, and the period of adjustment that required an open dialogue never occurred. The newspaper article was a blow to Fehn personally, but it also affected the studio, because commissions soon dried up. It was an anxious and, to a certain extent, isolating time, but Fehn seemed to be able to work around problems,

PUBLIC CONVERSATIONS 149

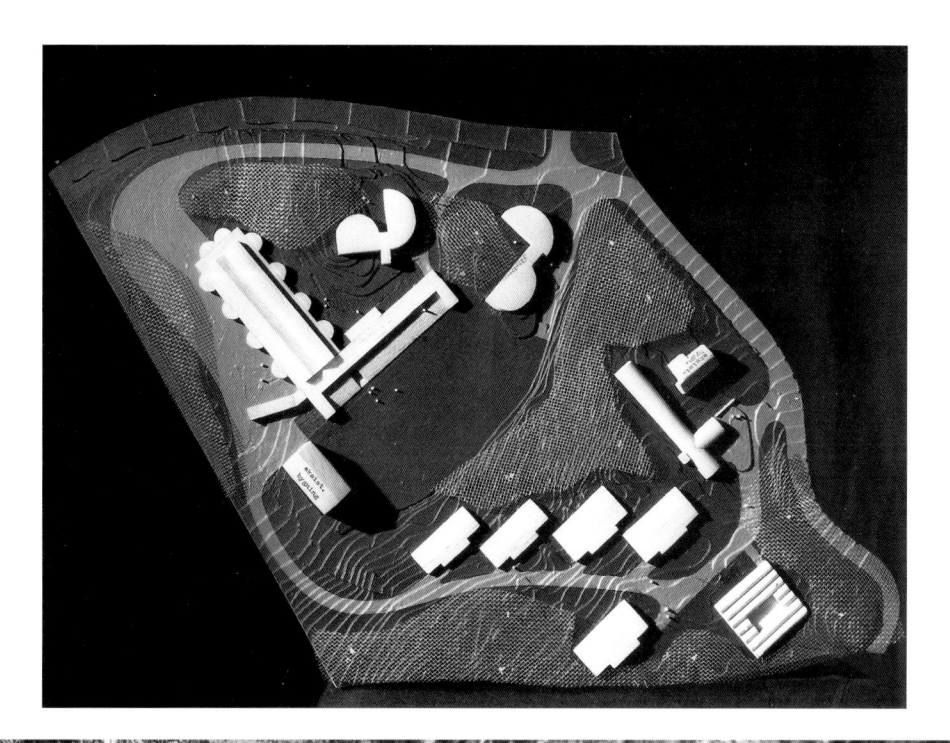

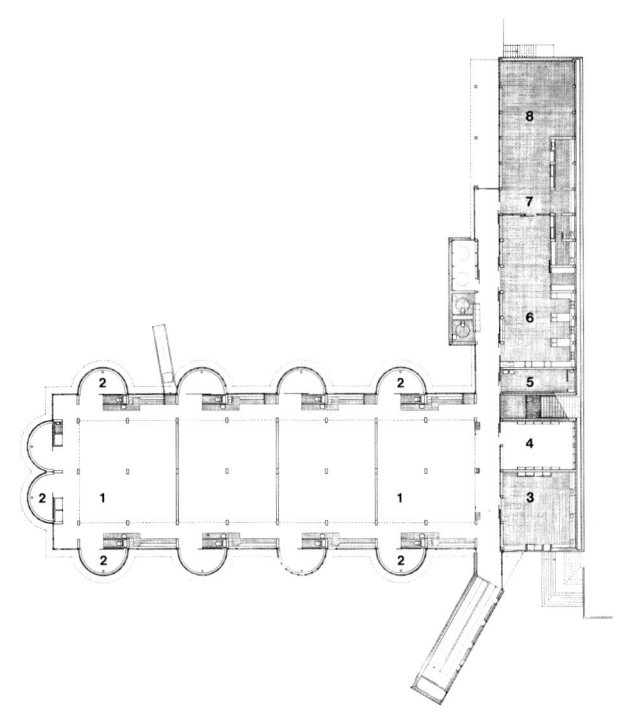

Skådalen School:
Plan of main building,
exterior view of main
building, exterior view
of dining room and
kitchen, exterior view
of main building.

PUBLIC CONVERSATIONS 151

Skådalen School: Observation rooms, interior of preschool, interior view of main building.

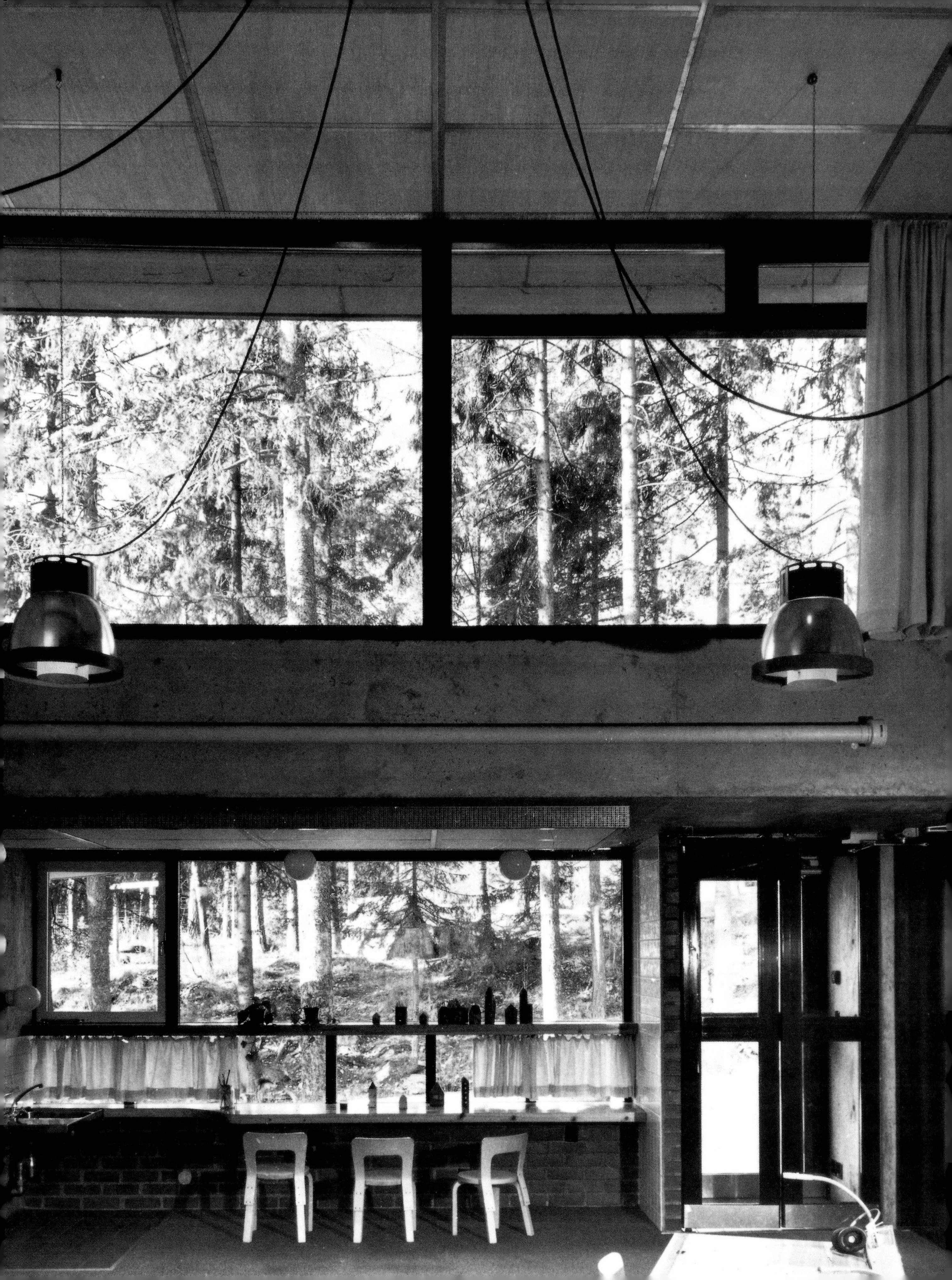

never losing concentration and always looking ahead. Without any major projects in the office he turned his attention to competitions and teaching at the Oslo School of Architecture. He continued to develop and rework concepts in relation to public architecture, but these concepts remained more or less in the classroom. Teaching was in fact the only testing ground for many of his thoughts and ideas.

It is the eye and sound that complete one's sense of space. It is your reflections that form space, and you discover its identity through sound and light. It does not exist before something hits it. I understand the sun's rays through the dust particles it strikes.

Once I visited Greece, and during the day I sat under a tree and smoked Golden Flake. I studied a sheepherder and his flock. I thought, Here is a person who walks in the landscape with his sound. He finds his sound constructions in his whistle. The man with the instrument had a sound dialogue with the landscape. The sheepherder found his own theater in the landscape. And then there were the church bells that defined each hamlet's geography. You lived within the church bell's limits. I remember from my own childhood that my day started with the horn from the shipbuilders at the Kaldnes factory in Tønsberg. This sound filled my room and gave it a dimension. The Middle Ages treated sound as an object. Sound was a part of the building, the tower, and space. Corbusier in the 1920s and 1930s searched for a sound out from the treatment of an inner room: a skin, a new layer that receives its own construction. It was first out in the forest with the trees that I had contact with the site at Skådalen. Sounds from the surroundings hit the soft ground, the trees, and the branches. This created for me a perfect room in silence. The most mysterious sound is the echo, when your voice is returned. You call out your word, the silence is broken, and this word is returned.

Like Bøler, Skådalen was in its intentions and spatial comprehension related to the more advanced architectural discourse taking place in Europe at the time. These new ideas included a more open relationship and stronger dialogue between the inhabitant and the space. One had to both participate and actively redefine one's own area within a public room. As daylight and fresh air began to be considered components with material qualities, a search for a new type of spatial lightness entered architectural discourse. The desire for a stronger place identity, through the reading of nature as site, was also evident in this search. Work would continue at Skådalen School over the years, but the difficult start meant that many important details were never thoroughly implemented and the wooded surroundings lacked the sensitive care in relation to the built complex that Fehn envisioned.

In 1967, a decade before the completion of Skådalen, Fehn won a competition to design housing for the town of Tønsberg. Although it became clear very early on that the project would never be built, for a long time Fehn had a small balsa-wood section model hanging on the wall in his office. Quite often he would refer to this project, and one can clearly see that it was an inspiration in relation to the Skådalen School. In each case, the landscape sets the cross section of the building. In the Spiraltoppen Restaurant and Hotel project, 1961, the section was again determined by the site, since each floor level was related to a specific site stratum. **As an architect I withdraw and let nature form my building.** In time, whenever he mentioned Spiraltoppen, he would also refer to the competition project for the Voksenkollen Medical Conference Center, 1978, which took the form of a horizontal plateau or shelf. This project allows the landscape to articulate the direction of the project. **The floor accepts the site. This is a place, a plateau, that has been inhabited before.** The moment the floor is placed in the terrain, terrain as place provides a precise dimension.

It is the characteristics of the landscape that give architecture its specific site capacity and direction. In the case of Voksenkollen, the competition brief asked for 280 hotel bedrooms, but the length of the site suggested instead 150 to 300. The landscape offered choices without compromising the architectural identity of the project. Nature's capacity to set architectural direction through the identity of place has always been part of Fehn's logic. He considered this project a room offered by nature, a clear resting place, a neutral place: **It is the boat and wagon that set a resting place and in turn set place. The horse** and the wind were able to find these places. **The motor does not have this capacity, since it is fuel that is most important. It generates the idea of motel, a lonely place accompanied by television.**

A 1972 competition project for a city block in Oslo, Tullinløkka Square combines a number of issues and elements from commissions that were in progress at the time. Fehn did not win, but the project set a standard for all the other projects and competition entries for this square. The site is located between the National History Museum, the National Art Museum, and the original campus of the University of Oslo and runs parallel to the

Sketch, 1982, "The sound, the space, and the sheepherder."

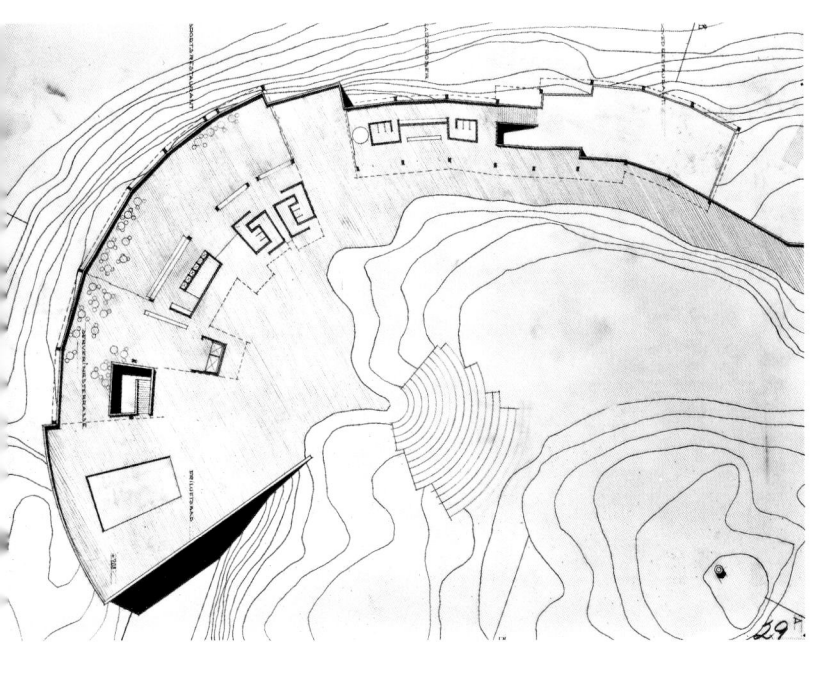

Spiraltoppen Restaurant and Hotel, Drammen, Norway: Plan.

Housing project, Tønsberg, Norway: Section model.

Sketch, Morocco, 1951.

OPPOSITE Sketches, 1978, of Voksenkollen Medical Conference Center, Oslo.

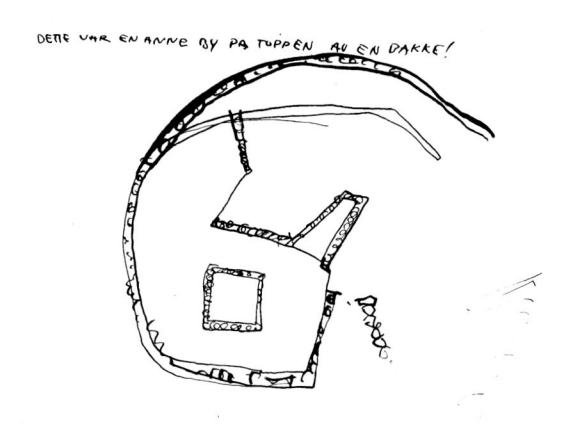

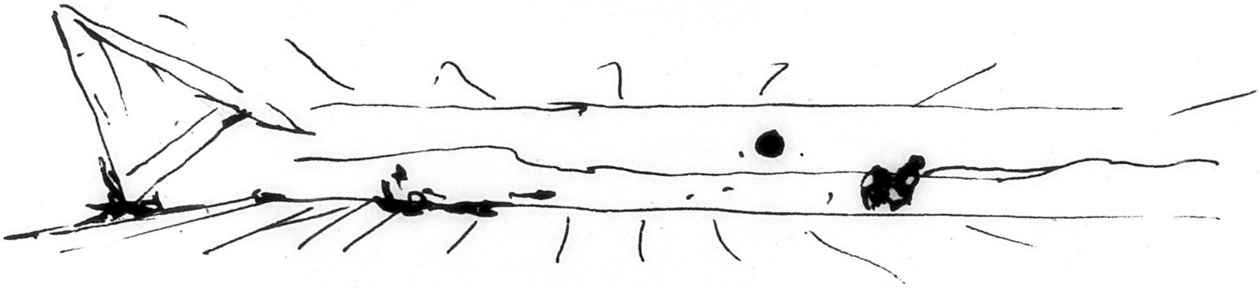

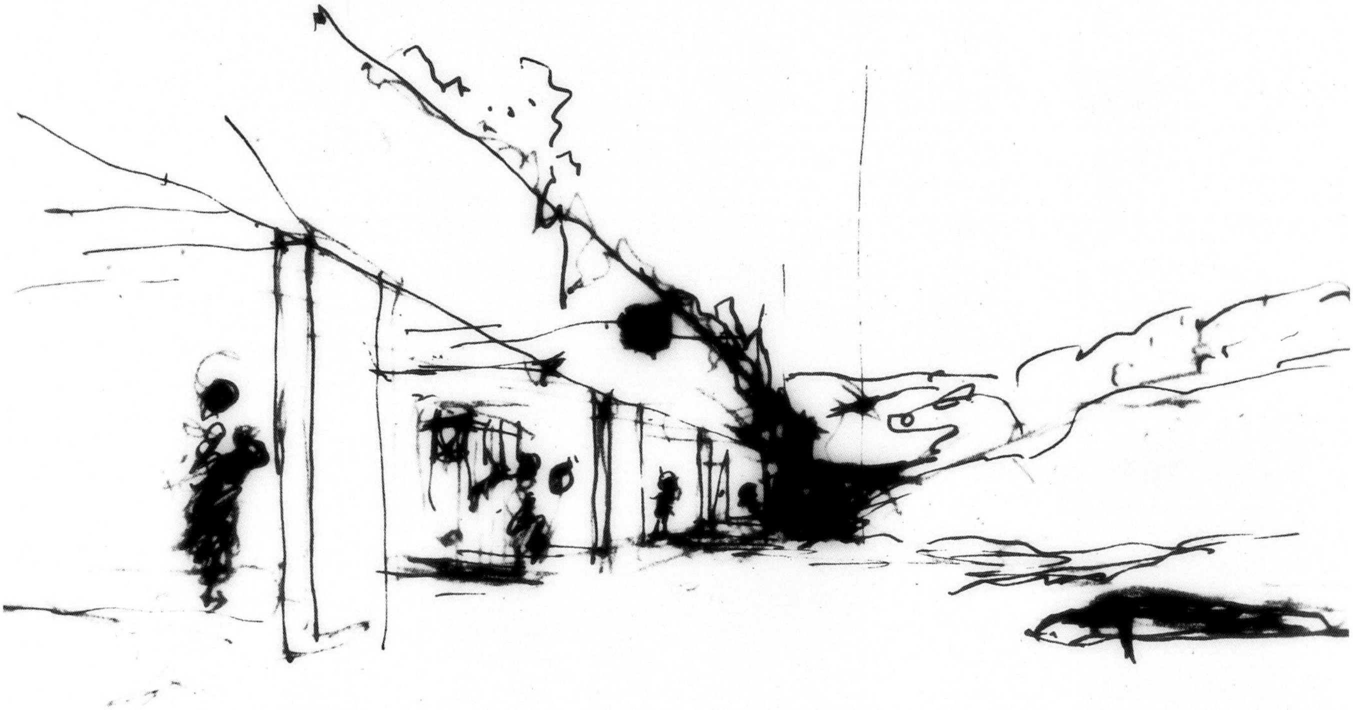

PLAN 2. ETG. 1:200

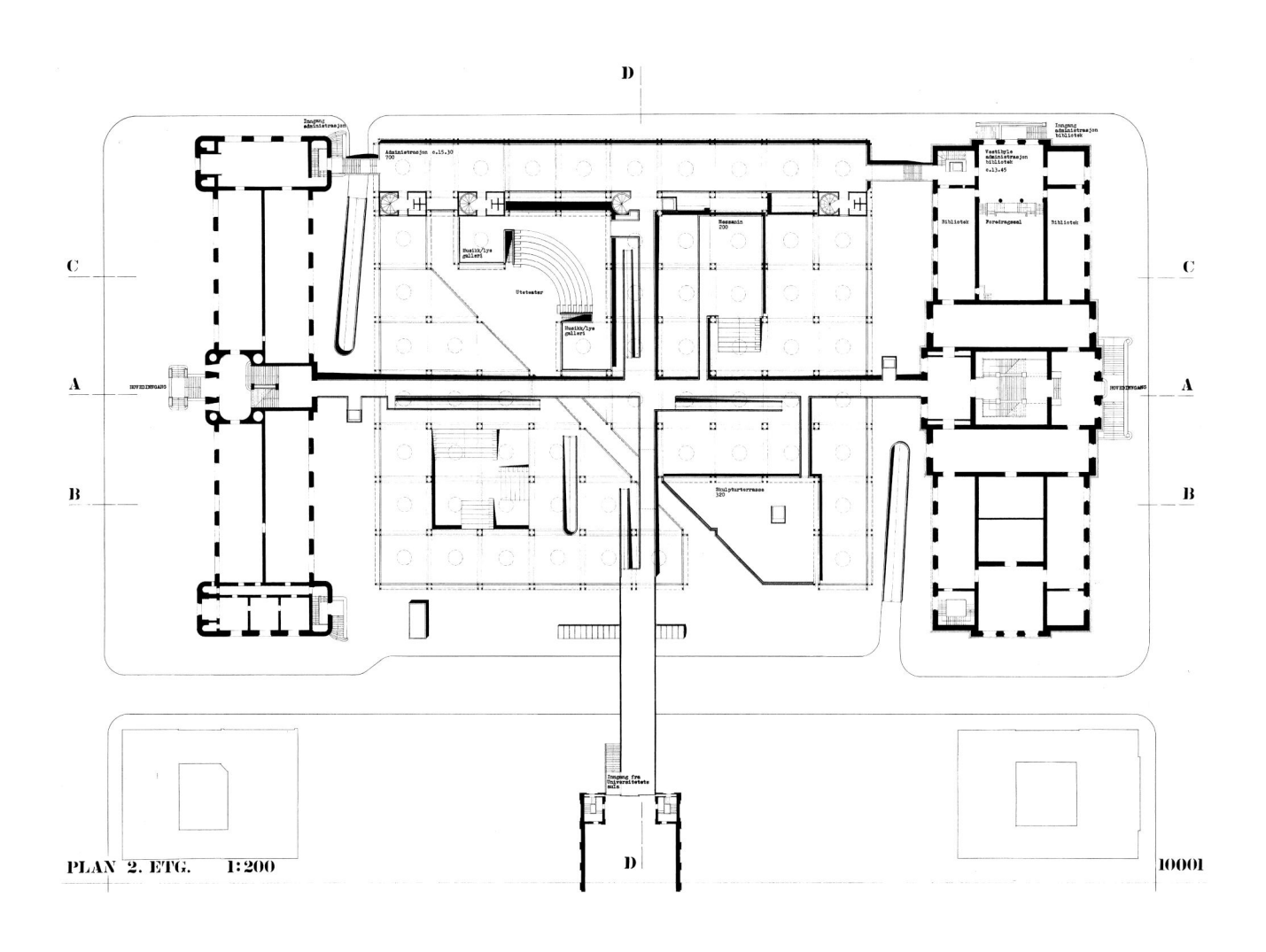

158 THE PATTERN OF THOUGHTS

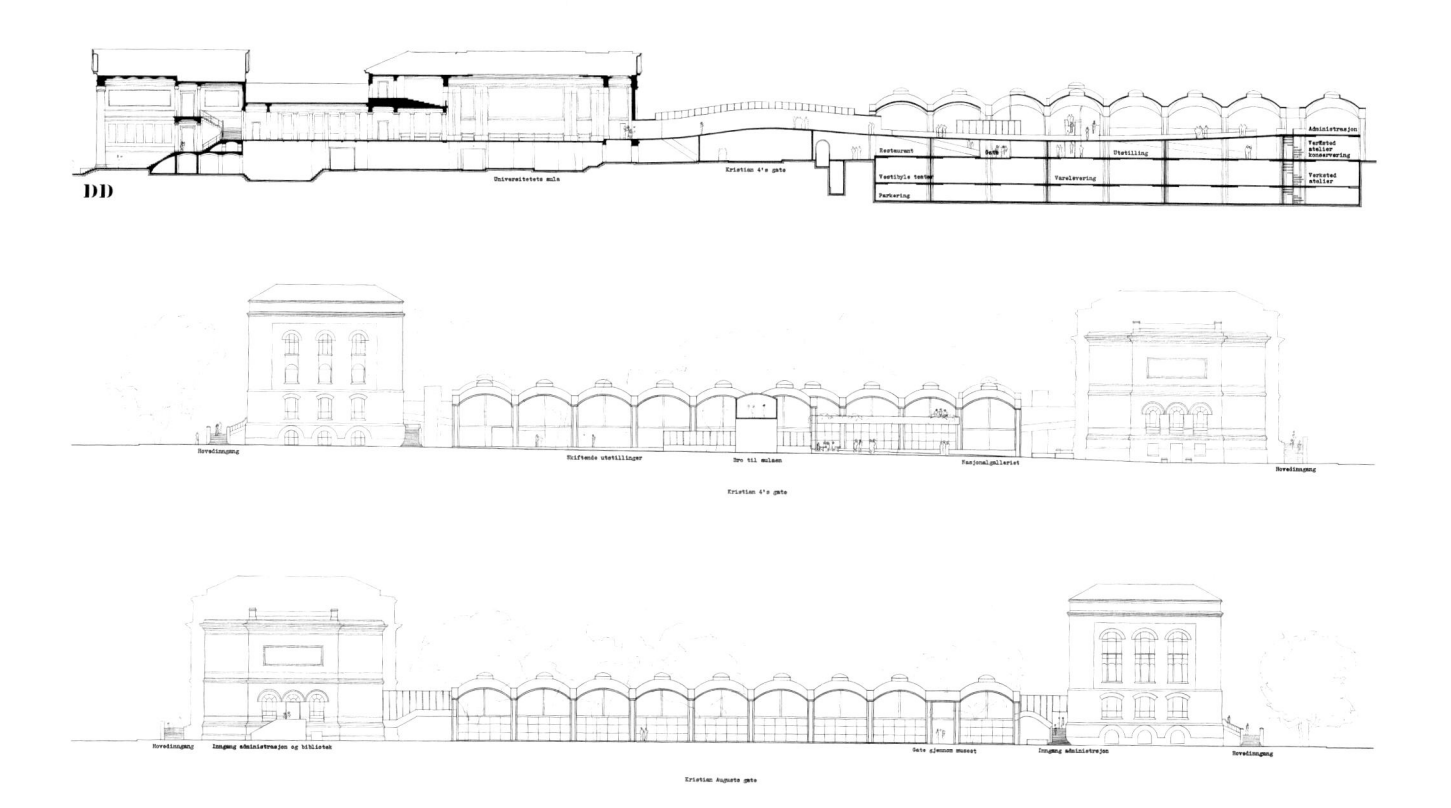

SNITT FASADER 1:200

Tullinløkka Square,
Oslo: Plan, sections.

160 THE PATTERN OF THOUGHTS

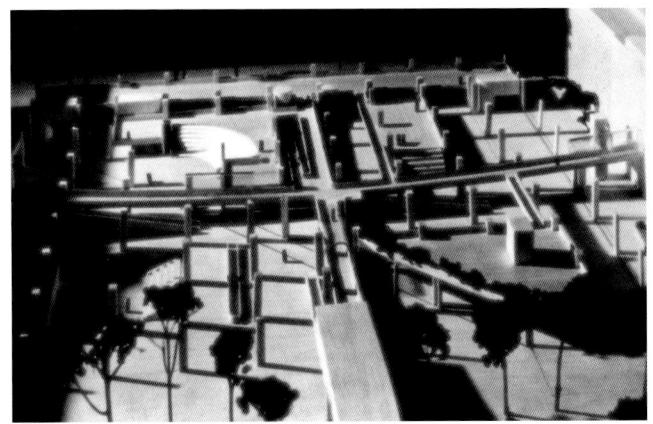

Tullinløkka Square:
Aerial view of model,
model with pedestrian
ramps, interior model.

New Palazzo del
Cinema, Venice:
Model views.

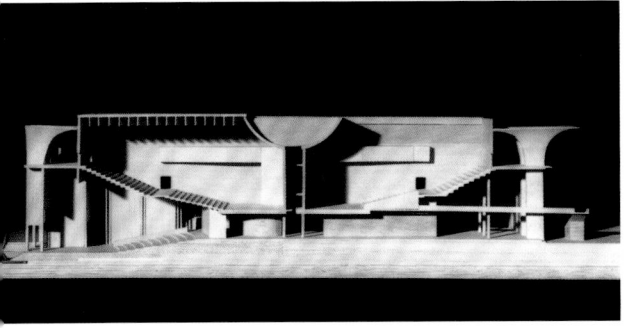

162   THE PATTERN OF THOUGHTS

city's main avenue, Karl Johans Street. Fehn envisioned the square as a pocket for various cultural activities. A light structure, almost tentlike, would contrast with the heavier surrounding buildings. The plan is based on a grid, and the spatial sequence works freely within this grid. Roof domes, each supported by four columns, were to be covered with blue ceramic tiles. Technical equipment would be housed at the meeting points between the structures. Into this floating blue composition Fehn inserted pedestrian ramps connecting the streets and the three surrounding public buildings. Over the years there have been many attempts to revitalize this square, either permanently or temporarily. There has also been a second competition, which again led to a stalemate, and the site remains a parking lot.

It would be some time before Fehn would land another large project. In 1991, he won first prize in an invited Nordic competition for the Mauritzberg Vacation and Conference Center. The site was Mauritzberg Manor, outside Norrköping, Sweden, which overlooked a small bay. The original brief included a golf course, three hundred vacation homes, tennis courts, business-leisure center, boat marina, and trails for riding and walking. Each vacation unit was to have an indoor-outdoor space to provide a sense of privacy within the communality of the center. Fehn envisioned the center as a place that would break up the monotony of the conference table, since the complex was to be used primarily for business retreats that offered a more relaxed and open form of communication. (The golf course was undoubtedly the largest conference table.) In many ways, the heart of this project was remote from Fehn's lifestyle; and he would sometimes complain facetiously about not having a hobby: the hunter, the fisherman, and the golfer all had their places, but not him. It was the housing units to which Fehn devoted most of his attention, and the project was never realized except for a prototype vacation home (see page 96). In his office, I found the site plan for the housing project in Tønsberg rolled up in the original drawings for Mauritzberg. In many ways, this confirms that there is an overall progression and consistency in his thought process around housing and careful utilization of the site.

In 1989, Fehn was invited to enter a competition for a new cinema complex in Venice, the Palazzo del Cinema on the Lido. He drew a beautiful project that interpreted, without mimicry, a Venetian architectural vocabulary. The project clearly reflects influences from Louis Kahn and Jørn Utzon, but only to the extent that Fehn let himself be influenced by other architects and their work. It was also a project that figured in his classroom lectures and discussions for a number of semesters. During this period, a large book on the Fenice Theater in Venice was never far from his desk. Fehn has expressed his fascination with the mask and with theater design in several remarks.
Rome in the Middle Ages was one big theater and the city's mask was its wall. Even its wine had its god where one could find comfort.

The actor's skin is his horizon, and his dressing room is where the most brutal acting takes place.

The mask freezes time: one works only with the mouth and eyes.

In 1983, Fehn participated in the competition for the Opéra de la Bastille in Paris together with a colleague from school, O. F. Stoveland, and his office, 4B Architects. The collaboration was successful in terms of a shared vision of design, but the broad teamwork was foreign to Fehn. While the entry was completed in a short time, it received no notice. Nevertheless, the conceptual thinking around the project generated a lot of energy and classroom discussion.

One must consider a theater as a concrete sound machine. One thinks of sound as something that wanders and disappears, but the problem is to keep the volume. Sound is like an object, and one regards it as a tactile mass. All the great leaders of armies were great speakers. They developed their vocal cords in a way that is unfamiliar to us today, and they had coaching from actors. But the most exciting element is the echo. One hears one's own voice. The sound quickly freezes and becomes an object. A recording conserves the sound in the same way one preserves words and thoughts in a book. John Cage felt that the best concert he had experienced was listening to his refrigerator. I remember *Poème électronique* [Corbusier's pavilion in Brussels, 1958] and Edgard Varèse, who was working in his office at the time. There was a film loop of images with this sound that was almost a frozen opera performance. One could feel the sound running through one's legs.

Winning the international competition for an extension to the Royal Theater in Copenhagen in 1996 was a victory for Fehn, and his hopes for building a large, prestigious building in an urban area soared. The project was important not only because he would be able to take advantage of Danish building skills, guaranteeing that the project's intentions would be carried out with great care, but also in relation to his position as an architect. With few exceptions, all his work is in remote areas in Norway and, to some extent, removed from the urban dweller. Fehn was gratified by attention and international prizes over the years, but these did not alleviate a sense of isolation. The architect was never content or satisfied, since the struggle was always the same as long as there was a project on the drawing board. So when Copenhagen decided to abandon his scheme, and soon thereafter a group with private funds commissioned another architect to build a new theater on another site, Fehn was disappointed. All his energy had gone into this project, and his health inevitably suffered.

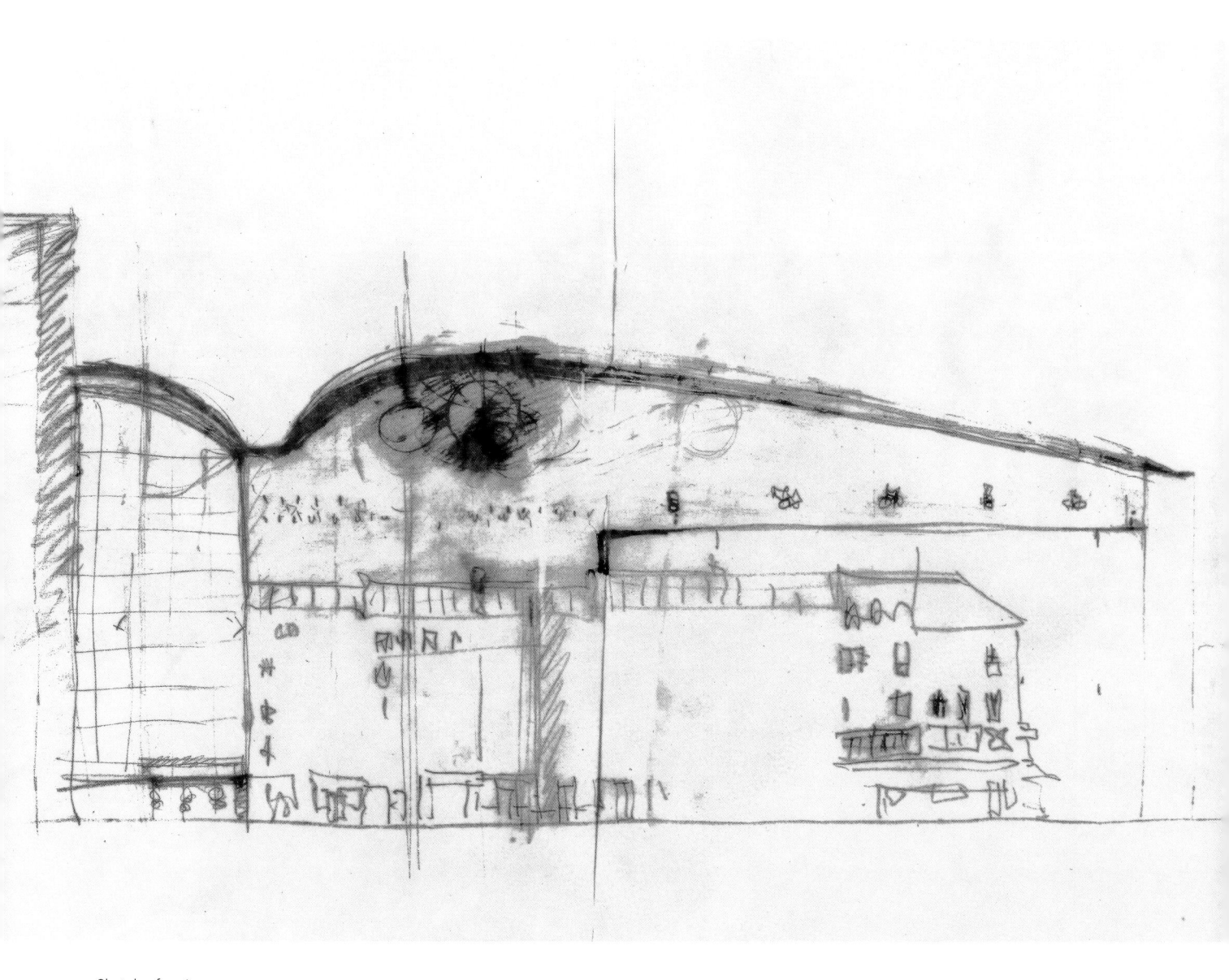

Sketch of main
facade of Opéra de la
Bastille, Paris.

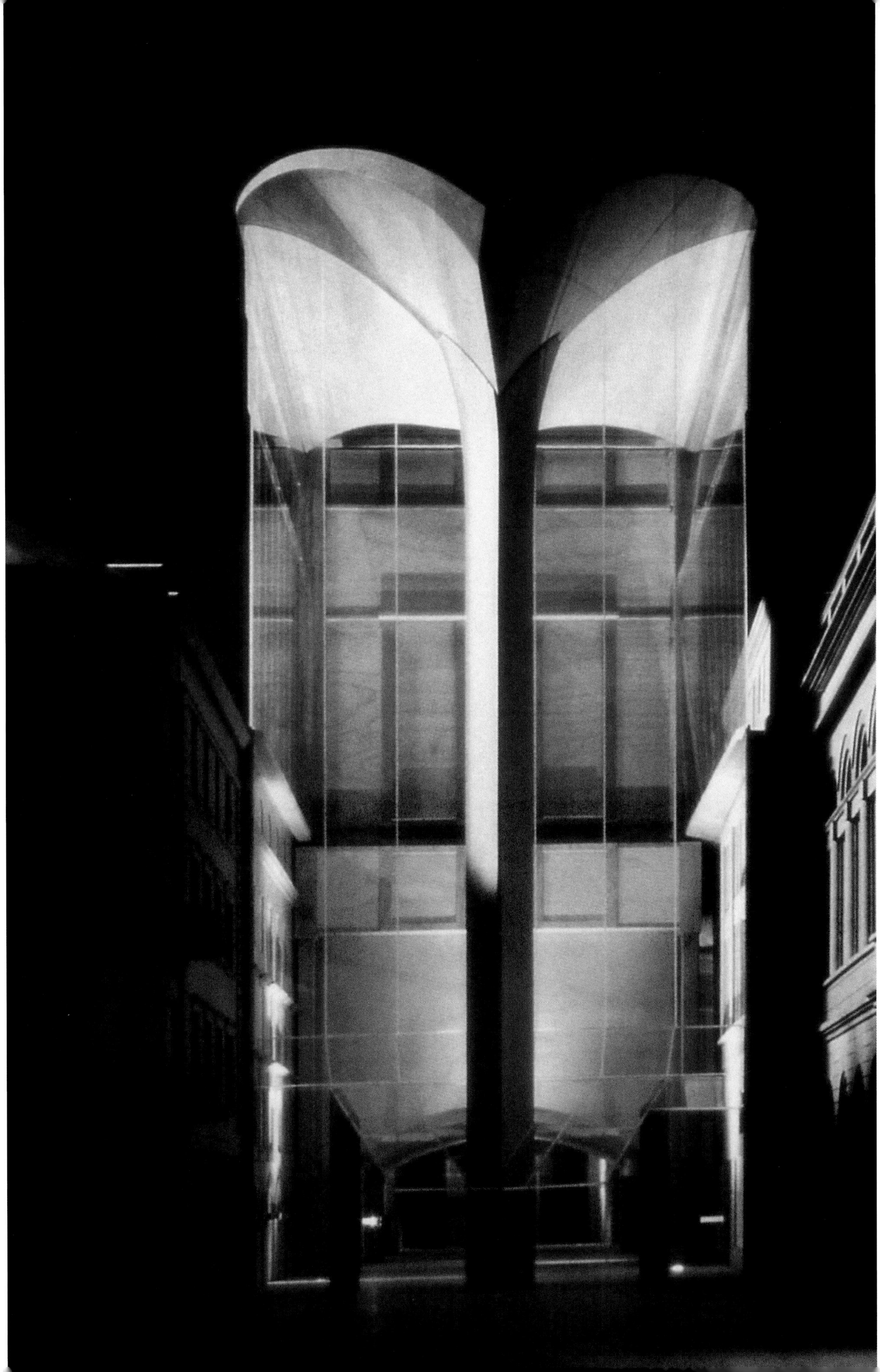

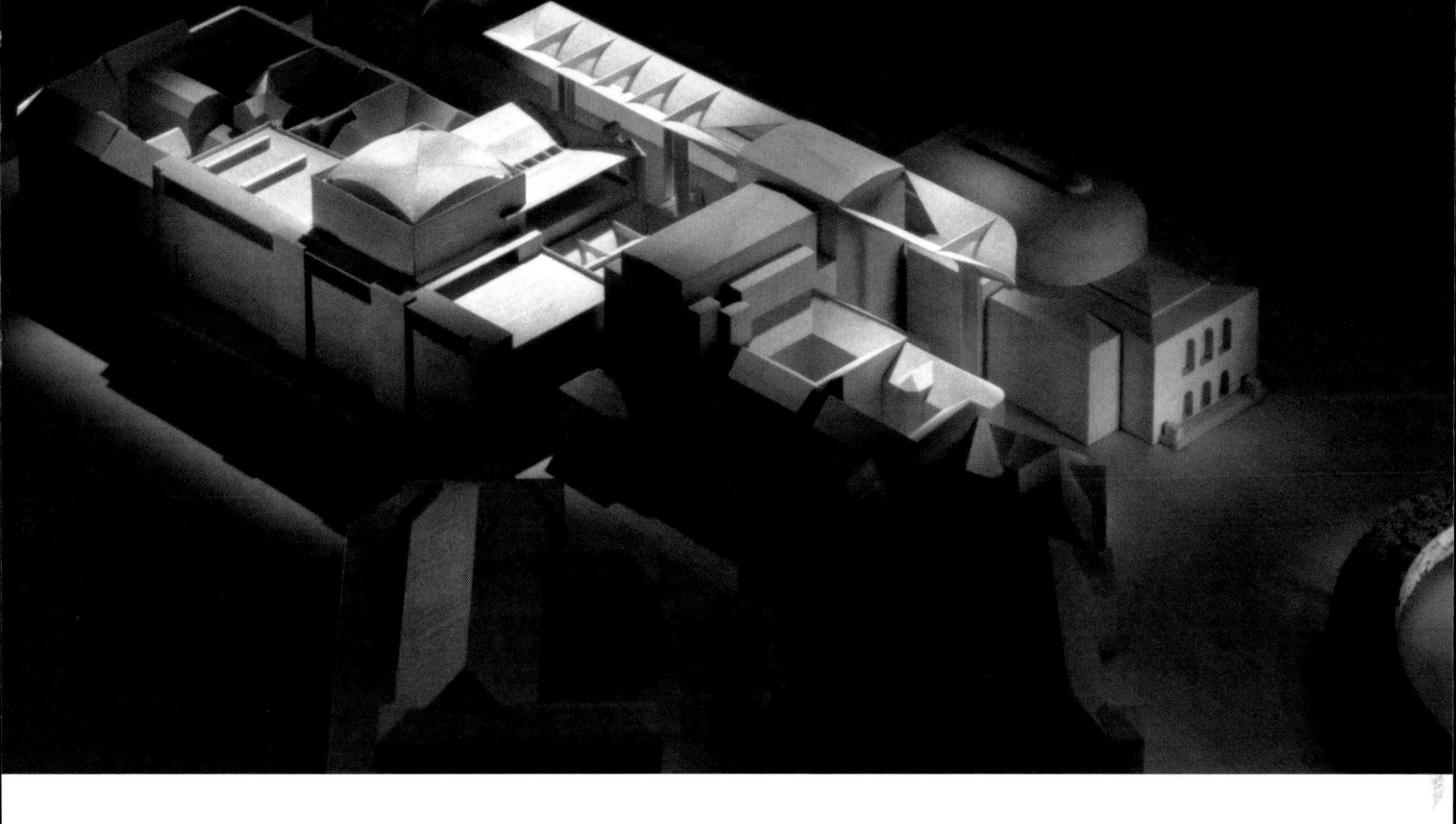

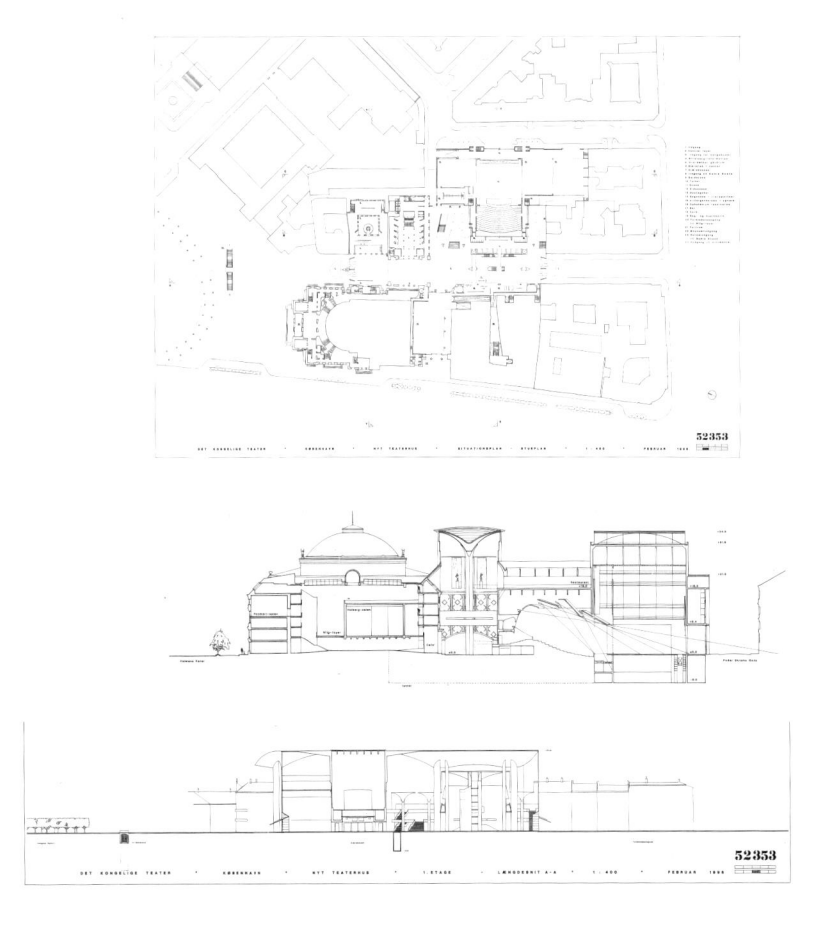

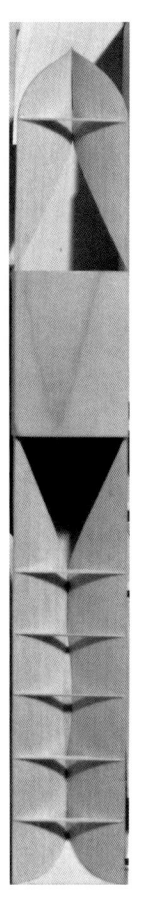

Extension of the Royal Theater, Copenhagen: Entrance model with "bird's wing," model showing extension, plan of main floor, elevation showing relationship between new and old, section, model showing roof detail.

PUBLIC CONVERSATIONS 167

Sketches, 1984, "The dialogue with nature is present. The dialogue with nature is broken," continuation.

The most striking element of this project is its interpretation of the existing urban site. Fehn effectively transformed a main street, which had once divided the different theater functions, into a foyer or large central hall. This expansive new common space connects the different activities within the buildings. From King's New Square, an important plaza directly adjacent to the site, the main entrance is clearly visible due to its height and the sculptured Y-shaped column that forms the entrance and the roof over what was once the street. This structure would allow a large amount of daylight to enter the central core of the theater extension. A full-size mock-up of the "bird's wing," as the Y structure was later called, was erected on-site to give the public an idea of what the building would look like. Fehn was skeptical of this move, commenting that the magic and energy found in the physical building would not be present in the mock-up, and he was right. The model became an event, a show, and left the project open to attack.

The importance of a directed and unadorned perception of the world in relation to Fehn's public built conversations was an ongoing preoccupation. His comments about two days of filming a biographical documentary in Morocco evidence his thoughts on this theme:

March 17: The film sequence in a library or Marrakech's great cultural center, the monastery. The small cells with the shutters are fantastic. None of the buildings have glass. I think about Lewerentz and all the patterns that cover the surfaces.

March 18: We found a village that I don't feel suited the day's recording, but we couldn't find the village I once visited. We left Marrakech after filming in a restaurant. It was difficult being filmed; it is a question of concentration or perhaps to find a place in oneself where there is silence or that one goes inside oneself. Especially when one should play oneself!

Strangely, a small episode that I experienced during a session at the International Laboratory of Architecture and Urban Design in Siena in 1986 seems to explain Fehn's comments and the often turbulent times he and friends of his generation experienced in introducing their humanistically derived spatial interpretations. Aldo van Eyck and I had a cup of coffee together one morning. We had been up most of the previous night with students, so the conversation was minimal. We dozed in the morning sun, the freshly starched tablecloth in front of us helped to make everything seem so quiet, and in my notebook I wrote this remark by van Eyck: "The world is around me, not in front of me."

PUBLIC CONVERSATIONS 169

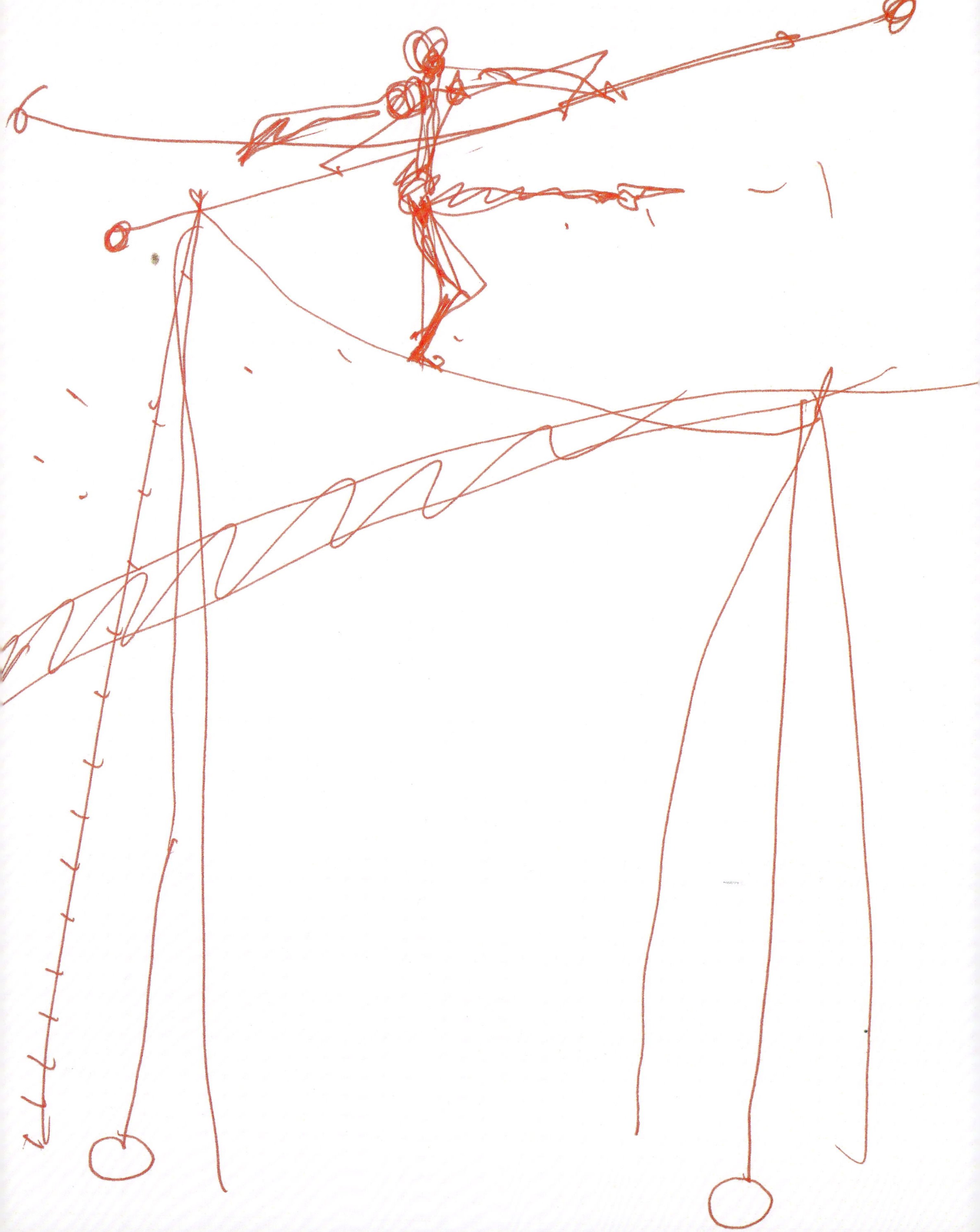

CHAPTER 7

A TWENTY-YEAR PIT STOP | In the middle of Fehn's career, from about 1973 to 1992, there occurred a span of almost twenty years in which the practice survived on a minimum of work, much of which consisted of exhibitions, a few private houses, and projects that were never realized. This was a period in which teaching at the Oslo School of Architecture gained a new prominence, since the situation in Fehn's office forced him to find other outlets for his creativity. Lectures, critiques abroad, exhibitions, and intermittent work on the museum at Hamar all contributed to further development of his architectural stance. It was early in this period that Fehn and I began to work on *Sverre Fehn: The Thought of Construction*, with weekly interviews and discussions that continued for several years. This process also prompted Fehn to focus on topics that were vital to him but that would come up only marginally in relation to commissions or classroom lectures. Just a portion of the material deliberated upon in this period made it into the book, but many of the ideas and topics would continue to develop and expand throughout this twenty-year span. This stage proved to be a time of incubation that gave Fehn an additional layer of theoretical content. Once his building career took off again later in life, the reflections and constant reworking of ideas that filled this period would directly affect how he approached and understood changes in architecture at the close of the century. The themes that run throughout his notes and lectures gave him the tools to face innovations and shifts in perception.

Architecture is not very complex, but the inspiration that creates good architecture is very complex, and constantly changing. It is the fantasies around themes that give you constructions. When I was in school we experimented with mass. We made casts over balloons and later popped them. All this about construction started early with me. When I was a child sitting in the chapel bored, I concentrated on the tension wires in the ceiling.

There were periods during this long "pit stop" when it was not feasible for Fehn to participate actively in international architectural discourse, and he felt deeply the distance from the rest of Europe. Communication with old friends and colleagues had to be kept up by mail, which required concentration and mental preparation. It was not unusual that his letters were never sent. It is a paradox that for all his curiosity and efforts to keep abreast of developments in architecture, correspondence with his colleagues abroad was sporadic and often neglected. But he was always apprised of his friends' work and what they were thinking and writing. No matter the financial straits in the office, the latest publications were strategically placed on tables and shelves. Fehn had a unique talent to grasp potential in the work of others and sense the coming of new tendencies in architecture (as well as their demise), but the distance from the rest of Europe also gave him time to allow this information to mature into a personal vocabulary. The book *Team 10 Primer* reveals in many of its chapters a thought process and approach—not in the political content but in the spatial and theoretical issues—that parallel Fehn's work of the same period. Van Eyck's "The Interior of Time" connects with many of the topics Fehn took up in his classroom. One of the members of Team 10 who steadfastly kept in touch and was eager to publish his work, built or not, was Giancarlo de Carlo, who produced the magazine *Spazio/Societá*. The Oslo School of Architecture was an early member of the International Laboratory of Architecture and Urban Design, and Fehn took part in some of the sessions in Urbino and Siena. At the opening of a session in 1989, De Carlo announced: "We are not here to look for something that is sure. Everything has to be invented, not to give a new theory but a comparison among friends. Scientists do not follow one theory, and we can no longer follow one theory. To establish an equilibrium that immediately gives equilibrium is not the premise from which we work. Reality comes from the overlapping of things. The whole program should be seen in this light."

During these sessions Fehn reconnected with old friends and acquaintances. These architects had clear attitudes toward their profession and shared in many ways similar destinies. None had that much work, and what work they did have often met hard critique. They all had periods of isolation. Most were able to counterbalance their circumstances with writings and other types of projects. The careers of Aldo van Eyck, Peter and Alison Smithson, and Giancarlo de Carlo are all examples of this. Fehn differed

At the blackboard; at the lectern.

PAGE 170 Sketch, 1984, of tightrope walker.

OVERLEAF Blackboard sketch.

slightly in that he was far more dependent on actively building to generate energy around a thought process. The only other outlet for Fehn was teaching in his close-knit, studio-like classroom tucked away in Oslo. His work and lectures were not easily available to the world abroad, since most lectures were held in Norwegian. In this respect, it is useful to mention his attachment to Finland. Reima Pietilä, Aulis Blomstedt, and Kristian Gullichsen had perhaps more insight into and shared experience of Fehn's working environment in this period. I know that he greatly appreciated these contacts and the invitations to give lectures and exhibitions in Finland. **Finland has a national holy place, untouched, virgin nature. Pietilä goes into nature's morphology, into its geometry. He no longer works with concrete constructively.**

Fehn's importance as a teacher must be emphasized. It was his personal impression of the world and how it works that made Fehn a superlative teacher. He has a unique ability to visualize and then simplify the most complex thoughts. In this sense, his teaching was similar to Louis Kahn's: they were both seductive, never imperative, in their approach. Both used the blackboard as one of their most vital pedagogical tools, which allowed an intuitive line to complement a verbal history or theme.

Fehn's lectures were an event, and at the start of each, a distinct hush spread over the classroom. Fehn captured and expressed content that allowed for a broad comprehension of architecture, pressing students to identify architectural potential and utilize it as a tool to find greater depth in a given task. Always

A TWENTY-YEAR PIT STOP 173

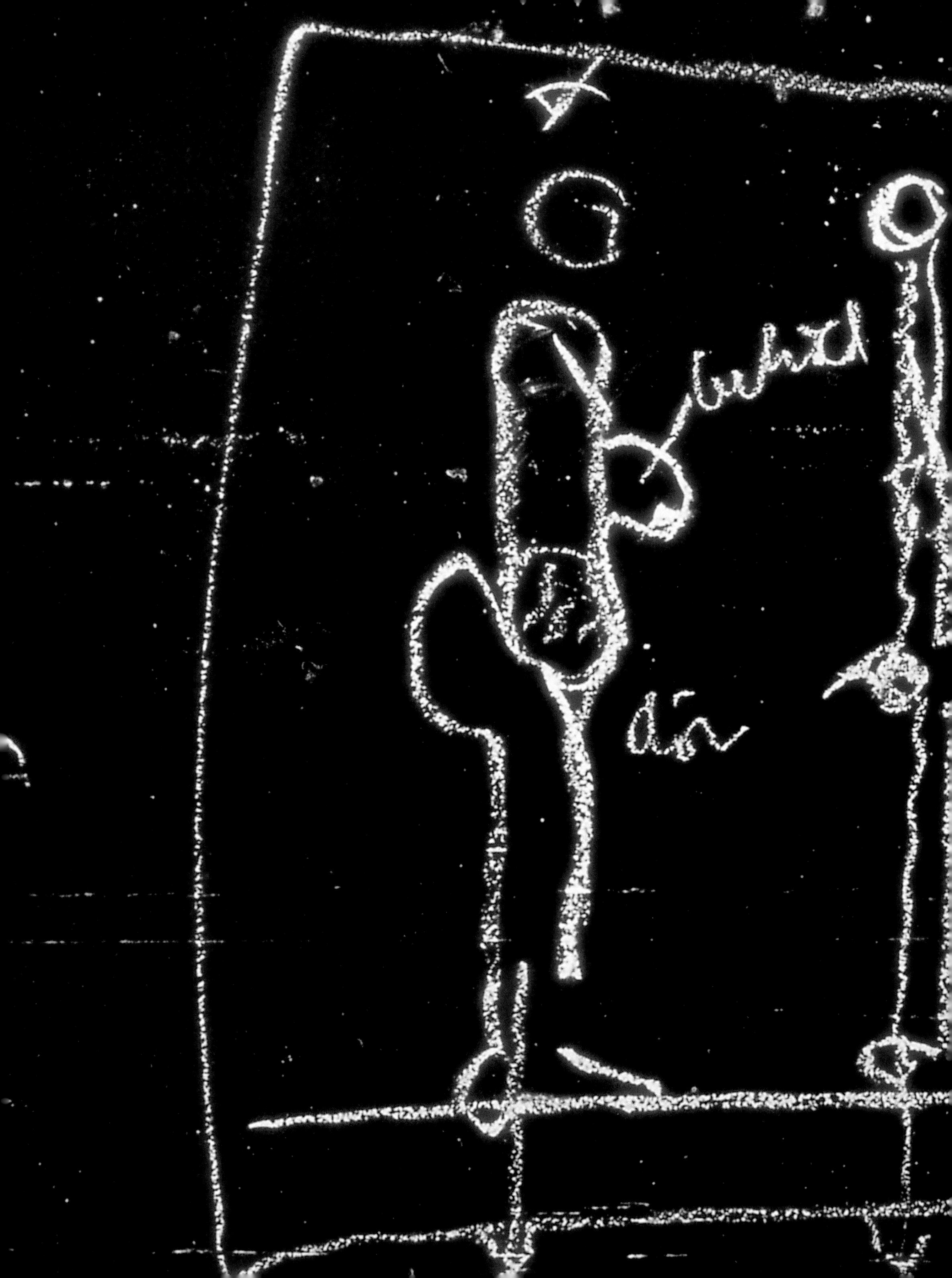

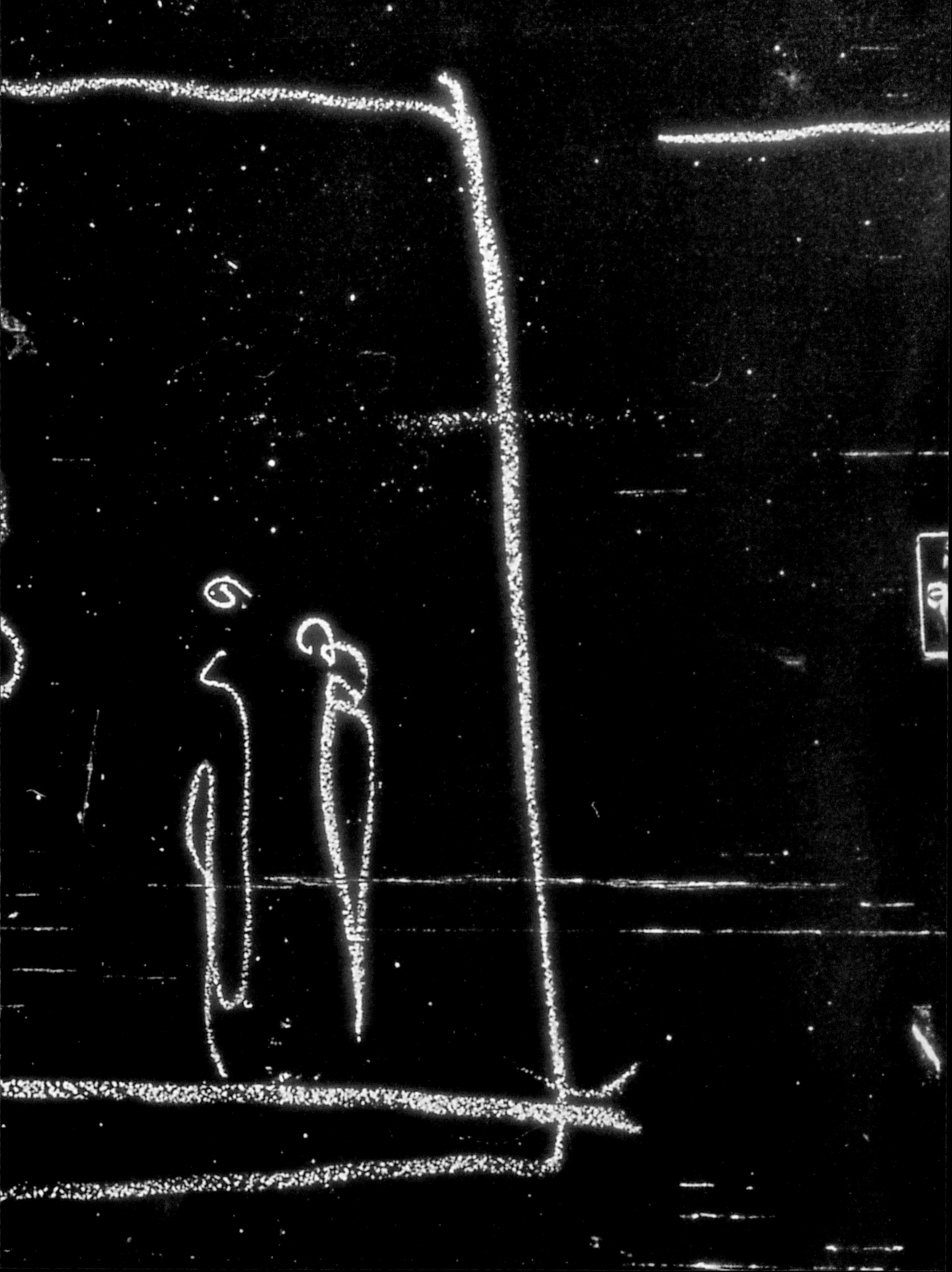

Sketch, "The rock on the ground, letters in stone. The imaginary scene. To stage your behavior. The architectural room shall give the imaginary room a place. The imaginary as the room."

OVERLEAF Sketches on scale; sketch, "The dimension of a child. The apple continues to fall from its branch. The skin and the tattoo."

revealed within the issues in a lecture was a spatial investigation that challenged the program content of a class or a semester. The students were mesmerized and engaged in the lecture stories; the moment the adventure was over, the students were once again alone with their project and its limitations. Each student was forced to confront his or her own working process and its weaknesses and strengths. Fehn never taught architecture as direct knowledge; rather, he turned to an intuitive understanding of potential. He seemed to have an unlimited reserve to go beyond the given task, dissect it, and reinvent its content. He had the intellectual and creative capacity to simplify the essential, and from this he gave each student an architectural platform that would lead toward maturity. In his approach, he once again reminded me of Kahn. Louis Kahn was never interested in addressing the problem straight on but preferred to investigate at a distance, seeking an angle no one else seemed to see. In Kahn's studio course the year I attended, one of the assigned projects was a library. Kahn spent most of the time discussing what type of person the librarian might be. In Fehn's office, it was much the same. He could look at a drawing and say, "Oh, is that what it looks like?" and you knew instinctively that it was time to start all over. His lectures were always well prepared, and the selected theme would unwind through carefully considered thoughts and images, but the topic never escaped the intuitive dimension. In a sense, Fehn's lectures never really had an end. They simply added layer upon layer to an ongoing architectural investigation.

Fehn often used the term *Rombilde* in relation to his creative process. In *The Thought of Construction*, I translated this term, quite literally, as "room picture." During one of the working sessions for that book, I asked Fehn, What drives your project after the first thought?

Deep in my mind I see a certain room picture that generates an image of what a specific space might be. In the beginning my drawings are not very clear in relation to the image, but as the idea gradually matures I extend the thought through my hand and continue to draw until what I have on paper fits my mental image.

This method may seem archaic in relation to today's reliance on expanding visual technology, its infinite capacity, and the corresponding use of media to give substance to a final image. But Fehn's process continues to have relevance. It is easy to underestimate the depth and content of his imagined room picture and its latent creative potential and concentrate instead on the linear development of the program and its preconceived solution; but in fact, the quality of the final project is contingent upon the depth and content of the room picture. For Fehn, the development of his internal images is a creative process of great complexity, and it is only the individual who can guide these images to a conceptual integrity. It is within the invention of various types of stories where the physical world and even what lies outside of it are at stake. Fehn's own stories, internalized through particular room pictures, were dear to him, but tales, phrases, and poems formulated by others could also inspire an entire lecture. It is in his unraveling of these stories that his gift for teaching comes alive. This complex repertory induces a creative, sensitive learning process instead of locking everyday instruction into a set pedagogy. It has an openness that seeks focus and attains an architectural precision. A simple childhood memory could elicit an architectural reflection: **I remember that as a child there was such a rush to depart when we would take a trip in the car, but my father would stop and picnic by the roadside as if he still had a horse to consider. A blanket was laid out and with this picnic the place was born again.**

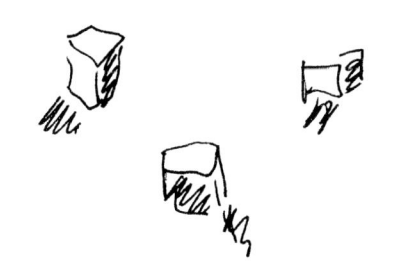

Scenene på makten
bokstaven sten.

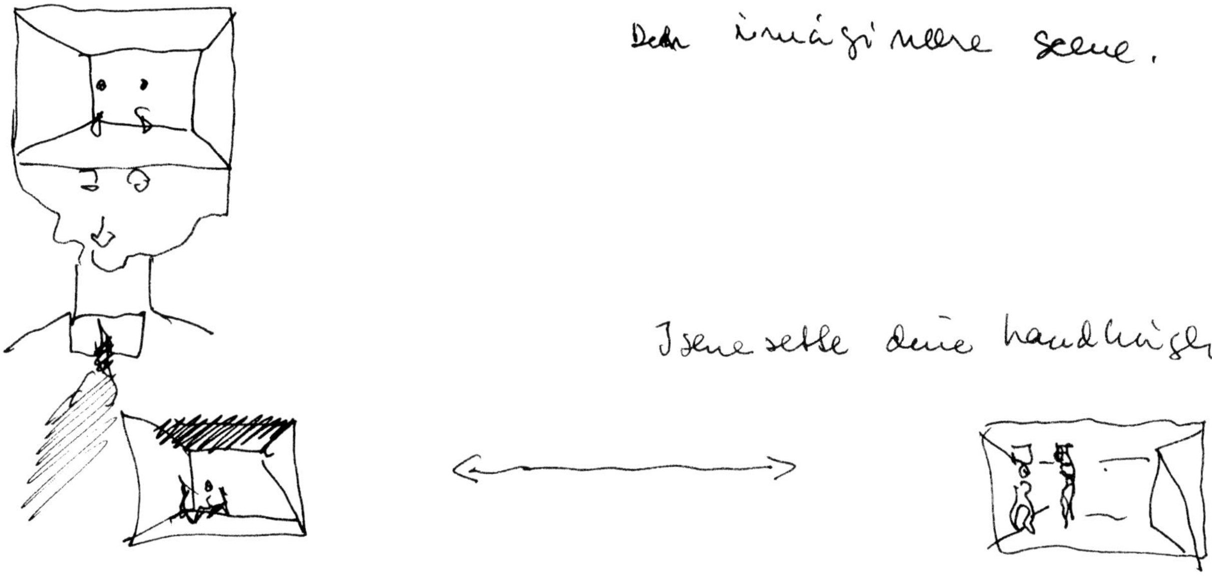

Den imaginære scene.

Isenesette dine handlinger.

⟷

Det arkitektoniske rom skal
gi det imaginære rom
plass.

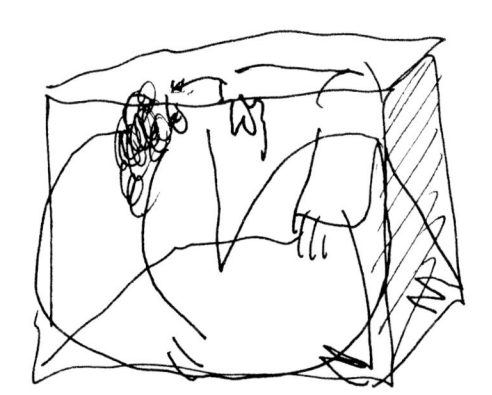

Det imaginære rom
rommet

B.

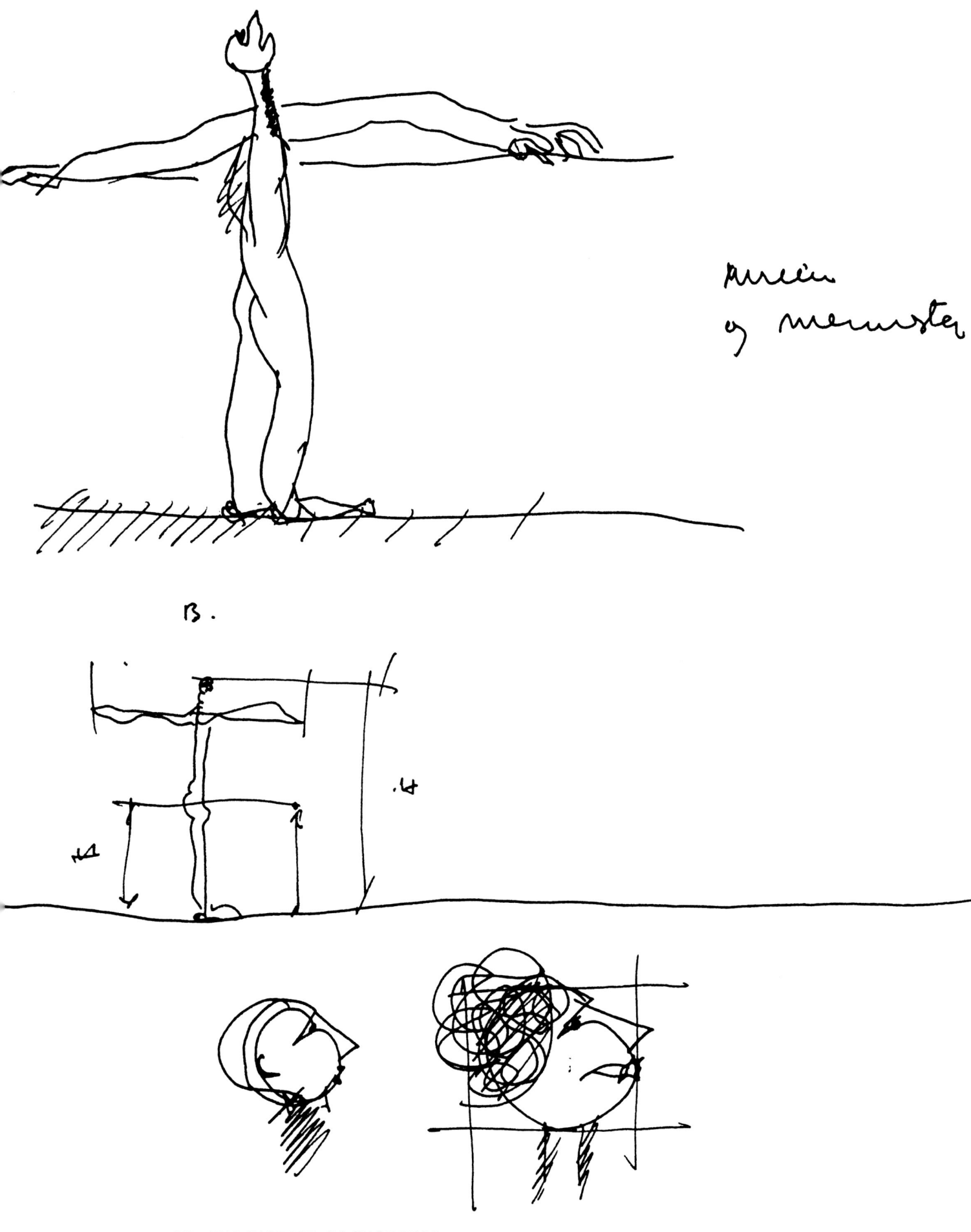

178 THE PATTERN OF THOUGHTS

? Bamet; störelsene ?

Eple   fodselses å falle ned av stammen

Huden og tatoveringen

During these rather precious lecture hours, it was not unusual for Fehn to comment on Utzon's work in particular to clarify a certain point. **Utzon's world lies outside of Europe. If he first finds his geometry, he also finds his construction. Instead of the European mechanic, he is a mathematician.** Or he might refer to his colleagues and friends: **I have a friend who is a master in making fur coats. To learn how to sew the skin together so it will be shaped for the body, he studied the sail maker's technique in cutting canvases. He discovered that there were no straight lines in any cut. And another thing: the square meters of sails on a medieval vessel could cover the cathedral.**

When Utzon was to realize his Sidney Opera House, he went to the geometry of a ball. By cutting sections out of the ball he found the exact shape for his shells. It was as if he moved into the past, destroyed the dome of the cathedral, and by gathering the pieces left on the ground, he suddenly had the tools to realize the poetic dream of the present.

To sketch or invent a story through a drawing was one of Fehn's most important teaching devices. His thoughts were focused on the drawing, and at the same time, the story line directed the drawing's development. His sketches reveal an architectural attitude, a basic understanding of a theme in motion yielding a spatial consciousness. Each sketch starts from a new point of departure. A slight change in the room picture induces a new approach and another round of drawings. Fehn's capacity to see the conventions of everyday events as an unfolding discovery belongs not only to his drawings but also to his spoken and written language. He established an open pedagogical platform that inspired students for nearly a generation. **A summer girl sits on a swing torn from her parents and the ground. That which preserves the child's weight lies in the earth. The constructive fantasy is in being able to realize the meeting with the earth.**

Fehn's Bygg 3 (Building 3) studio at the old Oslo architectural school on St. Olavs Street opened a door to a world beyond local issues and trends. It was an international studio where an updated architectural discourse was introduced sometimes long before the local profession had an awareness of it. Important architects would visit from time to time. Many of Fehn's students were perhaps most keenly aware of new movements and theories the year they graduated from his class. It was not really what he read or how much he read but his passionate working process that absorbed and comprehended the present. It is important to reiterate that if Fehn looked upon anyone as influential, it would have to be his former teacher Arne Korsmo; he too looked outward and brought home to his students what he found and experienced abroad. Each semester Fehn organized a class trip, and he knew every trick there was to enter a building anywhere in the world. He taught us that Norway was a small country, and that what happens here is not the only thing that happens in the world. Another city is another story. His first visit to New York provoked a change of emphasis in his spatial comprehension of cities. He began to move away from his earlier abstractions of the city wall and the concept of protection that connected them. He spoke about New York as a large forest, a forest that had exchanged its soul, the earth, for gold. The taller buildings were those that had exchanged the earth for a lot of gold; those whose ground was less "fertile" were smaller.

During these years, Fehn also discussed understanding life through a perception of death: this is a theme that has inspired and occupied him architecturally for a long time. This subject is not to be mistaken for a religious or mystical point of view; it is rather the observation of a fundamental life process. The meeting of these two absolute conditions is an abstract point in a physical situation. **If tragedy could be traced in a fabric, its expression would be that of violence.** This constructed thought has no clear beginning or end, but its ongoing nature generates creative energy. It is a demanding frame of mind in which everything is in the moment. Fear, too, constitutes a vital part of this discussion. Lectures, conversations, and built work consciously avoid a direct expression of sentimentality. There is a poetic brutality in many of his comments, yet they are also whimsical and, for Fehn, receptive to different interpretations; his comments opened rather than closed the discussion. Those that may appear to be naive carry a profound underlying critique or observation. **Concrete belongs to a mass concept that can take on any form: this porridge is as big as the earth and has no limits. It is the secret world calculation that has tricked its way into the mass. When the constructive thought is impoverished the line is straight.**

In his lectures, Fehn on occasion referred to sculpture and painting in a traditional sense to make a point. By restricting them to a traditional definition, he easily found his premise or argument. Yet this is not to say he was unaware of changes in method and approach as well as the broadening of the term "fine art." In the notes of one of our interviews, from around 1982, I found a page titled "Buildings," which in a simple way presents an interpretation or room picture with content that reaches beyond a set solution. **If one cannot manage the spiritual side of architecture, one almost immediately focuses on the practical issues. A sculptor's hand describes a surface without public interference, but the architect delivers his work to the next stage, the next group. The architect's hand describes a spatial phenomenon through drawings. With the sculptor it is the nearness of the body that is delivered, in that the hand is part of the process. Wherever the artist's hands have been, these places end up with me. No one has carried it further. Hamar just stands there with its love for its objects. With a rational standpoint one loses the intimacy and other elements. The more middle men, the more impersonal the architecture.**

Unfortunately, one no longer stands alone for long without the philosophic direction also changing. **One has difficulty because the proof does not come to the surface. One finds security in another place, and not in science's primitive system. The belief in the system is as strong as ever, and it is only to increase the system and everything will be in order.**

The small hut where everything is made of wood is a safe world to be born into. There is never anyone who says, "Fehn, you have gone too far." Rather, "We shall go further."

It must be clear that Fehn had nothing against teamwork, nor did he underestimate its complexities. Rather, he stressed the importance of finding and nurturing each student's creative capacity. His Bygg 3 studio was a testing ground. Without the opportunity to uncover and develop a student's strengths, office teamwork could reach only a limited understanding of aptitude and ability. Part of this individual creative approach was the acceptance of resistance forces that were stronger than the project itself, forces belonging to the unknown and forces of nature. Fehn has revealed his sensibility to such forces: **In the ancient Greek's row of columns, there arose a distance, a comprehensible distance, and this was necessary because infinity was still there.** Fehn has also elaborated on the birth of the column. **A point on the surface of the earth has a precise position. Socrates says, "Move so the sun is not blocked out for me." He stands alone again on the earth. He has left everyone. The column was born through this expression. Mankind was on its way to accept the point.**

Sketches, 1984 and 1985, of tightrope walker; sketch, 1982, of the car's meeting with the earth.

As well, the architect has aired thoughts on construction, not just as an important base within his own creative process but also as an essential element in his teaching. Clear spatial ideas always carry internalized structural attitudes. Structure is not an added layer; rather, it represents potential contained within the initial idea. **Construction is with me from the very beginning, but it takes time for the project to find its structure. The story I am seeking must be edited, and how much of the story shall structure decide? This time shall I allow just one image into the play between in and out? How large an opening shall I give the mask? What do you want to hide in your building? The entire architectural story plays into a purely symphonic work of construction.**

In your thoughts you have life and life after death with you all the time. The greatest constructive thought is the belief that there is a life after death. When our thoughts are inadequate the line becomes straight. Do you ever think of building a tree when you stand in front of a pile of wood planks?

Fehn ties the unknown to a concrete concept of the earth as mass, as a physical material that sustains an ever-present counterforce. His thinking on this notion would recur many times over in his teaching. **The earth is there and it gives constructive resistance, and this resistance is variable in relation to the earth's mass. The wetlands and mountains have different material qualities. We seldom think of the earth as a building material, but construction always has a duel with the ground.**

All architecture is dependent upon construction. Construction seeks the earth; it falls upon it. The eye, light, and thought, that which spatially disturbs these words, are construction.

Thought is the engineer, which is what makes the construction in its broadest definition. Construction is something you bring into nature, and you get the shadow for free.

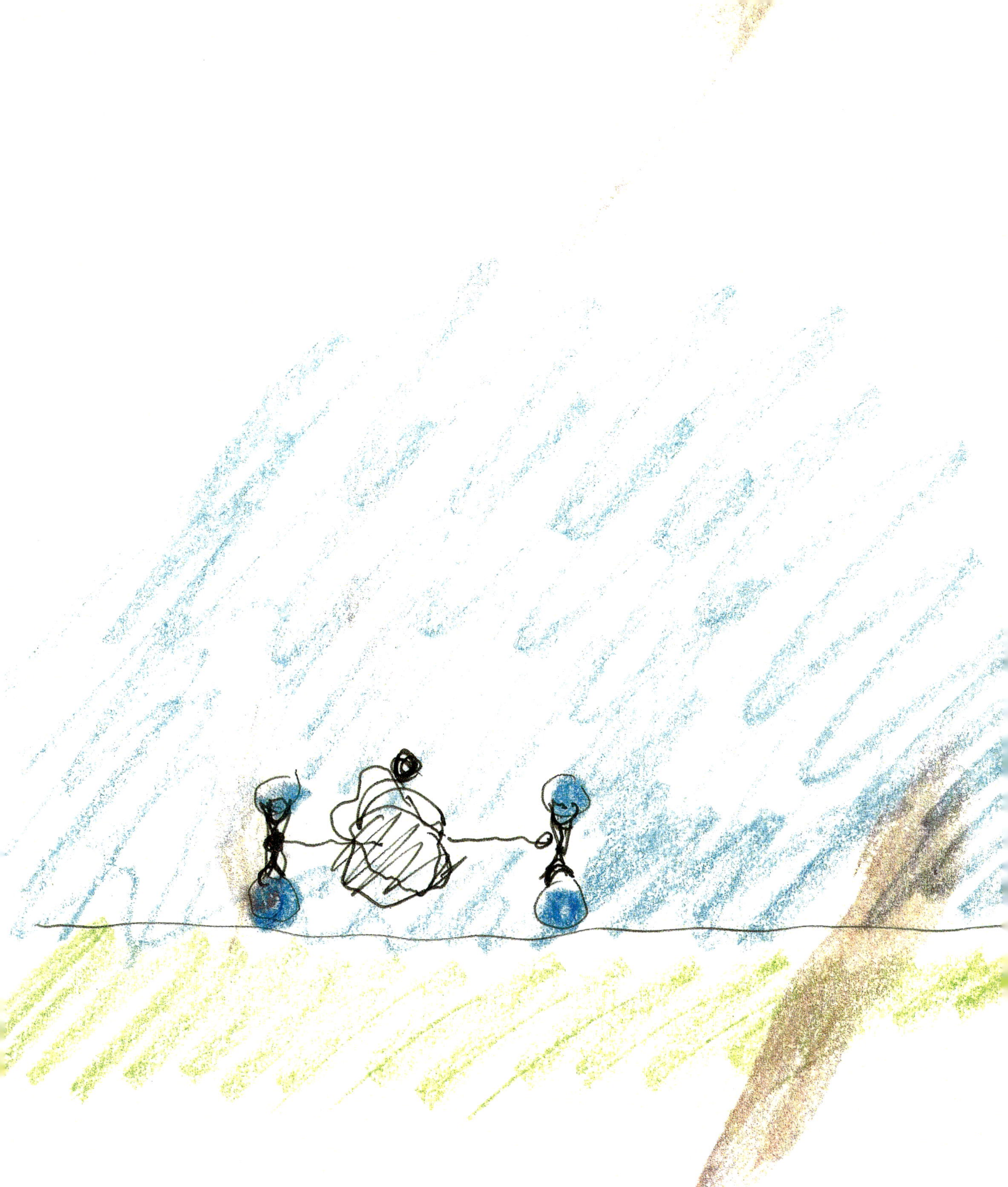

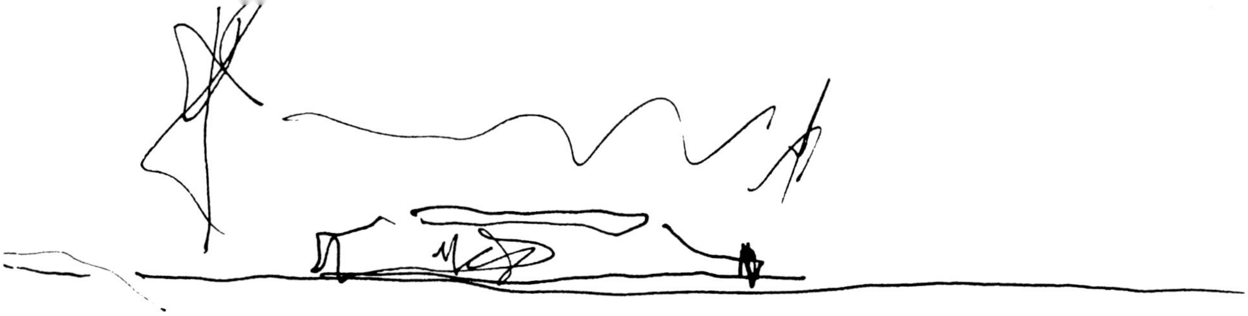

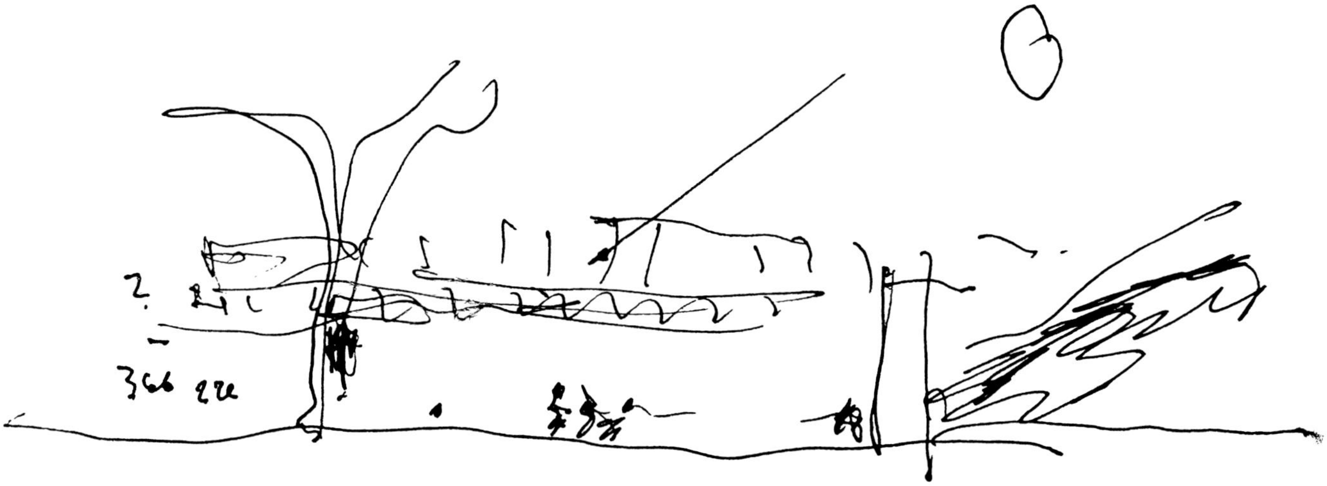

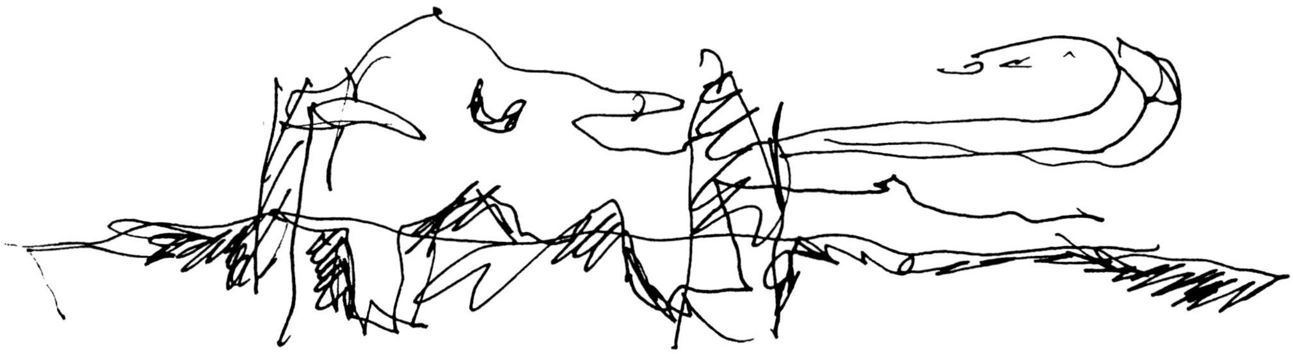

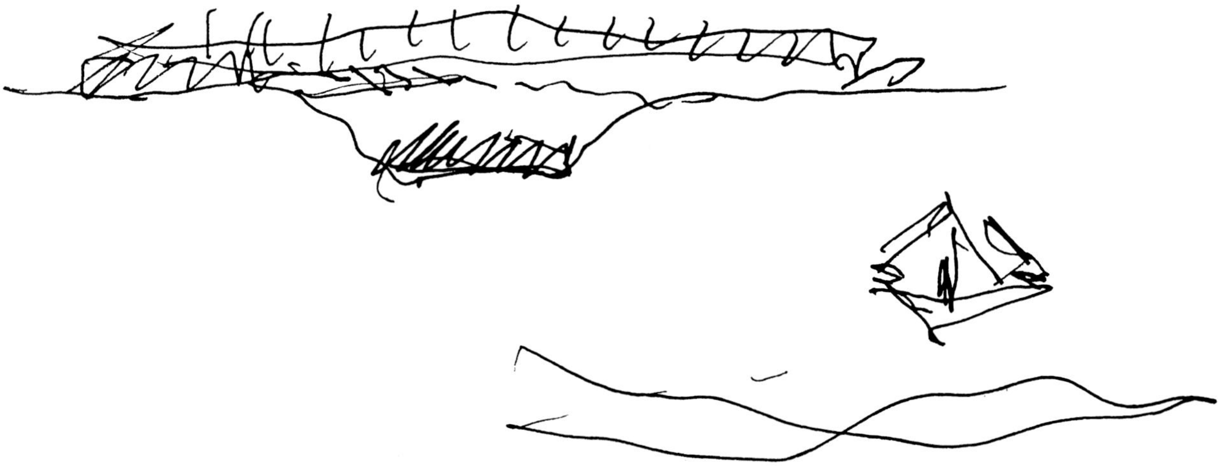

Construction hides and makes you selective in relation to what you see.

Whatever topic Fehn lectured on, whether at school or in a public forum, he almost always referred to cave drawings. From this, other stories followed. He would often joke, **I have only one lecture.** In his class, the physical model was a vital tool in conveying a spatial and structural attitude. It was imperative to comprehend the structural capacity of each material. Again, the earth is the base that initiates a relationship with all other materials.

There was a time when the earth and the content of its mass were regarded as unlimited. The cave as a climate zone defined where mass was soft or hard. The cave gave survival a dimension.

A brick is a constructive achievement; you can build with a stone that has the same measurements over and over again.

Sand, earth, and rocks are construction's mass concept. Wood is something else. It is understood through its size and belongs to limits. Glass is a transparent mass, a river that flows.

In relation to concrete, the mass is constant; it is the form one seeks. The architect is a poet who is thinking and talking with the help of construction.

The freedom the earth gives me is the vitality I seek in my structures. The Romans worked in a much more plastic manner: they poured the wall and reworked the opening.

You have no dialogue with architecture when construction disappears.

Fehn was also occupied with a type of structural autonomy, the interval before the structure meets the ground. Free from gravity, the building could gain vitality and signal new spatial possibilities. During this period, work by the Spanish architect Enric Miralles would come up in class. His urban work in particular evidenced this structural vigor. Miralles visited the Bygg 3 classroom on several occasions. **To have a sense of construction, one needs to enter the world of the acrobat. The entire history of great constructions can be represented through a tightrope walker. The excitement must belong to the structure. It must have something to tell; it is the storyteller.**

Sketch, "The stone is given a dimension."

OPPOSITE Sketches of Brussels pavilion, Venice pavilion, Hedmark County Museum, Røros Mining Museum.

Sketch, "The pyramid for one person. For tomorrow's moment. Philosophy. Religion. A momentary blink as architecture."

Fehn's year with Prouvé in Paris influenced not just his built work but also his teaching and his reflections on architecture. He was certainly inspired by the French architect's rational approach and by other lines of thought: **The wheel as a construction only touches the surface of the earth as a point. In this context, heaven and earth are one and the same, and the road becomes a horizon. In Prouvé's office, I learned that the car as a construction has heaven between it and the earth. The car is a construction that is placed directly on heaven.**

Much later, at a time when Fehn's lectures included comments on his trips to the United States and on his friendship with John Hejduk, he renewed his acquaintance with Aldo van Eyck. **As I write this note down from a lecture on construction at Easter in 1987 in Bygg 3, I suddenly remember a visit to Aldo van Eyck. I was staying in his house, and in the evening we were looking at photographs of a journey he had made in Peru. He kept circling around the theme of the stones in the ancient Peruvian walls. Why those rounded shapes, that precise masonry with its projecting points, this love of stone in this vast desolate landscape . . .**

Sometimes Fehn's work inspired his teaching, and sometimes teaching opened a door to a new story that would immediately affect his built work. Teaching for Fehn was an instrument that absorbed external input and changes. But common to both his teaching and his work in the office was an intense, enduring preoccupation with the importance of gravity and the horizon in the physical world of architecture. Fehn's teaching, in spite of its openness and its imaginative and sometimes irrational stories, required concentration and discipline. Along with endurance, it demanded one's absolute presence. **The key to every work is to get into position. If you are able to find a pencil and stay seated, you are well on your way. There is no other method that equals this one.** His teaching also emphasized that architecture cannot be everything: it has physical limitations. However, it is within these limitations that one finds a resistance force, that architecture discovers its uniqueness, its virtual presence embedded in physical space.

When Fehn retired from the Oslo School of Architecture, Giancarlo de Carlo sent this message: "For many years you have belonged to the school. It is you we have looked up to and admired each time you would come up with something none of us had ever thought of or recognized. I hope you will miss the admiration, and with this you will find the time to think about the years we were able to be together."

Pyramiden fr (A) menneske.

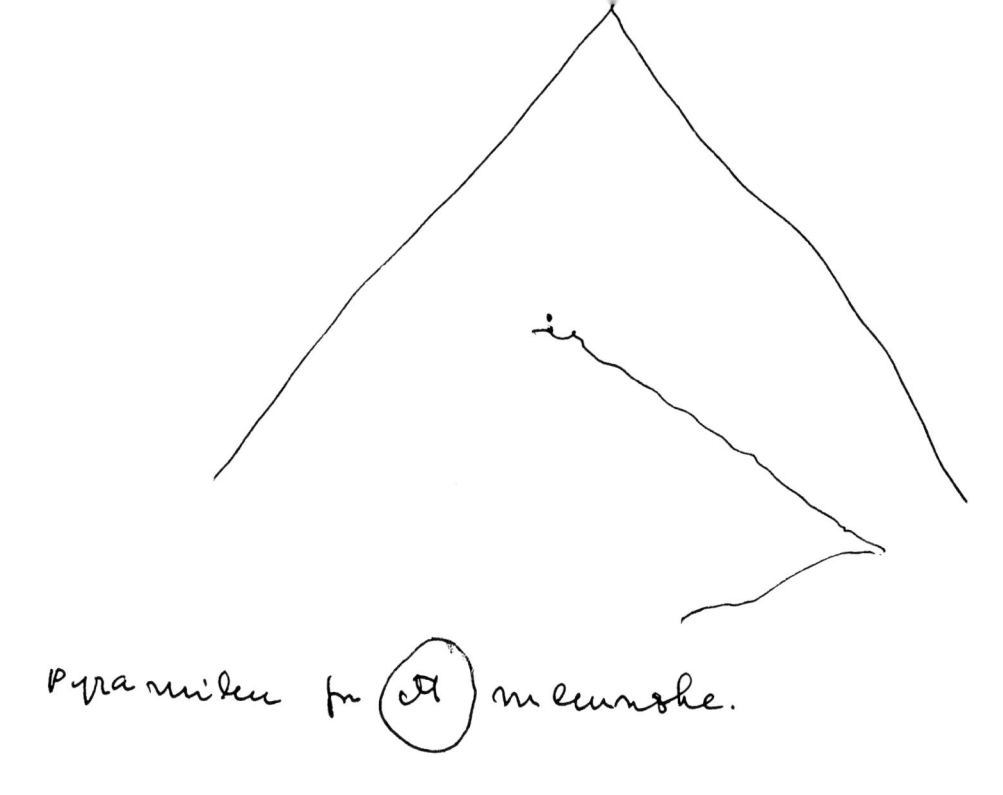

et morgen tåge billede

filosofi

region

øyeblikkets arkitektur.

CHAPTER 8

CONNECTING HEAVEN AND EARTH | The relationship between heaven and earth has always fascinated Fehn as an approach to architecture. His thought process as he works toward a better comprehension of this connection can be seen in his many sketches that reveal correspondences within the theme: fish and the sea, birds and the sky, the human being left standing alone on land, an in-between figure that tries to establish a dialogue. This figure has to make a space of its own, a new room attached to the surface of the earth and formed by human need and desire.

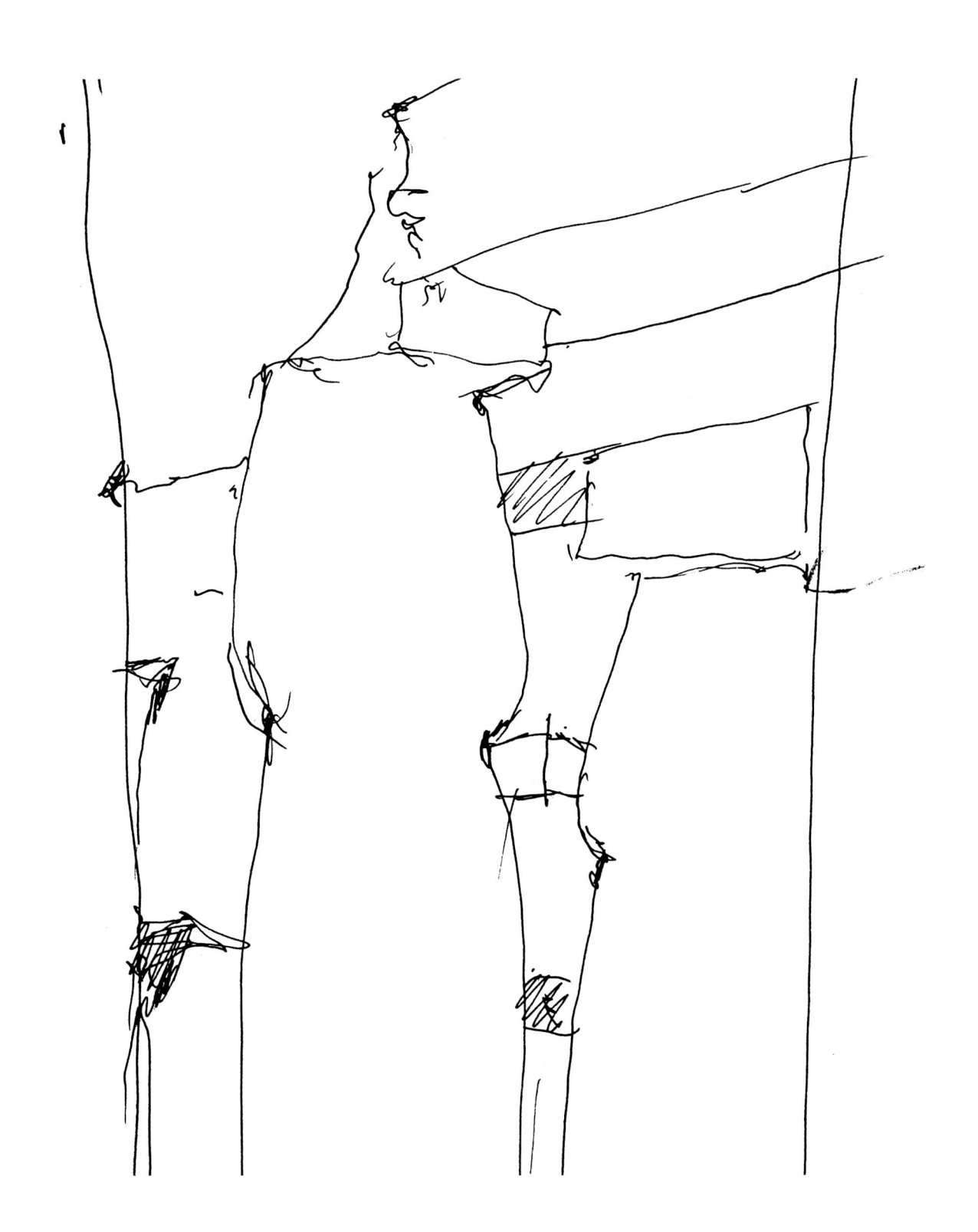

Sketch, "The human with its own shadow. The human together with the construction, the tree, and the shadows melt together."

OPPOSITE Sketch, 1992, of columns at Luxor, Egypt.

PAGE 188 Sketch.

In this room picture, the horizon serves as a mediator between the earth and the sky. The boat object has the ability to move the horizon. Sverre Fehn's work acknowledges the resistance force of gravity and the earth as its base; but his spatial dialogue belongs equally to the sky. Among the many conceptual images he used to broaden these discussions was the cut into the earth's surface, which allows the sky to enter the dark place below the surface and in so doing reveal the earth's secrets. This is quite different from the image of Aladdin's carpet, which requires a place in the sky. Architecture has its limitations, but the world that invents architecture does not. Because of its capacity to move the horizon, Fehn uses the boat as a kinetic link between the sea and the sky, just as he uses the tree as a fixed link between heaven and earth. The tree as nature's figure breaks the horizon while its structure reaches below the earth's surface. In this sense, the tree, which has a structure both below and above the horizon, is Fehn's most generous figure. Under the tree a person loses his or her shadow but gains shelter in the shade; under the surface the roots form a structure that supports the shelter. In his built work, Fehn considered each tree as precious and made a great effort to leave these elements of nature untouched as the site's connectors between heaven and earth. **The tree is a wonderful plant. It contains by nature a strong and magnificent structure. Each species of tree has been given its own distinctive form. There is a whole world of differences in expression between an oak and a spruce. The dramatic meeting between the sky and the earth is, however, common to them both. It is in the point of intersection, the horizon, that the tree gathers all its strength, reaches its maximum constructive size. From this, trees have directions toward minimal expressions; they stretch their roots down into darkness and their branches up toward the light. Between these extremities we find the dimensions of the tree that have inspired structures of use to men.**

As opposed to stone, iron, or glass, you can live with the tree next to your skin. The warmth it emits and its temperament offer the privileges of nearness. Viewing material in the dimension of time, the masonry wall belongs to history; the tree is transient and belongs to eternity.

The form given by the tree to our building arts is based on a straight line. It is the meeting with the sea (the water) that has given the material its great

CONNECTING HEAVEN AND EARTH

Sketch and notes for a lecture.

Fehn in Luxor.

OPPOSITE Sketch, 1993, "Landscape Symbolism: Heaven. The in-between. Hell. The *universal* room" (top left); sketch, 1994, "The numbers. The number → 0. The never-ending birth in the section belongs to the desert, the mathematics of the desert" (top right); sketch, 1982, "The fish and the bird" (bottom left); sketch, 1980, "Jorge Luis Borges. After reading his book A-Z, and other novels I end up with the important problems. 1. The mirror. You double yourself. And the negative-positive is the same. 2. Every short story ended with a knife or a sword. The one to execute yourself. Or if the perfection is brought to end it is no other solution than . . ." (bottom right).

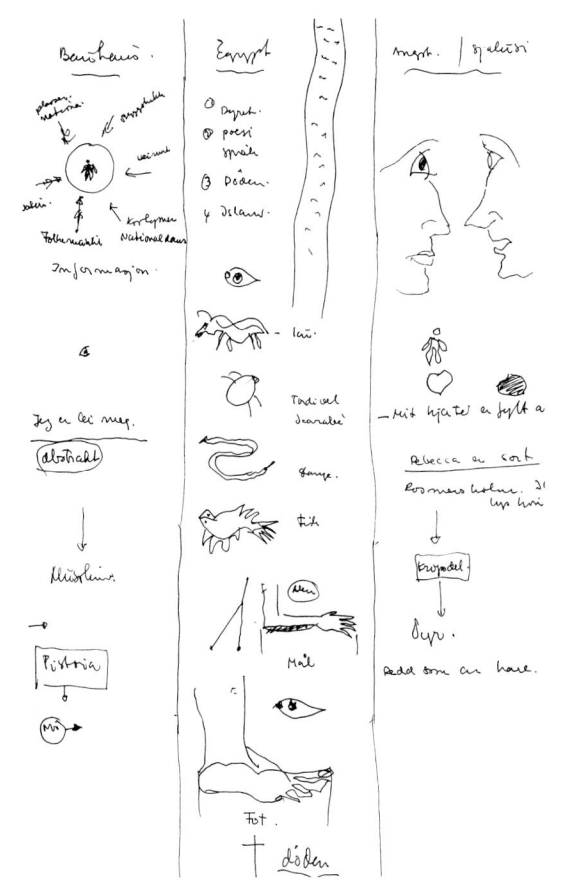

beauty. The curve of the branch has become the line of the vessel. The suppleness of the board has conquered the waves. The idea of the large enterprise was born not in the art of building on land but in the ship. The huge ships cleared the landscape of its forests and drifted out to sea as large communities, where men lived for years with the tree as their partner in hand, from the wooden spoon and barrel to the hull and the mast.

Until the end of his active career, Fehn hoped that he would one day build a church. The closest he came was his winning competition entry for a church at Honningsvåg (see page 142). Now and then, the community still attempts to realize the project, to have a "Fehn building," but so far without success. Just before he retired, Fehn worked on a project for a small chapel, St. Olav's Chapel, in the south of Norway; this too was never realized. Yet it should be understood that connecting heaven and earth was not particularly a religious theme. While it was related to the spiritual, it was more a way to appreciate the strong forces of nature and the vocabulary of earth, sky, sea, and horizon.

Two installations where the relationship between earth and heaven, the known and the unknown, were revealed through the object provided Fehn with the opportunity to realize issues related to a religious theme. Within a public space, he generates a personal space with the capacity to stimulate the connection. In an exhibition of Norwegian artifacts from the Middle Ages from the University of Oslo Archaeological Collection, first shown at the Henie Onstad Art Center in Høvikodden, 1972, and permanently installed at the National History Museum in Oslo, 1979–80, he investigates each object's inherent qualities for signs of possible connections. The expression of the displayed object conveys, distracts, strengthens, or reinvents the object's connection to heaven and earth anew. For the installation, Fehn puts a Jesus figure at rest and gives it earth as a pillow. The figure sleeps on a table with heaven as an urban room hovering above.

Landshapets Symbolikk

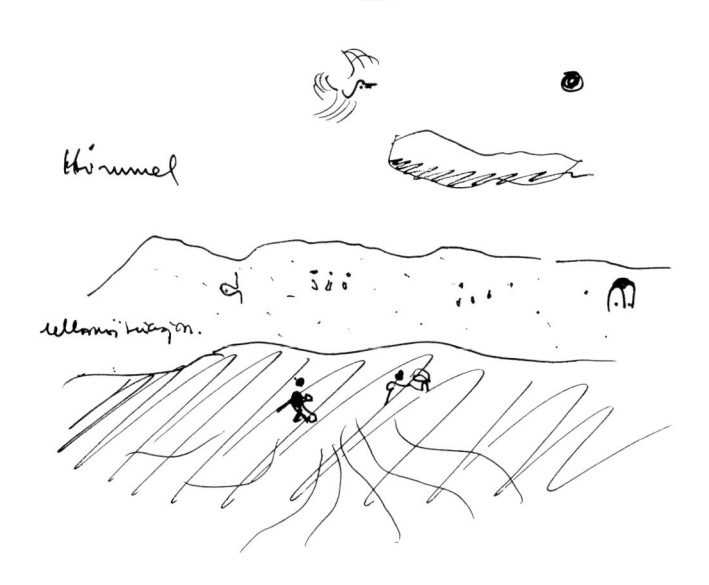

Himmel

ullomistasjon

nature

Det universelle rom.

The fish and the bird

tallene / 1.2.3.4.5
6.7.8.9.10

$\frac{1}{2}$ $\frac{1}{3}$ $\frac{1}{4}$

1 tallet. → O

Det uendelige fødsel i
antallet. — Ordenens
matematikk

Jorges Luis Borges. After reading
his work A–Z. and others novels
I end up in to important problems.

1

the mirror. You doble yourself.
and the negativ — positiv — is the
same.

2

Every short story ended with a
knife or a sord.

the end to execute yourself.
if the perfection is brought to end
it is no other solution than — ....

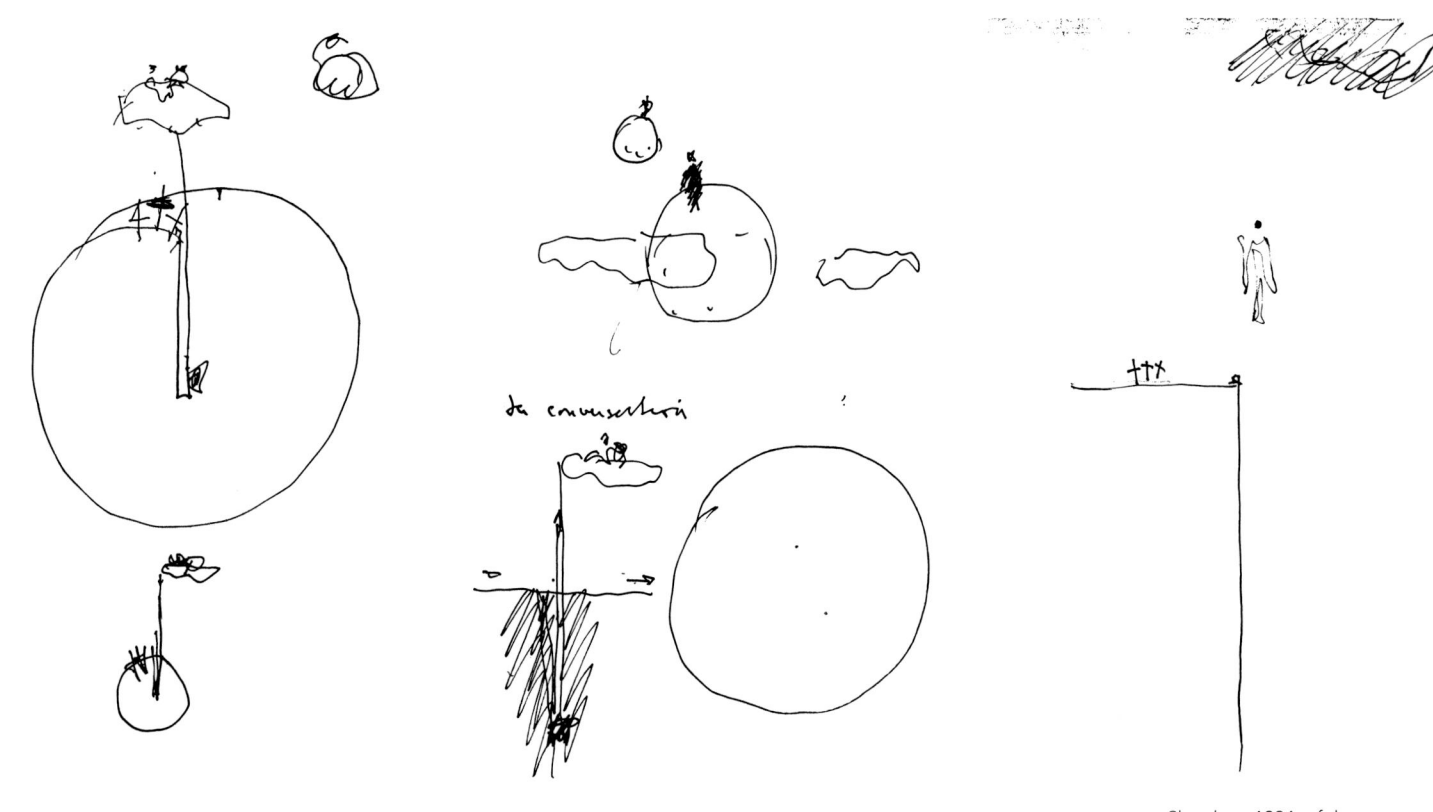

Sketches, 1994, of the religious story, "The story lives in your spirit; it is with you. Wherever you are, the room is your costume, forming a center."

194   THE PATTERN OF THOUGHTS

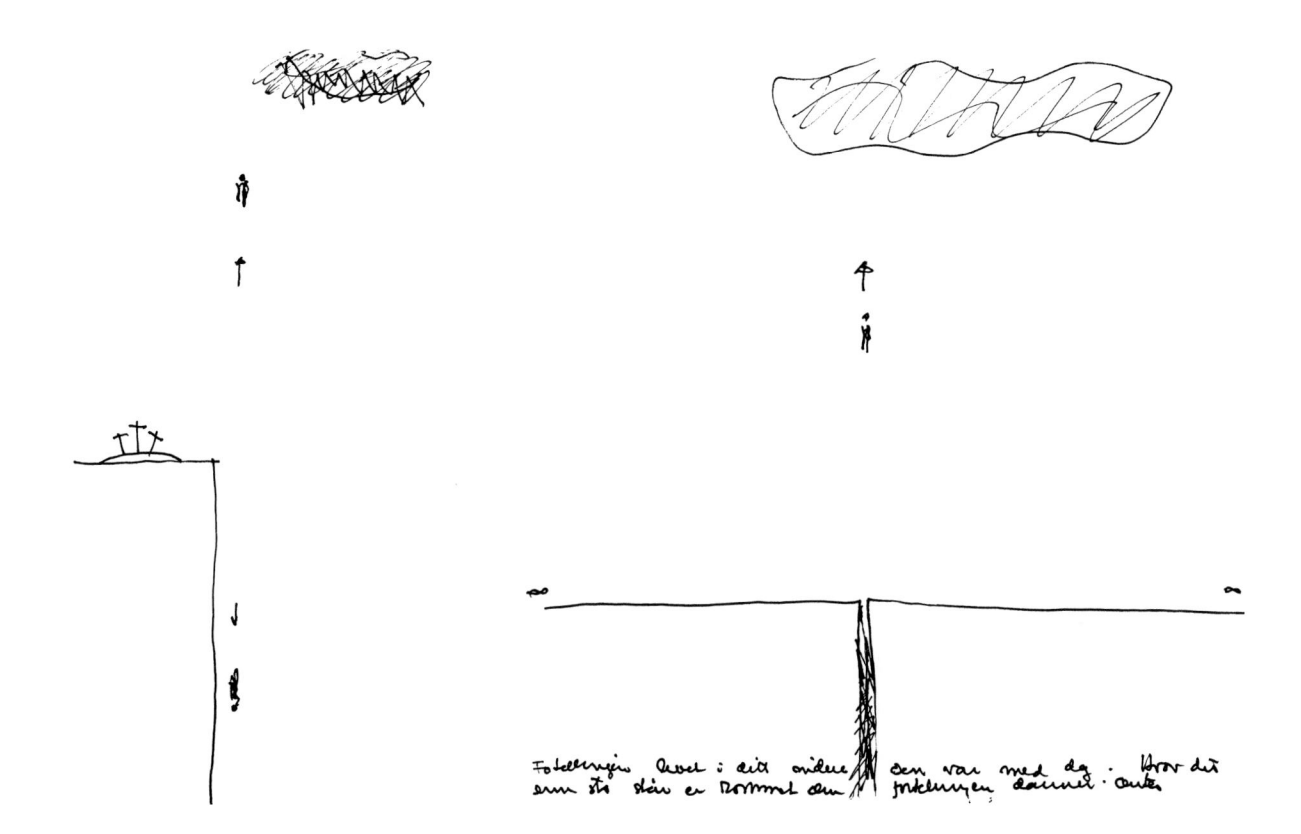

He replaces a lost disciple figure with an iron cross; upon the disciple's return, its place will be ready. **What about a reclining Christ figure? By placing the sculpture horizontally one comes closer to the details, and the tragedy of the crucifix is intensified. One has in any case freed the figure from time and space.**

In all of his exhibitions, Fehn's attitude toward the actual display structure was the same: it was never intended to compete with the object or risk draining its internal strength. For this reason, Fehn's installations remain just beyond symbolic connotation: the object is never able to escape its physical reality. The direct value of the object has never really interested Fehn; instead, it has always been the raw, straightforward physical existence of the object that is essential. It is the uncovering of this physical state that sets in motion a process of discovery of the unknown, and this is the story he wants to tell. But the unknown also contains a dimension that belongs to infinity. Thus, to comprehend the scale of each object in relation to the immaterial is also important. The aspect of infinity appears in two ways in Fehn's thinking: as numbers and signs, and as the horizon. Signs and numbers carry a dimension outside of nature's construction of heaven and earth; the in-between figure, the human, chooses the numbers—the idea of infinity—and forms a space of its own.

Fehn redrew quite often one particular motif in relation to the idea of size: a cave with a man huddled inside and a stone and an elk outside. The man has taken over the animal's cave; the animal, frustrated, stands outside. A cut stone in the drawing represents the dimension given by constructive thought. In time, man brings the animal's soul into the cave as a painting. **The cave is a building with the least resistance, and the hunter's prey is the only thing that clings to the earth. Therefore, the animal ends up as the great decoration of the cave. Within the animal's silence at the moment of attack and the duel between animal and man, one took spiritual possession of the animal.**

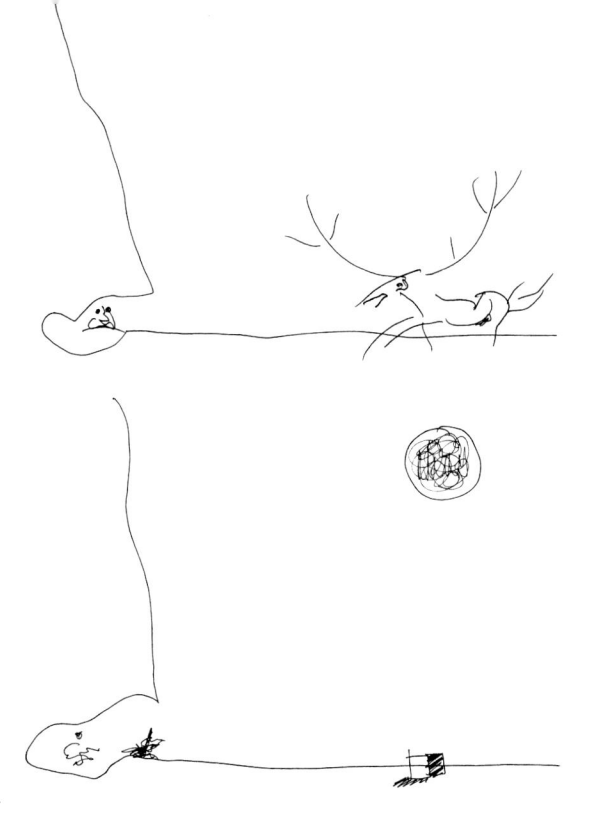

Sketch, 1982, of the cave.

OPPOSITE Blackboard sketch for the permanent exhibition at the National History Museum, Oslo.

OVERLEAF Exhibition of Norwegian artifacts, Henie Onstad Art Center, Høvikodden, Bærum, Norway: Views of installation.

After a class trip to Egypt and a short trip to Mexico in the mid-1980s, Fehn intensified and broadened his focus on the object and the animal. He was captivated by the placement and the meaning of the object as a human market caught between heaven and earth, life and death. His obsession with this quandary is evident in an interview I conducted for *Perspecta: The Yale Architectural Journal* titled "Has a Doll Life?" We talked for days, and in the end I asked, "Is the mask living, has a doll life?" **The bullet made a dent in the surface of the earth, and the size of the hole was the same as the bullet. Today's "bullet" has reached the invisible mystery, as it can destroy all life without rendering a mark on the surface of the earth. The spirit is now self-destructive. Matter has claimed a total victory. *The mask is left behind in conversation with the doll.***

Fehn's permanent installation at the National History Museum reveals a rigorous exploration of the object and its association with a dark, looming, implied heaven and earth. The massive stone building, designed by Henrik Bull and completed in 1903, establishes the framework around the display. Fehn brought history's sacred and mundane objects into a first-floor wing with turn-of-the-century gold-leaf ornamentation. A comb, a single shoe, and a bowl share a dim spotlight with an intricately carved portal and altarpieces; all are treasures. He was especially taken by a small wooden crucifix: **None of the figures fascinated me more than the Christ figure, who allowed himself to be crucified with gloves, with beautiful leather shoes, and with a diamond decorating his navel.**

Fehn focused on how a material could retain its essential substance yet simultaneously take on new and expressive roles. **The Nordic deities had a zealousness in their relationship to nature, but this continued even when there was a single common god. The objects emit a sound that describes their original room . . . and it is with the tree's dimensions that these wooden figures indicate their wealth. The tree works its way into the figure, its love and pageantry; everything is played out in the tree's dimension. It is the tree's qualities that express the clothing and folds in the dress.**

Fehn has said of the exhibition at the National History Museum: **When the room was about to be closed for the day and the main light switch and spotlights were turned off, there was a calm over the space and its objects. From the window facing the world, a natural shadow returned. And in this same moment, the urban space was born. Outside, there was once again a city with its life and time. I was thrown out into a world that was familiar, but at the same time it was also carrying the past. Inside, once the curtains were drawn, the spirit lives with the object.**

A temporary exhibition of nine of the famed Chinese terra-cotta warriors and two of their horses, 1984–85, also held at the Henie Onstad Art Center in Høvikodden, completes Fehn's spatial abstraction of the heaven and earth theme. The architect was faced with the challenge of conveying through these lone examples the army of almost seven thousand clay figures that had been buried to protect Emperor Qin Shi Huang's grave, which were unearthed in 1974. Fehn developed four important guidelines for the exhibition: the soldiers should be at once collectivized and individualized; the role of the warrior's weapon as tool of communication should be recognized; the light should remind viewers that the warriors have come from Hades; and the mirror is a means to join the real and the unreal. Inspired by the French poet Paul Claudel, Fehn often returned to a situation he called double infinity. He translates Claudel's struggle between the carnal and the spiritual into architectural content. (This typifies the way Fehn recasts his summer reading into a new setting.) Fehn's text for the exhibition explains the rest: **Is there a greater loneliness than eleven wooden crates from China with muslin-wrapped terra-cotta figures imprisoned in iron racks, torn away from their army of seven thousand**

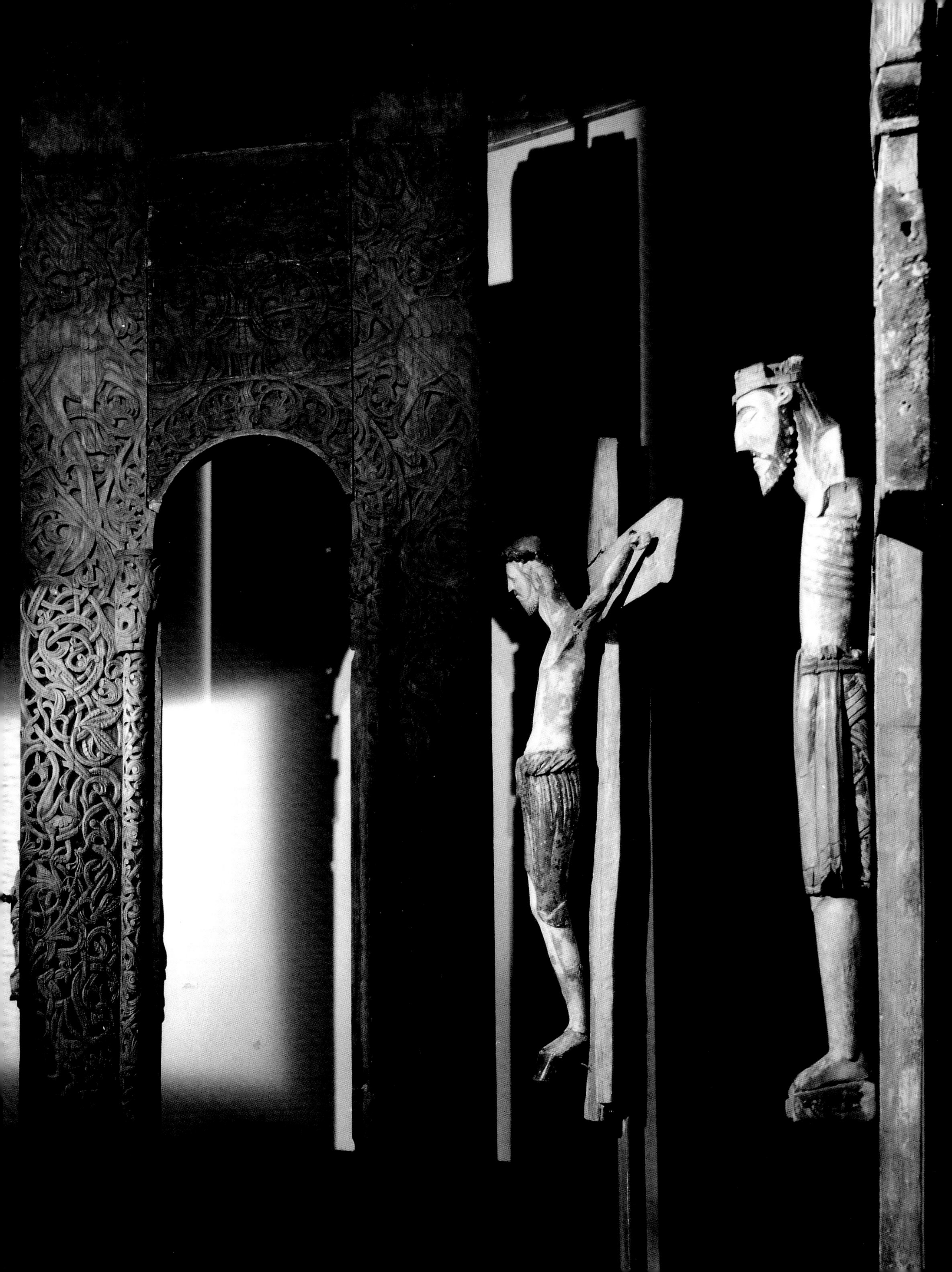

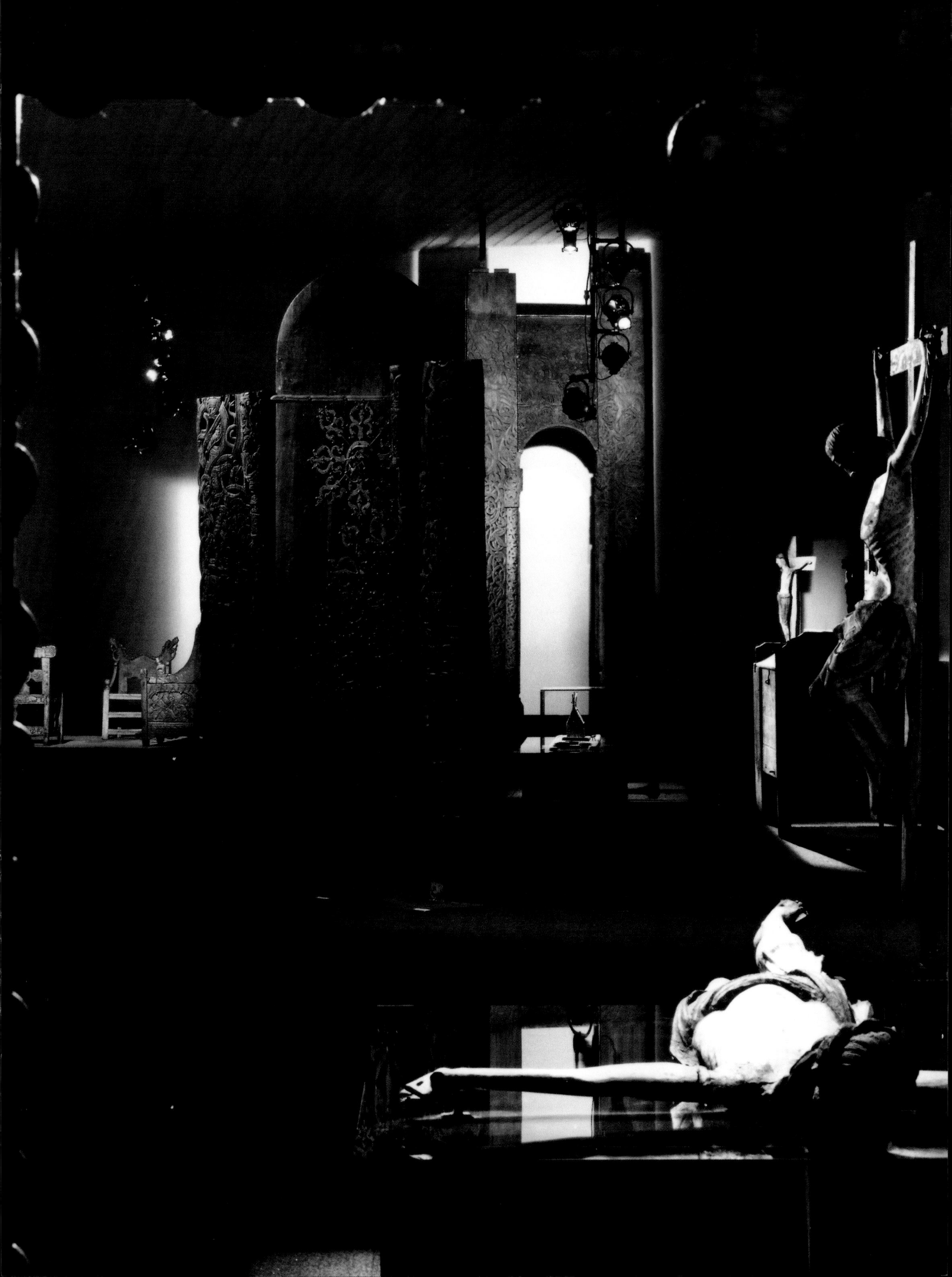

soldiers chosen for a trip to eternity with their Emperor Qin Shi Huang?

These offers for surgery of the earth's surface shall meet their new light at a point 9,100 kilometers from the place where they were burned and preserved. What is this fragment in the large prism hall in the Henie Onstad Art Center at Høvikodden?

A five-meter tower of mirror was built with sides parallel to the museum walls; on these walls were affixed mirrors of the same dimension as the tower. This tower became a great stage director for the six terra-cotta warriors, two archers, a stable boy, and two horses. Between the shadowless columns of mirror, the warriors again found their armies, an army of endless rows, and at the foot of the tower a sword; the weapon combined with the soldiers' skill brings you to eternity.

Jean Cocteau allows his Orpheus to go through a mirror to enter the realm of death in order to fetch Eurydice. If you go toward the mirror, illusion and reality both disappear into the thin surface layer.

The mirror was not just a device to visually increase the army of figures. Fehn often referred to the mirror as an instrument that releases intense loneliness; looking into the mirror is a search for confirmation and a response to loneliness. The soldiers see their comrades in the mirror, but they are not really

THESE PAGES AND OVERLEAF Exhibition of Chinese Terra-Cotta Soldiers, Henie Onstad Art Center, Høvikodden, Bærum, Norway: Views of installation.

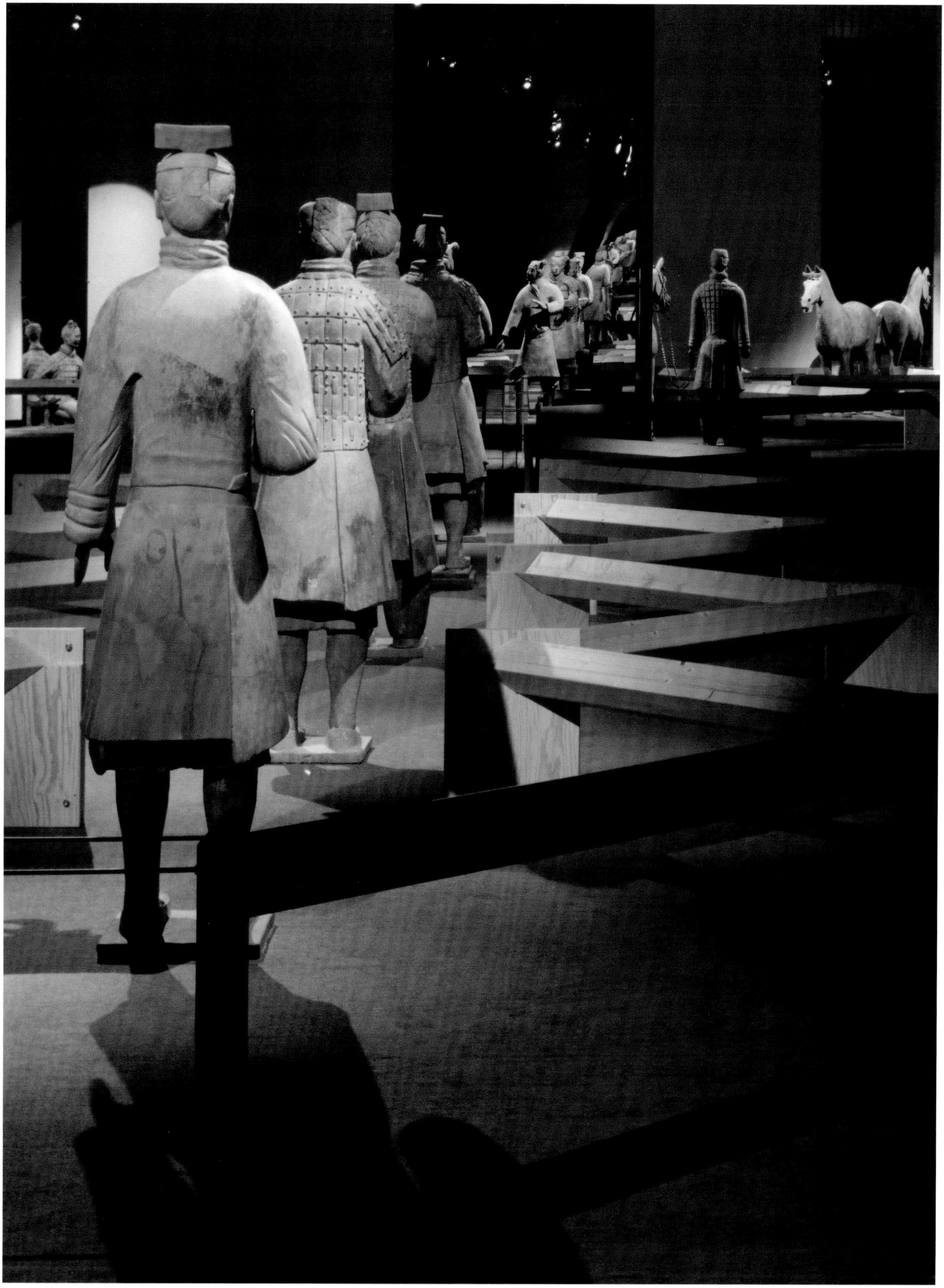

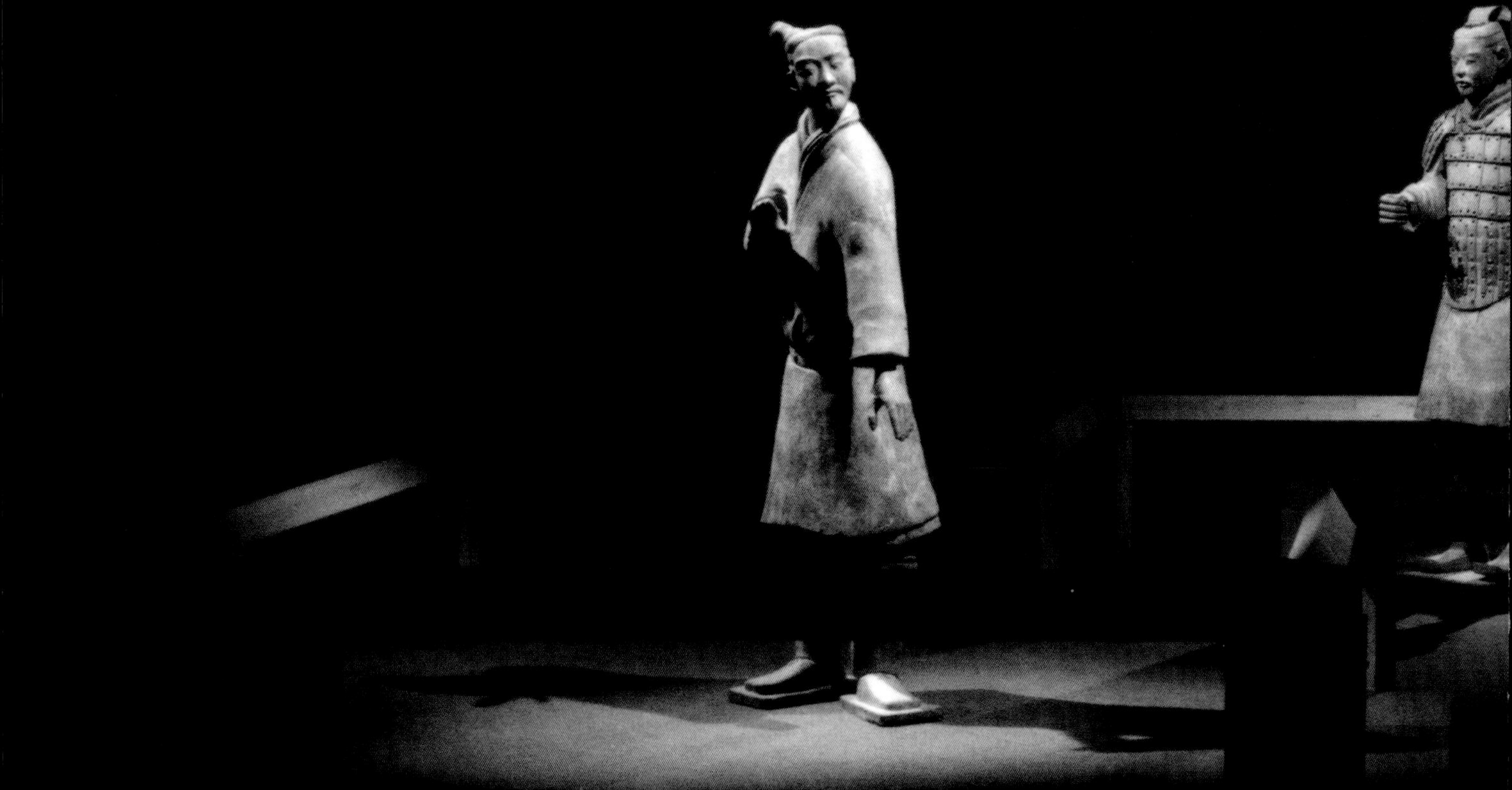

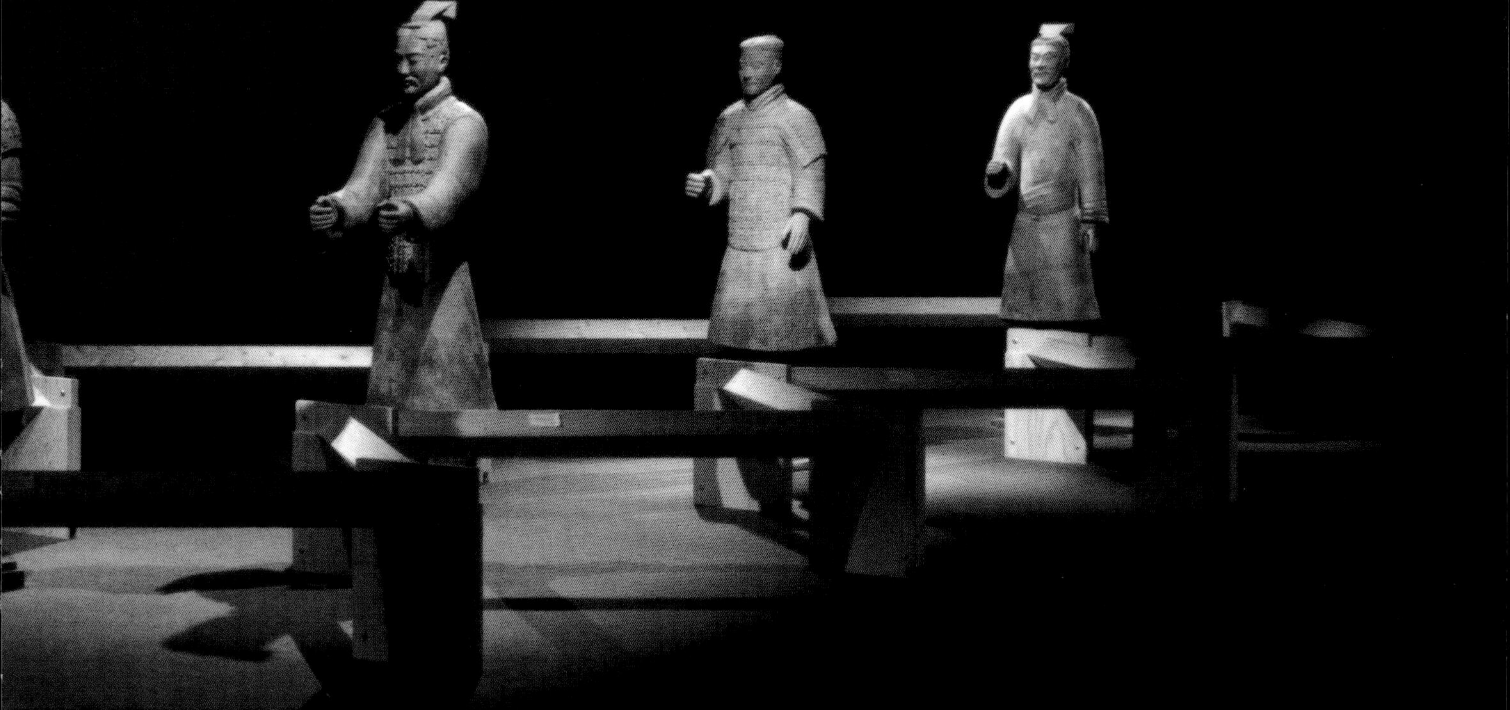

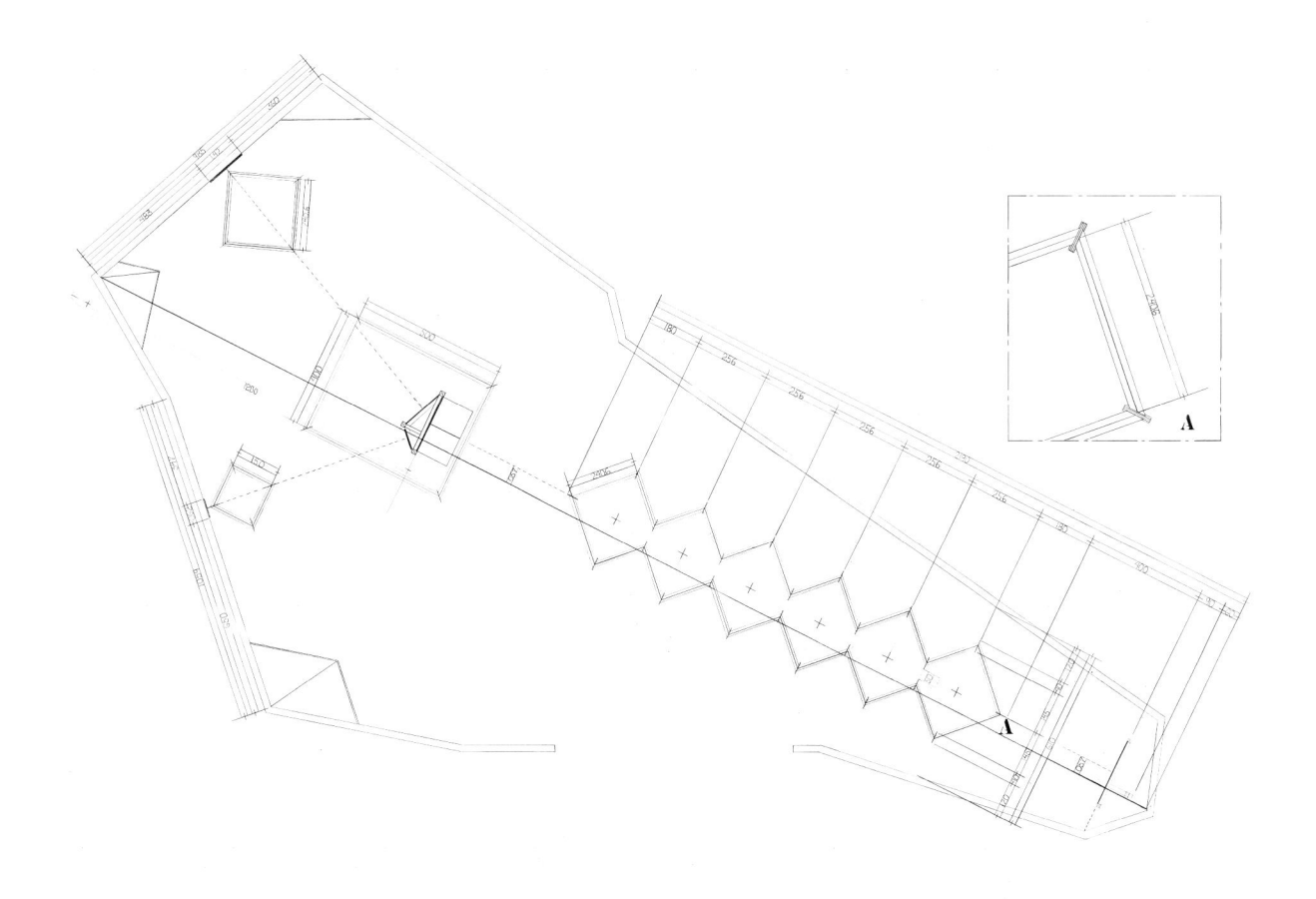

Exhibition of Chinese Terra-Cotta Soldiers: Plan.

OPPOSITE Sketch, 1992, of Luxor.

there. They are caught somewhere between heaven and earth in an untouchable image. Visitors to the exhibition sensed an endless dimension of silent horizon as thousands of perfect soldiers—the living dead—marched into infinity.

Fehn makes a connection between heaven and earth in his interpretation and display of particular objects. But the connection is more profound, for it is equally a discussion of transience and the immortal, and how humankind is trapped and must cope with the two conditions simultaneously. For Fehn, the abstract or the unknown has a clear room picture. The only force that can challenge this is another reality. **Fantasy is stored up in the heavens, but when we fly, there are no longer angels around us. The imaginary space has moved.**

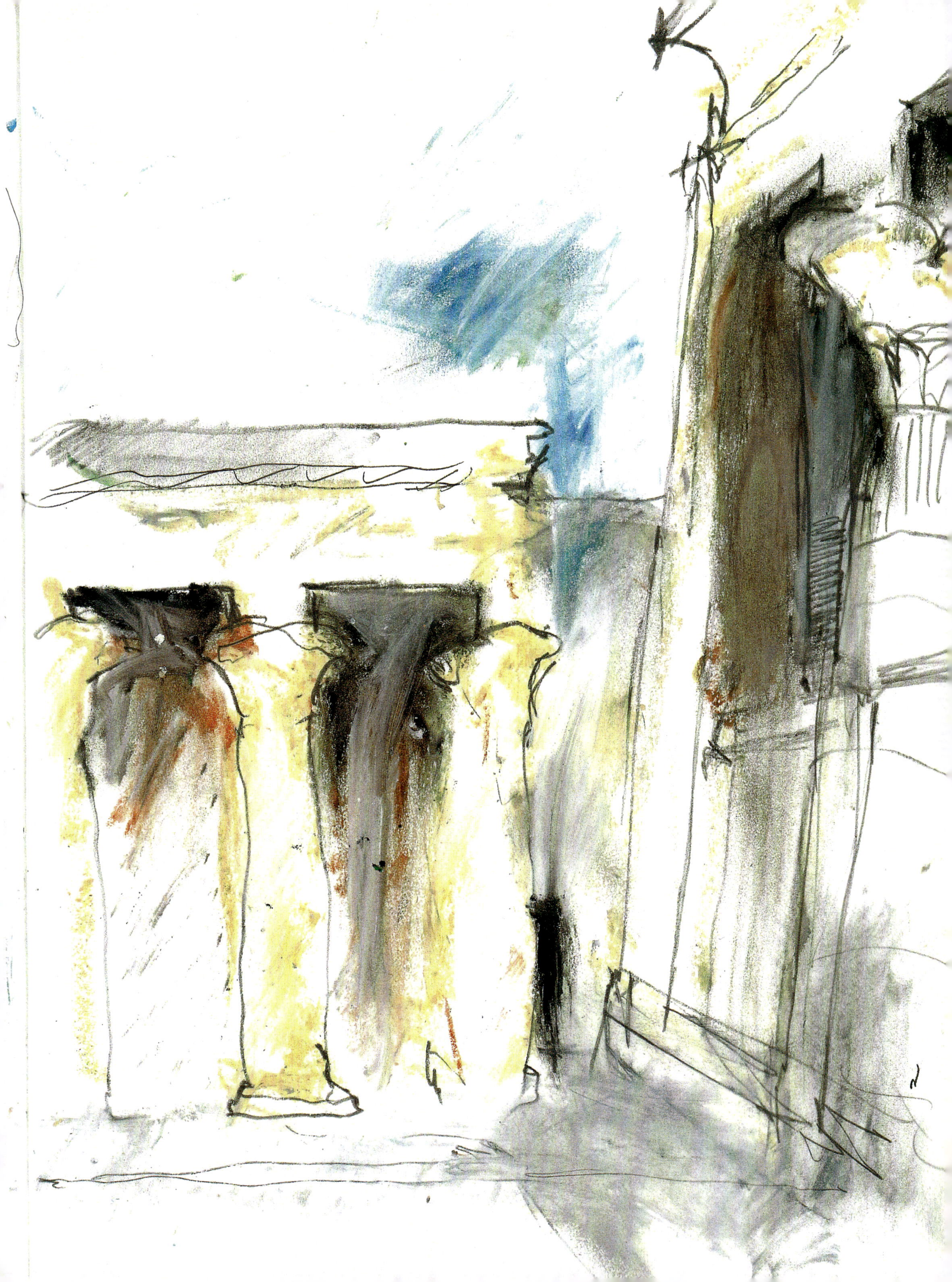

Enmoletin,
moral

CHAPTER 9

THE MASK AND THE CUT | With the full onset of postmodernism in the early 1980s, Scandinavian architecture, which had been firmly grounded in a Nordic sensibility, became polarized. The imagery of postmodernism was in conflict with the Nordic simplicity and sensitivity to material and its form, and a much tougher discussion evolved in relation to this change of attitude. Fehn had already experienced several lean years in his office, and while he did not falter in his architectural beliefs, there were some changes for him. For a number of years in this period, he was a visiting critic for the Architectural Association in London. Alvin Boyarsky was head of the school at that time, and the AA was a breeding ground for new ideas and architectural tendencies that went beyond postmodern trends. Committed students and teachers made Fehn's sojourns in London, usually the week before the summer break, an architectural feast.

At the Oslo School of Architecture, Christian Norberg-Schulz turned his attention toward a strong belief in postmodernism. For a while, this influenced his teaching and writings. Over time, there have been various interpretations of this rather radical shift. As a teacher at the school, I experienced this change first-hand, and I sensed that it did not make the relationship between Fehn and Norberg-Schulz any easier. Nevertheless, they had a strong respect for one another. Fehn also developed a closer association with Giancarlo de Carlo, founder of the International Laboratory of Architecture and Urban Design. ILAUD was quite active during this period, introducing ideas, projects, and important questions into the international architectural discourse. Almost every important figure in architecture visited its workshops. ILAUD's unique contribution was to situate architectural thought in a larger context. Toward the end of this time, Fehn took over from Norberg-Schulz as head of the School of Architecture. He was in a sense performing a balancing act between individuals and groups that did not necessarily agree or even travel in the same direction.

Sverre Fehn made several trips to the United States in the 1980s. The first was a short visit to New York with his friend Odd Østbye, and the second was as a guest professor at Yale University. But the visit that was to have a lasting effect was his guest professorship at Cooper Union in New York in 1986, an invitation from Dean John Hejduk. For some time, Fehn had presented elements of Hejduk's work in his classroom lectures. He was truly enthusiastic about the offer to teach at Cooper Union and, for the first time in many years, planned an extended stay abroad, leaving the office to fend for itself. In fact, this was the only time that Fehn offered his full attention to another institution for a lengthy period of time. He ended his stint with a three-week visit to Mexico and returned to Oslo with a whole new set of stories relative to his perception of architecture. Though many concerned distinct experiences, Mexico instigated a direct and brutal confrontation with his lasting preoccupations, the correspondence between humans and animals and between life and death. From this point on, Fehn and Hejduk would keep up a long and close relationship despite the distance. Admirers of each other's work, they could nevertheless disagree and go in different directions without affecting their friendship. In many ways, the time in New York was a creative haven from the frustration over lack of work in the office. Fehn would often return to Hejduk's poems, expressive paintings, and storytelling approach to architecture. Hejduk addressed the idea of unbuilt conceptual work as architecture head-on, developing a particular type of drawing and very precise models. As far as he was concerned, the projects were already built. Fehn concurred: **They contain all built information, every screw is there.**

The change in Fehn's work was immediately apparent upon his return to Oslo, although some aspects were clearly linked to his earlier fascinations. He had always been occupied with the concept of the tattoo as both an extension of the skin and a layer in its own right. Few of his lectures at school escaped a tattoo story. But after his trip to New York, the tattoo fell under the concept of the mask. This was clearly the influence of Hejduk, but Fehn, as usual, pulled the idea apart and reassembled its components into his own concept of an architectural mask. The architectural purity and spatial clarity that characterized his previous works were now enhanced with a more figurative and expressive layer, a mask. The facade and, in some cases, the form itself have an expository element that delivers an architectural explanation and a simplified form of discovery. Because this mask suggests a predetermined spatial interpretation, it requires less participation. Not only does the structure speak of its capacity as structure, but the material offers a separate story: it informs or expresses independent of structure. This distinct layer takes on content of its own; it takes on the mask.

I do not think Fehn was entirely aware of the extent of the change in his work, given that his creative approach remained more or less the same, but the adoption of computer drawing to some extent gave this process a new challenge. The rolls of pencil working drawings, on paper and foil, in Fehn's archive have many tracing paper sheets with sketches and notations. Very few of these sheets were attached to his rolls of computer drawings. Some of the immediacy of his working process was perhaps modified, and to compensate he drew in a 1:1 scale on his old office blackboard. The invention of a story or stories that enabled him to discover the core of a project continued, but now the interpretation was focused on producing a recognizable image. The story repeated its own story.

The first built project in which this is apparent is the Brick House, 1986–87, created for a housing showcase just outside Oslo called "Build for the Future." Fehn, representing the Norwegian Bricklayers Association, was asked to design a house. He was assigned a rather constricted site: narrow and steep, it had roads at the top and bottom and houses just meters away on both sides. Fehn exploited the full potential of the site by allowing the residence to follow the contours of the terrain: the rectangular building section is divided into three distinct layers. The upper part belongs to the living area and main bedroom; the middle to bedrooms; and the lower to garage and services.

Brick's language lies in the mortar joint. I repeat the size, but it is the joint that is a brick wall's language. It always reminds me of Lewerentz. To build in brick is an experience for me, since each course has its beauty. You would like to design, but in the end it is the brick that decides.

The feature that gives the house its particular identity is a large exterior chimney on the north front, which faces the valley and renders this facade as a mask. Smaller elements—spatial figures attached to the rectangular body—provide character.

While some of Fehn's earlier houses closed in on themselves, there was always one component or another that opened up to the landscape, to nature. The Brick House, however, turns completely inward. All that faces out is the mask. The exterior wall follows the terrain with great precision, shutting out streets and neighbors. An open court inside the wall provides a visual link to the sky and natural light, but like the rest of the house it is protected and screened, creating an urban sense of space. While the site does not enter the house, light from above and from the walled court articulates the interior. The brick

Sketch of John Hejduk lecturing.

PAGE 206 Sketch, 1997, "Loneliness's precept."

210 THE PATTERN OF THOUGHTS

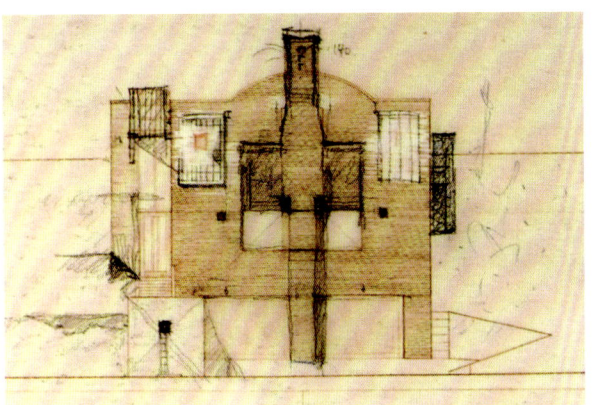

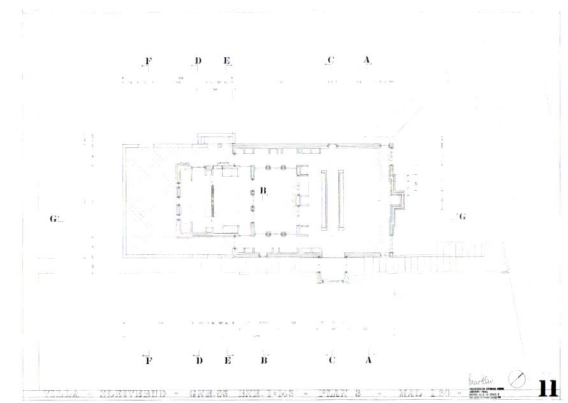

wall as mass takes on or forms masks that change in relation to context, both interior and exterior.

Inside, an intensity and textural variation, achieved through the use of different types of brick complemented by wood, delineate specific interior spaces. Texture as a separate layer heightens the sense of an architectural mask. In many ways, one is inside a spatial picture that varies according to color and light. **The fireplace is the central motif. The tile colors: green/white: summer/winter, fire/night: dark/white.** In the winter, the building is a cavelike structure, and in the summer, it opens in onto itself and its constructed exterior. Fehn drew this house with mature inhabitants in mind. His usual focus around a tight core of family life here gives way to an emphasis on separation.

I always felt the road up to this house was very tiring. The sun faced the wrong way, and the view was flawed. My reference was a man sixty years of age. The house is a drawer this man dreams of living in for the rest of his life. It reminds me of Beckett: the only thing he has left is a drawer, and the only key he has is the key to the drawer. Oh, he would like a little atrium where each morning he could go out in his pajamas after making his coffee in the little kitchen.

All of the architect's houses, independent of their clients, have the capacity to transform.

Brick House, Bærum, Norway: Exterior view, elevation sketch, plan of upper floor, main bathroom, kitchen and living room.

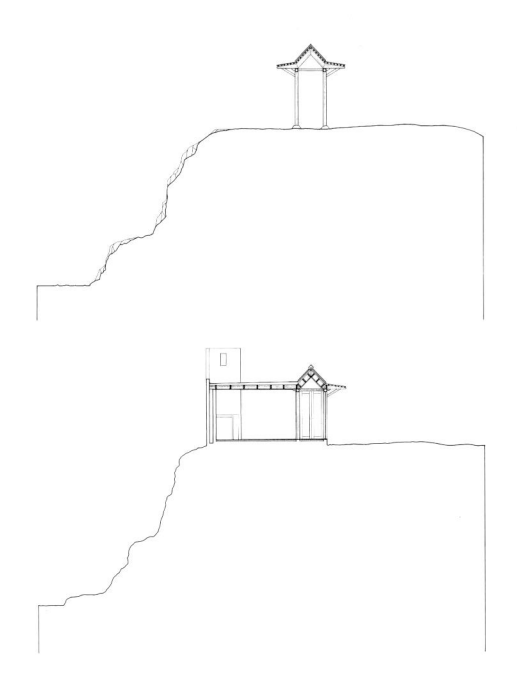

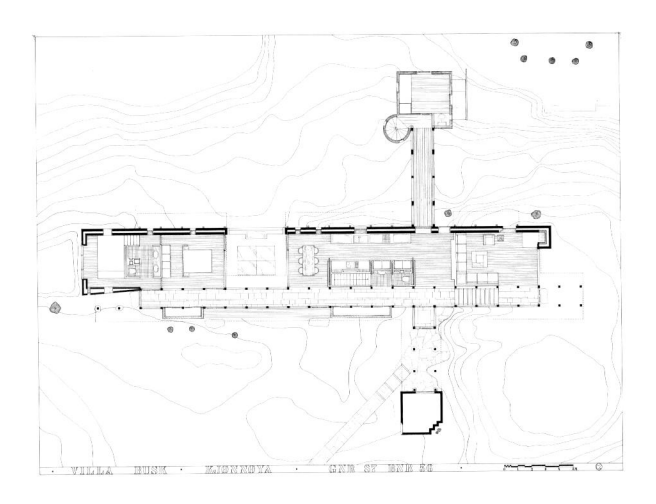

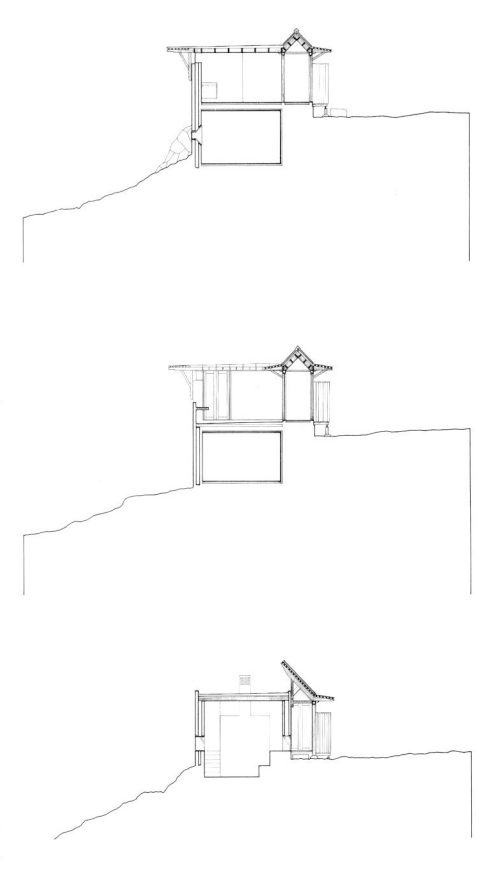

This is true of the Brick House as well, but one must go behind the mask. Fehn never really liked the house. I do not think the reason lies with the fact that he did not believe in applying an urban spatial attitude to a suburban area. Instead, it was that his imagined clients, a couple over sixty, became the actual owners. They moved in with their belongings and challenged his built mask with a mask upon a mask. The Brick House is a strange blend of before and after New York. Fehn, always sensitive to comments, was alert to what seemed to be two conflicting approaches within his thought process.

By the time the Busk House, 1987–90, was completed, the mask was in place. He had full control over the necessary precision of material and expression; the story of the mask and the physical presence were one. The Busk House is perhaps the only house by Fehn that may be understood on some level by all. He satisfied the need for observing a visual signpost before possessing the physical space.

The commission was quite different from the Brick House, not least because the residence was commissioned by real clients and not for a housing showcase. Terje Busk, a record producer, and his wife arrived for their first meeting with a portable television and video of the site. They were unfamiliar with Fehn's work, but just the same, it was agreed that he would draw a preliminary design. At the second meeting, Fehn and his only collaborator presented the project. The couple was silent throughout the meeting; after a long

Busk House, Bamble, Norway: Plan of main floor, sections, exterior view, sketch with site reading.

pause, Terje Busk proclaimed, "Ingenious! I'll buy it." Soon afterward, Busk and his family left for the United States to see the work of Mies van der Rohe and Frank Lloyd Wright.

The primary component of the house is a rectangular volume that meticulously follows the contours of the rocky site. Leading off one side of this main form is an entrance hall; on the other side, directly opposite, is a bridge that connects to a tower containing the bedrooms and bathroom for the daughters of the house. Running along the rectangular portion of the house is a narrow glazed passageway that functions as an introductory or access space to the other rooms. A concrete wall that extends the length of the house determines the overall direction and serves as the main structure. Other structural elements extend from this wall. **The Busk House was a fairytale project. I clapped together a summer and a winter house in one project. The site has a beautiful view and a fantastic rock formation clinging to**

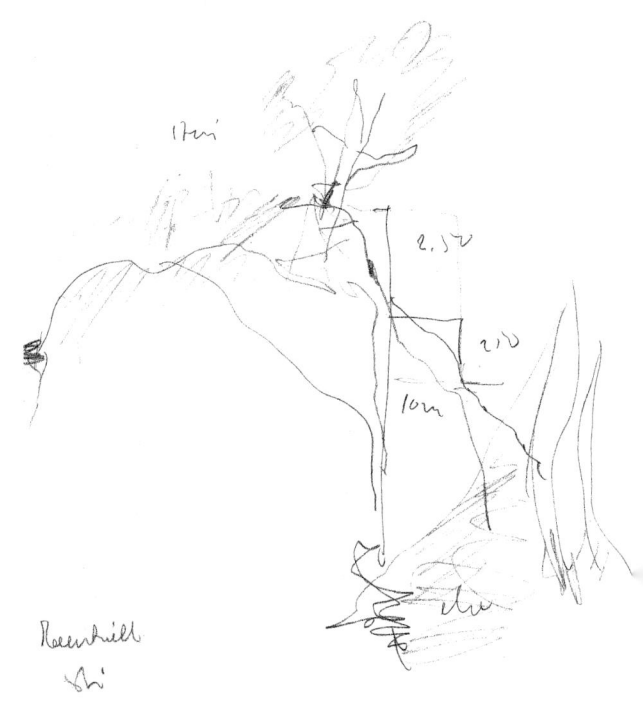

THE MASK AND THE CUT 213

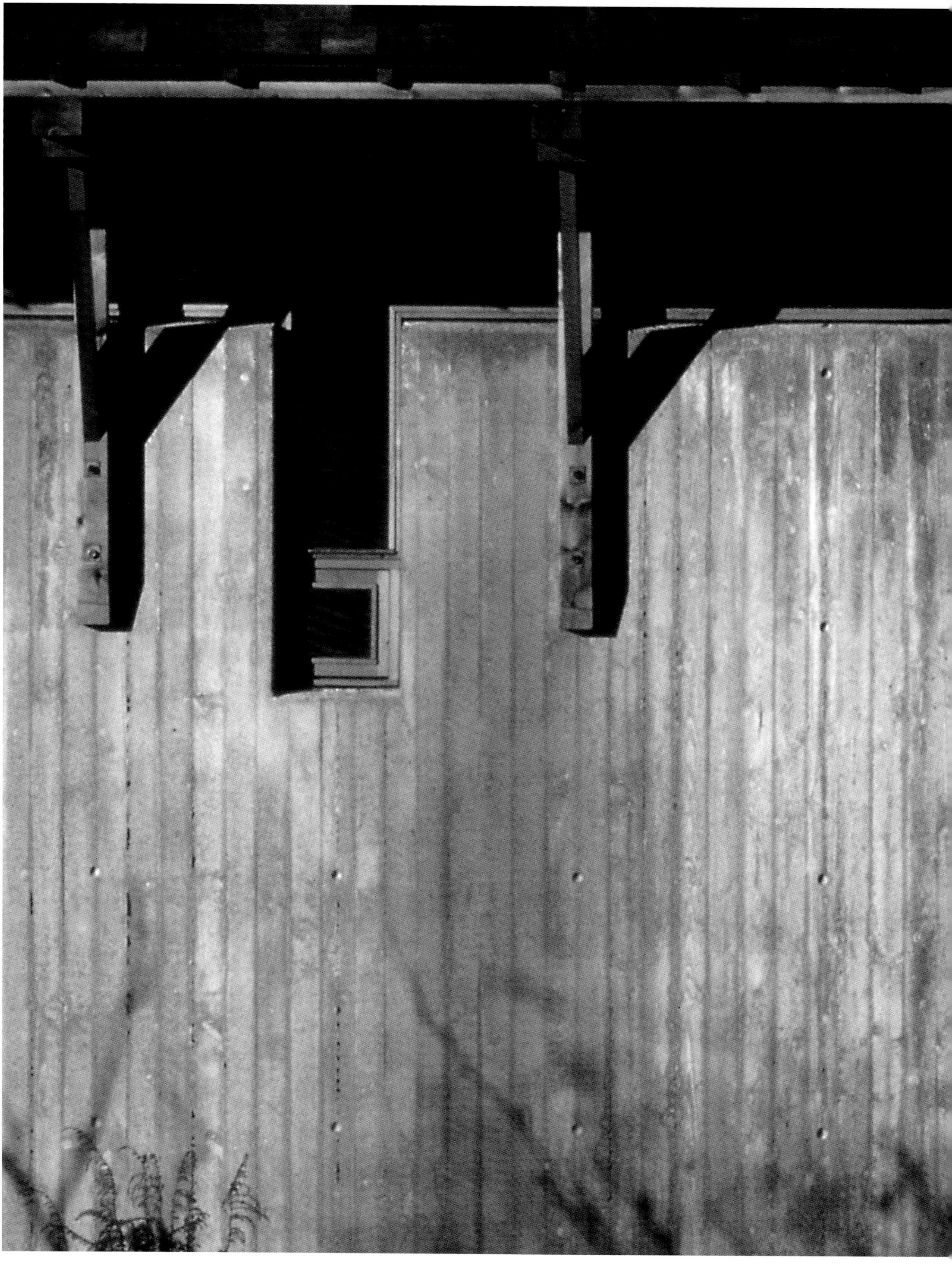

Busk House: Detail of structural relationship between wall and roof, tower for the two sisters, exterior view.

THE MASK AND THE CUT 215

366

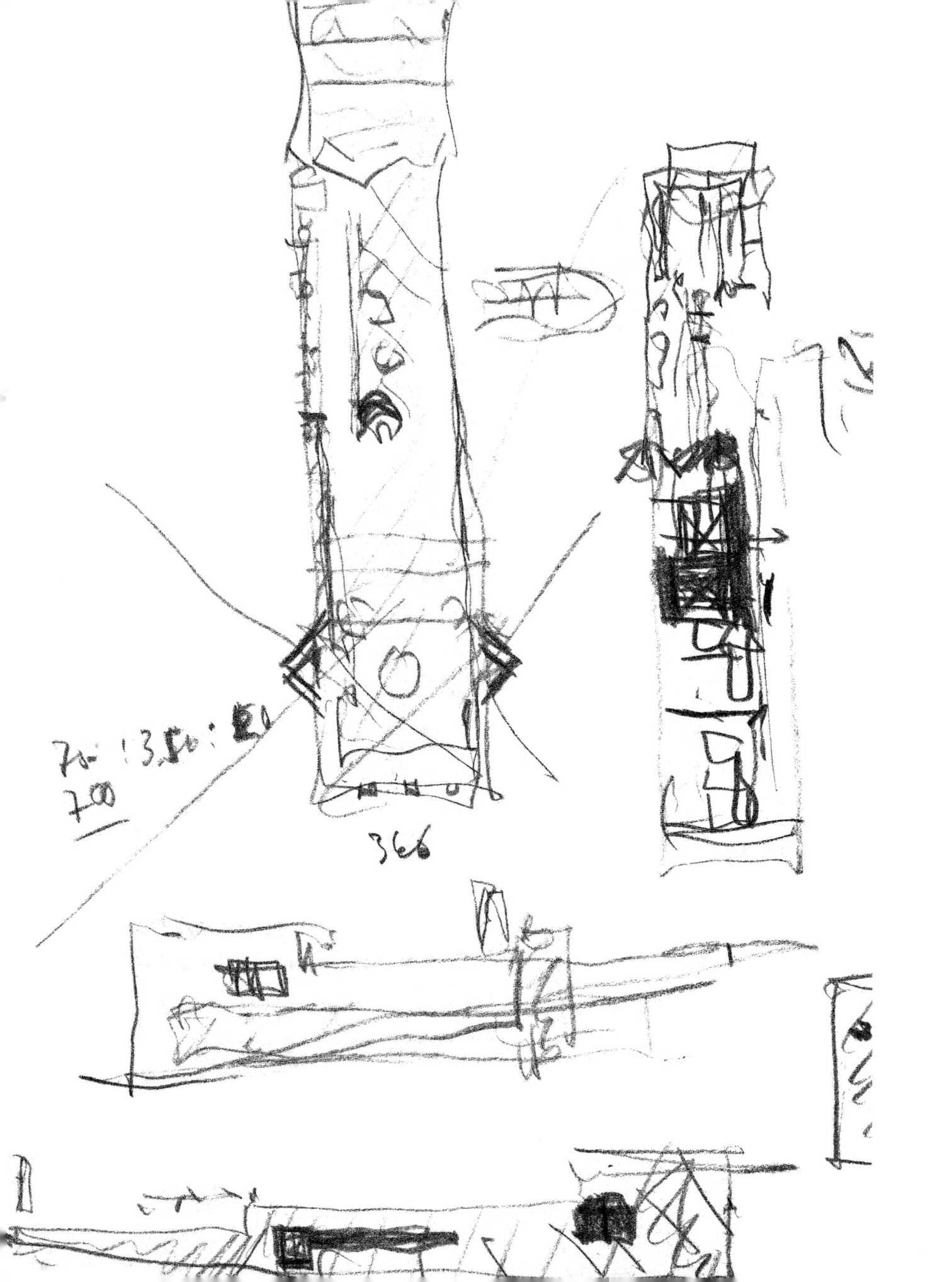

the sea. Here, as in Palladio's villas, summer breezes can ruffle silk shirts. What can sustain one when once again production is moved out into nature? Nature, the hillside, is untouched. You can run around in this nature and scream, "Here it is beautiful!" And the daughters—they will have their fairy tale: their home in a tower. There is something Asian about this house. It is something I have never seen or discovered before now.

Very few of Fehn's buildings have received such immediate popular acclaim as the Busk House, and I think this response surprised him to some extent. All of Fehn's other projects took their time, adjusting and maturing into public acceptance. Today, the house is on the National Heritage List. One reason is that this house is immediately recognized as a spatial figure. The tower, the bridge, and the traditional Scandinavian gallery or corridor are within seconds understood as belonging to a specific place. It wears a mask, and yet it communicates with the surrounding landscape. Christian Norberg-Schulz commented of the residence: "The function of the house is to make human comprehension of the world visible, as in a picture. This understanding is not a subjective product but rather an interpretation of the world; in other words, what it is to near an objective reality."

The refined duality between the inhabitant and nature is controlled by architecture. The catch in this duality is that the user must form an individual narrative within the architecture. Inside the house, a spatial flow follows the terrain. The resident confronts this natural

Busk House: Sketches of plan and section, kitchen, interior corridor.

Aukrust Center, Alvdal, Norway: The hollow wood columns en route, one column in place, plan, section.

spatial sequence with the formal aspects of the various sections: these are masks that form abstractions directed toward nature. This house is caught up in a dream that has diffuse roots in the past but the functional efficiency of the present. Where is the resistance force in this project? If anything, the resistance force is its inherent beauty as a spatial object. This is an architecture that clearly communicates with nature, but it is the mask that catches one's attention and fosters a belief related to harmony. One can provide a mask, a mask that promises identity. **Now architecture itself must be the object. One senses that one is adorning an abstract situation.**

For years, Fehn dreamed of receiving a commission for a long, narrow open space. At school we used to joke and call this type of project a "Fehn long-liner"—even Fehn used the term. He finally had the opportunity to do so when the Norwegian cartoonist Kjell Aukrust, known for his whimsical drawings and stories of rural village life, decided to commission a cultural center to house his work in his hometown of Alvdal, three hundred kilometers north of Oslo. The museum, 1993–96, is perched on a man-made plateau at the lowest point in the valley. It runs parallel to the main road and to the landscape, facing a distant ridge of mountains and a nearby river. An interior concrete "functional" wall serves as the main structure for the exterior walls and defines a distinct section for the building. This section was inspired by a simple room picture: **I made it the same way I used to place my skis against the wall after a ski trip.** On one side of the wall is a long triangular space that houses service functions; on the other, a long thin gallery. The gallery, oriented toward the landscape, has a facade that is broken by a row of large hollow wood columns. Daylight slips in between these columns and mixes with light from a narrow opening that runs along the top of the central concrete wall. Fanning

THE MASK AND THE CUT 219

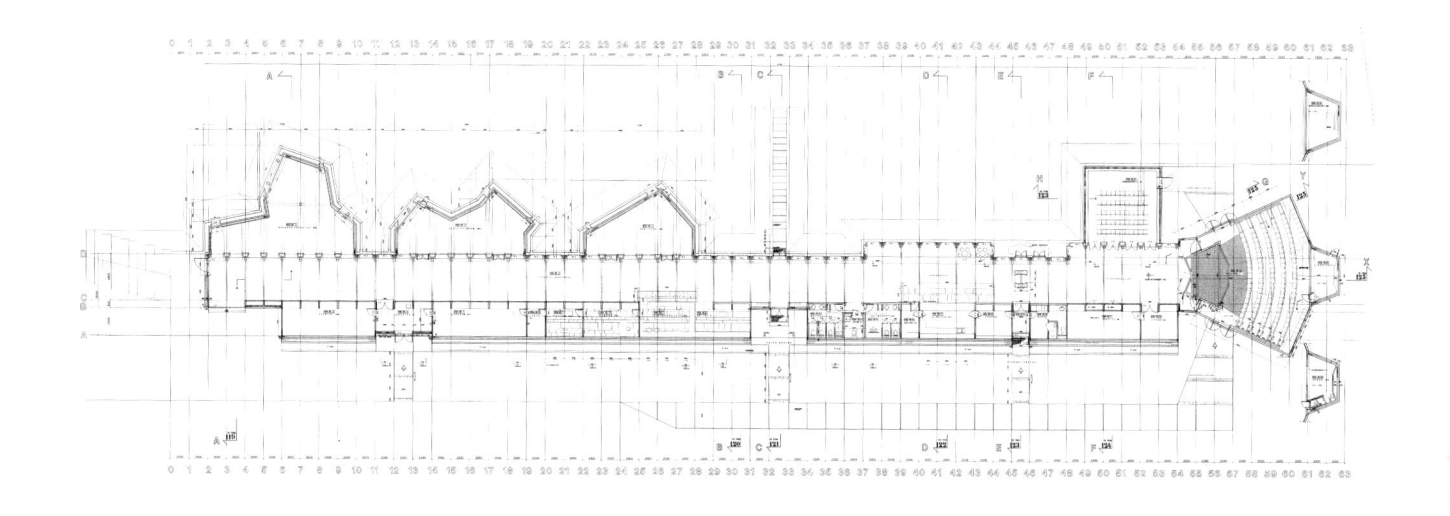

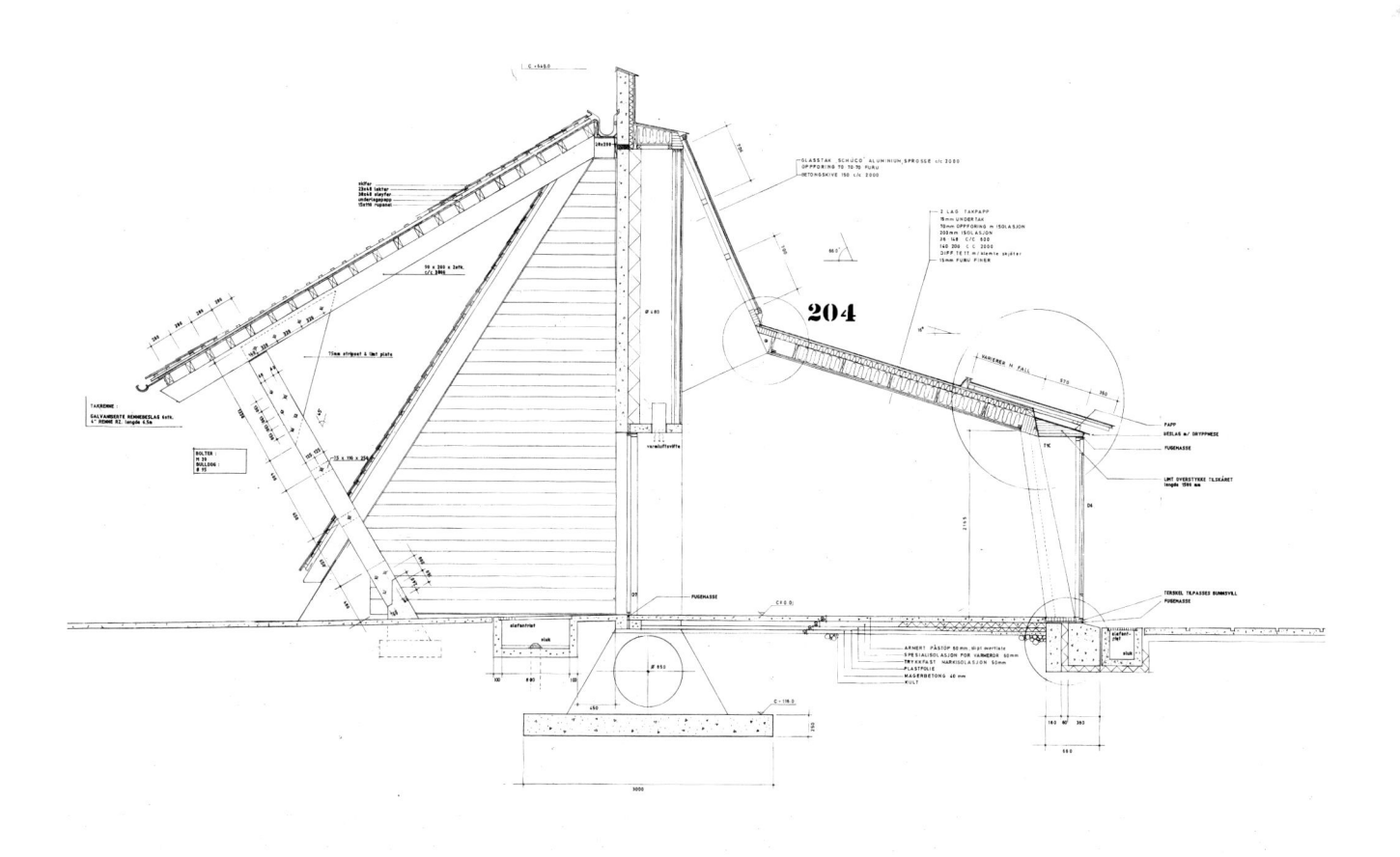

Aukrust Center: Fehn drawing the columns at full scale, interior views of long gallery.

THE MASK AND THE CUT 221

Aukrust Center:
Exterior views.

222   THE PATTERN OF THOUGHTS

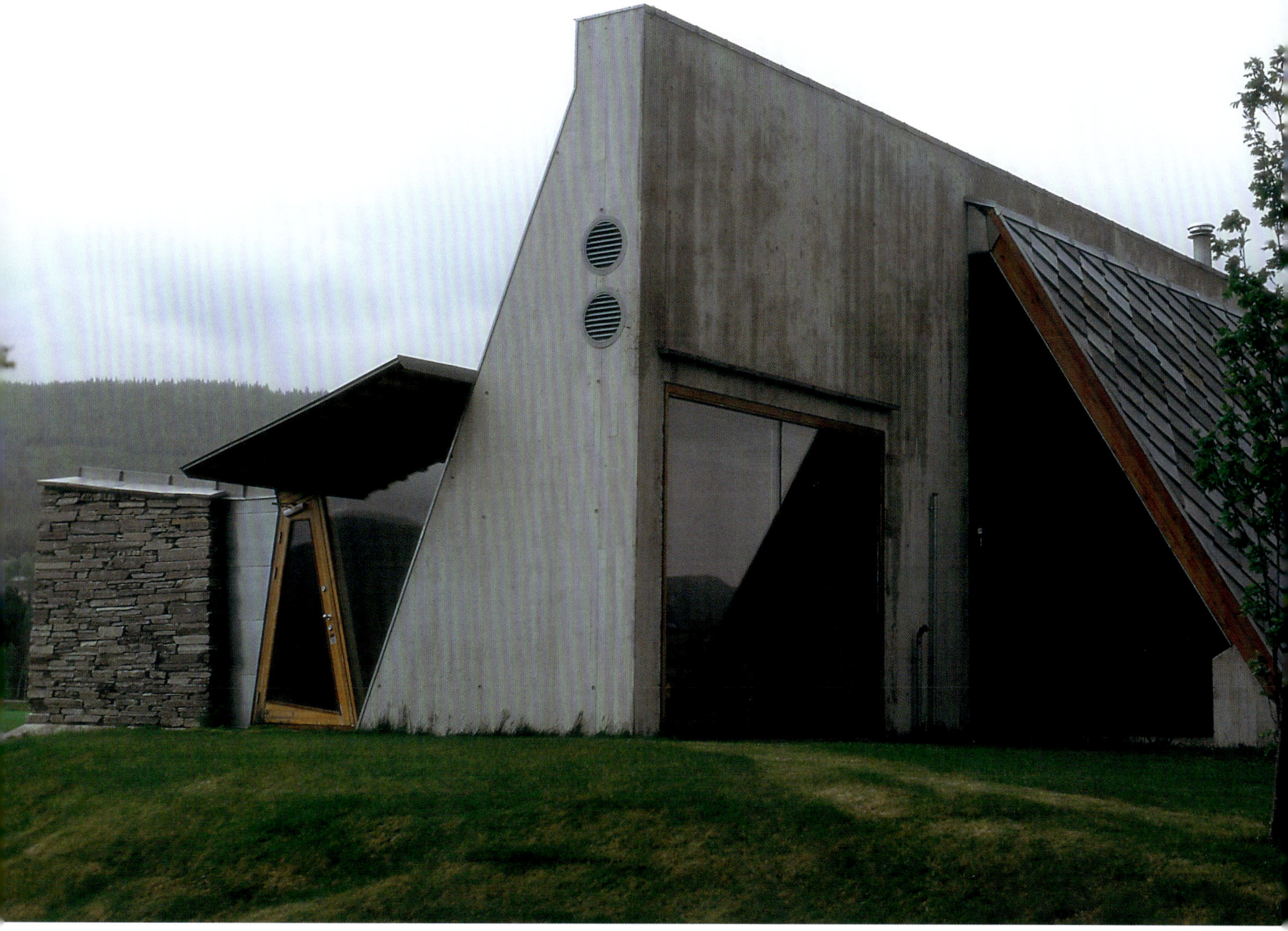

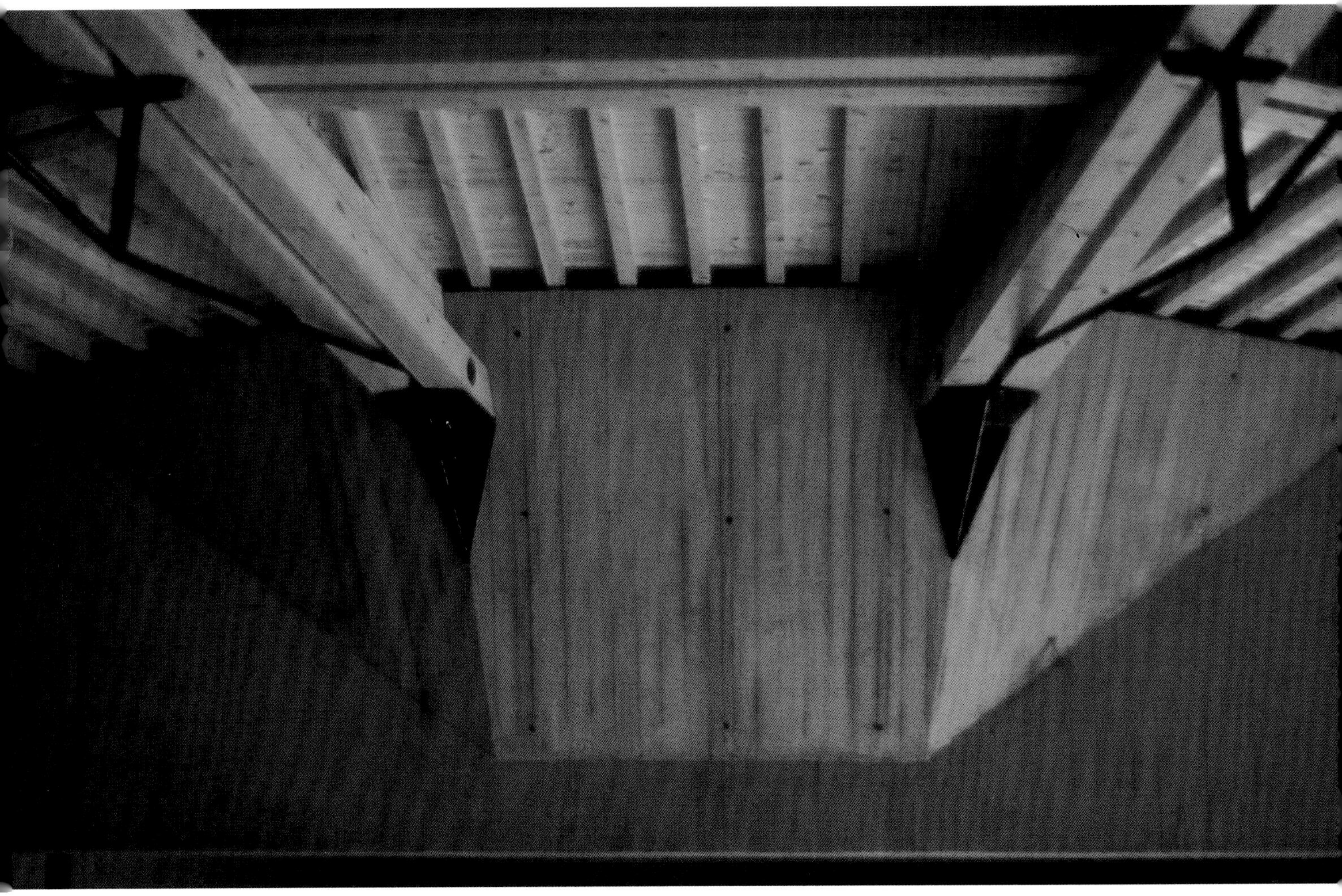

Aukrust Center:
Ceiling in auditorium,
exterior views with
built masks.

THE MASK AND THE CUT 225

Wasa Ship Museum, Stockholm: Sketch, "Life dozes off. Life after death. The joining in darkness"; section sketches; site plan and section.

out from the gallery are smaller, irregularly shaped exhibition rooms. While these have direct access to the main gallery, they retain an individual character.

The various materials, their uses and interrelationships, form another type of mask, one that is independent of the conceptual attitude of the project. Each material adds its tactile and visual character to the expression. The exterior is not a facade but a mask that faces the exterior surroundings. Once when we were driving up to the museum Fehn told me: **As you get older, it is what you wear, the clothes closest to your body, that are the most important. The material that touches your skin feels like a mask, a construction that you add to your body, and it becomes part of you. This is the way it is with architecture, too.**

Linked to his interest in the mask was Fehn's concept of the cut in the landscape, the cut in the skin of the earth. This too had a connection to the tattoo, but the cut had no mask, no preconceived image other than darkness. Instead, it revealed another type of spatial potential. At the point of the cut, the division between above and below ground is the straightest of all lines. The resulting horizon is inherent to this cut, and Fehn regards this as the starting point for all architecture, as the beginning. The image of the cut is something quite close to Louis Kahn's "sanctuary of art, the treasury of the shadows" in his silence and light diagram of 1968.

Fehn made a clear statement about the cut in his 1982 competition project for the Wasa Ship Museum in Stockholm. Using an old dry dock, he returned a seventeenth-century battleship, salvaged in 1961, to its position below sea level. The question of whether the boat belongs over or under the line of the sea is the critical one: should one wake this ship from its Sleeping Beauty state? Fehn chose the somber light and slumbering quiet below the surface. The ship keeps its horizon and its dim enclosure, and it is the visitor who makes the journey, entering with the light at the level of the top of the mast and walking down to the ship at the bottom of the sea. The shipwreck no longer has the capacity to move the horizon, but the cut freezes the moment of the journey.

In 1988, Fehn was asked to design a gallery at the tip of an island in the Oslo Fjord. There are a great number of islands in this area, some only granite boulders rising out of the sea. In fact, Fehn's own summer cottage was on Hvasser, a neighboring island. For years, Fehn kayaked, swam, and took boat trips in this archipelago, and the land- and seascape was the background for his boat and horizon sketches and watercolors. The site, a bare rock peninsula facing south, is called World's End. Its granite formations are large, polished boulders separated by fissures. Fehn did not need to gather additional information. His placement of the gallery intensified the space between the room of nature and the room of architecture. They share the same borders; the contours of the granite formation strengthen those of the built formation. Again, it is daylight that mediates the space between the two layers. The light, modulated by the new structure, generates new spaces, but as it enters into the rock crevice it remains the "old" light belonging to the cut in the landscape. In this project, Fehn performs a delicate balancing act between nature

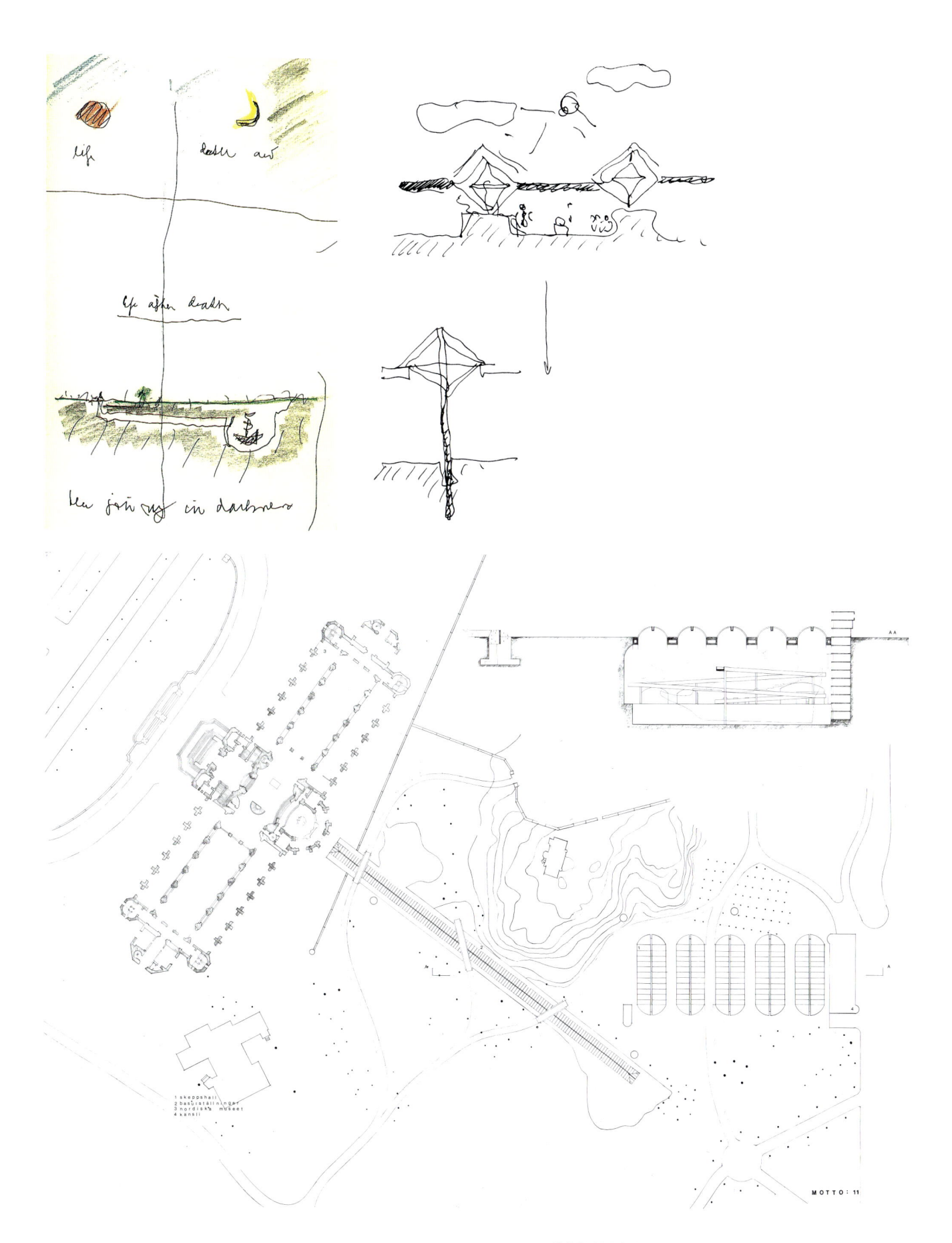

THE MASK AND THE CUT 227

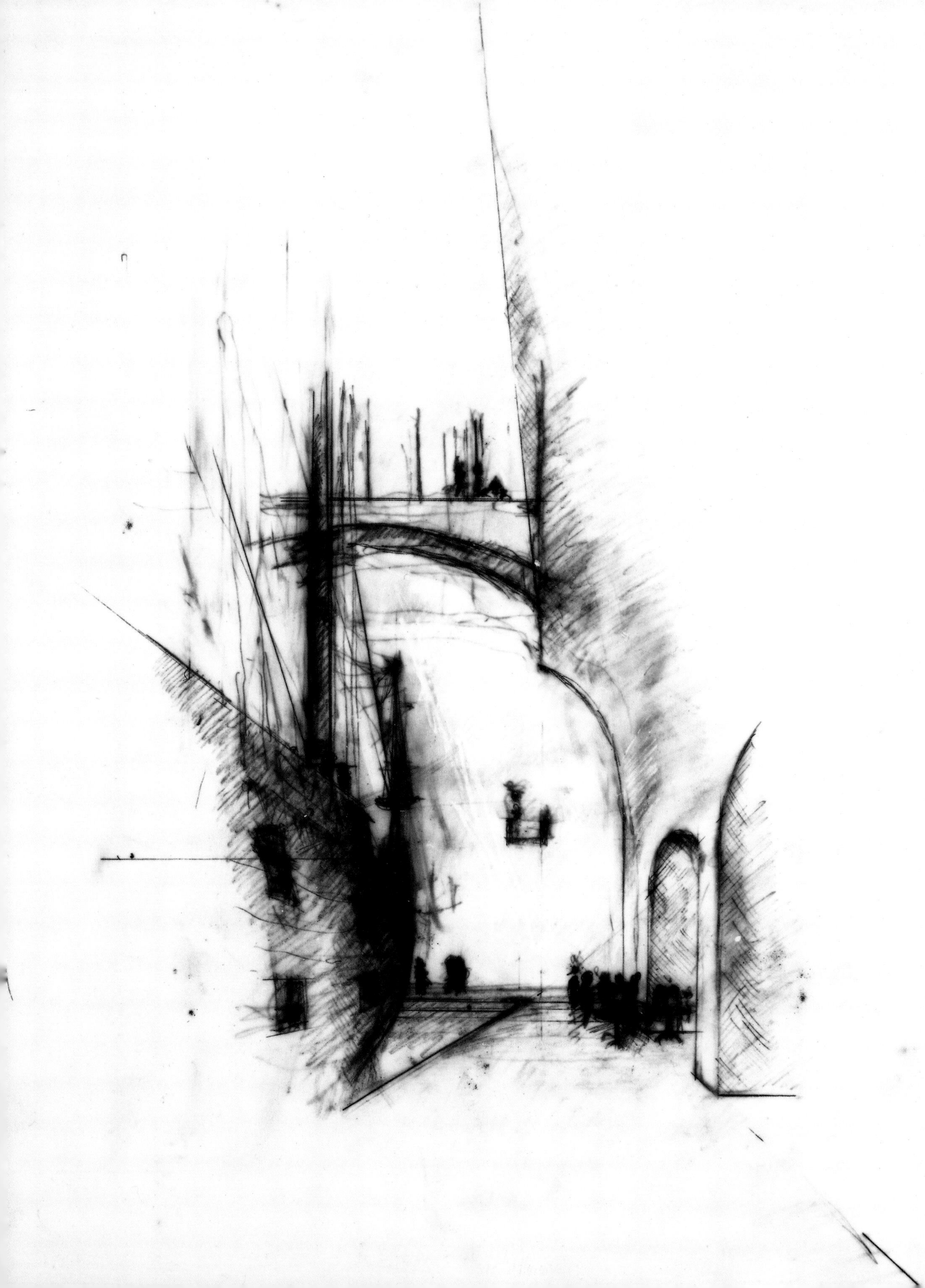

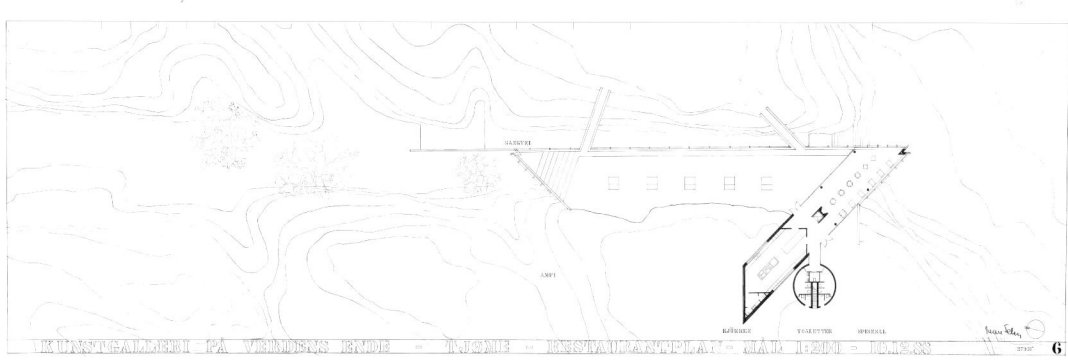

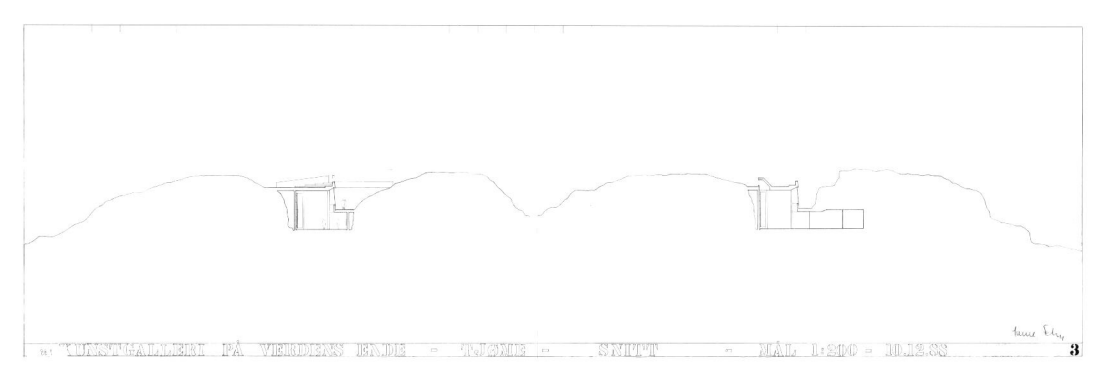

Gallery, World's End, Tjøme, Norway: View of the site, plan of entrance level, sections.

OPPOSITE Wasa Ship Museum: Interior sketch.

THE MASK AND THE CUT

and architecture. He sees the resistance force of nature as an intricate part of the scheme. The old light of the crevice is transformed into the light of the gallery, just as the illumination of the ruins at Hamar is transformed into the illumination of the added structure. Fehn is both precise and consistent in how he paraphrases nature. Once the room of nature and the room of architecture reach an agreement, the struggle is over and the visitor may enter.

Another event required Fehn's attention during this period. In 1989, the Oslo School of Architecture built one of Hejduk's projects, "Security," at full scale in front of the capital's old city hall. Fehn and Hejduk, whose friendship had withstood the barriers of distance and time, were brought back together at the opening celebration. Fehn wrote an introduction for the book that was published after the project was completed, which concludes with the following paragraph: **John Hejduk has created a world where the boundaries are erased. The architecture floats in a universe, extending from the cut of the surgeon's scalpel into the inner organs of the human body, to his own section through the veil of invisibility into the manifold activities of the angels, to the vast landscape where the site is cleared for "The Cemetery for the Ashes of Thought."**

The two architects shared certain elements of their vocabularies, though each manipulated them to different ends and to singular forms of expression. When Hejduk died in 2000, Fehn lost an intellectual companion and a connection that had eased some of the isolation he felt in Oslo. He added New York to his Paris-Venice vocabulary and from this drew personal energy and inspiration.

The mask and the cut are connected. The earth is a mask for forgotten objects; the cut discloses their hiding places. The cut has no will, no expression except as a border between light and dark. It is in the small opening between these two situations that Fehn finds his most intense expressions.

Sketch, 1987, "It is raining in New York."

Jag regner att i New York

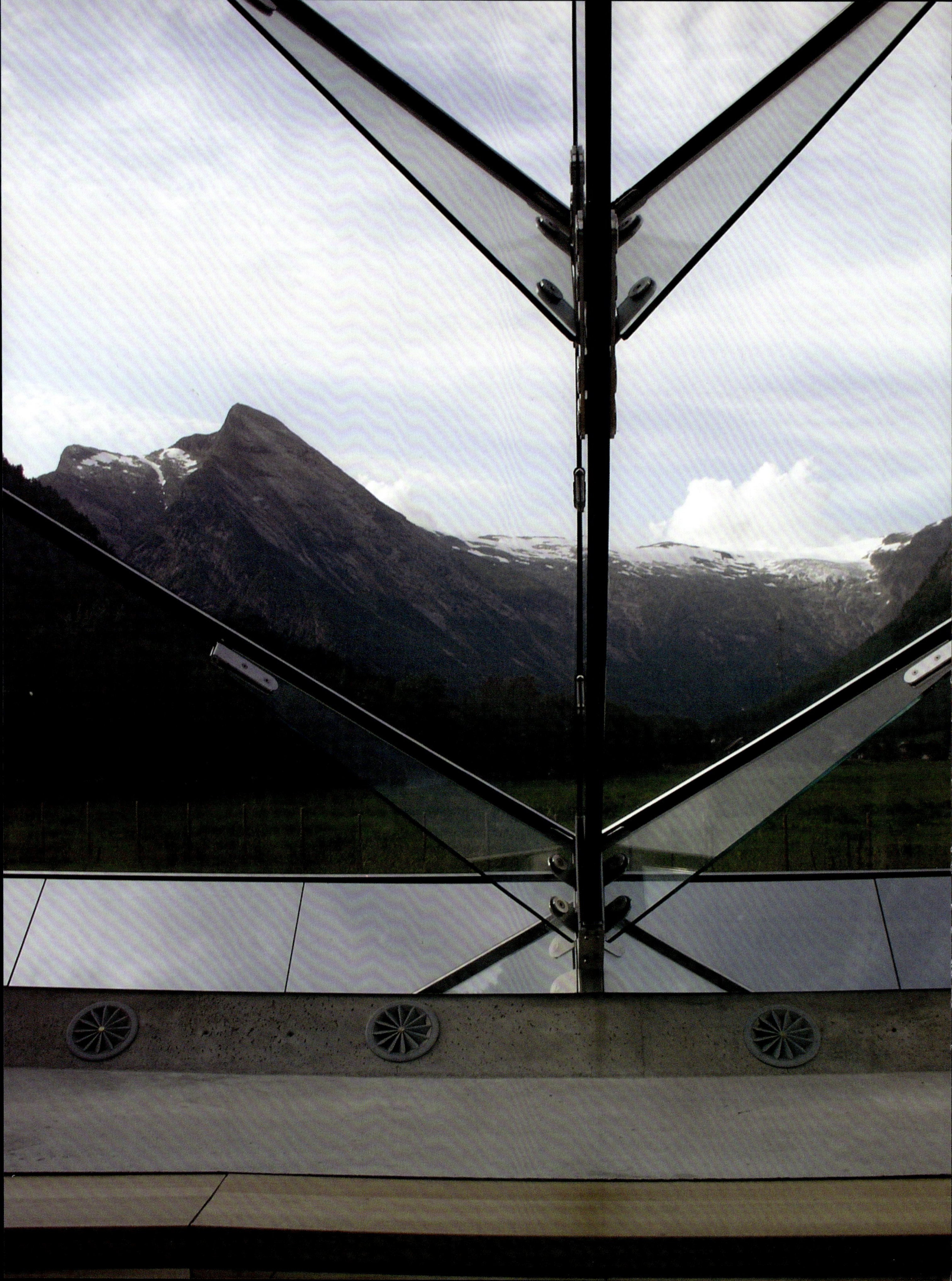

CHAPTER 10

PARAPHRASING NATURE

Nature as place has always been important to Fehn, but it is not easy to differentiate between his use of "earth" and "nature." Nature has an endless, eternal dimension; animals abide within this realm, while human beings seem to totter between infinite nature and finite earth. In concluding that humans are able to conceptually separate their individual presence from the ongoing presence of nature, Fehn envisions a spatial duality between that which is nature and that which is constructed, and in the long run, it is the constructed that capitulates to nature, not vice versa. The earth as a limited or determined base is the starting point for the added man-made structure. Equally, the association between nature and the concept of place has been for Fehn characterized by a vocabulary filled with confrontation. His most essential tool as an architect is the ability to read "nature" in its fullest sense and, from this, comprehend spatial potential. Once this reading is achieved, it is feasible to release these latent possibilities into architecture and its relationship to the bounded "earth."

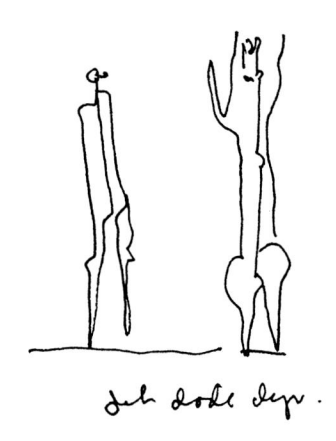

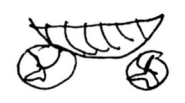

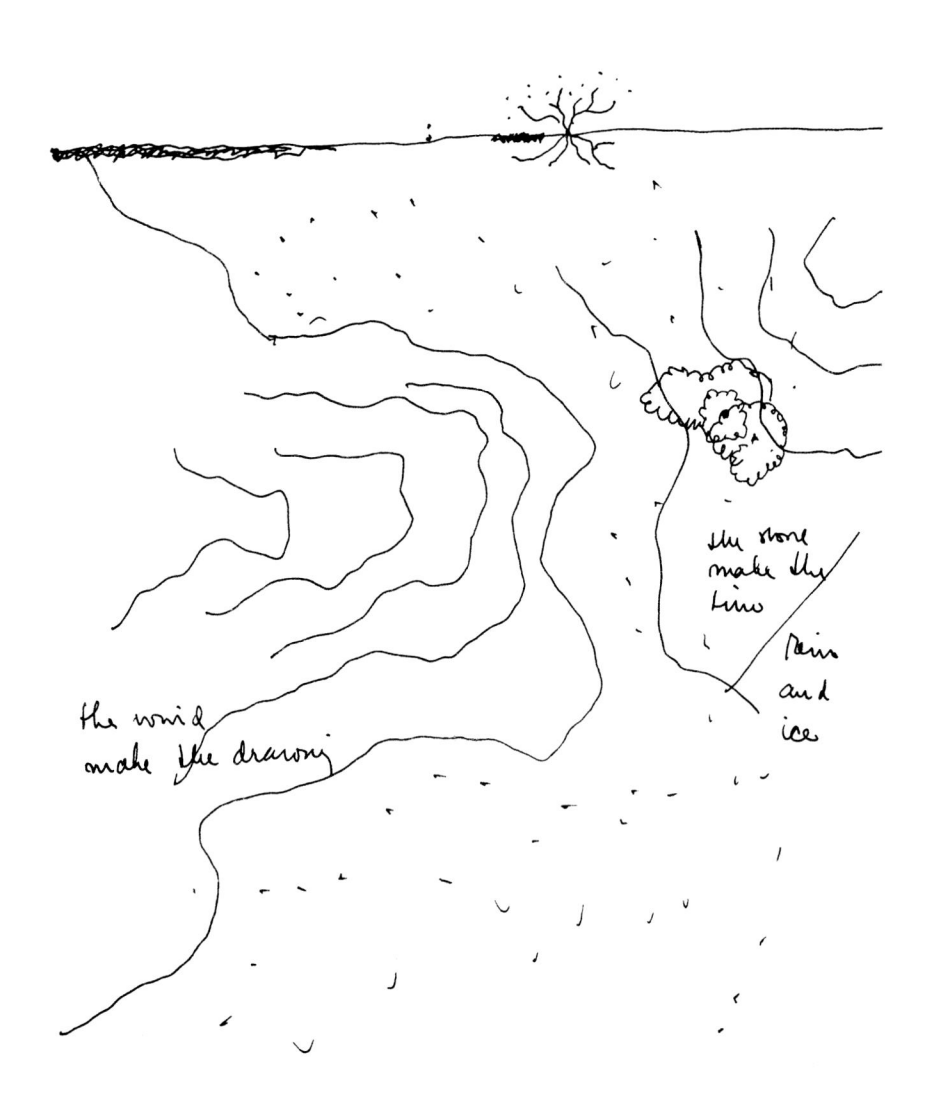

Sketch, 1998, "The dead animal"; sketch, 1982, "The wind makes the drawing. The stone makes the time. Rain and ice."

OPPOSITE Sketch, 1982, of animal in man and man in animal.

PAGE 232 Norwegian Glacier Museum, Fjærland.

The majority of Fehn's projects have been sited in relatively untouched landscapes. The architect often uses the word "nature" to refer to these landscapes, but nature can just as easily suggest an urban condition in the development of a project. It is merely the content and context that change. Fehn has always been able to read a given site with precision, not just in physical terms but also in terms of its architectural capacity. He takes great care in interpreting this tactile spatial identity and through this process gains a more precise sense of place. In a time when the limitations of the earth and the impact of architecture's consumption of material are more and more apparent, the elements of this creative approach are inspiring. Fehn draws a clear distinction between comprehending nature or a landscape at a distance and comprehending the potential spatial identity within this landscape.

The use of daylight has always been an essential part of the analysis of landscape. Decisions about where and how light should enter a built space evolve simultaneously with the interpretation of place; thus the light coming into each individual space is the result of this interpretation as well as of specific requirements. These requirements are found not in the client's program but in a reductive questioning of where and in what way light will be involved. This use of natural light is not a scientific approach but rather the result of a detailed investigation of the site's potential and the impact of Fehn's architectural "assault." Through this structural exploration, natural light arrives as an offering to the space.

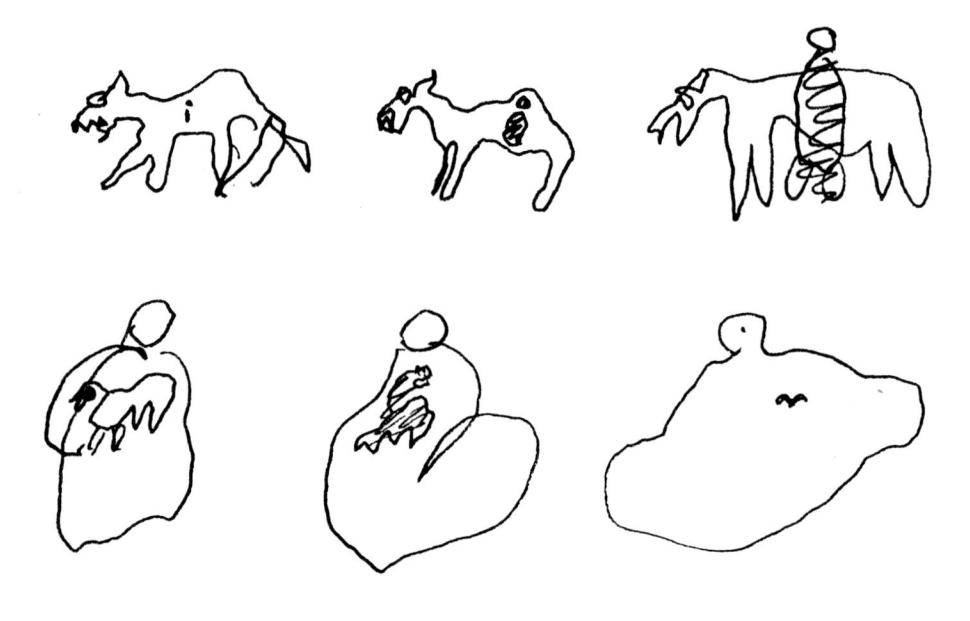

The competition project for the Norwegian Pavilion for the 1970 World Exposition in Osaka, Japan, is revealing in relation to Fehn's manner of paraphrasing nature. Pollution was the theme of the fair. Fehn's proposal is an interior public solution, a man-made nature, in which a given space—an existing wood structure—is filled with two balloonlike structures of transparent canvas, one on top of the other, that breathe air in and out like a lung. The smaller, upper balloon inflates and deflates with the changing air pressure, and the larger, lower volume maintains a constant pressure that holds or stabilizes the form of the balloons as a room. The pulsating motion within the space simulates a living organism. A platform in the lower balloon is accessed by two bridges that run the length of the volume.

When the object is left behind and one comes with a moral program called pollution, how can we exhibit this, how can we materialize it? Osaka is a large industrial "pot." I decided I would make an artificial unit, a lung, a limited area that could control its air, clean air. The building was like a crate without the ground, without the sky. I built into the old existing structure, thus imprisoning the progression of the spatial movement. Here, even construction was given limitations. It disclosed the repertoire between two balloons: first one inflates and then the other. Together they form a creature that lies there and talks. The two balloons symbolize breathing; inside it is possible to feel and breathe clean air and smell the fresh scent that contrasts with what lies outside.

In this project, it is the architectural object that stages a public discussion. Many years later, in 1992, he assigned a class project related to that year's World's Fair in Seville. His classroom lectures made it very clear that architects must face the consequences of their actions: **The world the Expo presents you with is your world. You cannot cover or hide from it. Now, when the whole world is presenting its individual "wholeness," one must accept more than ever the search for a common identity that does not exist, but one must find an answer anyway . . . How do you write dimension today when it no longer belongs to a sense of place?**

One theme that runs throughout Fehn's sketches and notations is the correspondence between a comprehension of life and death for humans and for nature. Architecture and the human life cycle have a connection, but architecture's true content is nature. In Fehn's architectural vocabulary, nature is not compartmentalized or separated from the connection of life and death. The landscape does not exist as a revolving door through which the same landscape will return over and over again. Its life has a death. The bond between humans and animals and the understanding of the animal in humankind is also part of this discussion. **The animal has a relationship to silence, and if one is going to be a great hunter one must near the animal's silence . . . In Mexico, all sculpture is about the animal. Humans appear in the animal's creation. One is in a sense the human in the animal. We have underestimated this relationship . . . Don't take from me the human in the animal! Wisdom came through the animal's eyes. One was able to read the animal through fear and silence, and one lived and settled in a concept of nature . . . The conversation with the heavens was through the rock on the ground, and the conversation with the horizon, through the steps in a stair . . .**

When the animal became an object, it began to separate the human from the animal. The animal is no longer in architecture or art. We see it as a monster, and it is no longer imprisoned. The animal has left us. Humans have lost the concept of nature that was once deciphered through the reflection in the animal's eyes. Plants and trees do not have the dimension the animal expresses.

One has freed the human that once lived in the animal. One does not sacrifice the human in the animal, one releases it; one frees humanness in oneself and releases another concept of nature. The animal thinks it will live forever, but once humans introduce a death concept, construction is born. The great constructions always evolve within a concept related to death.

Traces of the rhythm and movement the animal gave the human are left behind, but mankind is no longer able to create new places; it conquers them, plans them, as if one can see everything from above the earth, so that projects land on the surface. They don't grow up unless they find a rock or a step. The only thing that owns the earth today is the leaf as it falls in a stream . . . **Architecture was born of movement and sensibility to existence. It has always been connected to the realm of sensitivity. The animal knows the earth, its smells, its different winds. The animal's eyes are not directed to the heavens. When the animal left the human, our dialogue with nature was silenced . . .**

XX Y

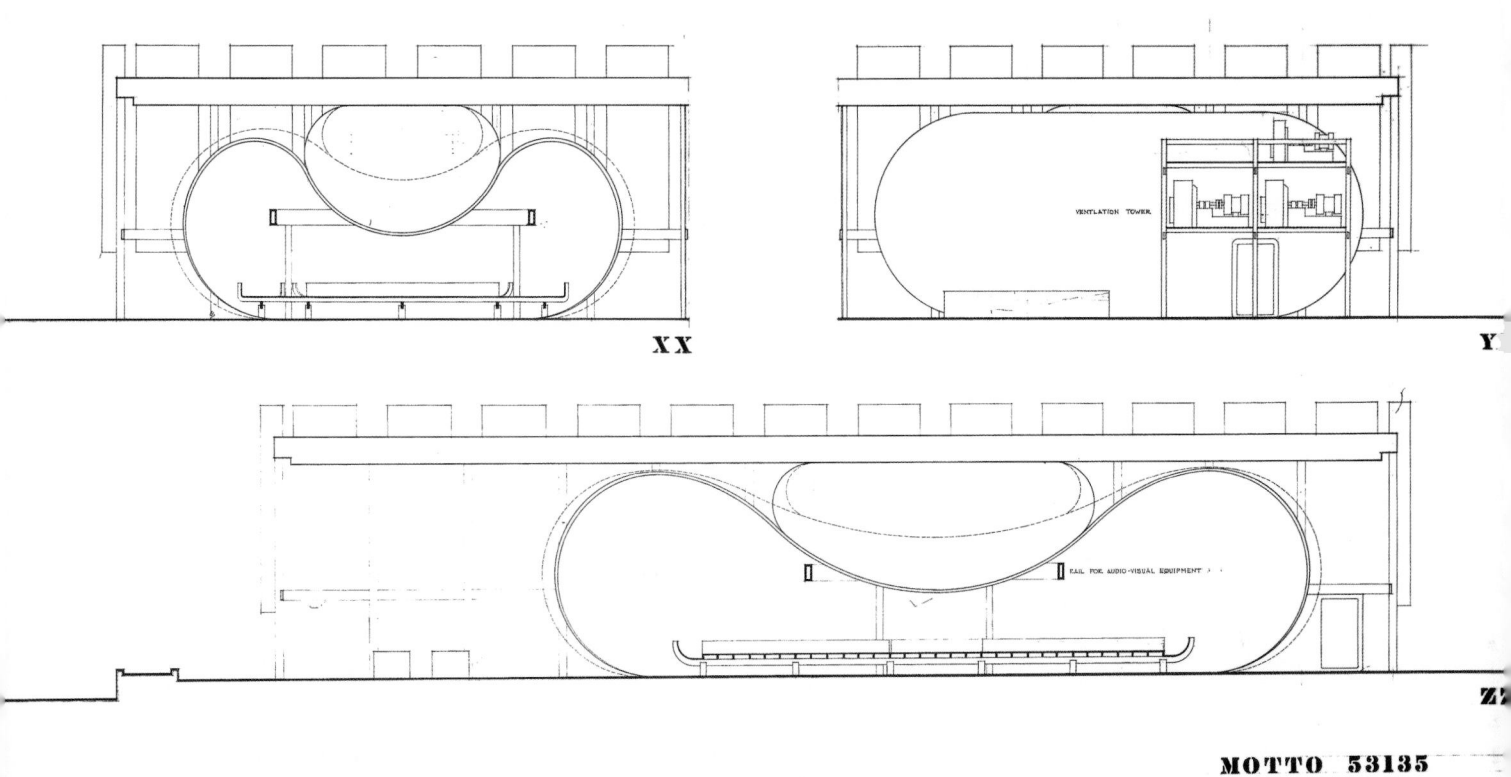

MOTTO 53135

Norwegian Pavilion for the World Exposition in Osaka: Sections, plan sketch.

PARAPHRASING NATURE

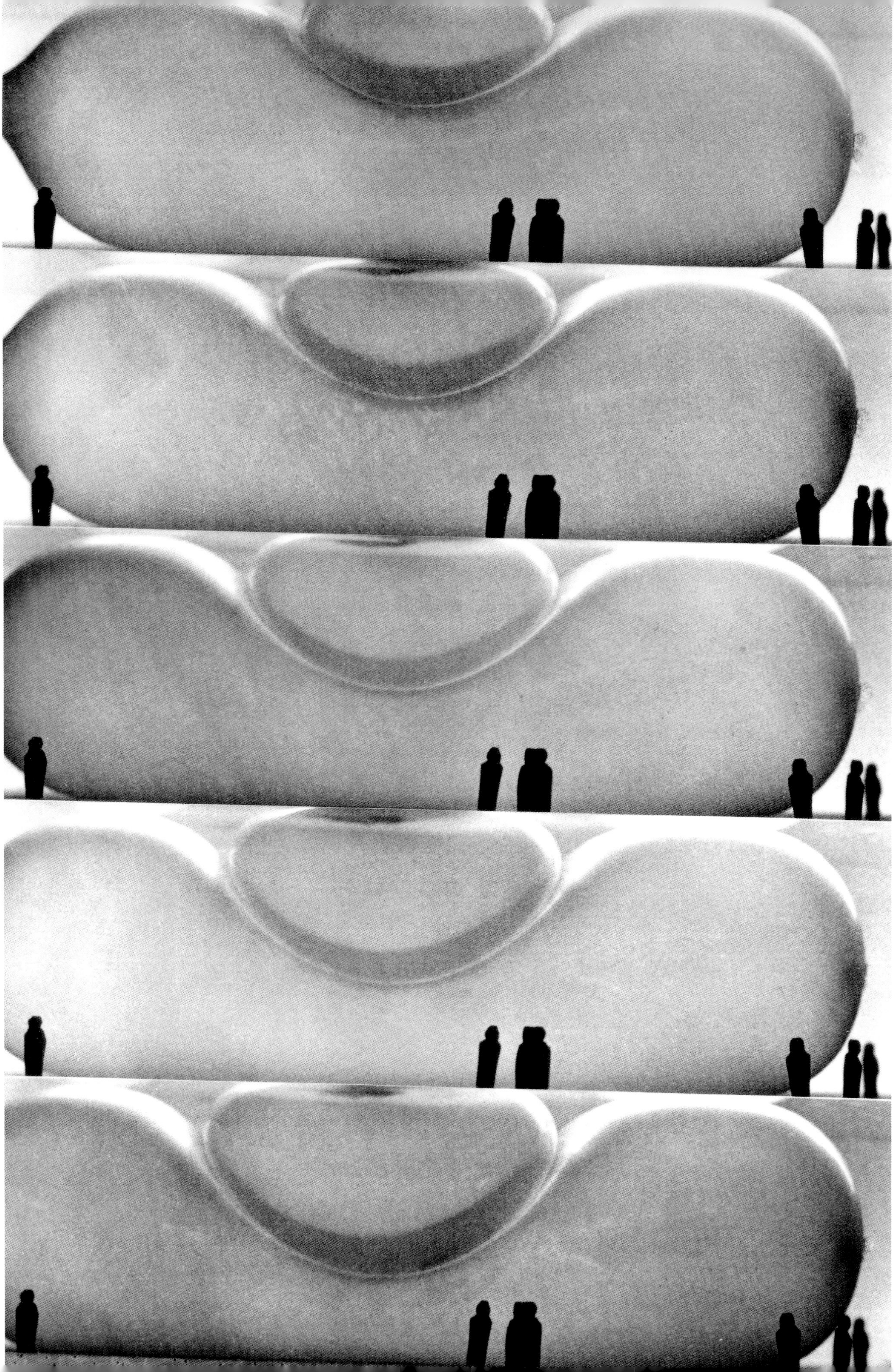

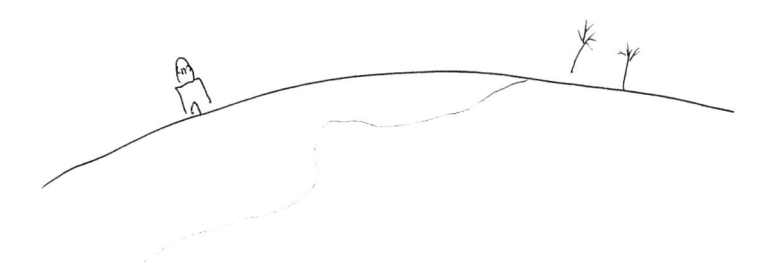

Sketch, "Aladdin's rug in a balloon"; sketch, 1993, "Towards lightness, a transparent architecture."

OPPOSITE Norwegian Pavilion, Osaka: The model at work.

PARAPHRASING NATURE

There is no dialogue today. Man has no place, and therefore he goes back into himself because nature is no longer internalized as instinctive knowledge. Humans live in a condition that is self-centered, and with this comes analysis. One revises and adjusts one's existence in relation to many points. The built stone is never placed correctly, and the dialogue with the animal no longer exists. We have created a correction, a revelation of a dream, and with the dream comes passion. In these dreams are new limitations, a little heaven. It is the dream that has become the new reformer in relation to the home.

Fehn has often commented that the Norwegian Glacier Museum in Fjærland, 1989–91, was the most difficult and challenging of all his commissions; he would return in 2006–7 to build an addition. The site and its surroundings are so immense that any insertion would be experienced as a mediocre intrusion. Relative to this kind of nature, even the most robust structure is too weak. Fehn solved this challenge in a surprising manner. The project did not develop from the idea of a building but from the forming of an object: the image was a hollow stone that had rolled down the mountainside and, like other stones in the area, nestled firmly in the valley. The main body of the museum is a rectangular concrete volume. Simple geometric forms superimposed on the rectilinear figure give an identity to the building and also offer a clear contrast to the strong site. Platforms atop the museum afford views to the Jostedal Glacier and the Fjærland Fjord. Inside, a cut along the length of the roof allows natural light to enter the main spaces.

The man-made stone of the museum has a unique ability to communicate with the powerful surroundings. A dialogue evolves between architecture and nature, and visitors experience the powerful landscape in a new and stimulating way through the building. In this sense, nature is not taken for granted; rather, it is tested. Visitors on the viewing platforms meet a synthesis of building and landscape. The interior rooms retain a specific character, but they are always secondary to the landscape "room." The hollowness in the image of the stone is important, since its limitations recognize nature's spatial enormity.

Norwegian Glacier Museum: Looking toward the site; the museum as a hollow stone in the valley.

The daylight that penetrates the interior through the slanted wall and the roof diminishes in intensity toward the far end of the building. This rather dim illumination reinforces the difference between inside and outside.

The strength of this primal building, the stone that has attached itself to the earth, is clear. The fog that surrounds the building or the rain that gives the concrete a new layer only enriches the understanding and experience of the environment. Fehn says that before construction, he was not sure either of his "room picture" or of how the inhabitants of the area would react to the building. The creative process was nerve-racking, and once again he risked uncertainty. The challenge first and foremost is the grandeur of the glacial site one experiences from atop the museum. One leaves something of oneself on the viewing platforms, something of the soul.

Fehn regularly brought up Nordic rock carvings from the Bronze Age in lectures and through projects. These primitive, symbolic cuts were almost an extension of Fehn's own sketches, hinting at a particular correlation between fact and invention. The boat, weapons, animals, sexual organs, tools, and small spatial indents that were carved not only sparked his imagination but also set in motion his conceptual understanding of space. He has commented that these figures do not refer to the horizon, that they float unencumbered in their own space. Without a horizon, there is no

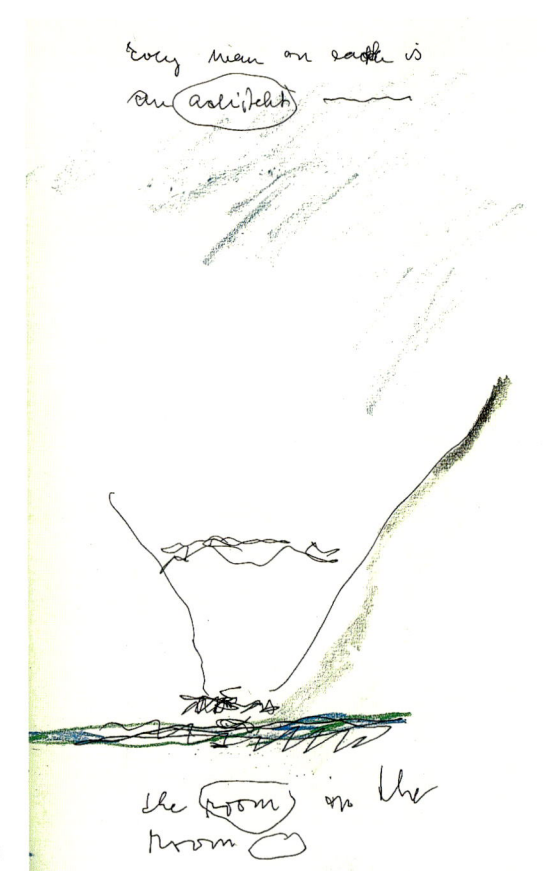

Sketch, 1996, "Every man on earth is an architect. The room in the room."

Norwegian Glacier Museum: Sections, plan, model.

OVERLEAF Norwegian Glacier Museum.

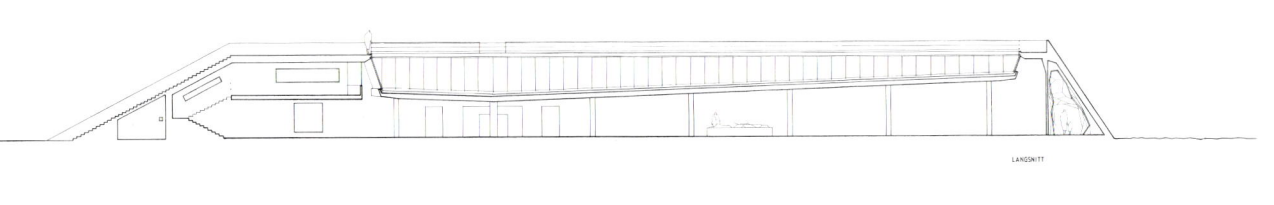

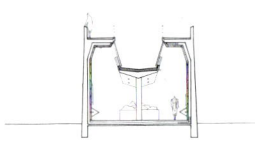

242 THE PATTERN OF THOUGHTS

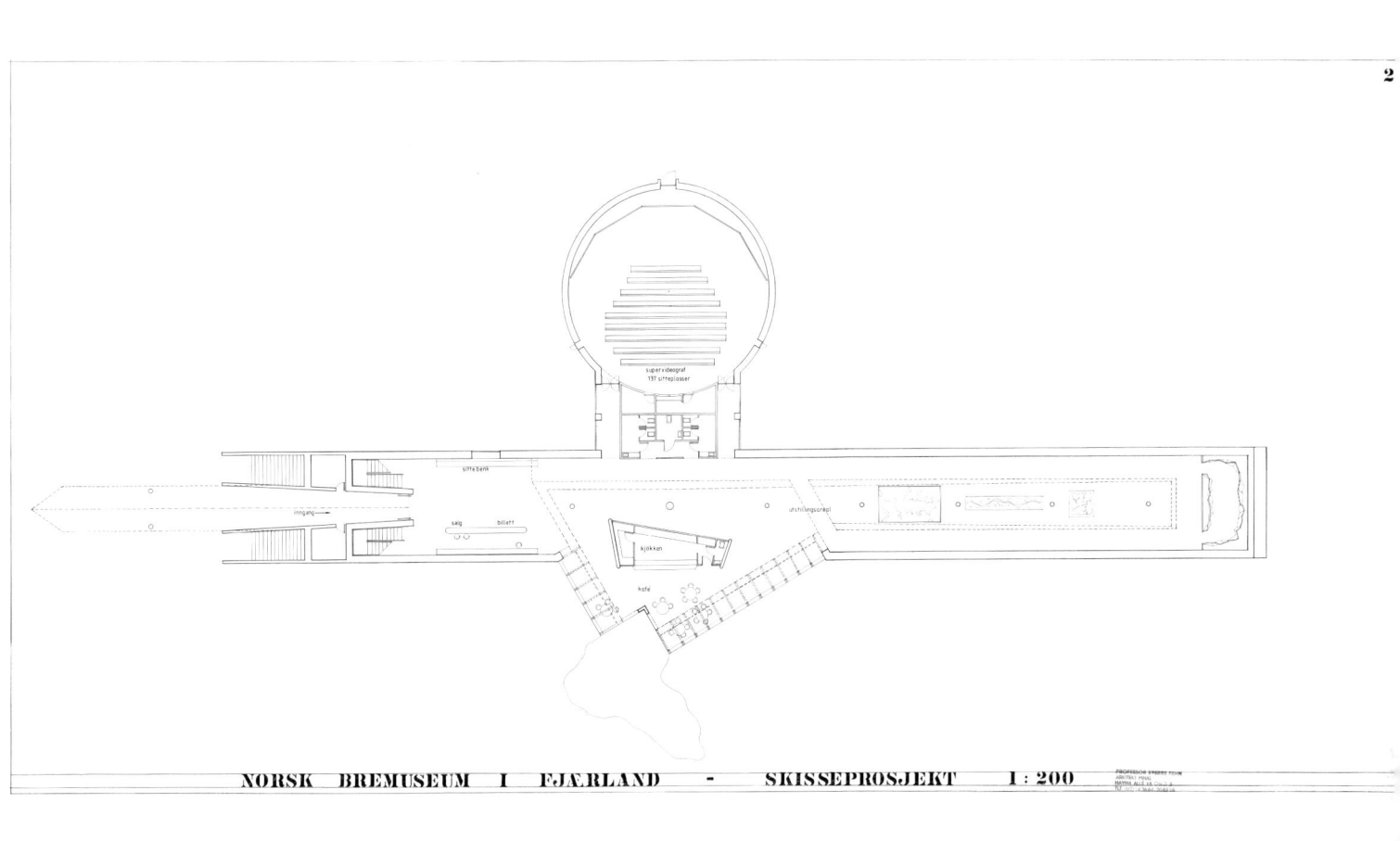

NORSK BREMUSEUM I FJÆRLAND - SKISSEPROSJEKT 1:200

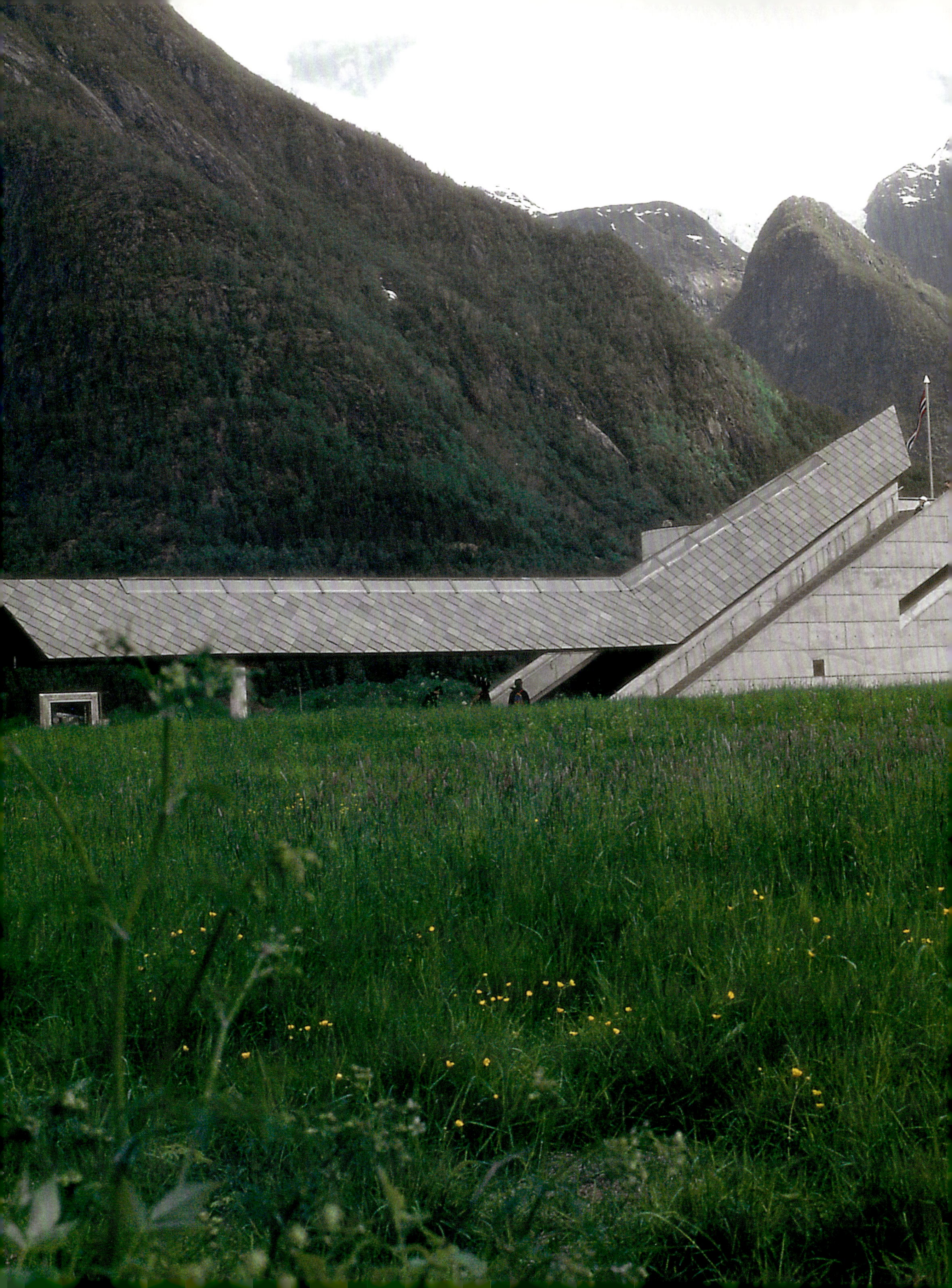

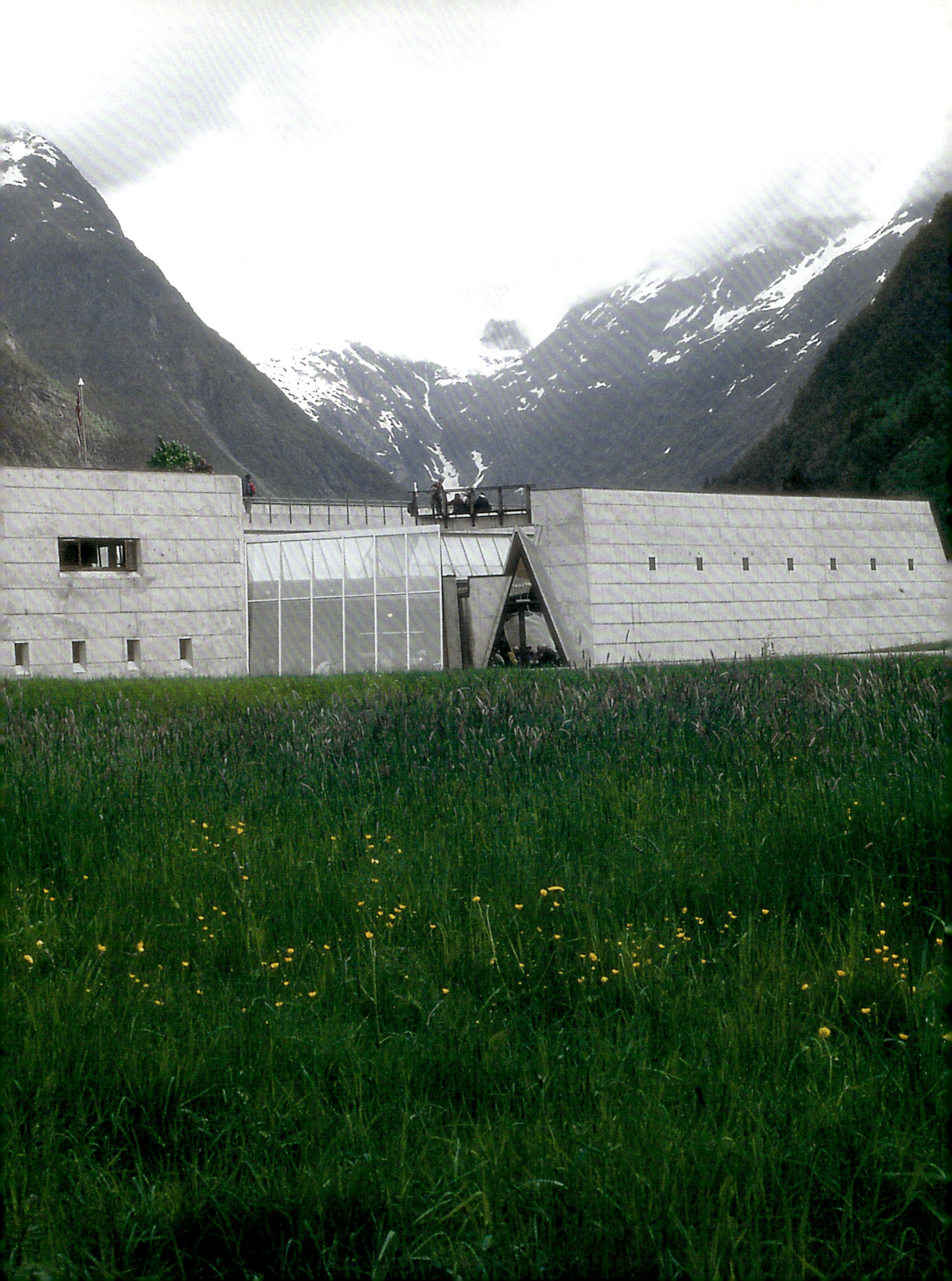

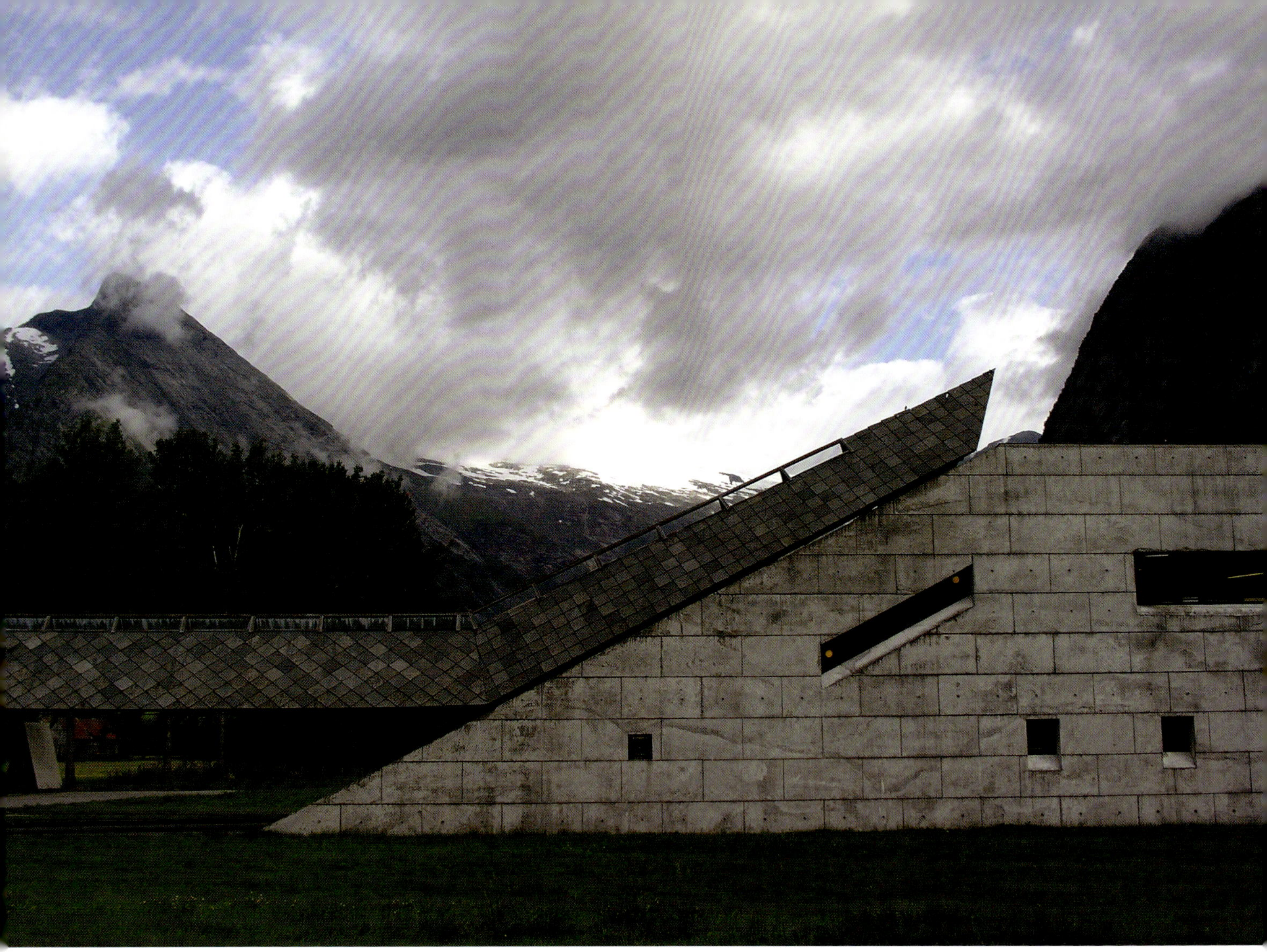

Norwegian Glacier Museum: Exterior view, view of addition, interior views.

PARAPHRASING NATURE 247

Norwegian Glacier Museum: Window details in addition, view of addition.

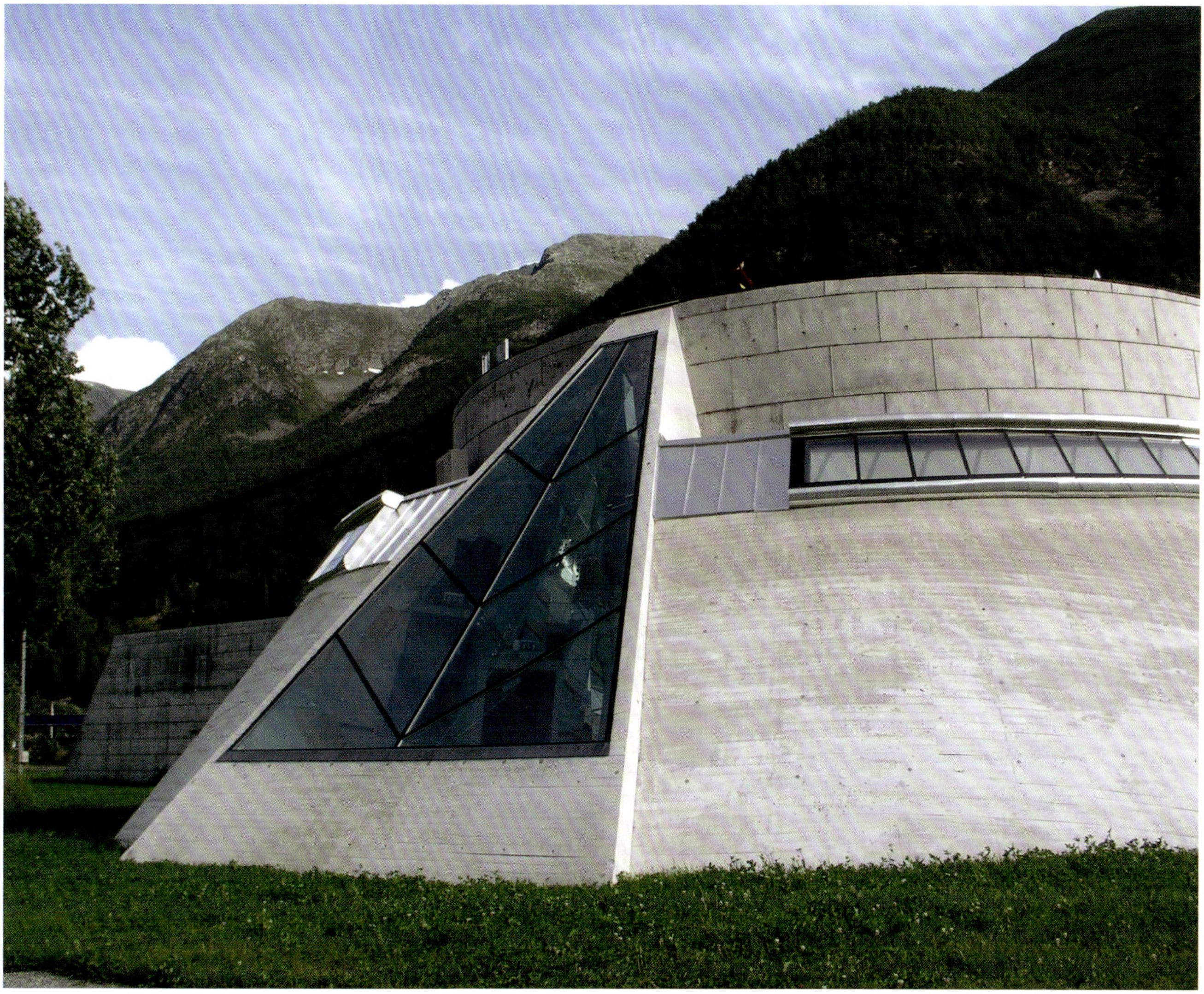

relationship between near and far; thus the object is not restricted by a precise scale or dimension. In this context, as objects free from the horizon, the rock carvings have a unique place in Fehn's conceptual work process. The architect refers to these figures as tattoos on the earth. As such, they are offerings to the sky or to the unknown "room picture," and their content belongs to the earth; this in turn transforms the earth into the one and only object.

Did Bronze Age humans have a sense of the earth as a traveling object in the universe? This question is not interesting in relation to an answer, but rather in relation to the ideas it raises concerning limits. For years, I dwelt upon what I called a bullet eye and how this was in the process of destroying architecture's sense of place. The human keeps itself within the limits of the horizon. The minute the bullet goes beyond and passes through the horizon, one is placeless and without the same sense of protection.

And when the bullet with its capacity to pass through the horizon is also searching for its prey, this uncertainty to place is only heightened. You can travel like crazy around the globe, but you have no possibility of dampening your fear. The bullet as an object has won over place. On an emotional level, it is difficult to understand that we have become placeless. We can only go straight down into the earth.

Fehn's competition project for the Rock Carving Museum at Borge, 1993, is an extension of the landscape, a cut in the rock. A pitched roof starts at ground level and rises, like the cover of a book, to a viewing platform on the roof; the open side of the "book," facing the hill and Bronze Age rock carvings, is a glass wall. Visitors walk over the roof into the site or view the carvings through the open glass facade that faces the red granite rock. The internal space of the museum is a direct result of the cut, a wound between two surfaces. There is an interior silence, a sense of a cavelike place. Slanted structures—Fehn called them "pyramidal columns"—hold the gap open, allowing for a particular type of subdued light. Fehn views these piers as hollow wooden trunks that cannot be separated from the earth, much as the carvings cannot be separated from their surface. Fehn included in his competition scheme a series of large columnar objects that direct a path into the built landscape. These elements would extend the earth by giving the flat landscape a direction toward the sky, almost an architectural mask facing the unknown and searching for a dialogue with another type of content.

Rock carvings have no horizon; they are in space. The canvas is the earth itself. The sun, the moon, and heaven's symbols are scratched into the surface; large and small figures are placed in a picture of the universe. The symbols are on nothing else but the earth's surface. And as such, what is the content of a rock-carving museum? Is it about finding a key to heaven or to the landscape? Or is it an associative method to understand ourselves?

Similar in theme to the Rock Carving Museum was the competition project for the Borre Viking Museum and Information Center, 1993. Several Viking burial mounds are close to the proposed site, and only a short distance to the south is the famous Oseberg Burial Mound, which once contained the largest of the Viking ships (now at the Viking Ship Museum in Oslo); more mounds and historic sites are scattered throughout the area. This is also some of the most fertile land in the country, characterized by rolling hills and the Oslo Fjord with its many small islands. How does one touch a landscape so deeply ingrained in a nation's picture of its heritage? **It is an incredibly sensitive**

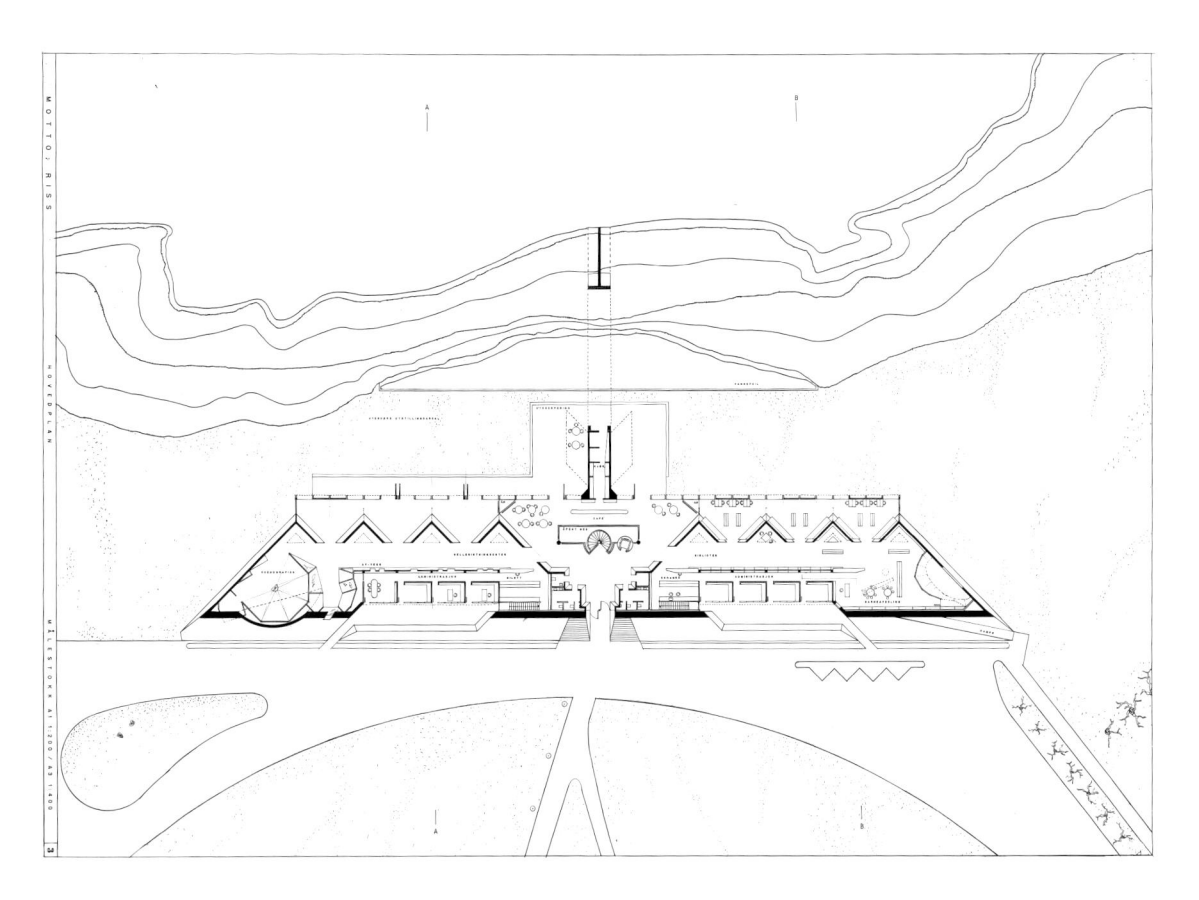

Rock Carving Museum, Borge, Norway: Plan.

landscape, Edvard Munch's landscape. To build a museum where there is no object, the museum becomes the object and architecture the story. It is a search into the surface of the earth. The plowed field stretches toward a dark, large sea—out there the light is stronger. The building becomes a figure that begins to resemble a boat; one builds a furrow. The cut is carved, giving exposure. Architecture leaves. The invisible becomes visible.

The architecture signals a voyage into the horizon; the cut in the landscape is the building itself. By seeking a spatial sequence that is both over and under the earth, the project reflects the realm of the dead in the center of the burial mound. Shaped like the blade of a plowshare, the roof cross section slices the surface of the earth. A long ramp takes visitors up to a built plateau; another leads to the depths of the building. Hanging between ceiling and floor, the interior ramp moves from a dim central volume down to the well-lit beginnings of the story. This sequence is articulated by the ever-changing daylight that trickles through the roof construction. The placement of the ramps and the amount of daylight are direct consequences of the section and its continuous transformation. The sharpness of the cut into the landscape and the straight lines produced contrast with the gentle coastal setting and provide a clear framework for the visitor amid the sanctuary that is buried within the earth mounds.

Neither the Borge Rock Carving Museum nor the Borre Viking Museum was realized. Yet in these projects Fehn is clearly searching for an architectural expression suitable for the physical remnants of a journey founded on a belief in life after death. His capacity to abstract historic content into a thought of construction is decisive for the projects. It is the boat that seems to be an

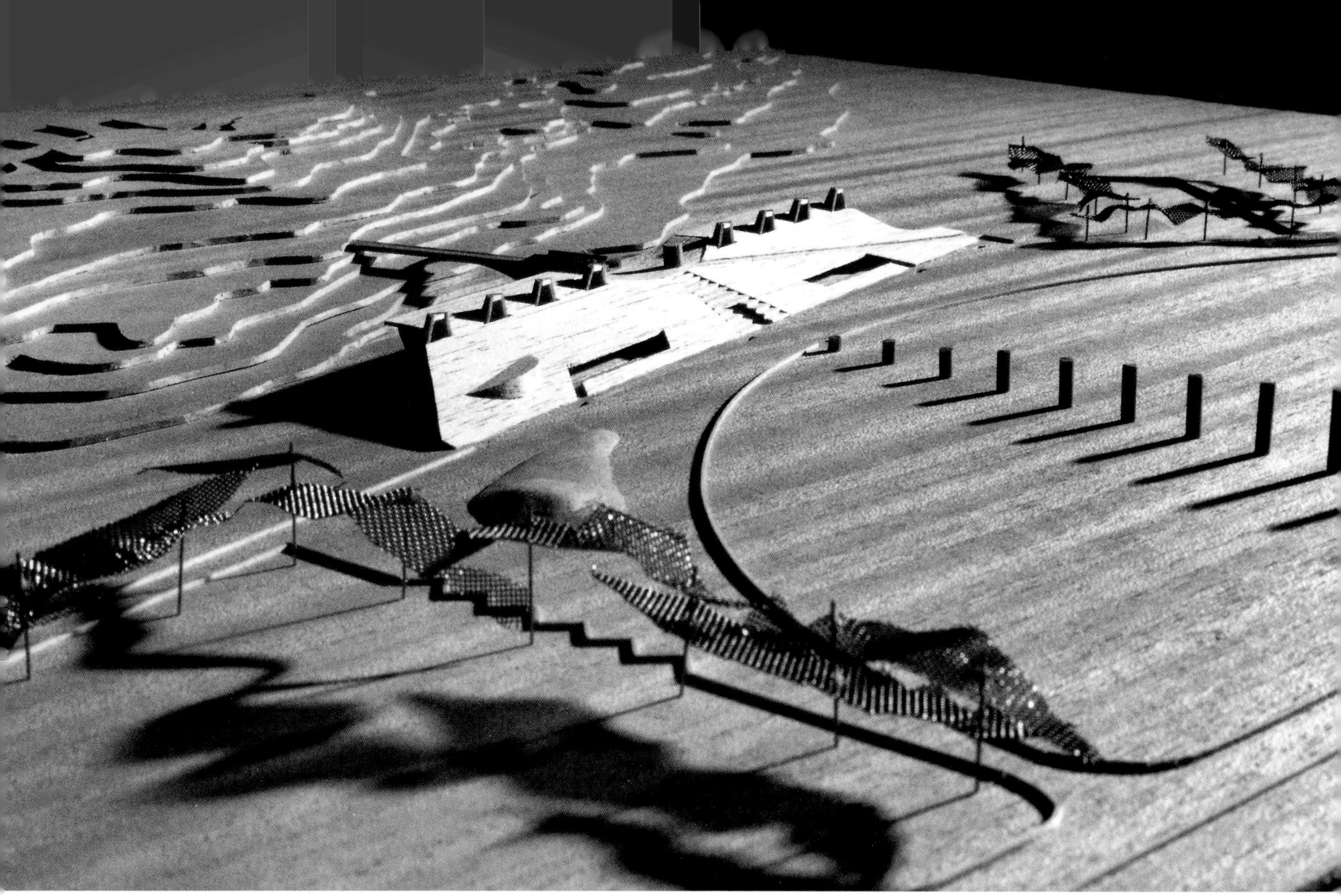

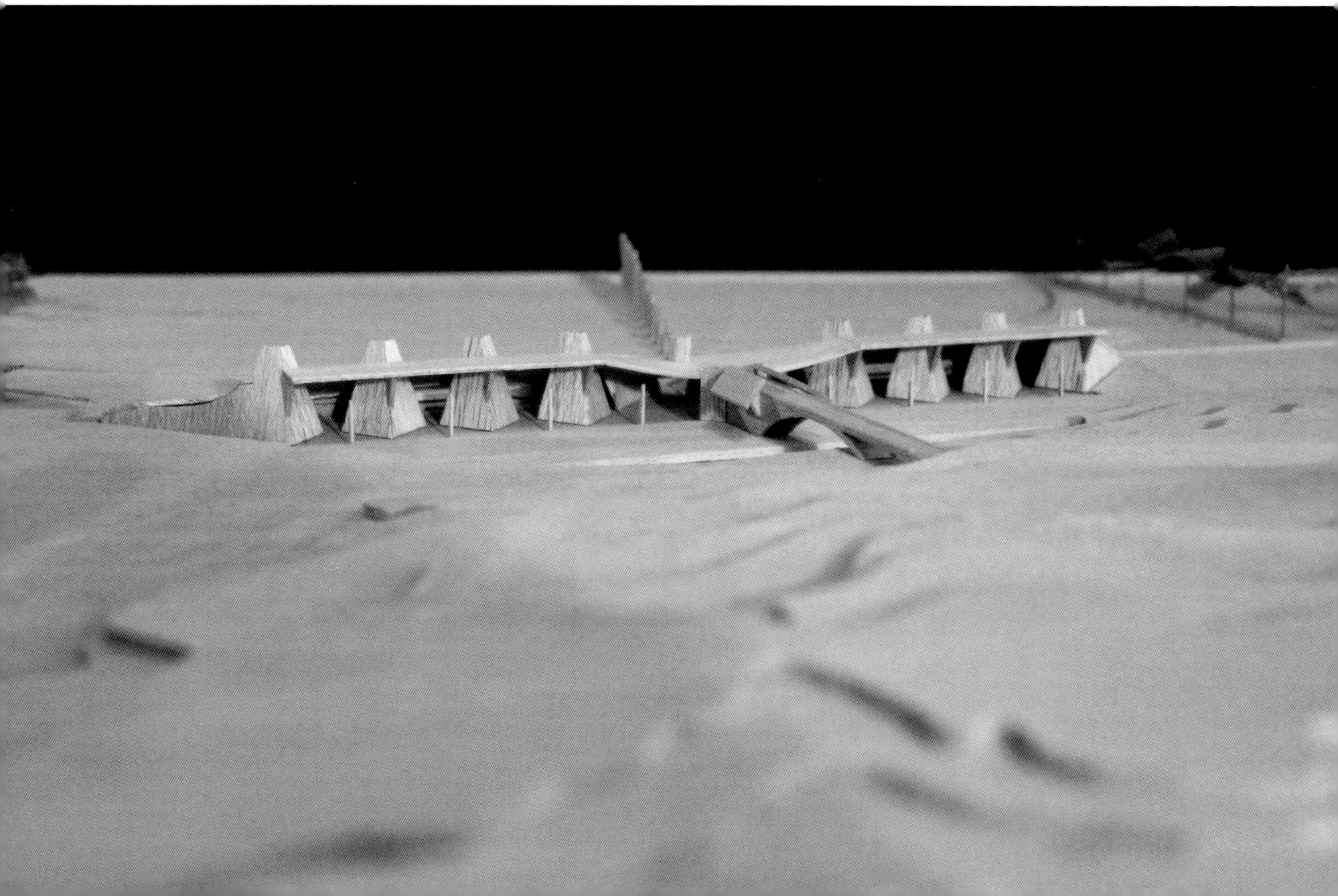

Sketch, 1992, "*Calm* landscape, the sweet horizontal lines."

OPPOSITE Rock Carving Museum: Model views toward entrance and toward glass wall.

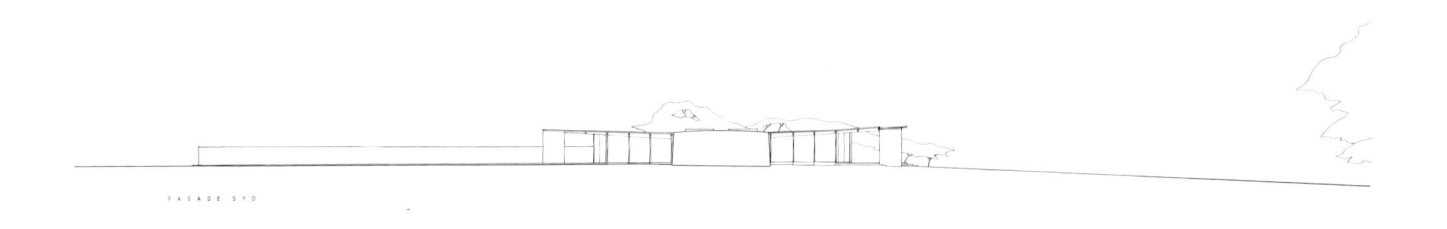

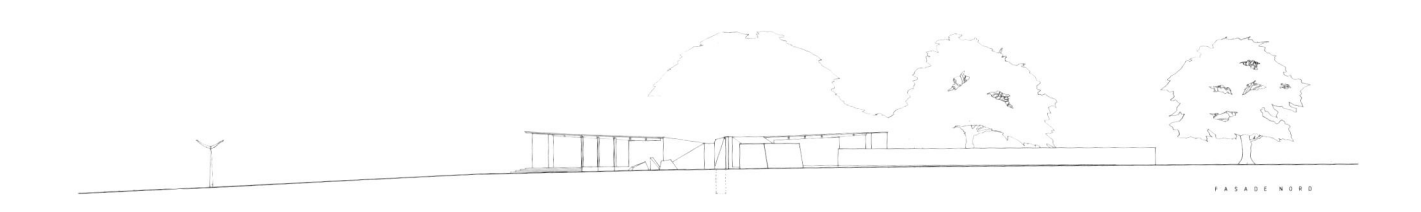

Viking Museum and Information Center, Borre, Norway: Sketch, south and north elevations, plan, sections, model.

254 THE PATTERN OF THOUGHTS

PARAPHRASING NATURE 255

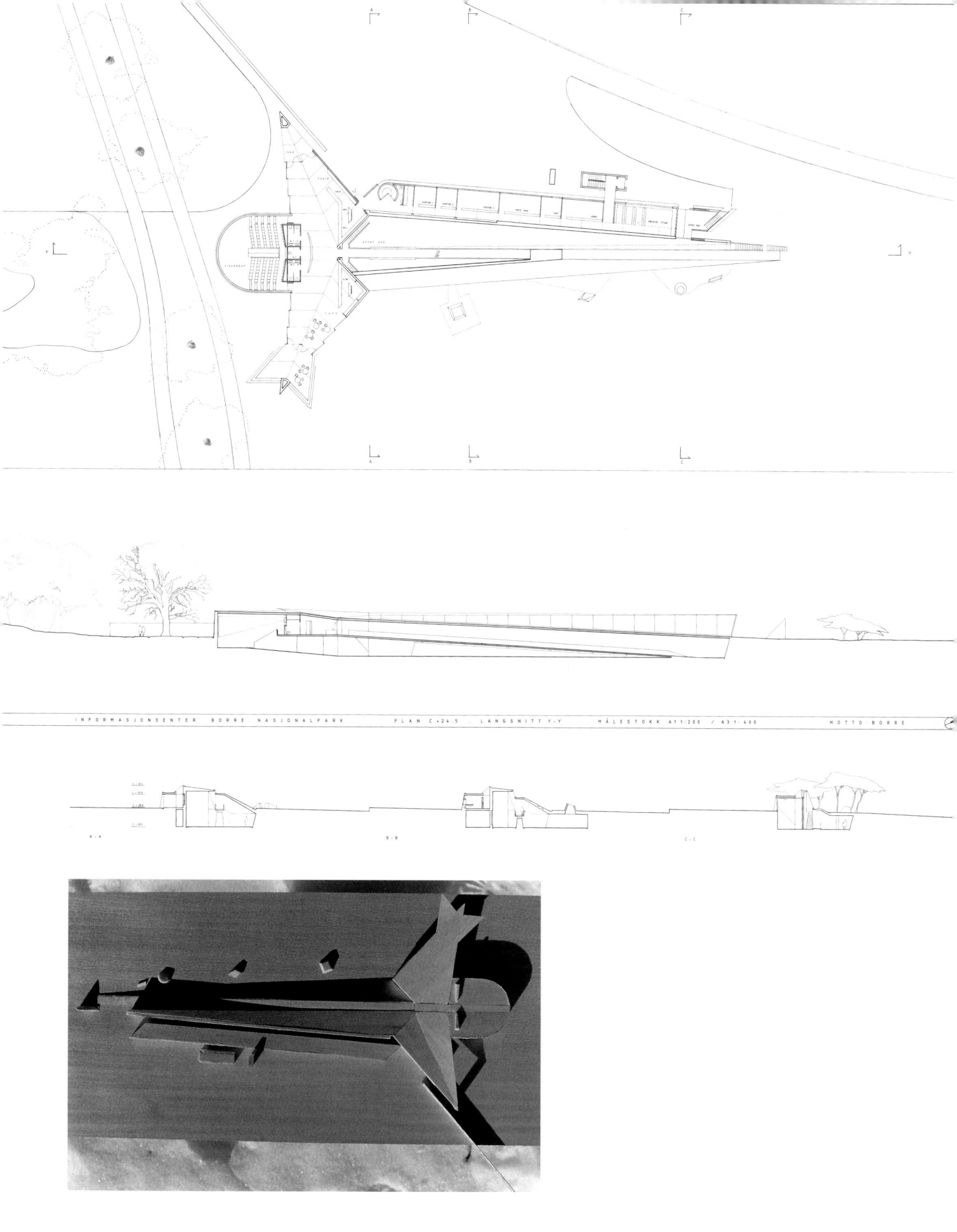

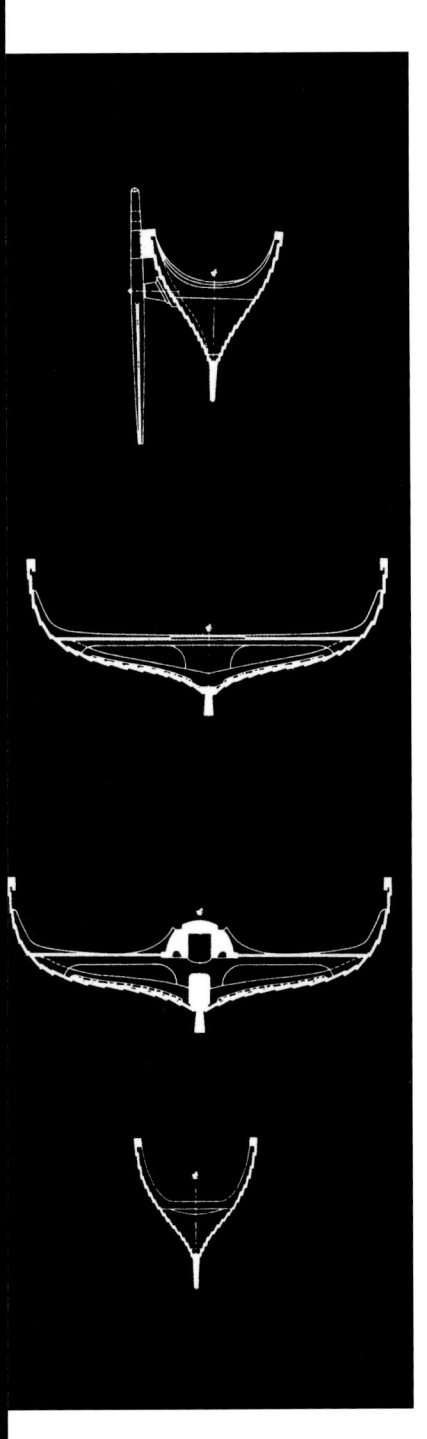

Sections of Gokstad Viking ship (drawn by Bruce Bergendoff).

OPPOSITE Sketch of the sun and the stone (for the Norwegian Glacier Museum).

essential link in his connections between sky and earth, life and death. The boat carries an implicit belief in other places. There is a longing to reach an elusive horizon, to create a bridge between earth and sky. It is just a matter of making the connection, and this is why the boat is, for Fehn, a pivotal object. Fehn asked one assistant, who as a student had made some striking drawings of the Gokstad Viking ship, to draw the Wasa with the same accuracy for that competition.

The competition project for the Hydro Energy Museum in Suldal, 1994–95, is yet another project that internalizes the terrain within the core of a design. The site clings to a rocky mountain face and includes three waterways. These elements make up the physical platform for the museum. Fehn considered three components important: the dam and its placid reservoir, the waterfall and its potential energy, and the cultural landscape that had developed around the river. Visitors approach the museum via a bridge that crosses the river and a road that winds through the landscape. A new bearing wall along the hill reinterprets ancient city walls and the protection they provided, only in this case the protection is from the water's force.

The competition scheme offers a duality between two distinct walls. One follows the contour of the rocky hillside; the other is straight and angular, facing the river below. Between the wall following the curves of the terrain and the roof is a slit where light "falls" into the building. The moment daylight enters the large open space and spreads out over the floor, the building as a machine comes into play.

In all of Fehn's creative thinking around architecture, he never shirks or sets aside nature. Every project faces the site and its context as a positive force. Yet he is clear in both his work and his teaching that architecture is a demand on the earth's surface. Precision lies in how well the concept of paraphrasing nature is understood. **A door never has the perfect height. A foxhole always has the same height. Its builder has no inner voice, no death concept. The hole in itself is perfect, and mankind's calculations will never reach a comparable perfection. We cannot cover up the stars' positions and their place within the heavens. Everything must be read through the animal and the mask.**

Within the architect's vocabulary, there is an attitude of "deep" ecology. If nature is to be appreciated and respected, not exploited, the built space must exercise an ability to reinforce nature's spatial potential. Fehn's evaluation of his own work depends on the project's capacity to paraphrase nature.

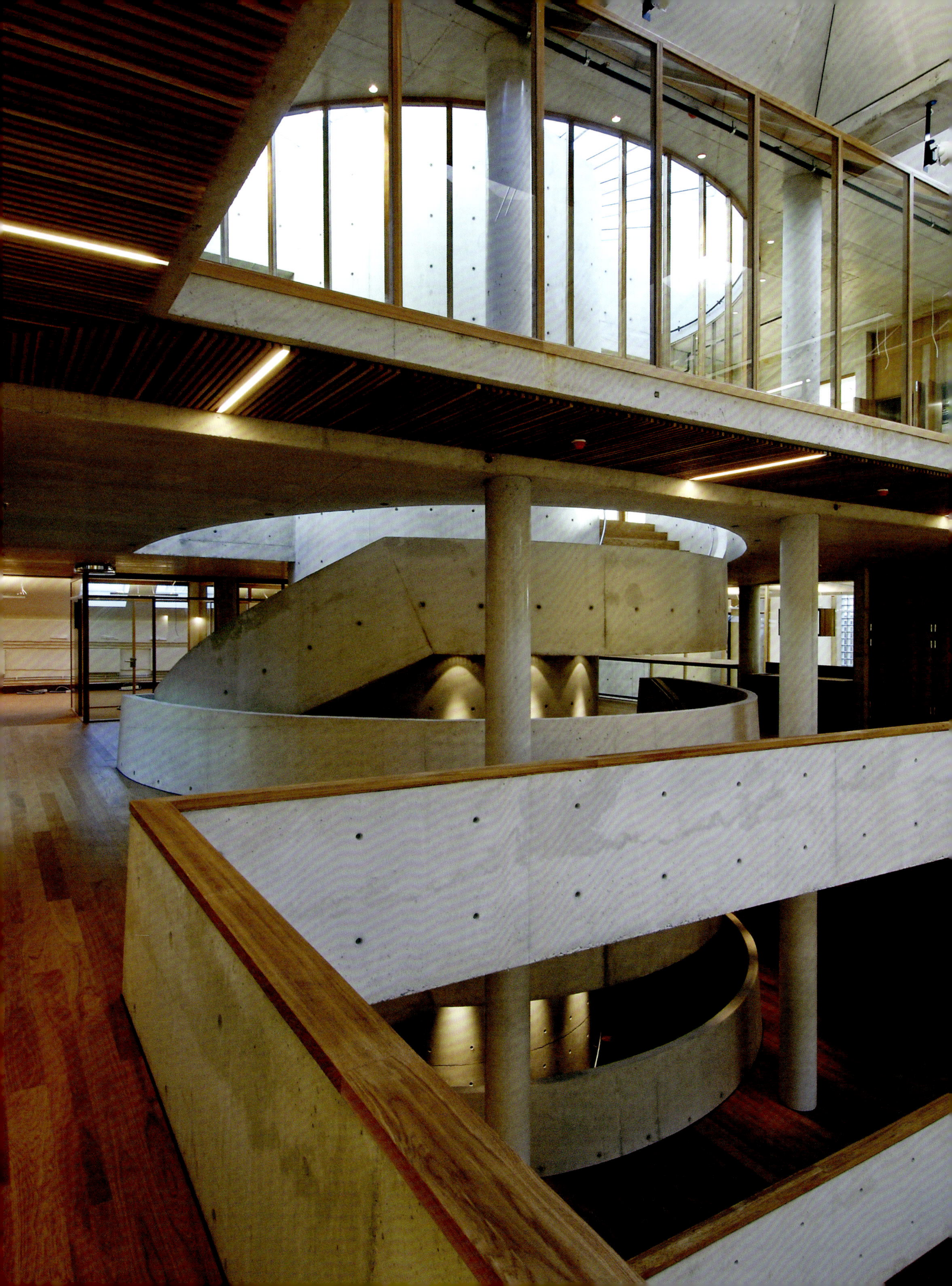

CHAPTER 11

BEFORE CLOSING THE GATE

After Fehn retired from his position at the Oslo School of Architecture in 1994, he devoted all of his time to his practice. After so many years at the school, the change, though welcome, was noticeable. It was hard to replace the day-to-day contact and inspiration from students and colleagues; but fortunately, Fehn had enough work to keep a talented team of young architects in the office. Much of this work consisted of projects that had been in the office in one form or another for some time, but there was also an upswing of interest in Fehn that led to a number of new commissions.

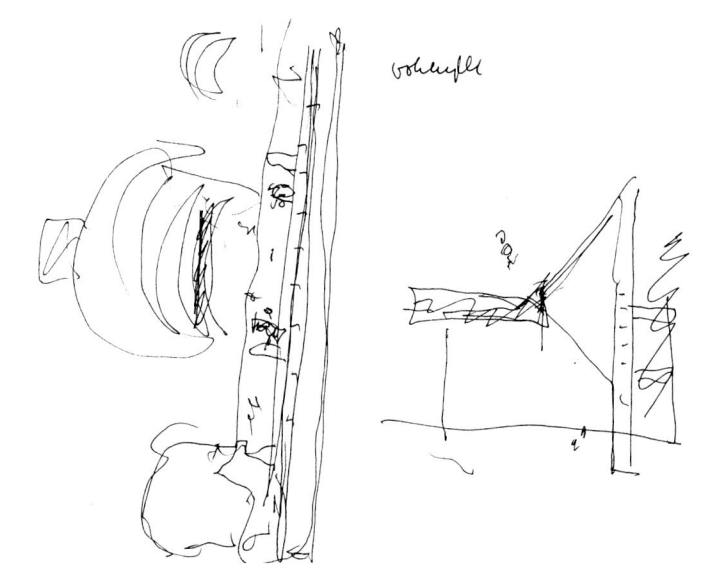

Ivar Aasen Museum, Ørsta, Norway: Plan and section sketches, 1996; entrance to auditorium.

PAGE 258 Offices for Gyldendal Publishing Company, Oslo: Atrium and central stair.

The Ivar Aasen Museum in Ørsta, 1996–2000, was the last project in which Fehn would personally push the boundaries of his creative capacity in relation to the development of a building from start to finish. Dedicated to Ivar Aasen, a leading figure in the establishment of Norway's second language, Ny Norsk, the museum is dug into a hill, forming a cave. The "cave" opening is the source of light for the building and also affords a view of the valley. From a distance, the structure appears as a slanted glass facade set into the hillside. Fehn seemed to expand on all his old spatial images and at the same time reject them. Every signature element is here, remixed and tested in provocative combinations. Each section of the building has an individual identity: his formal expression has never been more active. The museum carries both a personal architectural vocabulary created solely for this place and a design language drawn from his early sources of inspiration. Awarded so late in his career, this work represents a final testing ground for Fehn's architectural thinking and expression.

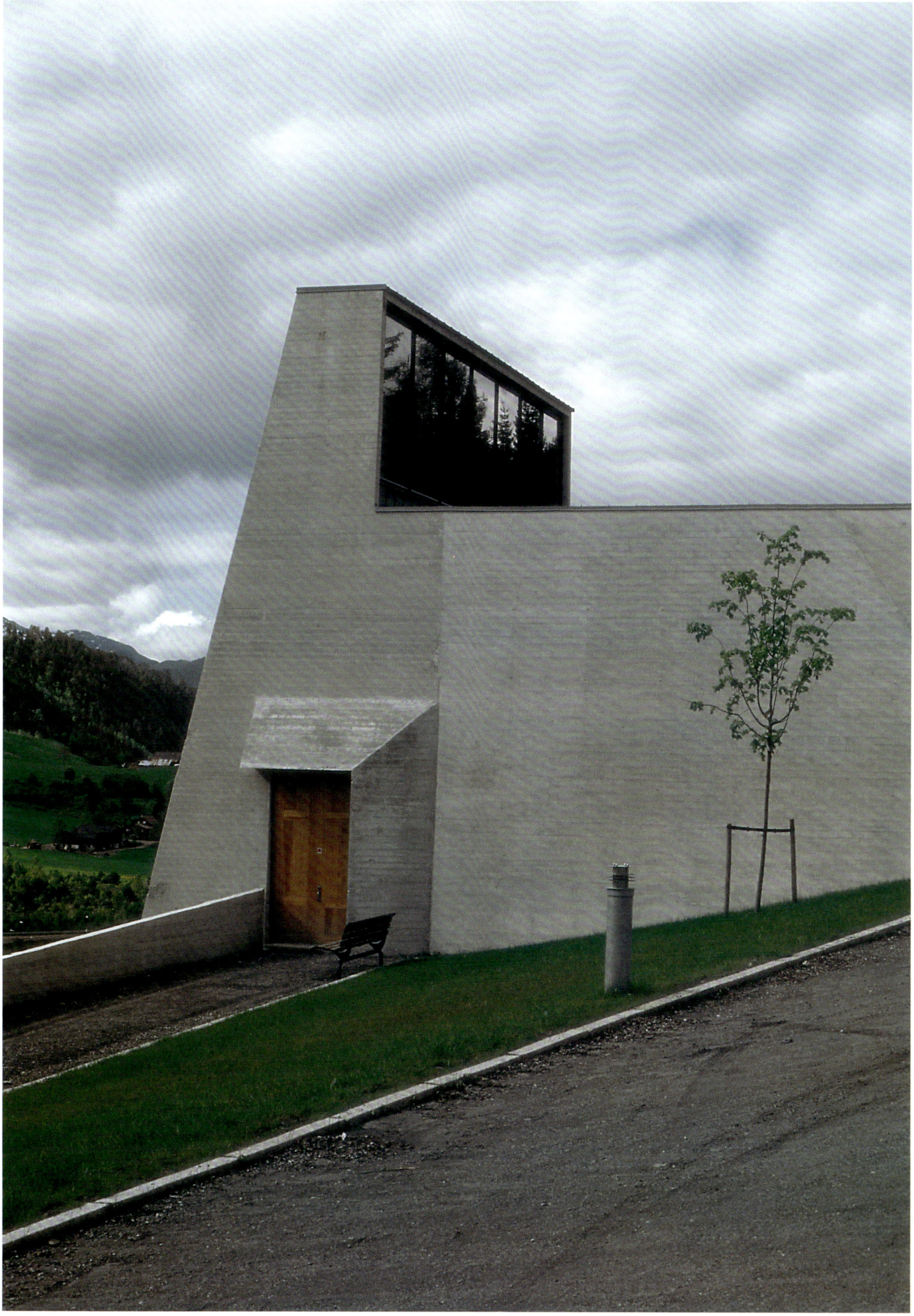

Ivar Aasen Museum: Sketch, 1996, of plan; exterior corner.

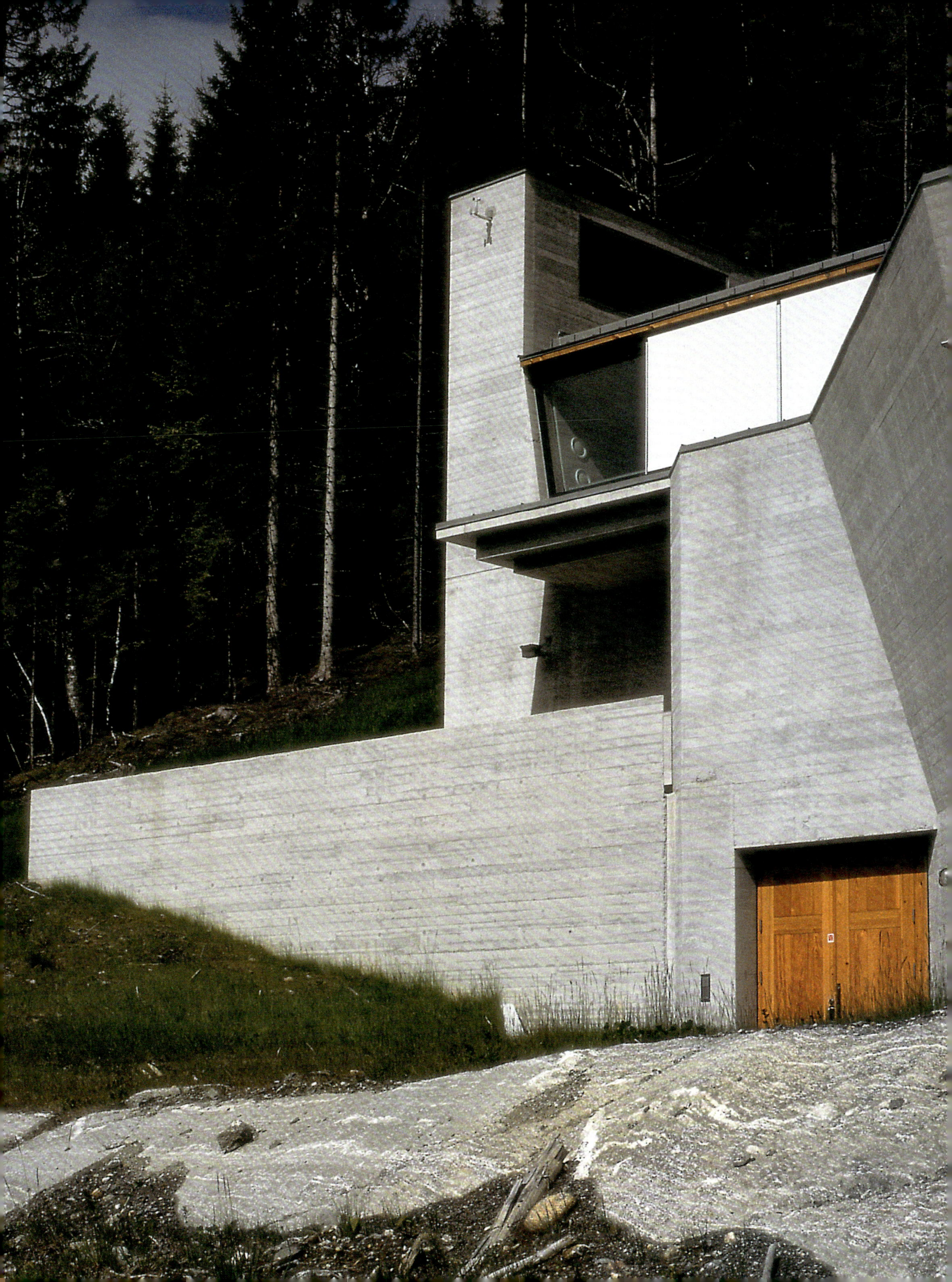

264 THE PATTERN OF THOUGHTS

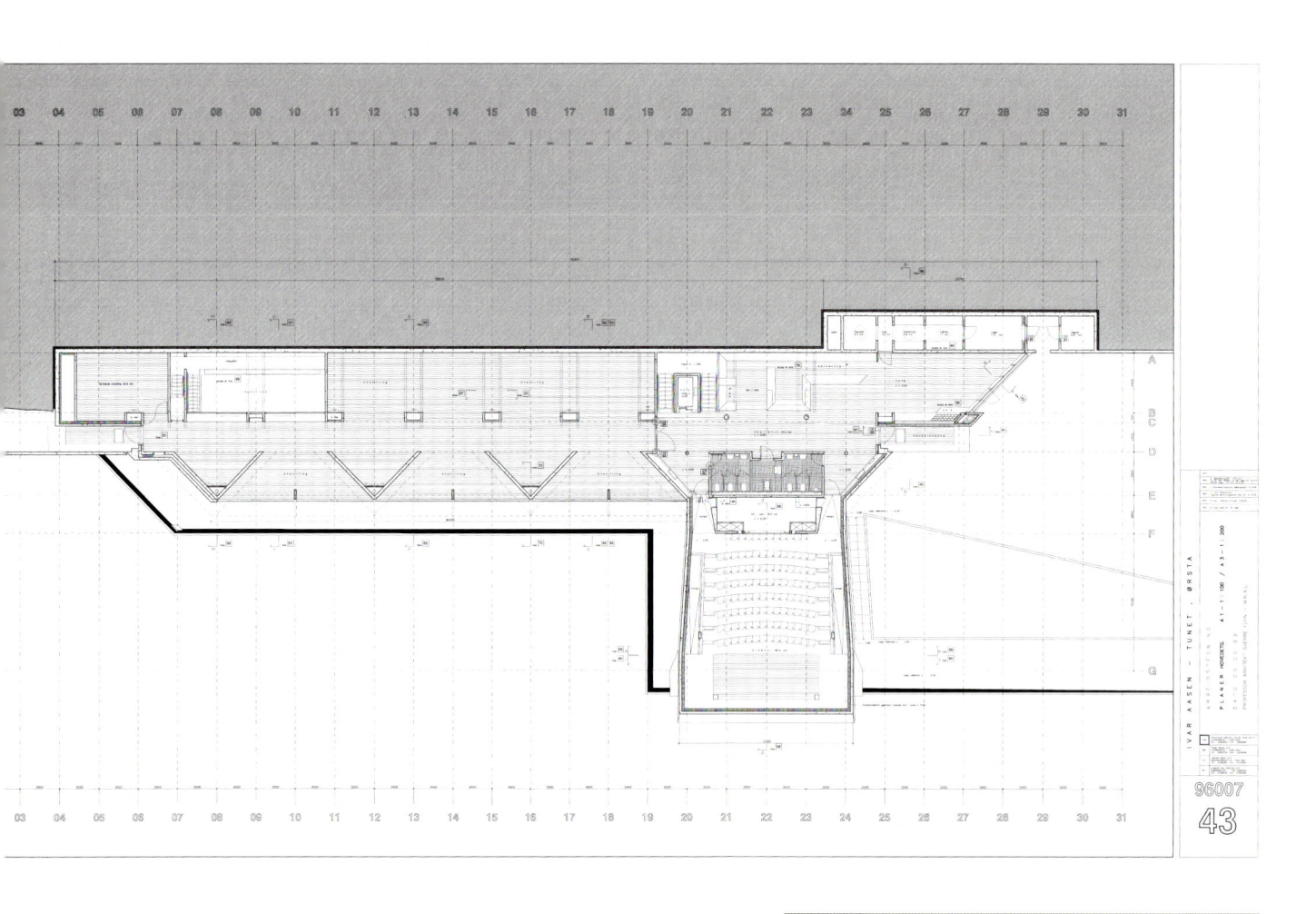

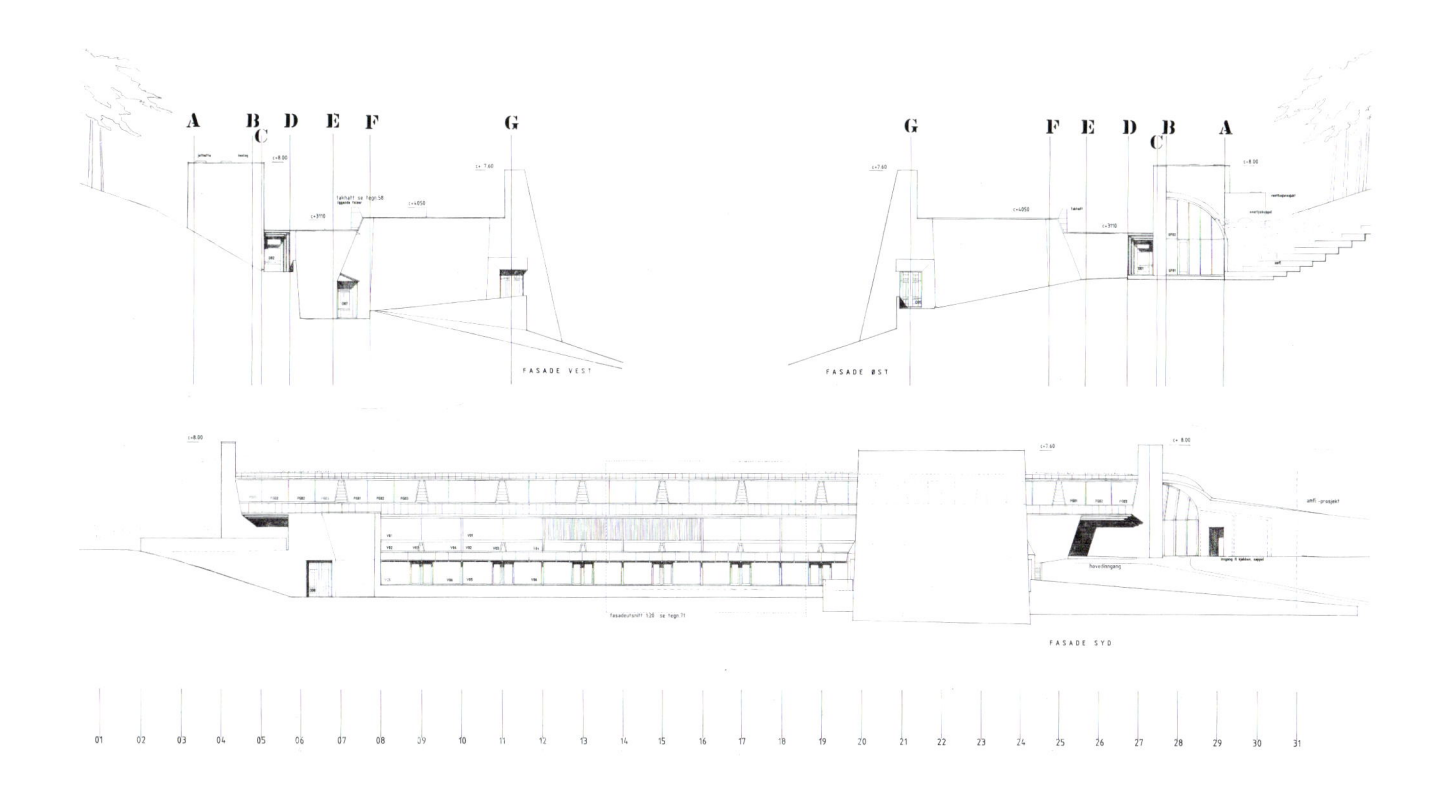

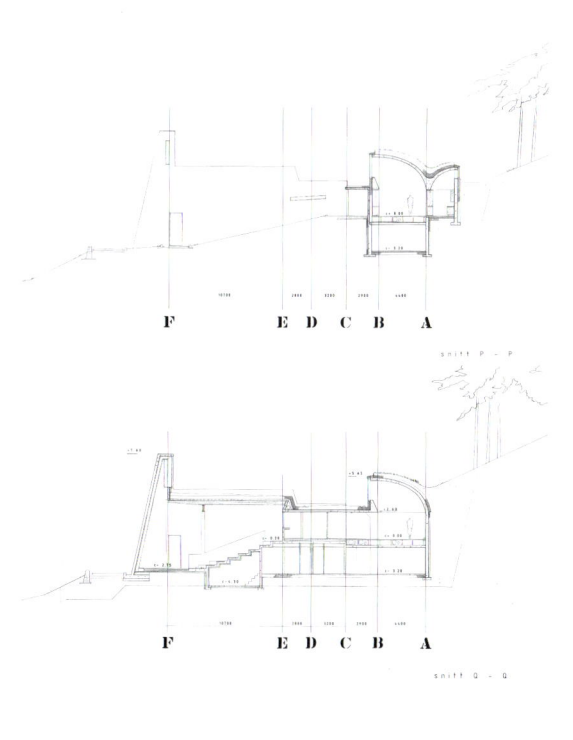

THESE PAGES AND OVERLEAF Ivar Aasen Museum: Plan, section sketches, interior column, sections and elevation, exterior detail, exterior view.

BEFORE CLOSING THE GATE 265

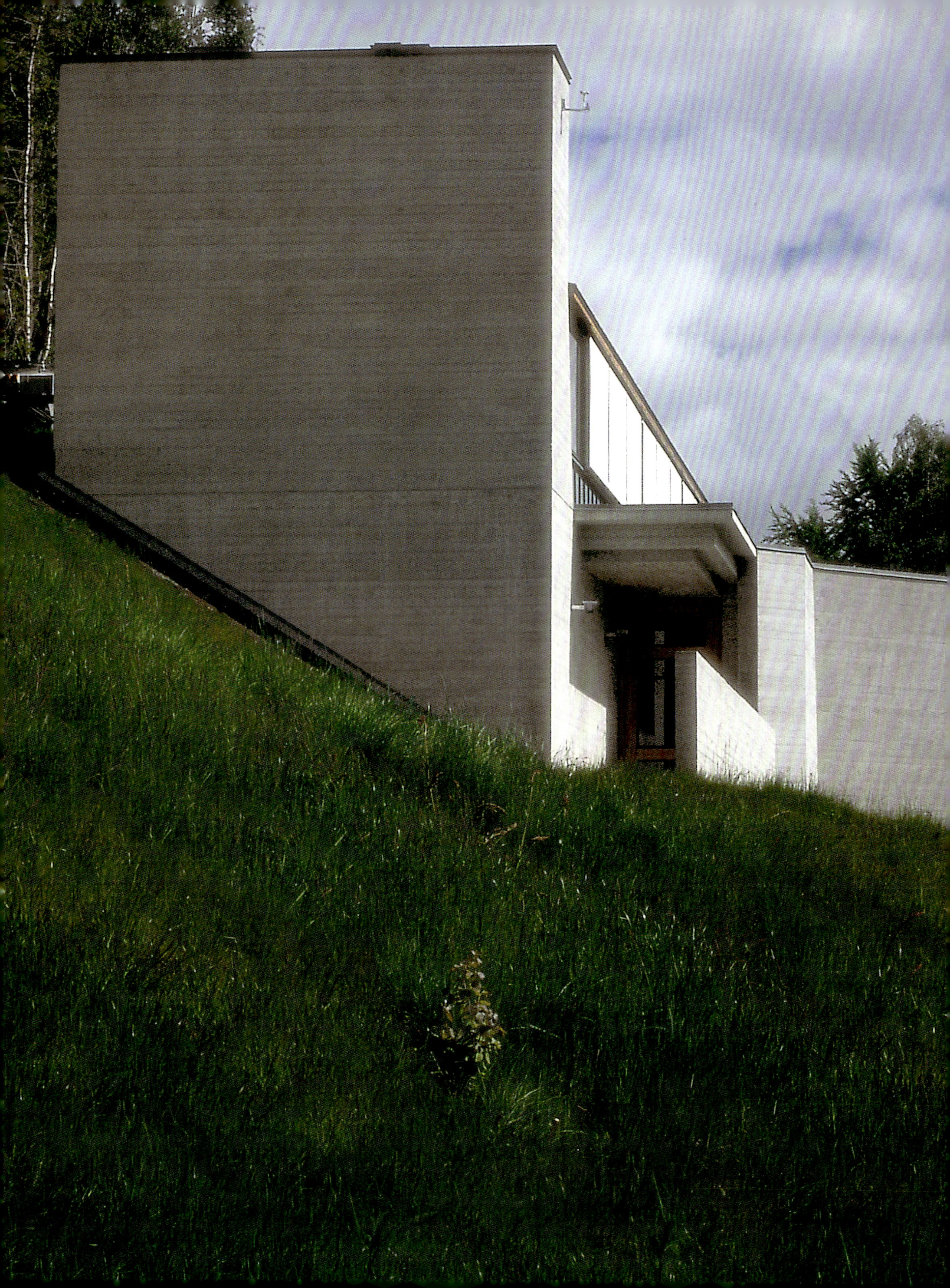

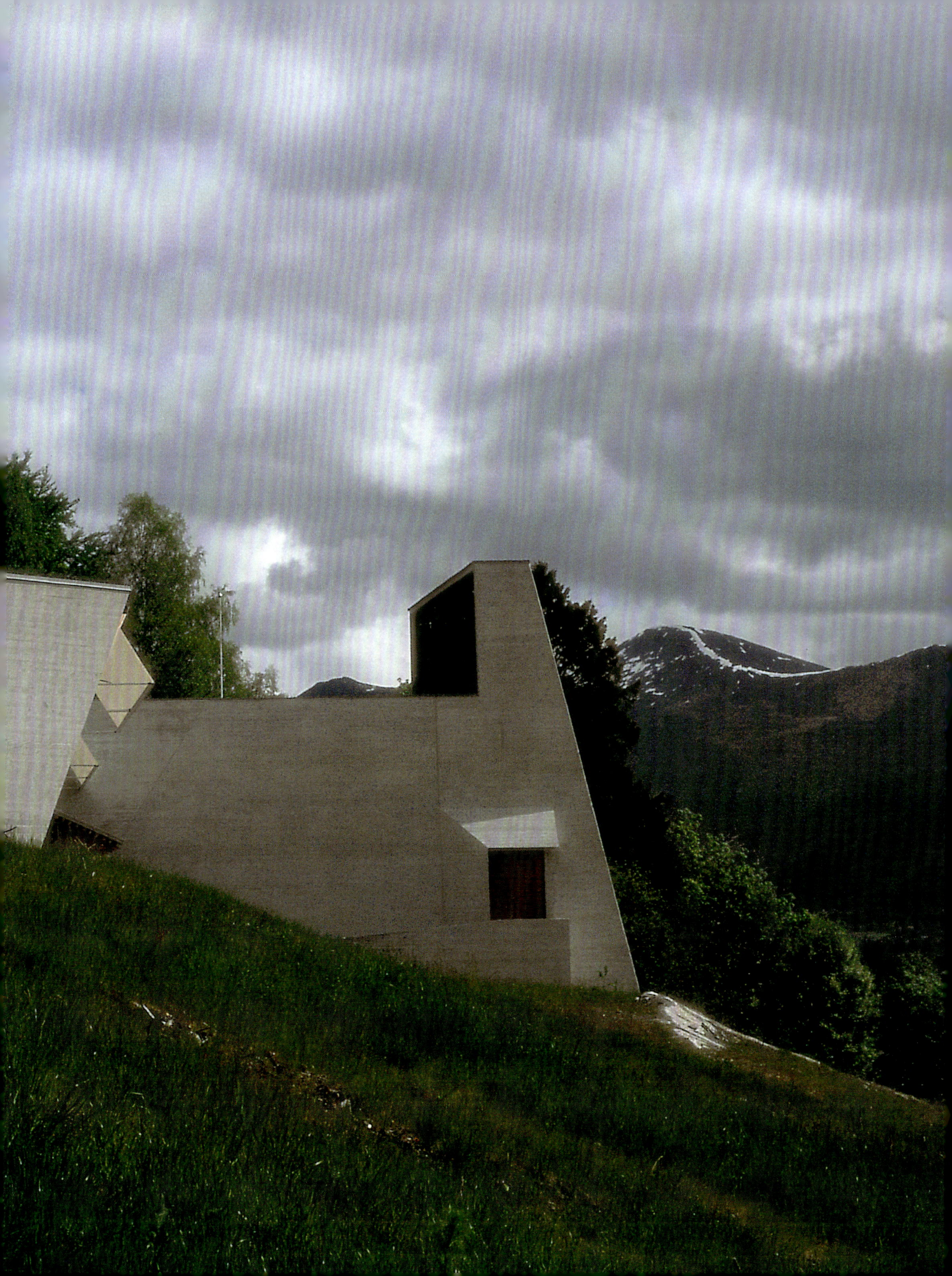

Ivar Aasen Museum:
Interior views.

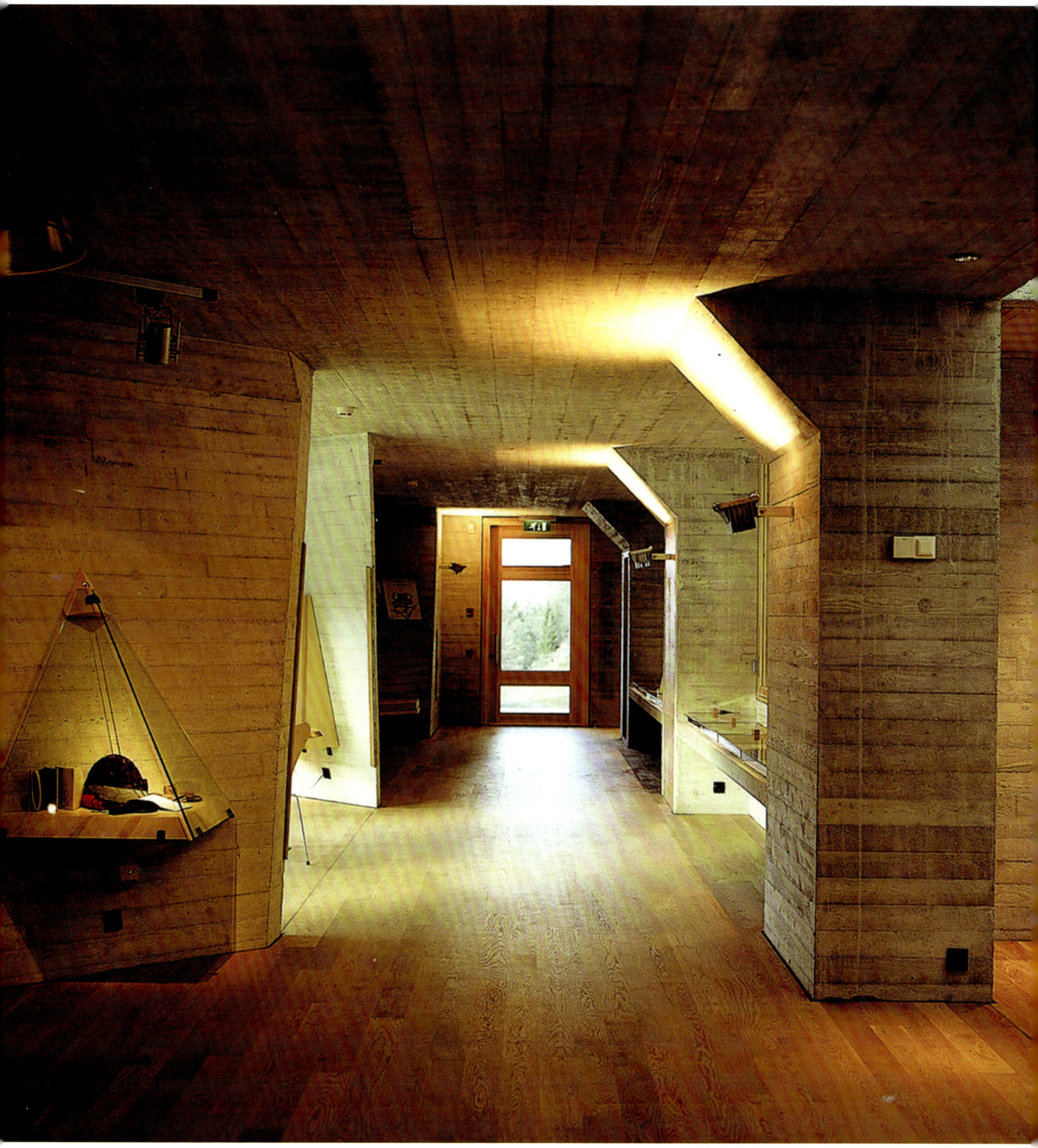

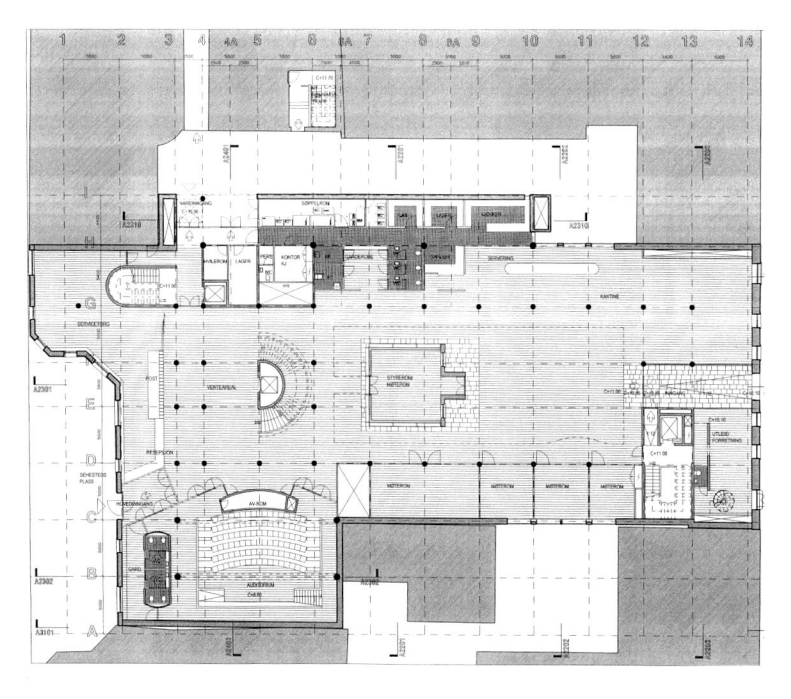

Offices for Gyldendal Publishing Company: Plan of entrance floor, section.

Two new urban projects would challenge the rather misleading notion that the architect designed only for remote natural settings. In fact, a significant number of his many unbuilt projects had an urban context, and all were informed by his reflections on city life. In 1995, Fehn landed a commission to build a large office building in the center of Oslo. The brief was for a transformation of the offices of the Gyldendal Publishing Company, which were located directly across from the National Gallery and a few minutes walk from Tullinløkka Square, the site of a competition the architect entered in 1972. Fehn uncovered the hidden architectural potential within the cluster of old buildings and their urban tissue. He kept the facades of the structures facing the museum as a kind of mask; inside, he gutted the buildings to form a large central space that controls and supports the functional aspects of the building. The main entrance is through this five-story public space, which also holds a replica of the original Gyldendal headquarters in Copenhagen, known as the Danish House. This object establishes a scale and image for the public room. Eighteen pyramidal "daylight" lanterns, which function as skylights, fill the room with muted light. A deflected illumination enters from the sides as well. Within a relatively traditional urban setting and using rather conventional materials, Fehn created a completely new and surprising connection between interior and exterior. Unfortunately, his health failed when the project was about to be realized. But the concept was fully developed, and the architects in Fehn's office completed the project with his characteristic precision. While he was not able to supervise the construction, his energy and foresight are manifest in the early work on the design.

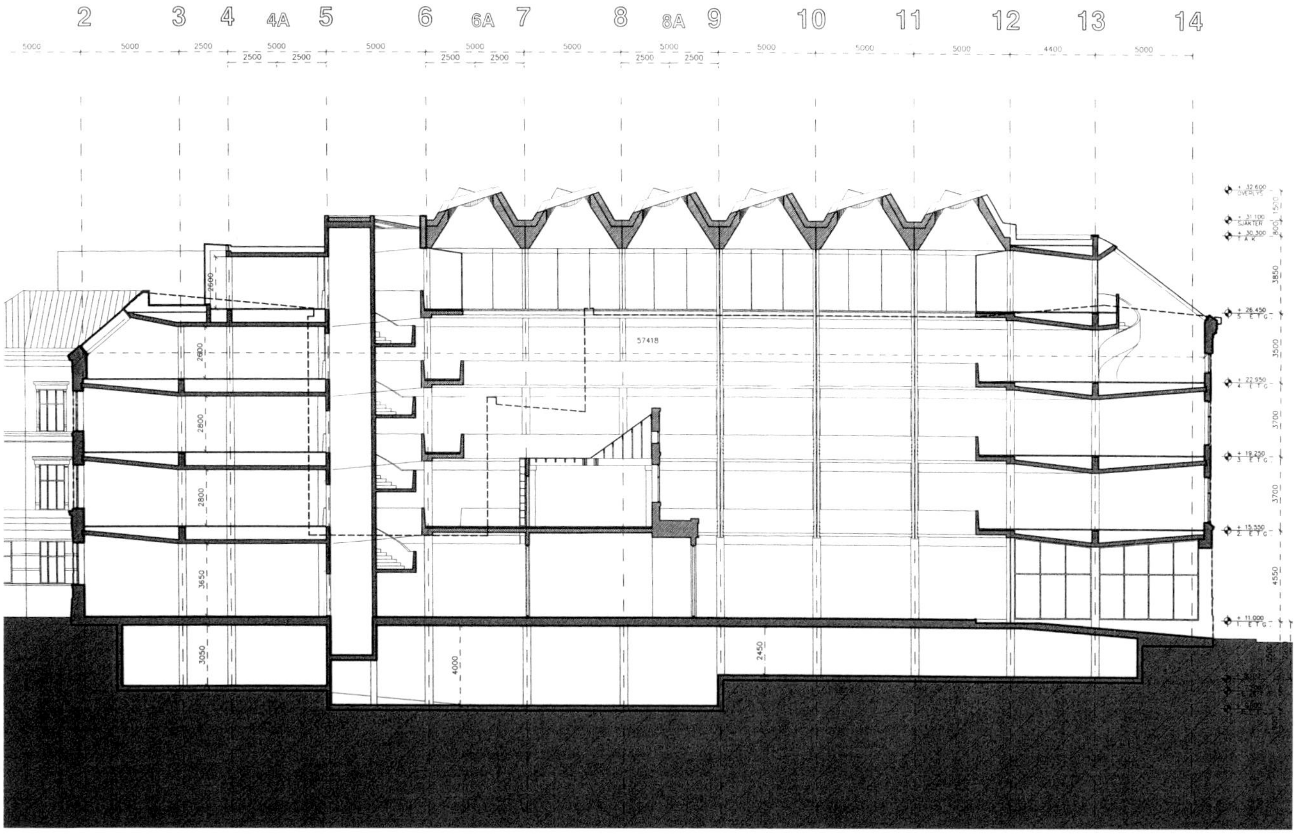
2
3
4
4A
5
6
6A
7
8
8A
9
10
11
12
13
14
57418

Offices for Gyldendal Publishing Company: Section, interior view with Danish House.

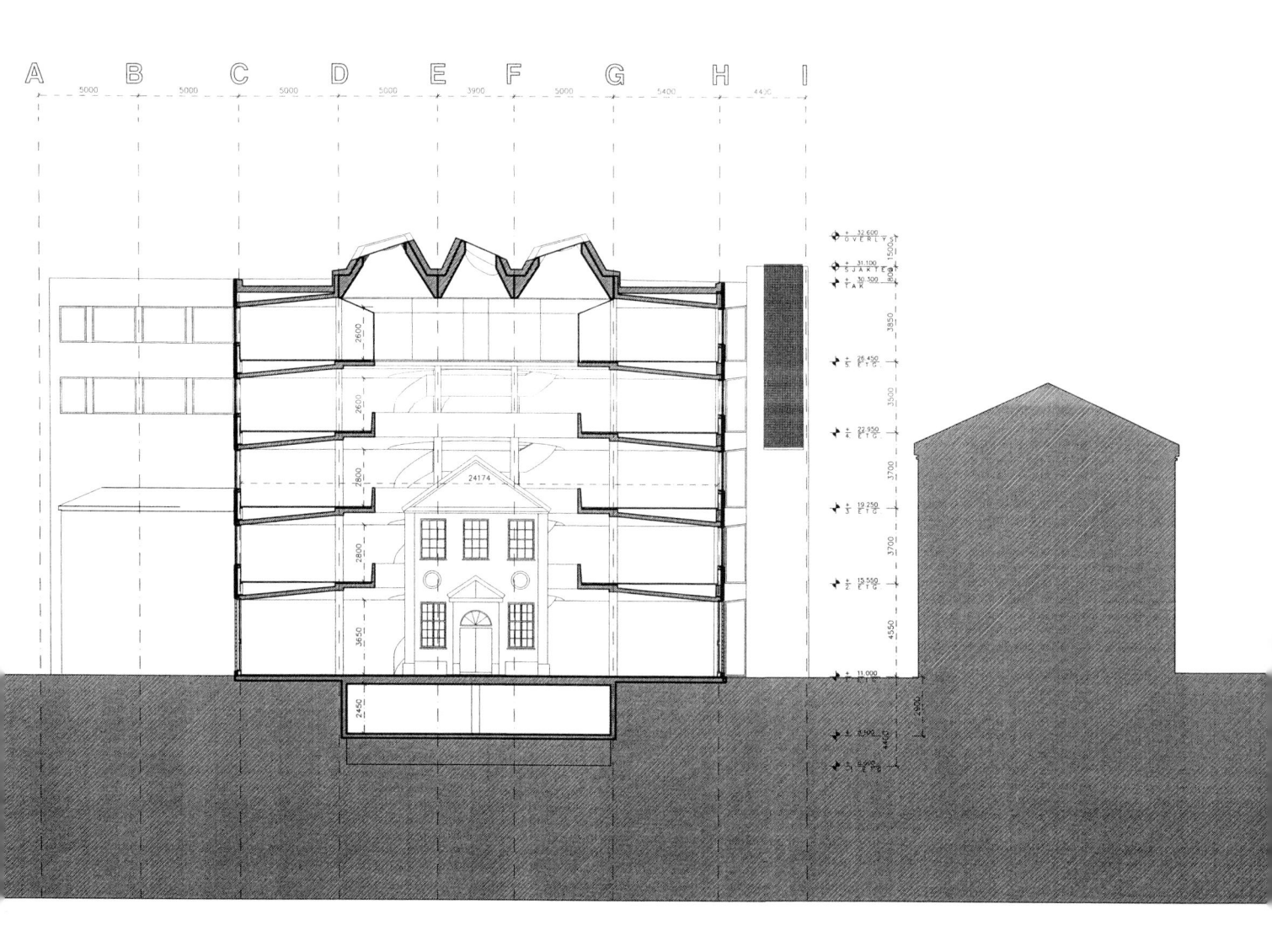

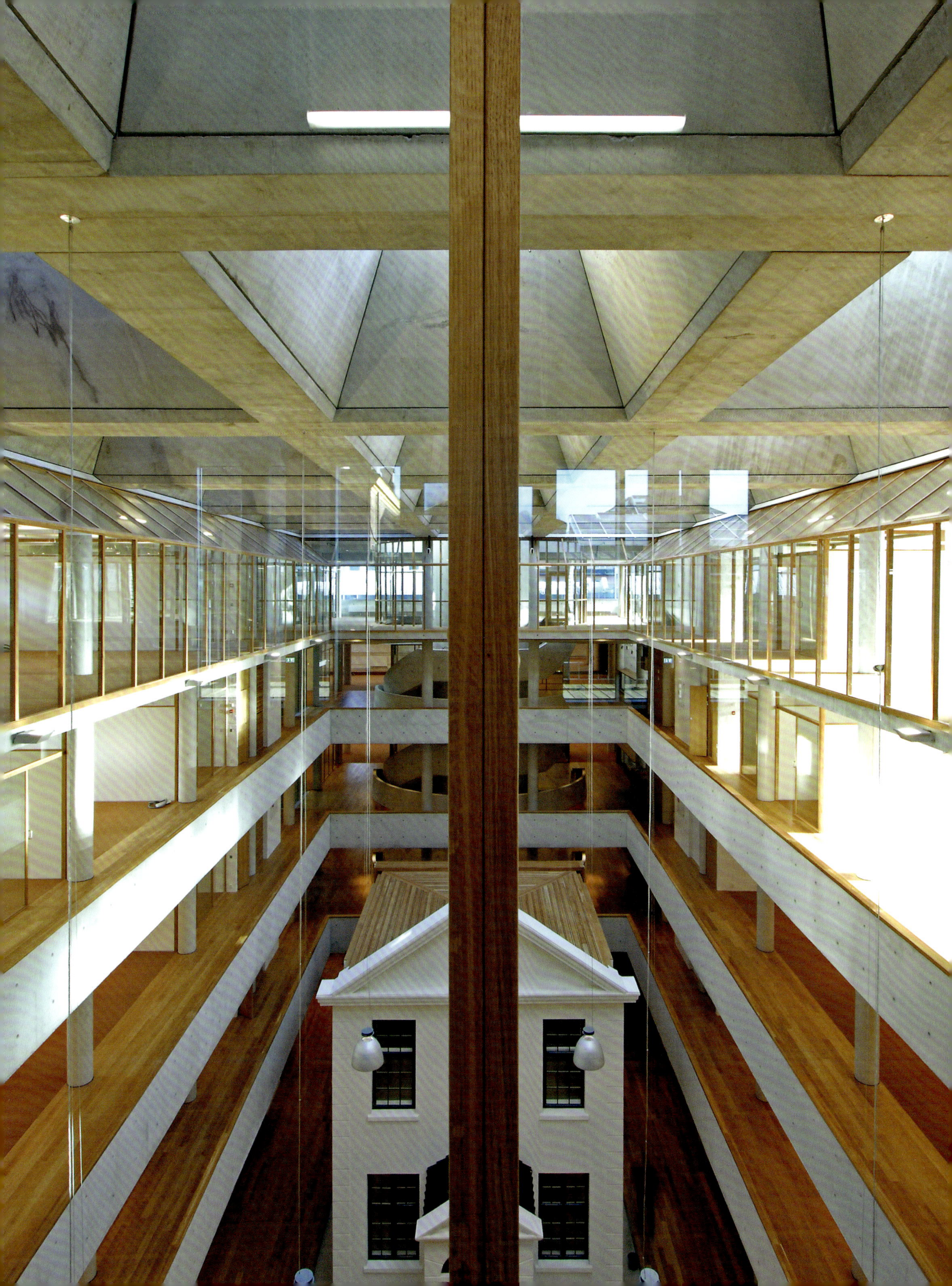

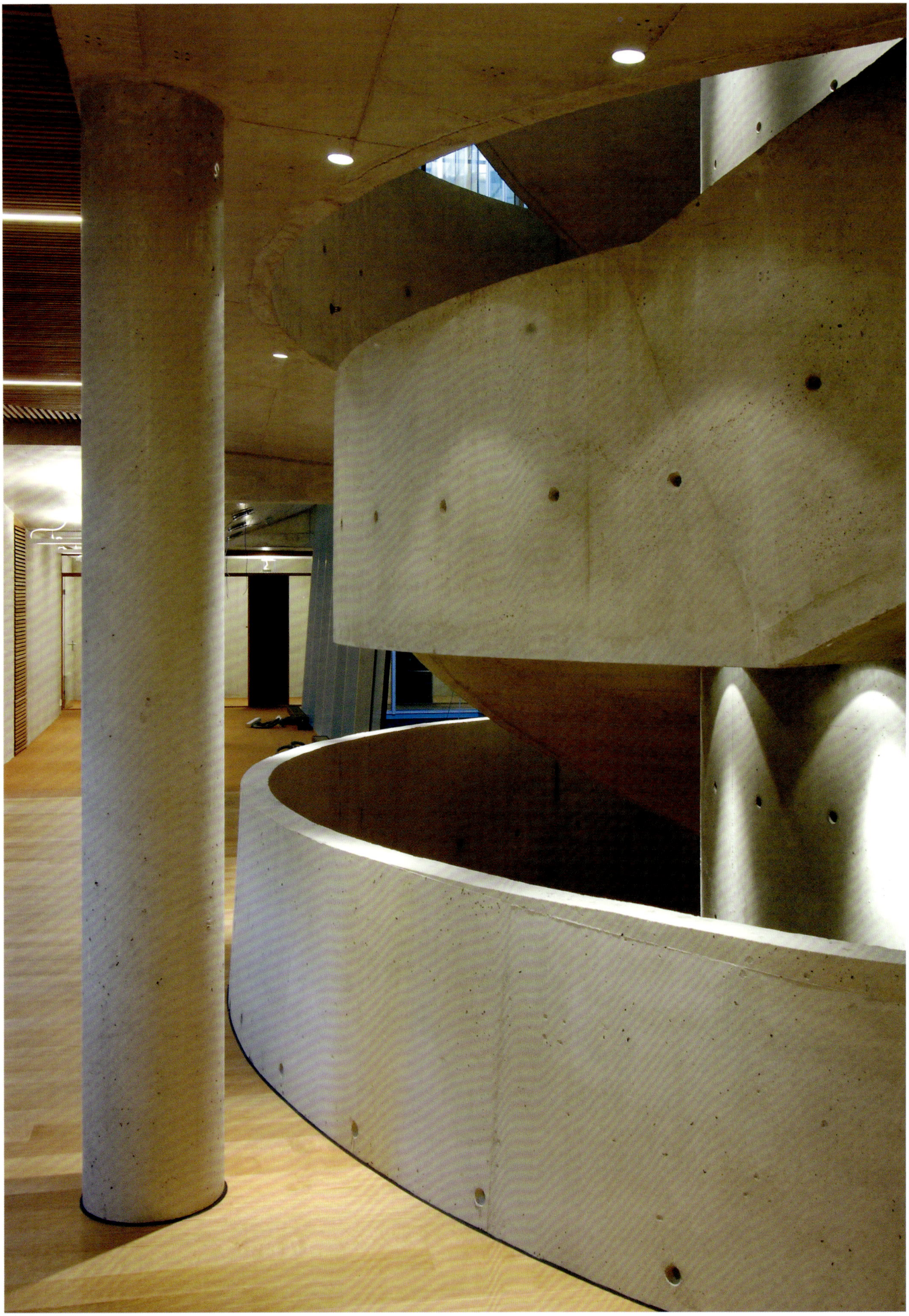

Offices for Gyldendal Publishing Company: Detail of central stair, "daylight lanterns" in central space.

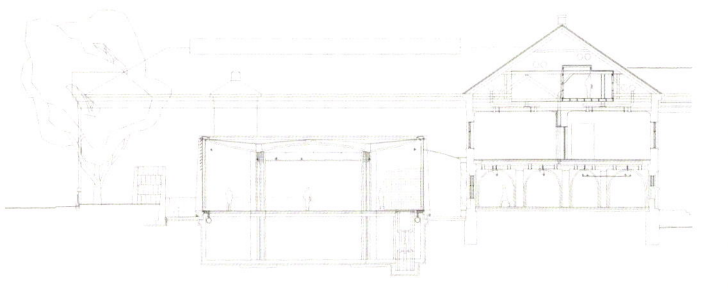

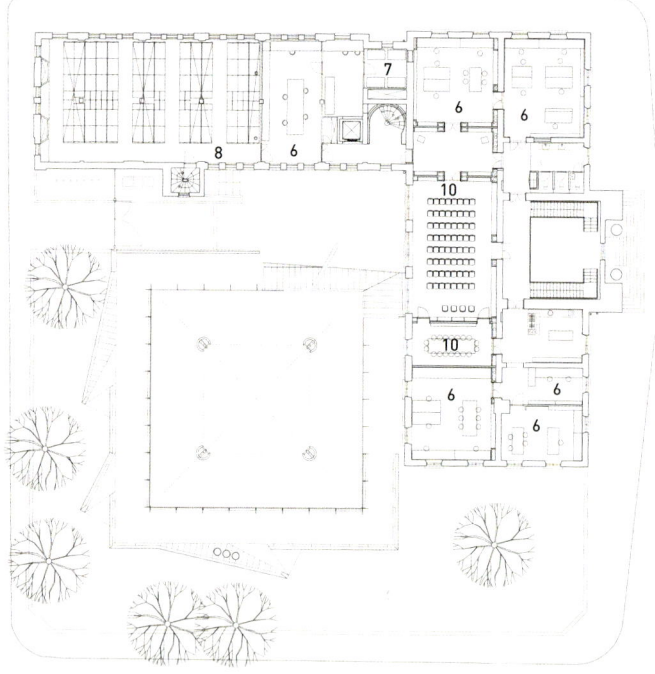

Norwegian Museum of Architecture, Oslo: Section, relationship between new and old, plan, detail of exterior.

During this same period, Fehn was asked to restore a classical nineteenth-century building by Christian H. Grosch as the new home of the Norwegian Museum of Architecture in Oslo. In addition to developing offices, archives, and exhibition areas, Fehn designed a pavilion for temporary exhibitions. The new glass object attaches itself to the existing building mass in an unconventional but resolute way—no intermediate space links them—forming a direct relationship between old and new. Four large hollow concrete columns support the concrete roof. Outside, the glass wall of the pavilion is surrounded by a concrete wall that faces the street; the tight space in between serves as an extension of the exhibition space as well as a buffer zone from the busy street on the other side of the concrete wall.

Curiously, this last project, a precise square glass pavilion, refers back to Fehn's first international work, the Norwegian Pavilion for the Brussels World's Fair. The structure and space are different, but both pavilions introduce inside-outside interstitial space in which light penetrating a surface is important. The small pavilion in Oslo also shares the strict geometry so evident in Fehn's early work. He was not able to follow the construction in person, but bedside reports and photographs kept him apprised. Once in a while, the young team in the office would coax him down to the site.

Just as both commissions were secure, with working drawings in progress, Fehn's wife, Ingrid, died. Ingrid had been Fehn's office manager, gatekeeper, organizer, and source of unquestioning support; suddenly, late in life and with more work than ever, Fehn was without his partner. Coupled with his failing health, this meant that he never really had a chance to step back and assess a body of work or enjoy unhindered time with his family. In many ways, this situation dampened the excitement over his two projects in Oslo.

Sometimes Fehn would replace the word "infinity" with the word "emptiness" in a lecture, and I would wonder if it was a slip of

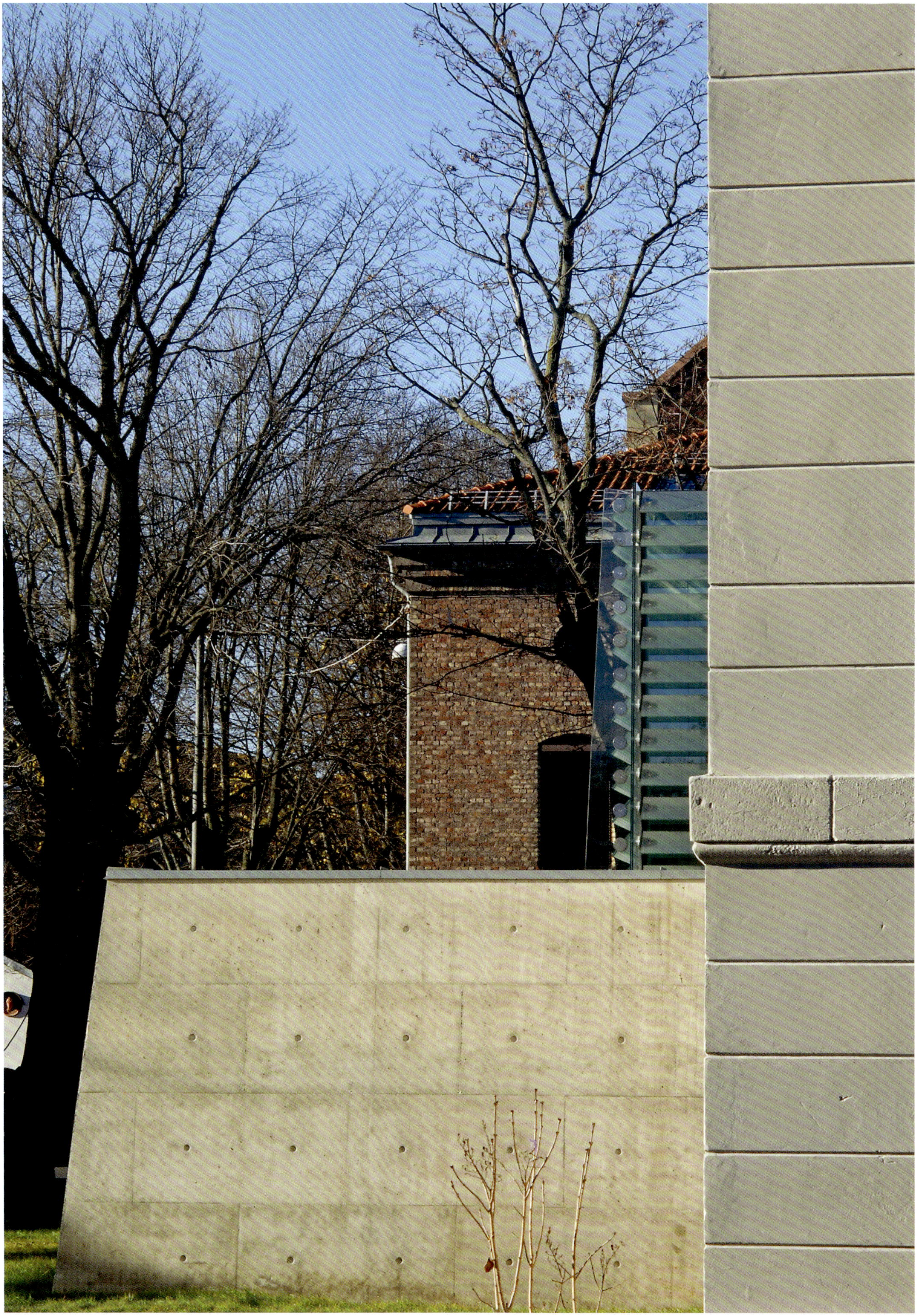

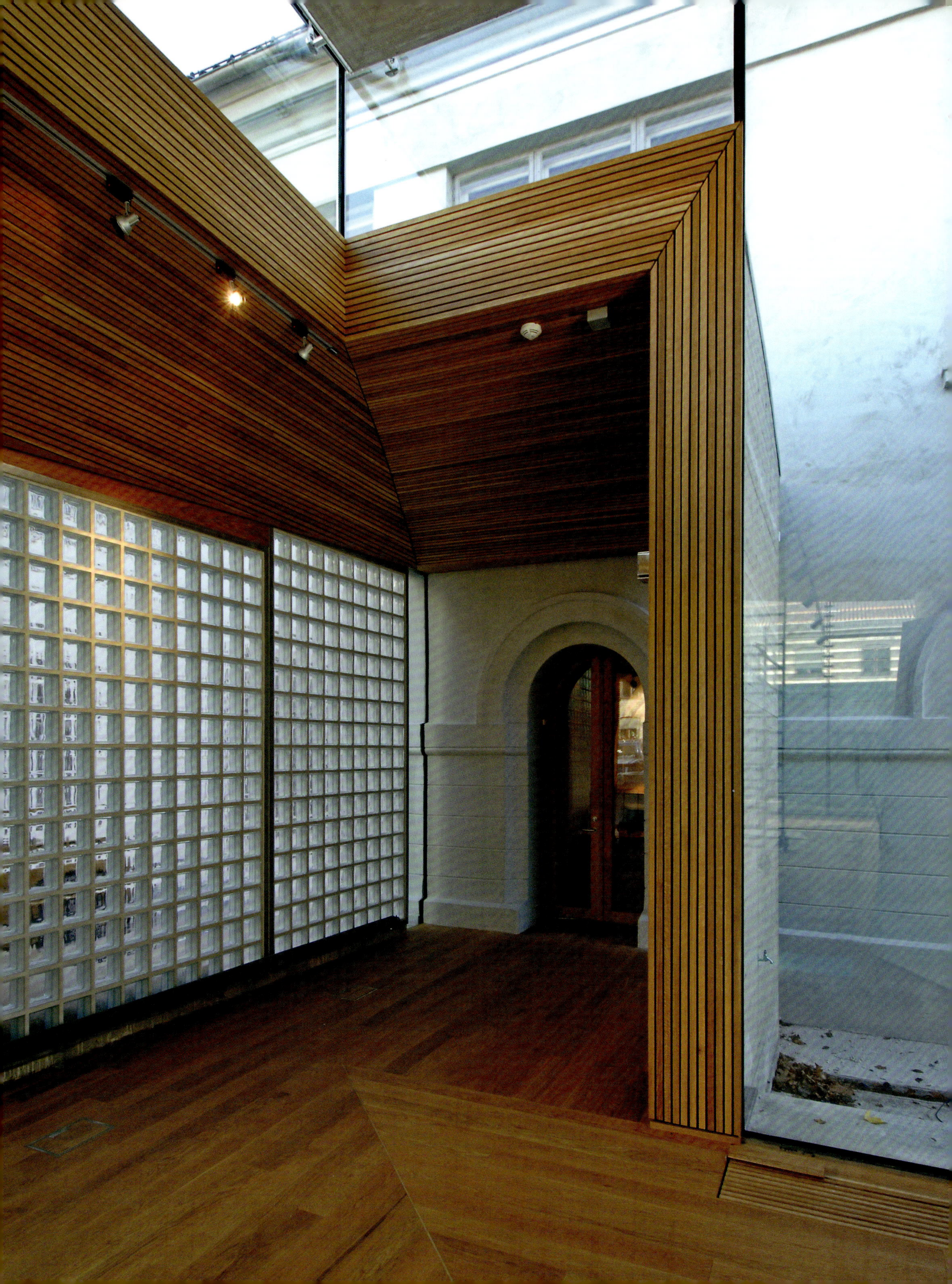

Norwegian Museum of Architecture: Interior views.

Sketch of angels flying in the sky.

the tongue or if he really was referring to emptiness. He returned to the idea of loss relative to the unknown time and time again. This was a topic even in the interviews for *Sverre Fehn: The Thought of Construction* back in the late 1970s. At that time he described it very simply: **Once one is able to cross over a mountain and see the other side, the potential of mystery and dreams is less; one loses a dimension in relation to the unknown, and one is unable to satisfactorily substitute this loss with anything else.**

Another topic that he connected to the unknown is fear. Modern society's need to buffer the physical experience of fear results in a reduction of the understanding of the dimension and impact of fear; its mystery is all but gone. In Fehn's opinion, fear and the unknown have come to be perceived as solely negative input; thus, there seems to be no need to replace these spatial concepts with something of equal strength. He was attracted to the energy embedded in fear and applied it straightforwardly to his work. His argument was that the approach to spatial information has become too direct. Fehn asked for another methodology, one that would incorporate problem solving into a more basic core knowledge or perception. The latent spatial potential found in the unknown, in fear, in emptiness, is Fehn's door to creative energy. Within the moment of fear is a reality one cannot escape. It has no buffer, no alterations. **Reality is always worse than the copies. One is always trying to be finished with one's own play, loneliness.**

In a time when architecture is again seeking a connection to a resistance force in nature or in life, Sverre Fehn's work reveals a sharp line between nature and architectural limitation. It is not work that intrinsically maps out future directions, but it is an approach that offers an opening for a discussion around spatial integrity. Fehn's architecture does not overlook or dismantle the physicality, the life-death cycle within nature's space, and it is through this attitude that he finds a human dimension that accepts the earth as its base, a spatial limitation that gives architecture its precision.

Today, architecture as a profession is exceedingly vulnerable to commercial and media pressures. Buildings must be entertaining and provide quick economic returns, and to meet these demands architecture must consume, on all levels, material, energy, landscape, and even society's sense of place and culture. The lifespan of a construction is no longer measured through material but through a strategy based on economics and the viability of architecture as a visual diversion. Fehn's passion and interest in architecture has always concerned its relationship to the inherent limitations of physical space, and within these limitations he has constructed small worlds around the human and the object.

Why didn't Sverre Fehn's career move toward a more demonstrative and international use of public image? Why didn't he have large commissions all over the world? There is no one answer, but when I look at the careers of architects

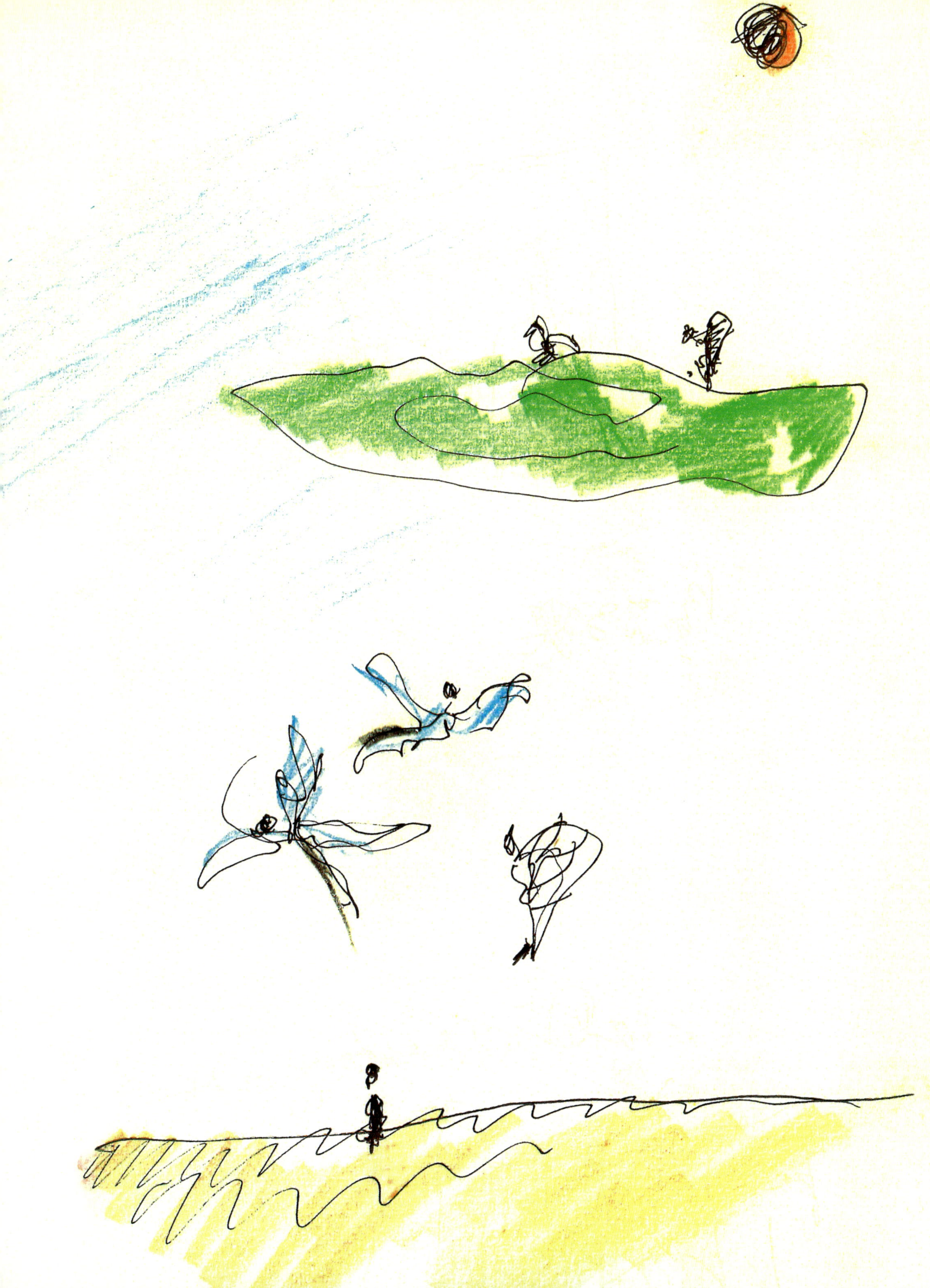

what is architecture

Sketch, 1993, "That is architecture"; sketches, 1992, of museums, Norwegian Glacier Museum, Mining Museum at Røros, Hedmark County Museum, Voksenkollen Medical Conference Center, and Wasa Ship Museum.

① Reisen inn i historien.
② Huren om himmen om hygge / i vinter lyset   det horisontale

③ Your footsteps on earth is —

④   A.

Reisen mellom himmel og jord.

B.

Reisen over elven.

C.

Båtens reise.
Objektets stillen over piren vinden.

Reisen inn i det visle

he admired there are clear similarities. There is no architectural compromise in Fehn. This lies deeper than the actual physical work—it is also present in his thought process, his understanding of what is essential—and this is what occupies his boundless energy and focus. Fehn's work has an element of chance. In the early twenty-first century, a profound need for predictability in architecture has evolved. While it may be presented in new packaging, an unspoken but clear requirement that the client feel secure in architecture as an investment, whether it is a public or commercial undertaking or even a private house, hangs over much of the creative process. Fehn's ability to step outside of this pressure, to keep his focus within a poetic interpretation that never loses sight of an earthbound existence, is his strength.

In 1997, Fehn summed up his career in a lecture: The Venice pavilion as a space was a maximum minimization of a game, and Villa Norrköping had something of the same. It is architecture with discipline that has no relation to a world of motifs or topics. Both projects contain a poetic world, a minimalist story. Over the years, as you talk more, the conversation with architectural space and history should become larger. There are many stories I would like to tell. In some of the more important conversations, it is possible that some of the architectural strength disappears or at least is different.

The year I built the Brussels pavilion, it was a wet and muddy winter. I was the project leader and got very little help from a thankless comet. The contractor said I was too young; all the countries had the same contractor. The expensive hotel ate up the entirety of my fee, and afterward I was broke and had no work. I was made fun of by the Norwegian press at home, and at times there was full confusion. On the whole, I think it was the worst building project I ever experienced. I never saw Corbusier there, but I did see Pietelä quite a bit. But he was fired and they blocked out all the overlights in his pavilion.

The Venice pavilion with its minimal story is without a determined pattern of movement and as such belongs to all objects; Hamar is my greatest story in this respect. Lewerentz also had a lot he would have said, Gehry has colossal stories, Mies had simplicity, and Wright had the use of material. My affinity is with Prouvé's technology. This is found in the structures of the pavilions in Brussels and Venice. I am careful in copying my own youth, but I am surprised at the confidence I had in dimensioning. I am pleased with the precision and simplicity these first works radiate.

Niemeyer's last building—the little gallery clinging to the hillside—manages to hold tight to all its simplicity. One is always attracted to architecture with simplicity, because motifs are not fighting over room in a space. Just the same, the Aukrust Center infiltrates other histories. Brussels and Venice are much simpler.

I have never been that interested in complicated technical buildings, great comforters that lie there breathing, hovering over the earth and surrounded by their regulations, like a child that shouldn't freeze but at the same time must take care of itself. In this respect, the Brussels pavilion was a summer experience. Venice also belongs to summer, and Hamar too.

Sketch, 1984, "1. The journey into history. 2. The wall that finds its shadow, the horizontal winter light. 3. Your footsteps on earth . . . 4. The voyage between heaven and earth. The trip over the river. The boat's journey, the object's position over the earth's rushing wind. The journey into the unknown."

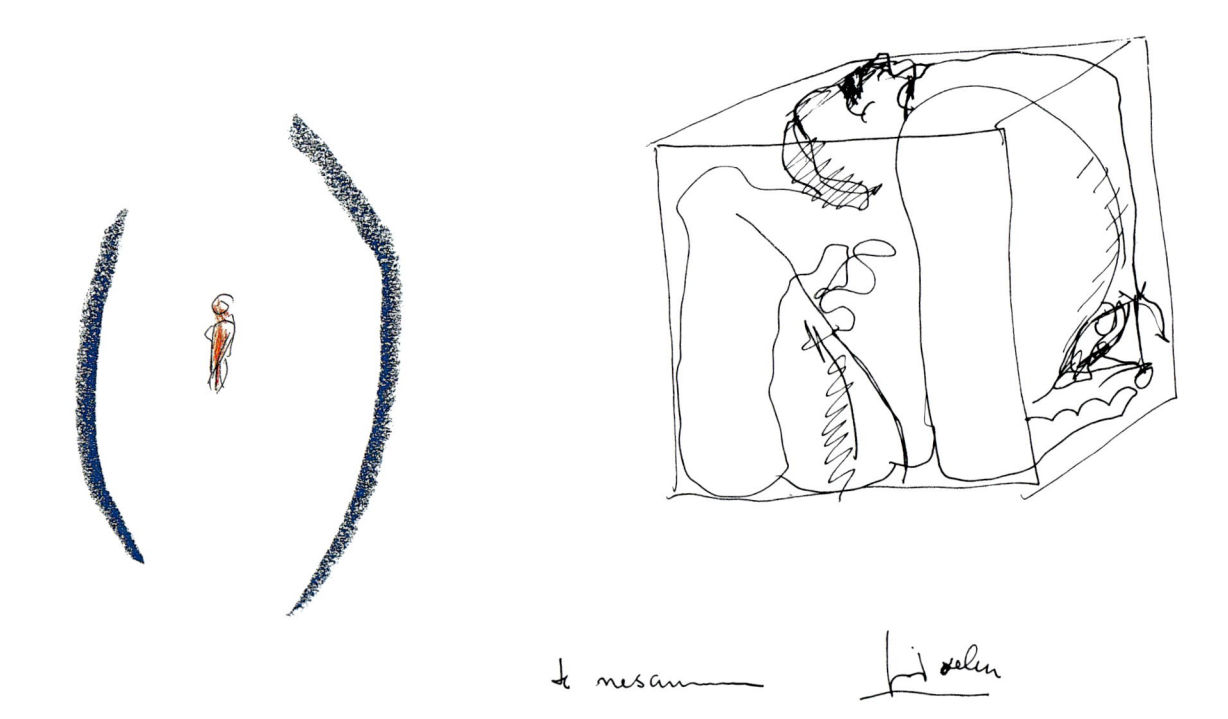

Sketch, 1996, of the man and the room; sketch of misery.

OPPOSITE Seasonal changes, a photograph from the exhibition at the Norwegian Pavilion for the World Exposition in Brussels.

Over the years, Fehn received a great number of awards and prizes. Yet he remains an architect on the periphery of Europe. During his active career, he did not lack for friends and contacts abroad, but he was very careful with his time. International lectures, exhibitions, and publications were often turned down when they began to intrude on or pressure day-to-day work and, more important, time to think. He was not a strategist.

To visit a Sverre Fehn work is to listen to one of his stories. His buildings speak for themselves, with clear references and memories. Fehn made his architectural voyage intuitively, but with energy and strength. His years of teaching produced a steady flow of young architects, many of whom are internationally recognized. His work and teaching have quietly and poetically opened a less used door to the future, where the earth serves as solid base and nature as a resistance force gives to architecture its precision.

Architecture speaks with the past. Each house on earth has significance, and this is found in the pleasure of coming inside. My mother's bench is architecture. It is a story told with love and poetry. You can't say that it is necessary or that it is bad or good. Most important is that it is a story that is told, that it has an absolute meaning. You send a Christmas card and it has its poetic value. It is like the bench with my mother and the sunset.

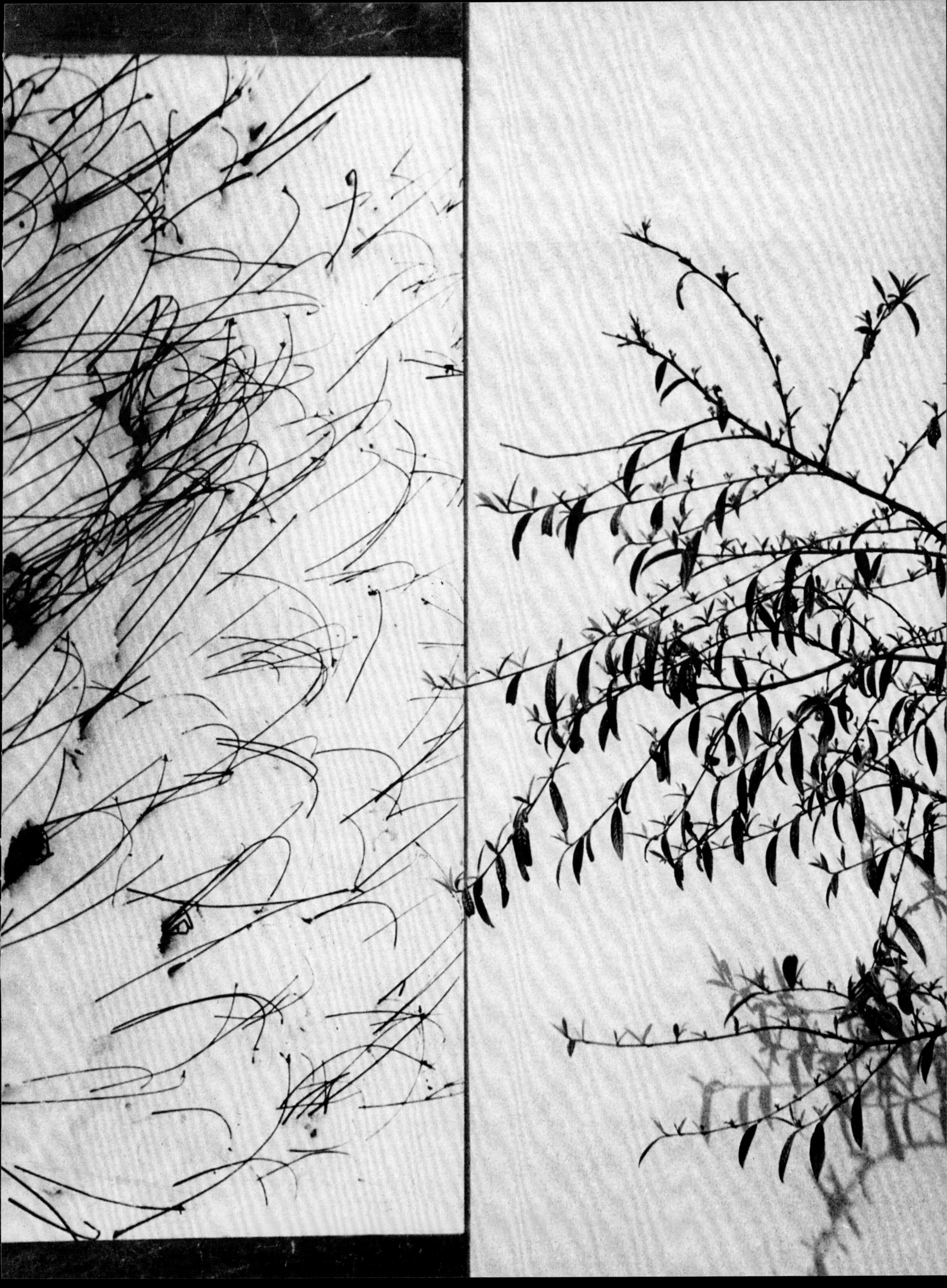

NOTES | For the most part, Sverre Fehn's notebooks contain sketches along with brief, personal captions that refer to the subject of a lecture, a course he was teaching, or observations from a trip. In his earliest notebooks are some rather long notations, but over time he came to rely more and more on his drawings as a form of reflection and as a tool to develop an architectural concept. Drawings that directly concern his built work and its design process are seldom found in these notebooks.

My own notebooks span from my time as a student under Louis I. Kahn to the present. These books include my notes for the first book on Sverre Fehn, 1978–80, as well as notes from his lectures and conversations at the Oslo School of Architecture, private conversations and interviews for articles, and public lectures. These books also include notations from lectures and conversations with Fehn's friends and colleagues as well as from my many years of involvement with the International Laboratory of Architecture and Urban Design. I took down my notes directly and as accurately as possible; none of the material has been transcribed from recordings.

MIDSUMMER FRAMES

14 Architecture shall be human . . . *Byggekunst: The Norwegian Review of Architecture*, 1953, no. 6: 195.

15 I am not able to teach within . . . POF notes, 1980.

15 The key to the formal expression . . . POF notes, 1980.

20 When the construction was completed . . . *Byggekunst: The Norwegian Review of Architecture*, 1985, no. 6: 304.

21 I had to keep a workbook on . . . POF notes, Aug. 1, 1995.

THE BEGINNING OF NO RETURN

29 In 1949, Jørn Utzon and Arne Korsmo . . . POF lecture notes, 1995.

30 We drew this after . . . POF lecture notes, 1988.

31 Utzon followed in Korsmo's wake . . . POF interview notes, 1978–80.

34 The breeze from an opening . . . Per Olaf Fjeld, *Sverre Fehn: The Thought of Construction* (New York: Rizzoli International Publications, 1983), 152.

34 My French was soon much better . . . POF notes, 2007.

39 When I was living in Paris . . . POF interview notes, 1978–80.

39 I don't really know what . . . SF notes, Nov. 2, 1951.

42 It is in the desert . . . POF lecture notes, 1987.

42 I went to Morocco . . . POF lecture notes, n.d.

EARLY FAME

46 I stayed in a good hotel . . . POF notes, 1978–80.

47 It became very apparent . . . POF interview notes, 1997.

47 The project had silence . . . POF interview notes, 1997.

48 I visited various museums . . . POF interview notes, 1997.

48 Corbu denied Newton's fall . . . POF lecture notes, March 25, 1988.

54 The goal is to rediscover . . . *Byggekunst: The Norwegian Review of Architecture*, 1962, no. 4: 110.

54 Venice is a city that has . . . POF notes, 1987.

59 Some days before the opening . . . POF interview notes, 1978–80.

61 After the Venice Pavilion . . . POF interview notes, 1978–80.

64 I remember my short meeting . . . POF lecture notes, July 4, 1988.

64 [Scarpa] is in material . . . POF lecture notes, n.d.

64 How much should structure . . . POF lecture notes, July 4, 1988.

BEYOND THE IMAGE OF HOME

68 Architecture must travel . . . POF lecture notes, Oct. 23, 1987.

68 If you know how to . . . POF notes, 1989.

70 Tragedy arrived when . . . POF interview notes, 1978.

70 The bathroom is an extension . . . POF interview notes, 1978.

73 The night gains an incredible . . . POF interview notes, 1978.

73 The radical plan and use . . . Béatrice Glase, "Kom Helst Utan Flyttlass," *IDUN Vecko Journalen*, Nov. 19, 1965, 46–49.

80 The house is constantly giving . . . POF lecture notes, Oct. 9, 1987.

80 Corbusier: How are things . . . POF lecture notes, 1978.

80 The interior is . . . POF lecture notes, Urbino, 1979.

89 The Arne Bødtker house is . . . POF interview notes, 1981.

89 A house is not nature . . . POF lecture notes, Oct. 9, 1987.

96 The house welcomes you . . . POF lecture notes, Oct. 9, 1987.

99 I have to confess . . . POF notes, 1996.

99 When you build with brick . . . POF notes, 1989.

104 The child holds himself up . . . POF notes, 1989.

THE RETURN OF THE HORIZON

108 The Second Horizon . . . POF interview notes, 1985.

110 The moment it is again . . . POF notes, n.d.

110 Where between heaven and earth . . . POF notes, n.d.

110 The secret of the boat . . . Per Olaf Fjeld, *Sverre Fehn: The Thought of Construction* (New York: Rizzoli International Publications, 1983), 27.

112 The Norwegian Forestry Museum . . . POF lecture notes, Sept. 29, 1993.

116 My story is where do I put . . . POF lecture notes, Sept. 1985.

116 My interest is not to continue . . . POF lecture notes, Oct. 6, 1986.

127 The time an artwork can feel . . . POF lecture notes, Oct. 4, 1978.

128 To exhibit an object . . . POF notes, Oct. 4, 1979.

128 The largest museum . . . *Byggekunst: The Norwegian Review of Architecture*, 1982, no. 4: 169.

131 Someone without an urban . . . POF notes, 1978–80.

131 The building mimes the diagonal . . . POF interview notes, 1978–80.

134 Rock carvings have no . . . POF lecture notes, Rome, 1993.

PUBLIC CONVERSATIONS

138 The minute interest was legal . . . POF lecture notes, 1987.

139 He knits his light . . . POF lecture notes, 1985.

142 When constructing a church . . . Dag Roglien, ed., *Treprisen: Ten Norwegian Prize-Winning Architects* (Oslo: Norwegian Association of Architects, 1978), 36–37.

142 I was so tired of the large mass . . . POF lecture notes, July 4, 1988.

142 The boatbuilder is familiar . . . POF lecture notes, Oct. 23, 1987.

144 The Child and the Old Man . . . SF notes, 1988. The story was originally written for a piece called "Five Short Stories." At the last minute this story was dropped; the others were published as "Four Stories" in *Architecture and Body* (New York: Rizzoli International Publications, 1988).

154 It is the eye and sound . . . POF lecture notes, Oct. 1, 1984.

154 As an architect I withdraw . . . POF lecture notes, Sept. 6, 1988.

154 The floor accepts the site . . . POF lecture notes, Sept. 6, 1988.

155 It is the boat and wagon . . . POF notes, Sept. 1985.

163 Rome in the Middle Ages . . . POF notes, 1983.

163 The actor's skin is his horizon . . . POF notes, 1984.

163 The mask freezes time . . . POF notes, 1983.

164 One must consider a theater . . . POF notes, 1983.

168 March 17: The film sequence . . . SF notes, 1987.

168 The world is around me . . . POF notes, Aug. 1989.

A TWENTY-YEAR PIT STOP

172 Architecture is not very complex . . . POF notes, n.d.

172 We are not here to look . . . POF notes, Siena, 1989.

173 Finland has a national . . . POF notes, 1992–93.

176 Deep in my mind I see . . . POF notes, 1978–80.

176 I remember that as a child . . . POF lecture notes, 1981.

180 Utzon's world lies outside . . . POF lecture notes, 1984.

180 I have a friend who is . . . SF notes, c. 1986–87.

180 A summer girl sits on a swing . . . POF lecture notes, March 25, 1988.

181 If tragedy could be traced . . . Per Olaf Fjeld, *Sverre Fehn: The Thought of Construction* (New York: Rizzoli International Publications, 1983), 152.

181 Concrete belongs to a mass . . . POF notes, 1984.

181 If one cannot manage the spiritual . . . POF interview notes, 1982.

181 In the ancient Greek's row . . . POF lecture notes, 1984.

181 A point on the surface . . . POF interview notes, 1982.

182 Construction is with me . . . POF lecture notes, 1984.

182 In your thoughts . . . POF interview notes, 1982.

182 The earth is there . . . POF interview notes, 1982.

185 I have only one lecture . . . POF notes, 1984.

185 There was a time . . . POF lecture notes, 1984.

185 To have a sense of construction . . . POF interview notes, 1982.

186 The wheel as a construction . . . POF interview notes, 1982.

186 As I write this note down . . . Marja-Riitta Norri and Maija Käinen, eds., *Sverre Fehn: The Poetry of the Straight Line* (Helsinki: Museum of Finnish Architecture, 1992), 4.

186 The key to every work . . . POF lecture notes, 1988.

186 For many years you have . . . POF notes in diary, 1994.

CONNECTING HEAVEN AND EARTH

191 The tree is a wonderful . . . Dag Roglien, ed., *Treprisen: Ten Norwegian Prize-Winning Architects* (Oslo: Norwegian Association of Architects, 1978), 36–37.

196 What about a reclining . . . *Byggekunst: The Norwegian Review of Architecture*, 1975, no. 3: 58.

196 The cave is a building . . . POF notes, Jan. 1993.

196 The bullet made a dent . . . Per Olaf Fjeld, "Has a Doll Life?" *Perspecta: The Yale Architectural Journal* 24: 40–49.

197 None of the figures fascinated . . . *Byggekunst: The Norwegian Review of Architecture*, 1982, no. 4: 169.

197 The Nordic deities . . . POF notes, 1981.

197 When the room was about . . . POF notes, 1981.

197 Is there a greater loneliness . . . *Byggekunst: The Norwegian Review of Architecture*, 1985, no. 6: 353.

204 Fantasy is stored up . . . POF lecture notes, 1992.

THE MASK AND THE CUT

208 They contain all built . . . POF notes, n.d.

209 Brick's language lies . . . POF lecture notes, 1989.

211 The fireplace is the central . . . POF lecture notes, 1989.

211 I always felt the road . . . POF lecture notes, 1989.

213 The Busk House was a fairy-tale . . . POF lecture notes, 1989.

217 The function of the house . . . POF lecture notes, 1994.

218 Now architecture itself . . . POF notes, 1994.

218 I made it the same way . . . POF notes, n.d.

226 As you get older . . . POF notes, n.d.

226 Sanctuary of art . . . From the Louis I. Kahn Collection, University of Pennsylvania. Reprinted in Alexandra Tyng, *Beginnings: Louis I. Kahn's Philosophy of Architecture* (New York: John Wiley and Sons, 1984).

230 John Hejduk has created . . . Sverre Fehn, "John Hejduk," in *Security: A Work by John Hejduk*, ed. Astri Thån (Oslo: Aventura Forlag, 1995), 9–10.

PARAPHRASING NATURE

236 When the object is left . . . POF notes, 1978.

236 The world the Expo presents . . . POF notes, 1992.

236 The animal has a relationship . . . POF notes, 1979–81.

250 Did Bronze Age humans . . . POF lecture notes, 1985.

250 Rock carvings have no horizon . . . POF lecture notes, Sept. 1993.

250 It is an incredibly sensitive landscape . . . POF lecture notes, May 1994.

256 A door never has . . . POF notes, 1979–81.

BEFORE CLOSING THE GATE

280 Once one is able . . . POF notes, 1978.

280 Reality is always worse . . . POF notes, 1983.

285 The Venice pavilion as a space . . . POF lecture notes, 1997.

286 Architecture speaks with the past . . . POF notes, 1978–80.

CHRONOLOGY OF WORKS

BUILT PROJECTS ARE LISTED IN **BLACK**.

MUSEUM FOR THE SANDVIG COLLECTION, Lillehammer, Norway, 1949–56; with Geir Grung; competition project, first prize
The spatial potential of the topography gives the museum its scale and identity. The building is based on a modular order; its structure forms an essential expression within the space. The spatial openness and the relationship to the displayed object were considered modern for the time. The built museum was modified in relation to the competition project of 1949.

CREMATORIUM, Larvik, Norway, 1950; with Geir Grung; competition project, first prize

HOUSING PROJECT, Oslo, Norway, 1951; with Jørn Utzon and Geir Grung; submitted to CIAM, 1953

YACHTING CLUB, Bergen, Norway, 1951; with Geir Grung; project

NORWEGIAN MARITIME MUSEUM, Oslo, Norway, 1952; with Odd Østbye; competition project

CHURCH, Harøya, Norway, 1955; with Odd Østbye; competition project

ØKERN HOME FOR THE ELDERLY, Økern, Oslo, Norway, 1952–55; with Geir Grung
The flat site for this building was originally part of a farm, and Fehn and Grung preserved a row of large linden trees that once lined the driveway. The facade was designed as prefabricated structural modules of 2.7 by 2.5 meters, which were to be placed by a crane, but due to lack of expertise the concrete was poured on site. The building consists of reinforced load-bearing walls, prefabricated-concrete floor elements, and a flat concrete roof slab. Inside are seventy-eight single rooms and twenty double rooms. The total built area including the interior open courtyards is 880 square meters.

CHURCH, Harstad, Norway, 1955; with Odd Østbye; competition project

UNIVERSITY LIBRARY, Bergen, Norway, 1956; competition project

NORWEGIAN TRADE EXHIBITION HALL, Oslo, Norway, 1956; with F. R. Hougli; competition project

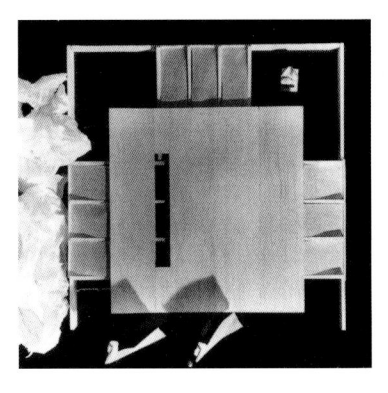

NORWEGIAN PAVILION FOR THE WORLD EXPOSITION IN BRUSSELS, Belgium, 1956–58; competition project, first prize; dismantled
The theme of the exhibition was "Life through Light." The pavilion, 37 meters square, used only a portion of the assigned lot of 2,400 square meters; the remainder of the site continued as terraces and vegetation. The building was enclosed on three sides by prefabricated-concrete wall elements. Four one-meter-deep laminated-wood beams set five meters apart carried the roof. A secondary set of laminated-wood beams one meter apart completed the roof structure. Nylon webbing stretched between the primary beams and sprayed with a quick-drying plastic substance, Co-Coon, was utilized for the transparent roof section. Inside, Fehn used cruciform Plexiglas columns in an attempt to find a structure that would cast no shadow. The floor of the pavilion, both inside and outside, was covered in Norwegian slate.

KING HÅKONS CHURCH, Copenhagen, Denmark, 1956; competition project

LIE VACATION HOME, Oppdal, Norway, 1957; project

MUSEUM COMPLEX, Kinshasa (formerly Léopoldville), Democratic Republic of the Congo, 1958; competition project

NORDIC PAVILION FOR THE VENICE BIENNALE, Venice, Italy, 1958–62; competition project, first prize
The Nordic Pavilion (shared by Norway, Sweden, and Finland) is situated on a flat site between the United States and Danish Pavilions. Two concrete walls at the northeast and southeast form a right angle that faces the United States Pavilion and a slight rise in the terrain. A large concrete beam spans between the northeast wall and a Y-shaped column at the west corner. Large glass sliding doors enclose the two remaining facades, which meet at the column. A double layer of concrete beams forms a gridded roof that prevents direct sunlight from reaching the exhibition room and also has the structural capacity to form openings for preexisting trees. The 2.2-meter depth of the roof grid, determined by the trajectory of the Venetian summer sun, gives a diffuse, shadowless light. The grid openings and the original slate floor (it has been replaced with marble) use an ancient Egyptian building module of 52.1 centimeters. Curved fiberglass sheeting tops the open roof construction. The column-free interior space is 470 square meters and the overall ceiling height is 4.46 meters. The outdoor pyramidal stair emphasizes the slope of the hill.

T. NOER HOUSE, Svartsskog, Norway, 1959; project

NYKÖPING CITY HALL, Nyköping, Sweden, 1959–60; competition project

SÆTHREN HOUSE AND WORKSHOP, Ski, Norway, 1959–62; expanded, 1969

SCHREINER HOUSE, Oslo, Norway, 1959–63
The house clearly distinguishes between public and private exterior space. The front facade, facing the street and neighbors, is a closed wall with a main entrance and garage. The opposite wall, which looks west, is a series of glass sliding doors that open fully to the untouched wooded landscape of an adjacent national park. The plan, 120 meters square, is organized around a module of one square meter, and the wood post-and-beam construction is adapted to this module. The central unit is 3.66 meters high; the general height for the rest of the interior spaces is 2.4 meters. The joints between floor and walls and ceiling and walls are caulked with a rubber hose that is pumped to create a vacuum; this system quickly adapts to the ever-changing levels of moisture in the wood frame. Brick is used only in the center unit around water and the fireplace. The walls and ceiling are Norwegian pine, and the floor is terrazzo. All the doors and windows are frameless; the same profile is used for both the slide-hang and conventional sliding doors. Electric panels in the ceiling provide heating, and adjustable vertical floor-to-ceiling louvers offer natural ventilation.

ZONING AND PLANNING FOR RESIDENTIAL DEVELOPMENT, Kringsjå, Oslo, Norway, 1959; project

CAMERA STORE, Oslo, Norway, 1960; demolished
Fehn adjusted the floor level so that it would have direct access to the street outside. A new facade of glass replaced the massive old brick facade. A small glass showcase box within this glass wall extended into the street. The back wall was covered with a large photograph by the Norwegian artist Carl Nesjar; the other walls consisted of glass and cabinets made of Oregon pine.

UNDERLAND HOUSE, Ski, Norway, 1960–62

RESTAURANT AND EXHIBITION AREA FOR SEVENTH OF JUNE SQUARE, Oslo, Norway, 1961; competition project

AUDITORIUM, Norwegian Agriculture College, Aas, Norway, 1961; competition project

SPIRALTOPPEN RESTAURANT AND HOTEL, Drammen, Norway, 1961; competition project

UNIVERSITY OF STOCKHOLM, Stockholm, Sweden, 1961; competition project

ARNE BØDTKER HOUSE, Oslo, Norway, 1961–65
The house, a parallelogram in form, sits on a steep site along a hill. A wooden bridge connects the entrance to the slope. Three V-shaped brick cavity walls serve as the main structure of the house, organizing space and guiding movement on both floors. The secondary structure is a timber frame. The living and dining areas and kitchen are on the upper floor; below are bedrooms, baths, and storage. Norwegian pine is used for floors and ceilings. The total area is 280 square meters.

ZONING AND PLANNING FOR A RESIDENTIAL AREA NEAR VEITVET, Oslo, Norway, 1961; project

T. IDLAND VACATION HOUSE, Bjerkøya, Norway, 1962

JERMAN HOUSE (part of a duplex in connection with Skagestad House), Oslo, Norway, 1962–63; first project

EEK HOUSE (part of a duplex in connection with Skagestad House), Oslo, Norway, 1963; second project

SKAGESTAD HOUSE, Oslo, Norway, 1962–64; final project

WESSEL HOUSE, Oslo, Norway, 1962–65

BØLER COMMUNITY CENTER AND LIBRARY, Oslo, Norway, 1962–72
The project, comprising a community center and a library building, was designed for a new suburb of Oslo. The library is 576 square meters and the community center 1,296 square meters. The structure for both buildings is a 9-meter-square grid of concrete columns supporting a waffle roof slab with a modular subgrid of 1.5 meters square. The principal materials are concrete, ceramic tile, and Norwegian pine. Dekaphan, a transparent plastic material, set into wooden frames forms the exterior walls of the community center. The main multipurpose room in the community center, 5.6 meters high, accommodates 220 people and can be easily subdivided. In both buildings, Fehn drew the fixed interior furnishings and some individual pieces in meticulous detail.

BØLER RECREATION HALL AND INDOOR SWIMMING POOL, Oslo, Norway, 1971–75; project

KARL JOHAN CITY SQUARE, Oslo, Norway, 1963; competition project

HENIE ONSTAD ART CENTER, Høvikodden, Bærum, Norway, 1963; competition project

VILLA NORRKÖPING, Norrköping, Sweden, 1963–64; competition project for "Villa Parade: House of the Future" exhibition, first prize
The house is located in a large green park outside Norrköping. The neighboring residences are also part of the housing exhibition. The area of the house is 150 square meters. Primary materials are brick and local pine. The plan is a Greek cross with a raised central core; the core houses all functions having to do with kitchen, bath, toilet, and water heater. The load-bearing brick cavity walls make no distinction between

interior and exterior. The roof is a system of wooden beams that sit directly on the brick walls. Sliding wood doors/walls expand the house from one to nine rooms. The four corners of the house are the main sources of natural light for adjacent rooms. Two of these corners have pivoting floor-to-ceiling windows that open to give unhindered access to the exterior. The house is heated by electric panels incorporated into the ceiling, and the floors are covered with coconut-fiber carpeting. Fehn designed all the built-in furniture, closets, and shelves. All materials retain their natural color and texture.

ETERNIT PROTOTYPE HOUSE, 1963–64; competition project

REBUILDING OF COLOSSEUM THEATER, Oslo, Norway, 1963–83
The rebuilding of the Colosseum Theater after a major fire included the dome, a new movie theater, restaurant, bar, outdoor café, and service areas. Little remains of the project except for the distinctive copper dome.

HENRIKSEN BOATHOUSE, Tjøme, Norway, 1964

DANTE HOUSE, Oslo, Norway, 1964; project

CHURCH, Honningsvåg, North Cape, Norway, 1965–67; competition project, first prize

UNDERLAND VACATION HOUSE, Oppdal, Norway, 1965

ZONING AND PLANNING FOR RESIDENTIAL AREA, Skedsmo, Norway, 1965; competition project

EDVARD GREIG CONCERT HALL, Bergen, Norway, 1965; competition project

ISAKSEN VACATION HOUSE, Oppdal, Norway, 1965–66

NORWEGIAN FORESTRY MUSEUM, Elverum, Norway, 1965; competition project

CARL BØDTKER HOUSE, Oslo, Norway, 1965–67; addition, 1982–85
A covered pergola attaches the house to its hillside site. The central core is a brick light well set diagonally within a second square; the spaces resulting from this geometry determine the living and dining areas on the top floor and the bedrooms below. Attached to the square brick volume is a long, rectangular two-story service wing. The house has load-bearing brick-cavity-wall construction. Laminated-wood beams set the pattern of the ceilings, and the floors are oak planks with wood dowels. The total area of the house is 320 square meters. The residence uses hot-water radiators. In 1985, Fehn added a second house. The original pergola serves as the connecting bridge between the two. A pool was added parallel to the pergola. The materials and construction of the second house are in keeping with the original.

SPARRE HOUSE, Skedsmo, Norway, 1965–67

CHURCH, Rossabø, Norway, 1966; competition project

HOTEL AND CONFERENCE CENTER, Riyadh, Saudi Arabia, 1966; competition project

MUSIC PAVILION, Tønsberg, Norway, 1966; project

HOUSING PROJECT, Tønsberg, Norway, 1967; competition project, first prize

CHRONOLOGY OF WORKS 295

TELEMARK AGRICULTURAL COLLEGE, Nome, Norway, 1967–70
The main materials of the multipurpose college building are brick, laminated wood, and Norwegian pine. Although alterations requested by the board toward the end of the project affected some of Fehn's spatial ideas about schools and student life, his detailing and spatial concerns of the period are apparent in the project.

HEDMARK COUNTY MUSEUM, Hamar, Norway, 1967–2005
The museum has had a number of construction and restoration periods. The first and major period, 1967–71, includes the main museum building and the exterior ramp in the courtyard. The largest part of the installation design was done between 1978 and 1980. There have been small adjustments over the years. In 1996, the first design work began on two outbuildings close to the main museum building; these were finished in 2005.

The museum, 1,980 square meters in all, is divided into three major parts: the north wing, which is devoted to folk art; the west wing, with the ramp over the archaeological excavations and an exhibition of medieval artifacts; and the south wing, containing the administration, lecture hall, and area for changing exhibitions. Building components that existed prior to construction were left as untouched as possible. The concrete ramp that runs throughout the museum and courtyard allows much of the ground to remain untouched and available for archaeological research. The simple pitched tile roof reflects the form of the original barn. Glass roof tiles in a few areas give light to the interior. Inside is revealed an elaborate post-and-beam construction laid atop the historic stone walls. The principal materials are concrete, glass, and laminated wood. The floors are concrete or Norwegian slate, and the ceilings are paneled in pine. Only the south wing is heated, with electric panels set into the floor.

JOHNSRUD HOUSE, Bærum, Norway, 1968–70
The house, originally designed for a couple and a child, was built on a flat suburban site on the outskirts of Oslo. The area of the building is 160 square meters. The structure consists of load-bearing brick cavity walls and post-and-beam timber framing for the floor and roof. The dimension of a standard brick set the overall module for the house, and the wood frame was based on standard timber sizes. The interior is brick, laminated wood, ceramic tile, and pine veneer, and the raised central core has a height of 3.66 meters. All interior partitions were originally moveable; only the kitchen and bathroom had permanent walls. The various service units—kitchen and bath—are located on the periphery of the house.

WIGGEN HOUSE, Stockholm, Sweden, 1968–72; project

NORWEGIAN PAVILION FOR THE WORLD EXPOSITION IN OSAKA, Japan, 1970; competition project

PLATEAU BEAUBOURG, Paris, France, 1970; competition project

PROTOTYPE HOUSE IN POLYURETHANE, 1971; project

SKÅDALEN SCHOOL AND ACCREDITATION CENTER FOR CHILDREN WITH HEARING IMPAIRMENT, Oslo, Norway, 1971–79; adapted as teacher competence center, 1997
Located in a wooded suburb within Oslo city limits, the Skådalen School was the first open-classroom school in Scandinavia for children with hearing impairments. The school, 4,808 square meters, consists of six dormitories; main

building with kitchen-dining room, classrooms, administration, workshop, and observatory space; and restoration of an existing building to contain a gymnasium and swimming pool.

Brick-cavity-wall construction and concrete interior columns supporting a concrete slab serve as the basic structure in the main building. Some of the smaller buildings have a concrete-vaulted-roof structure. Brick, concrete, and laminated wood are used throughout the interior. The tactile qualities of each material combined with a focus on spatial clarity determined the design choices for the project. The heating is provided by electric cables in the floor. Fehn designed the original built-in furniture and some individual pieces. Most of the complex was completed in 1974, but work continued intermittently until 1998 as the complex took on other related jobs and became a center for teacher training.

TULLINLØKKA SQUARE, Oslo, Norway, 1972; competition project

EXHIBITION OF NORWEGIAN ARTIFACTS FROM THE MIDDLE AGES, Henie Onstad Art Center, Høvikodden, Bærum, Norway, 1972

ORGAN FOR MARIA CHURCH, Bergen, Norway, 1973–74; project

PUBLIC LIBRARY, Trondheim, Norway, 1977; competition project

MEDICAL CONFERENCE CENTER, Oslo, Norway, 1978; competition project

PROTECTIVE COVERING FOR A PREHISTORIC ROCK DRAWING, Svartskog, Norway, 1978; project

EXPANSION OF THE FRENCH EMBASSY, Oslo, Norway, 1978–79; project

CULTURE CENTER, Stavanger, Norway, 1979; competition project

MINING MUSEUM, Røros, Norway, 1979–80; project

EXHIBITION OF NORWEGIAN ARTIFACTS FROM THE MIDDLE AGES, National History Museum, Oslo, Norway, 1979–80

WASA SHIP MUSEUM, Stockholm, Sweden, 1982; competition project

GABRIELSEN HOUSE, Oslo, Norway, 1982

OPÉRA DE LA BASTILLE, Paris, France, 1983; with O. F. Stoveland/4B Architects A/S; competition project

EXHIBITION OF CHINESE TERRA-COTTA SOLDIERS, Henie Onstad Art Center, Høvikodden, Bærum, Norway, 1984–85

ØSTMOE HOUSE, Oslo, Norway, 1985–87; project

VESTSIDEN PRESCHOOL AND KINDERGARTEN, Nesodden, Norway, 1986–87; project

CANOPY FOR THE VIGELAND MUSEUM, Oslo, Norway, 1986; project

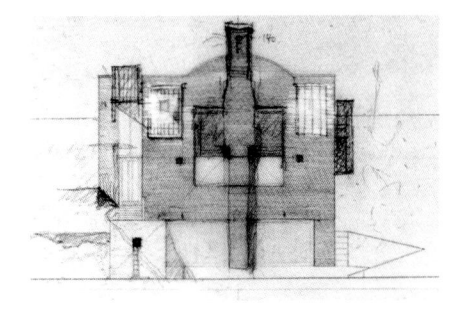

BRICK HOUSE, Bærum, Norway, 1986–87; for "Build for the Future" housing exhibition
Commissioned by the Norwegian Bricklayers Association, the house follows the steep slope of the site. There is little contact between the immediate surroundings and the interior. An open courtyard in the center of the principal rectangular volume gives a visual link to the sky and natural light. Double-cavity brick walls, rectangular in form, carry the vaulted roof. Norwegian pine and glazed brick are used throughout the interior. The arched plastered ceilings and limited natural light give a subdued calm to the interior.

KISE HOUSE, Skien, Norway, 1987–90

BUSK HOUSE, Bamble, Norway, 1987–90
The long rectangular body of the house carefully follows the terrain. At one side of this main volume is an entrance hall and on the opposite is a bridge connecting to a tower for the two daughters. Along the front of the rectangular portion of the house is a narrow glazed passageway giving access to all the other rooms. A concrete wall running the length of the house provides the main bearing structure and determines the overall direction. Laminated-wood columns and other secondary structures resting on or extending from the wall complete the house. Fehn drew most of the furniture for the house.

GALLERY, World's End, Tjøme, Norway, 1988; project

NEW PALAZZO DEL CINEMA, Venice, Italy, 1989–90; invited competition project

NORWEGIAN GLACIER MUSEUM, Fjærland, Norway, 1989–91; addition, 2006–7
The site for the museum is a flat open valley pocket where the Fjærland Fjord meets the Jostedal Glacier and surrounding mountains. The main body of the museum is a rectangle; a simple circular form for the auditorium, superimposed onto the rectangle, identifies the building and offers a clear contrast to the strong landscape. The roof of the cylinder also serves as a platform to view the glacier and the fjord. The stair leading to this platform gives monumentality to the rectangular volume of the museum. A cut along the length of the roof allows natural light to penetrate the main room; the amount of natural light entering the museum gradually decreases toward the far end of the gallery. Concrete is the main material. Fehn did not design the installation. An addition connected at the circular auditorium opened in 2007.

ENTRANCE FOR HÅKONSHALLE, Bergen, Norway, 1991; competition project

MAURITZBERG VACATION AND CONFERENCE CENTER, Mauritzberg, Sweden, 1991–92; competition project, first prize; Mauritzberg Prototype House, Mauritzberg, Sweden, 1991–92
The house was Fehn's first ecological structure. A prototype built in connection with the development of the Mauritzberg Vacation and Conference Center project, this unit was intended to explore the many house design variations planned for the center. Though it was regarded as an experiment in ecological building materials and methods, Fehn did not compromise his usual focus on spatial quality. The walls, coated with a dyed lime mixture, are 10 percent clay and 90 percent straw. The roof structure consists of prefabricated double-plywood arches covered with wood paneling, cork, bark, and earth. The service unit is attached to an interior path that runs the length of the house, giving a sense of separation from the living areas. An open interior court serves as a light source and also offers more privacy both within the house and within the vacation center. The house was built by students from the Nordic countries under the supervision of craftsmen specializing in these building methods.

VIKING MUSEUM AND INFORMATION CENTER, Borre National Park, Borre, Norway, 1993; invited competition project

ROCK CARVING MUSEUM, Borge, Norway, 1993; invited competition project

SERVICE STATION BESIDE NORWEGIAN GLACIER MUSEUM, Fjærland, Norway, 1993–95

INFORMATION CENTER, Bud, Norway, 1993; invited competition project

AUKRUST CENTER, Alvdal, Norway, 1993–96
Built to house a collection of drawings and other works by the artist/writer Kjell Aukrust, the museum stretches the length of its flat site parallel to a main road. A central concrete service wall or spine, 170 meters long, divides the building in two. Each side has a distinct section and visual identity. Toward the village and main road are the service functions; toward the valley are the main public room and adjacent galleries. On the valley side, large hollow half-circular pine columns support the roof. Between these columns, large glass doors and windows give access to the terrace and light to the main room. Three small, irregularly shaped exhibition spaces project out from the main gallery and have a dry stone wall as an exterior layer. A secondary tilted structure on the side of the road rests on the primary internal concrete structure. This secondary volume is covered in large slate roof tiles. Fehn designed the installation.

HYDRO ENERGY MUSEUM, Suldal, Norway, 1994–95; competition project

NORDIC ECOLOGICAL HOUSE, Kolding, Denmark, 1994–96
The house in Kolding utilizes the plan and building methods of the Mauritzberg Prototype House. Similarly, professional craftsmen assisted during the construction, but architectural students from the Nordic countries carried out most of the work.

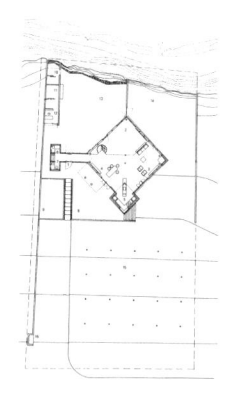

HOLME HOUSE, Holmsbu, Norway, 1995–97; earlier projects, 1972–75
The house sits diagonally on the site, taking advantage of a rock formation to the rear of the building. The strict geometry of the plan gives the house its spatial pattern and sequence. The exterior is raw concrete and untreated larch. Interior steel columns support a roof that tilts from the exterior into the central square core. Brick, pine, concrete, and steel, each of which retains its individual tactile identity, highlight the sense of a geometric space. Fehn designed all of the built-in furniture as well as several freestanding pieces.

INFORMATION CENTER FOR LOCAL HISTORY AND CULTURE, Ulefoss, Norway, 1995–96; project

EXTENSION OF THE ROYAL THEATER, Copenhagen, Denmark, 1996; competition project, first prize

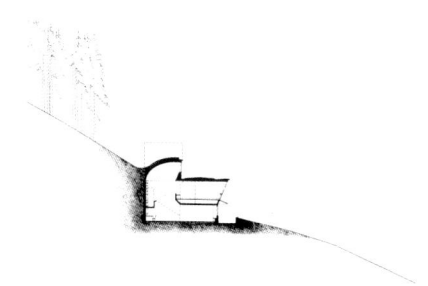

IVAR AASEN MUSEUM, Ørsta, Norway, 1996–2000
The building is dug into its very steep site, resulting in a strongly directional but broad view to the valley and an equally directional source of natural light. The main material is light-colored concrete, with an extensive application of glass in the main facade. Fehn designed the installation, in which the use of wood, steel, and glass found in earlier display work is echoed and developed.

PREUS MUSEUM, Horten, Norway, 1997–2001; partially dismantled
The photography museum is in the top floor and attic of a former naval warehouse. Fehn restored the old brick walls and massive arched roof construction of the interior. The exhibition cabinets of glass, steel, and mirrors were custom made for each object. Oiled oak was

used for the interior furnishings and the matching oak floor. All technical fixtures were channeled through the attic and brought down into the exhibition space through the arches, with minimum disturbance to the original space. Much of the Fehn-designed installation has been dismantled.

HOMANSBYEN METRO STATION, Oslo, Norway, 1997–2001; project

CHAPEL AT OLAFSSUNDET, Sogn, Norway, 1999; project

KISTEFOS ART MUSEUM, Kistefos, Norway, 1999–2001; project

SOLA GOLF COURSE, Sola, Norway, 2000; project

OFFICES FOR GYLDENDAL PUBLISHING COMPANY, Oslo, Norway, 1995–2007
The new offices, with an area of 9,000 square meters, are installed within a conglomerate of several existing buildings. The original facades were retained, but the interiors were gutted. A large, five-story public space controls and supports the functional aspects of the building. In this area is a copy of the original Gyldendal publishing house in Copenhagen, left standing as a spatial object. Inside this "Danish House" is an exhibition room for rare books, with access from the ground floor, and a boardroom, with access from a bridge. The publishing offices surround the main public space in tier-like balconies. Above are eighteen pyramidal concrete skylights set into a concrete grid. Concrete columns and beams are the basic structural elements throughout the building. An intricate infrastructure provides technical services. The floors in all public areas and the built-in furniture and fittings are light oiled oak.

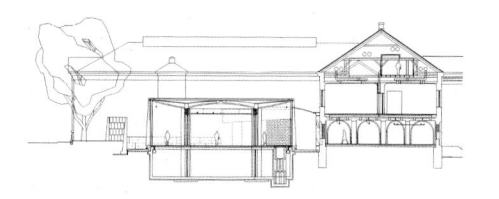

NORWEGIAN MUSEUM OF ARCHITECTURE, Oslo, Norway, 1997–2008
When the National Museum of Art, Architecture, and Design was established in 1993, the Norwegian Museum of Architecture was allocated a new location in a nineteenth-century building by Christian H. Grosch. Fehn's office restored and updated the old building, developing offices, archives, and exhibition areas as well as a new pavilion for temporary exhibitions. The concrete roof of the new pavilion is supported by four large hollow concrete columns; together with seven meters of glass wall, they give scale to the exhibition space. The floor and interior walls are in oak. The glass pavilion is enclosed by a concrete wall that faces the street, forming a tight interstitial space that is both an extension of the interior exhibition area and a buffer from the busy downtown street.

COLLABORATORS AND CONSULTANTS

The following architects have worked in Sverre Fehn's office:
Knut Aasen
Bruce Bergendoff
Eilif Bjørge
Kristoffer Moe Bøksle
Martin Dietrichson
Guy Fehn
Per Olaf Fjeld
Inge Hareide
Henrik Hille
Baard Hoff
Tore Kleven
Bjørn Larsen
Marius Mowe
Truls Overum
Jon Kaare Schultz
Ervin Strandskogen
Haakon Viksnes
Alexander Wærsten
Tom Wike
Thomas Willoch

The following architects were tenured colleagues in Sverre Fehn's Building 3 (Bygg 3) studio:
Per Olaf Fjeld
Neven Fuchs-Mikac
Turid Haaland
Finn Kolstad
Terje Moe
Ole Fredrik Stoveland

Consultants:
Almost all of Sverre Fehn's work used the same two civil engineers, Arne Neegård and Terje Orlien. Neegård started with Fehn in 1956 with the Norwegian Pavilion for the World Exposition in Brussels. The architect has often remarked on the engineer's ability and advice in finding technical solutions, in particular the roof structure for the Nordic Pavilion for the Venice Biennale and the first building stage of the Hedmark County Museum. Terje Orlien joined Neegård's office in 1967. His first jobs with Fehn were the Bøler Community Center and Library and the Telemark Agricultural College. When Neegård died in 1970, Orlien and another engineer, Karl B. Bjørseth, took over the firm, but Bjørseth left after completion of the first stage of the Skådalen School. From this point until he retired, Terje Orlien worked on almost all of Fehn's projects including the first stages of the Norwegian Museum of Architecture in Oslo. When Fehn moved the office out of his home at Havna Allé, he shared office space with Orlien. On a number of occasions, Fehn would ask him to teach or advise students in his department at the Oslo School of Architecture; many of these students would return to Orlien as their consulting engineer.

SELECTED BIBLIOGRAPHY

MAGAZINES/PAMPHLETS

Abitare, Milan: April 1972, Feb. 1994.
Architects' Journal, London: Nov. 9, 1988.
The Architectural Review, London: Aug. 1981, Feb. 1986, June 1990.
Architecture and Urbanism, Tokyo: 320 (1997).
L'Architecture d'Aujourd'hui, Paris: Sept. 1957, June 1959, Sept. 1962, April 1965, Feb.–March 1968, June 1993.
Arkitekten, Copenhagen: 1964, no. 17.
Arkitektnytt, Oslo: 1961, no. 17; 1961, no. 18; 1963, no. 5; 1964, no. 6; 1965, no. 8; 1965, no. 17; 1966, no. 13; 1967, no. 11; 2005, no. 19.
Arkitektur: Swedish Review of Architecture, Stockholm: 1994, no. 6.
Arkitektur DK, Copenhagen: 1963, no. 1; 1980, no. 1.
Baumeister, Munich: Nov. 1994.
Byggekunst: The Norwegian Review of Architecture, Oslo: 1950, no. 3; 1952, no. 5; 1952, no. 6–7; 1956, no. 4; 1958, no. 4; 1964, no. 5; 1964, no. 8; 1968, no. 4; 1971, no. 2; 1973, no. 4; 1975, no. 3; 1978, no. 6; 1982, no. 4; 1984, no. 1; 1985, no. 6; 1994, no. 7; 2001, no. 1; 2006, no. 5.
Le Carré Bleu, Paris : 1969, no. 3–4.
Casabella: International Architectural Review, Milan: April 4–15, 1994; Jan. 1996.
Domus, Milan: Aug. 1958, Dec. 1963, March 1965, Dec. 1969, Oct. 1975, July–Aug. 1991.
GA Houses, Tokyo: April 1977.
IDUN Vecko Journalen: Nov. 19, 1965.
Lotus International: Quarterly Architectural Review, Milan: 1978.
Møbel & Decoration: International Review, Stuttgart: 1958, no. 8.
Museumsbygget i Storhamerlåven, Hamar, Norway: 1973.
Perspecta: The Yale Architectural Journal: 24 (1988).
Progressive Architecture, Stamford, Conn.: Feb. 1994.
Scala: Nordisk Magazine for Architecture and Design, Copenhagen: 1986, no. 4; 1992, no. 27; 1994, no. 30.
Spazio/Societá: International Journal of Architecture and Environmental Design, Milan: 1980, no. 10; 1982, no. 17; 1992, no. 60; 1994, no. 64; 1994, no. 65.
Statsbygg Ferdigmelding–Nationalmuseet–Arkitektur, Oslo: 2008

BOOKS

Architecture and Body. New York: Columbia University/Rizzoli International Publications, 1988.
Fjeld, Per Olaf. *Sverre Fehn: The Thought of Construction*. New York: Rizzoli International Publications, 1983.
Flora, N., P. Giardiello, R. Guadalupi, G. Postiglione, S. Raffone. *Sverre Fehn: Architetto del Paese dale Ombre Lunghe*. Naples: Fratelli Fiorentino, 1993.
Giurgola, Romaldo, and Jaimini Mehta. *Louis I. Kahn*. Boulder, Colo.: Westview Press, 1975.
Kaspar, Karl. *International Shop Design/Ladenbauten–International*. Stuttgart: Verlag Gerd Hatje, 1967.
Leatherbarrow, David. *Uncommon Ground: Architecture, Technology, and Topography*. Cambridge, Mass.: MIT Press, 2002.
Lefaivre, Liane, and Alexander Tzonis. *Aldo van Eyck, Humanist Rebel: Inbetweening in a Post-War World*. Rotterdam: 010 Publishers, 1999.
Norberg-Schulz, Christian, and Gennaro Postiglione. *Sverre Fehn: Opera Completa*. Milan: Electa, 1997. English edition, *Sverre Fehn: Works, Projects, Writings, 1949–1996*. New York: The Monacelli Press, 1997.
Pedersen, Ragnar, and Jan Haug. *Storhamarlåven: En visuell oppdagelsesreise i Sverre Fehns arkitektur*. Hamar, Norway: Hedmarksmuseet og Domkirkodden, 2004.
Schofield, Maria, ed. *Decorative Art and Modern Interiors*. London: Studio Vista, 1978.
Smithson, Alison, ed. *Team 10 Primer*. Cambridge, Mass.: MIT Press, 1968.
Stiller, Adolf, ed. *Sverre Fehn, Architekt*. Salzburg: Verlag Anton Pustet, 2001.
Trujillo, María Antonia. *Sverre Fehn: Museo en Hamar*. Madrid: Ministra de Vivienda, 2005.
Yvenes, Marianne, ed. *Arkitekt Sverre Fehn: Intuisjon, Refleksjon, Konstruksjon*. Oslo: Nasjonalmuseet for Kunst, Arkitektur og Design, 2008.

PHOTOGRAPHY CREDITS

NUMBERS REFER TO PAGE NUMBERS.

O. Akhøj/Sverre Fehn Archive: 166, 167
Jim Bengston/Sverre Fehn Archive: 19 bottom
Gay Bjercke: 10, 16–17
Nils Petter Dale: 258, 273, 274, 275, 276, 278, 279
Ling Fan: 118
Guy Fehn/Sverre Fehn Archive: 220, 252, 268 left, 269
Ferruzzi/Sverre Fehn Archive: 44, 58, 60, 62–63, 65
Per Olaf Fjeld: 14, 15, 19 top, 23, 25, 57, 94, 97, 100–101, 104, 112, 116, 117 bottom, 122–23, 124, 125, 130, 149, 150, 192, 210, 213, 214, 215, 217 right, 218 right, 221, 222, 223, 224, 225, 241, 244–45, 247 bottom right, 261, 263, 264, 265, 266–67, 268 right, 277
GA Houses 2/Sverre Fehn Archive: 92 top
Lars Hallén/Sverre Fehn Archive: 98
Jiri Havran/Sverre Fehn Archive: 217 left
Svein Erik Helgersen/Sverre Fehn Archive: 247 bottom left
Hervé Photo/Sverre Fehn Archive: 50, 51, 52, 53
Henrik Hille/Sverre Fehn Archive: 95, 218 left
Mona Holtmoen: 232, 240, 246, 247 top, 248, 249
Siri Norén Jensen/Sverre Fehn Archive: 229
Suburb Club evening seminar, 1989–90, Oslo School of Architecture: 2, 172, 174, 175
Oslo School of Architecture Archive: 18
Sverre Fehn Archive: 20, 34, 40, 46, 47, 49, 115, 134, 173, 255, 287
Inger Lise Syvertsen: 101, 102, 103
Teigen Foto/Sverre Fehn Archive: 28, 31, 32–33, 35, 55, 66, 75, 76, 77, 78, 79, 83 left, 84, 85, 87, 88, 90, 91, 92 bottom, 93, 96, 106, 114, 117 left and top, 118 top, 120, 121, 132, 133, 136, 142, 143, 145, 146–47, 151, 152, 153, 156, 160, 161, 162, 197, 198–99, 200, 201, 202–3, 238, 243
Richard Weston/Sverre Fehn Archive: 211
Tom Wike/Sverre Fehn Archive: 83 right, 129